Fodor's
MAUI

Welcome to Maui

"Maui no ka oi" is what locals say—it's the best, the most, the top of the heap. To those who know Maui well, there are good reasons for the superlatives. The island's miles of perfect beaches, lush green valleys, and volcanic landscapes, as well as its historic villages, top-notch water sports, and stellar restaurants and resorts, have made it an international favorite. Maui is also home to rich culture and stunning ethnic diversity, as reflected in the island's wide range of food and traditional activities.

TOP REASONS TO GO

★ **Beaches:** From black-sand beauties to palm-lined strands, each beach is unique.

★ **Resorts:** Opulent spas, pools, gardens, and golf courses deliver pampering aplenty.

★ **Hawaiian culture:** From hula to luau, you can experience Maui's diverse culture.

★ **Road to Hana:** This famed winding road offers stunning views of waterfalls.and coast.

★ **Whale-watching:** Humpback whales congregate each winter right off Maui's shores.

★ **Water sports:** Surfing, snorkeling, and sailing are just a few top options.

Contents

Fodor's Features

MAPS

Chapter 1

EXPERIENCE MAUI

22 ULTIMATE EXPERIENCES

Maui offers terrific experiences that should be on every traveler's list. Here are Fodor's top picks for a memorable trip.

1 Walk on a Black-Sand Beach

When molten lava meets the ocean's waters, it shatters into tiny pieces of basalt, creating black sand. Waianapanapa State Park's Pailoa near Hana is such a beach, but beware—while it's beautiful, it's also sharp and heat-saturated. *(Ch. 1,2, 8)*

2 Watch for Whales

Humpback whales hang out in the Auau Channel every winter; boats leaving from Lahaina can be in the midst of these gentle giants within 15 minutes. *(Ch. 10)*

3 Find Your Aloha at a Luau

Luaus are a time for Hawaiians to come together to feast, tell stories, and remember their past. Old Lahaina Luau gets high marks for authenticity. *(Ch. 3)*

4 Hike a Bamboo Forest

Haleakala National Park's 4-mile round-trip Pipiwai Trail, which many consider the island's best hike, is a dramatic realm of plunging waterfalls, archaic ferns, and an immense bamboo forest. *(Ch. 9)*

5 Eat at Mama's Fish House

Many Maui restaurants serve delicious seafood, but the most delicious old Hawaii blended with Tahiti experience is found at Mama's, a casual, beachside eatery in a North Shore coconut grove. *(Ch. 7)*

6 Beaches, Beaches, Beaches

One of Maui's greatest appeals is its beaches. You'll find soft sands, sunny skies, clacking palm leaves, and refreshing blue waters all around you; it's the quintessence of paradise. *(Ch. 1, 2, 3)*

7 Go Fish!

Maui may not be Hawaii's primo sportfishing spot, but you will find unsuspecting places to successfully troll your line, especially on one of the Island's many fishing charters. *(Ch. 10)*

8 Duffer's Paradise

Maui is heaven for any golfer. Perfectly stunning weather, gorgeous views, and fantastic course layouts are here for any skill level. *(Ch. 10)*

9 Sweet, Sweet Pineapples

The sun-blessed tropical flavor of pineapples exudes Hawaiian happiness and Maui boasts the country's only tour of a working pineapple plantation, courtesy of Maui Pineapple Tours. *(Ch. 6)*

10 Explore Oheo

This serene valley is highlighted by a crystal-clear, basalt-lined stream that gurgles into the sapphire sea along the rugged Kipahulu coastline. *(Ch. 2, 9)*

11 Drinks with a View

Stick a plumeria behind your ear and saunter up to the bar. You'll know you've found paradise when you feel the breeze in your hair and hear the sounds of the surf crashing nearby. *(Ch. 3, 4)*

12 Hang Ten!

Beginners, or "Grommets" are in luck—Maui boasts more beginner surf breaks than any other Hawaiian Island. To watch the big kahunas, head to the North Shore's Hookipa Beach. *(Ch. 7)*

13 The Road to Hana

One of the world's most famous drives, this dangerous road has more than 600 curves and crosses some 50 gulch-straddling bridges in 52 coastline miles. *(Ch. 8)*

14 See the Sunrise

Haleakala National Park's Puuulaula Overlook is Maui's highest point and the best place to see the sunrise. On a clear day, you can see Molokai, Lanai, and Hawaii Island. *(Ch. 2, 6)*

15 Listen to the Ukulele

The ukulele is the heart and soul of Hawaiian music. Many places offer live music while you dine. *(Ch. 4, 5, 11)*

16 Dive the Cathedrals of Lanai

These lava tubes comprise one of Maui's primo diving spots (technically off Lanai) boasting a variety of multicolored fish, eels, turtles, dolphins, and octopi. *(Ch. 12)*

17 Snorkel Molokini Crater

Tropical fish thrive at Molokini Crater, a partially submerged crater about 3 miles off Maui's southern coast that serves as a fortress against the waves. *(Ch. 10)*

18 Historic Lahaina

Once an active hub for whaling, pineapple, and sugar, Lahaina is a busy town with restaurants, shops, and galleries. *(Ch. 1, 3)*

19 Small-Town Charm

Discovered by hippies in the '70s, Paia continues to be a hip and happening place with galleries, eateries, antique stores, and, of course, surf shops. *(Ch. 7)*

20 A View from Above

Much of Maui's breathtaking landscape is remote, but helicopter tours zip you into Haleakala's Martian landscape, down Hawaii's tallest waterfall, and over the secluded Wailua Valley. *(Ch. 10)*

21 Take a Hike

Maui in general is a hiker's paradise, and one of the best hikes is Keoneheehee (Sliding Sands Trail) inside Haleakala's crater, the world's largest dormant volcano. *(Ch. 6, 10)*

22 Visit Iao Valley

Central Maui's iconic, green-mantled natural spire rises 1,200 feet above a verdant valley; go early in the day before clouds obscure the views. *(Ch. 2, 6)*

Maui Today

Hawaiian culture and tradition here have experienced a renaissance over the last few decades. There's a real effort to revive traditions and to respect history as the Islands go through major changes. New developments often have a Hawaiian cultural expert on staff to ensure cultural sensitivity and to educate newcomers. A number of Maui public, private, and charter schools now offer full-time coursework in *olelo Hawaii* (Hawaiian language).

Nonetheless, development remains a huge issue on Maui and all islands as land prices continue to skyrocket, putting many areas out of reach for locals. Traffic can also be a major problem, as some of the main routes on Maui are just two-lane roads, creating bottlenecks and gridlock when closed for landslides, accidents, and other mishaps.

SUSTAINABILITY

Although sustainability is an effective buzzword and an authentic direction for the Islands' dining establishments, 90% of Hawaii's food and energy is imported, and the state's limited natural resources are being seriously tapped; there are ongoing battles over the allocation of precious water resources. However, solar and other renewable resources are making significant inroads in power production. Solar panels are a common sight on Maui homes and businesses. Large-scale solar farms opened in Kihei and Lahaina at the end of 2018, and towering wind turbines are visible on the ridges above Maalaea in South Maui and on the remote Kaupo coast.

Most of the agricultural land in Hawaii was used for mono-cropping of pineapple or sugarcane, both of which have all but vanished. Pioneer Mill in Lahaina conducted its last sugar harvest in 1999, and Hawaiian Commercial & Sugar Co. in Central Maui followed suit in 2016. When Maui Pineapple Co. halted production in 2009, a group of former employees started Maui Gold Pineapple Co., cultivating fields on the lower slopes of Haleakala to supply the fresh fruit market with its sweeter, less acidic pineapple variety. The loss of large-scale agriculture is slowly opening the door to more diversified farming, including coffee, fruit orchards, livestock grazing, and biofuels.

BACK-TO-BASICS AGRICULTURE

Emulating how the Hawaiian ancestors lived and returning to their simple ways of growing and sharing a variety of foods have become statewide initiatives. Localized efforts from groups such as the Maui County Farm Bureau are collectively aiding the organic and sustainable agricultural renaissance. Many Maui locals buy fruit and produce from farmers' markets, which often feature exotic in-season crops at reasonable costs, and the farm-to-table food movement is thriving in Maui's restaurant industry as more and more chefs form partnerships with local growers and fishermen. Even Oprah has her own organic farm on Maui, some of which is used at local farm-to-table restaurants. From home-cooked meals to casual plate lunches and fine-dining cuisine, these sustainable trailblazers enrich Maui's culinary tapestry. The recent boom in food trucks offering familiar and fresh ethnic flavors also uplifts the overall quality of life.

TOURISM AND THE ECONOMY

Tourism is the largest single source of private capital for Hawaii's economy, making the state vulnerable to financial market fluctuations that impact travel spending. The visitor industry roared back from the 2008 financial meltdown with its sixth consecutive year of record-breaking numbers in 2017, when 9.4 million tourists enjoyed the Islands while spending $17 billion. The 2.7 million tourists who visited Maui that year represented a 4% increase in arrivals and $4.8 billion in spending. In 2021, during the pandemic, Maui's 202,000 visitors spent $352 million compared to $378 million in pre-pandemic November 2019, with over 230,000 visitors.

Attuned to local attitudes and visitor demand for more authentic experiences, the tourism industry has adopted more ecoconscious practices. Many Maui residents feel development shouldn't happen without regard for impacts on neighboring communities and the natural environment.

The belief that an industry based on the Hawaiians' *aloha* (welcome, love and fellowship) should protect, promote, and empower local culture and provide more entrepreneurial opportunities for local people have become more critical of tourism businesses. More companies are incorporating Hawaiiana programs and traditional cultural values in their policies and practices, and aim not only to provide a commercially viable tour but also to ensure that visitors leave feeling connected to their host.

The concept of *kuleana,* a word denoting both privilege and responsibility, is a traditional value. Having the privilege to live in such a sublime place comes with the responsibility to protect it.

SOVEREIGNTY

Political sovereignty issues continue to divide Native Hawaiians, who have formed diverse organizations, each operating with separate agendas and lacking one collectively defined goal. Ranging from achieving complete independence to solidifying a nation within a nation, existing sovereignty models remain fractured and their future unresolved. However, the sovereignty movement began gaining new traction in 2019 as Hawaiians formed a protest site at the base of Mauna Kea to prevent the building of the Thirty Meter Telescope at the summit of the mountain, a place considered sacred by many. The camp of the "protectors" (their preferred name) includes daily protocol that includes hula, chanting, and prayers, as well as free health care, meals, and a university. Ripple effects from this protector movement have been seen across the Islands, particularly on Oahu, and a new political party has formed to address issues of particular interest to Native Hawaiians.

The Native Hawaiian Government Reorganization Act of 2009, introduced by the late Senator Daniel Akaka, would have granted Native Hawaiians federal recognition similar to Native American status. Despite 12 years of lobbying, the "Akaka Bill" never mustered enough votes to pass.

RISE OF HAWAIIAN PRIDE

After the overthrow of the monarchy in 1893, a process of Americanization began. Traditions were duly silenced in the name of citizenship. Teaching the Hawaiian language was banned from schools, and children were distanced from their local customs.

But Hawaiians are resilient people, and with the rise of the civil rights movement they began to reflect on their own national identity, bringing an astonishing renaissance of the Hawaiian culture to fruition.

The people rediscovered language, hula, chanting, and even the traditional Polynesian art of canoe building and wayfinding (navigation by the stars without use of instruments). This cultural resurrection is now firmly established in today's Hawaiian culture, with a palpable pride that exudes from Hawaiians young and old.

WHAT'S WHERE

1 West Maui. This sunny leeward area with excellent beaches is ringed by upscale resorts and condominiums in areas such as Kaanapali and, farther north, Kapalua. Also on the coast is the busy, tourist-oriented town of Lahaina, the former capital of the Hawaiian Kingdom and a former whaling center with plenty of shops, restaurants, and historical sites.

2 South Shore. The leeward side of Maui's eastern half is what most people mean when they say "South Shore." This popular area is sunny and warm year-round; Kihei, a fast-growing town, and Wailea, a luxurious resort area with some outstanding hotels, are here.

3 Central Maui. Between Maui's two mountain areas is Central Maui, home to the county seat of Wailuku and the commercial center of Kahului. Kahului Airport, Maui's main terminal, is here.

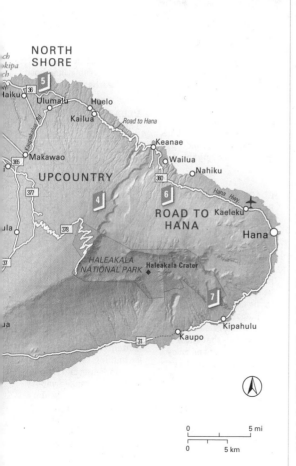

NORTH SHORE

UPCOUNTRY

ROAD TO HANA

HALEAKALA NATIONAL PARK Haleakala Crater

Haiku
Ulumalu
Huelo
Kailua
Road to Hana
Keanae
Wailua
Nahiku
Makawao
Kaeleku
Hana
Kipahulu
Kaupo

4 Upcountry and Haleakala National Park. Island residents have a name they use affectionately to describe the regions climbing up the slope of Haleakala Crater: Upcountry. This is a great place for agricultural tours.

5 North Shore. The North Shore has no large resorts, just plenty of picturesque, laid-back small towns like Paia and Haiku—and great windsurfing action at Hookipa Beach. The towns are good spots for a break if you're heading out along the Road to Hana.

6 Road to Hana. The Island's windward northeastern side is largely one great rain forest, traversed by the stunning Road to Hana. Exploring this iconic, winding road with its dramatic coastal views can be the highlight of a trip. The tiny town of Hana preserves the slow pace of the past.

7 East Maui. Located between Hana and Upcountry, East Maui invites visitors to really get off the beaten path. Past Hana are incredible ocean vistas, historic churches and cemeteries, and the back side of Haleakala National Park.

Maui's Best Beaches

HAMOA BEACH

Visitors who keep going past the town of Hana are rewarded with the salt-and-pepper sands and vibrant blue waters of Hamoa Beach. The shore break can be a bit rough at times, but don't let that keep you from enjoying this quiet cove.

BALDWIN BEACH

The soft, golden sand of this nearly 1.5-mile-long beach is one of the many things that draws visitors and local families to this North Shore locale. Baldwin is a lovely spot for that long walk on the beach that you've been planning, especially in the early morning or at sunset. The shore break can be rough, but extended, shallow, calm areas on the east and west end. Baby Beach lies on the west end and is an excellent place for kids to play and adults to enjoy the cozy sand and beautiful views.

BLACK ROCK BEACH

Puu Kekaa, known as Black Rock Beach fronting the Sheraton Maui, offers excellent snorkeling and a chance to enjoy locals showing off their cliff jumping abilities. This beach is a laid-back area in the northern part of Kaanapali Beach, where the ocean is relaxing, with deep waters that allow you to float out and enjoy more of the Pacific. As part of their cultural program, stick around for sunset to watch the Sheraton's nightly torch-lighting and cliff jump.

MAKENA (ONELOA) BEACH

This long, wide stretch of golden sand and translucent offshore water is worth the effort. The icing on the cake is that this long beach is never crowded. Use caution while swimming because the steep onshore break can get big. There are no hotels, minimarts, or public restrooms nearby—instead, there's crystal-clear water, the occasional pod of dolphins, and drop-dead-gorgeous scenery. You can grab a fish taco and a drink at a nearby food truck for a tasty lunch. Makena Beach includes both Big Beach and Little Beach (which can sometimes host nude beachgoers).

ULUA BEACH

This cozy cove is a favorite among snorkelers and scuba tour proprietors. Kids can enjoy the tide pools while adults experience the excellent snorkeling. It also makes a good starting point for beach hopping, as both Keawakapu Beach and Mokapu Beach are within walking distance.

MALUAKA BEACH

Maluaka Beach is known by many names among locals, including Turtle Town, and it often lives up to that name. It offers sandy-bottom ocean areas for swimming; reef and rocks for snorkeling and calm waters that make a variety of activities possible. You'll also likely see turtles grazing and lounging, couples getting married in this picturesque area, and kids playing in the sand.

Napili Beach

WAILEA BEACH

Often considered one of the top beaches in the world, it's no wonder that Wailea Beach fronts some of the more posh resorts on the island. There's plenty of people-watching on this busy beach (including the occasional celebrity), and a lot of activities happen here, including swimming, snorkeling, boogie boarding, and lots of relaxing on the soft sand. Visitors can spot Molokini, Kahoolawe, and Lanai as they search the horizon for whales.

KAHEKILI (OLD AIRPORT) BEACH

Anyone who loves snorkeling will be overjoyed to spend some time at this beach with a huge reef and mild surf. It's great for older kids and inexperienced swimmers to get comfortable snorkeling, though there isn't much sand past the beach (it's almost all reef), so playing in the water along the shoreline isn't the easiest. Fish, turtles, and whales are often frequently seen (and heard) in the area.

NAPAILI BEACH

This resort-fronted beach in West Maui is lovely for families thanks to the reef, which keeps the water calm most of the time. Kids will love the turtles that snack on the *limu* (seaweed) growing on the lava rocks. This sometimes crowded crescent-shaped beach offers sunbathing, snorkeling, swimming, bodysurfing, the occasional whale sighting, and a spectacular sunset.

PAILOA BEACH AT WAIANAPANAPA STATE PARK

This rustic black sand beach will capture your heart—it's framed by lava cliffs and backed by bright green naupaka bushes. Ocean currents can be strong; if they're too strong for swimming, relax on the beach and enjoy the views that include seabirds, a blowhole, a sea arch, and more.

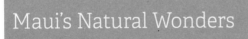

Maui's Natural Wonders

NAKALELE BLOWHOLE
It's a bit of a hike to the blowhole, approximately ¾ of a mile one way, but it's a great place to see rainbows in the morning mist, watch for whales, and enjoy a hike through dramatic lavascapes. While you're facing the blowhole (a safe distance from the water) a bit to your left, turn around and you'll see the Instagram-famous heart-shaped rock cutout.

ROAD TO HANA WATERFALLS
The Road to Hana is well known as one of the most beautiful drives in the world with 620 curves and 59 bridges. Waterfalls of all shapes and sizes trickle onto the asphalt below; some create stunning pools. Get out of the car and hike to discover even more treasures.

MOLOKINI
To enjoy some of the best snorkeling available on Maui, visit Molokini, a volcanic crater just off the South Maui coast that has been designated a state marine life and bird conservation district. Though the landmass section of the crater is closed to visitors, the cove is open to the public.

IAO VALLEY STATE PARK AND IAO NEEDLE
This park has plenty of greenery, as it's the second rainiest area in the island chain. Many travelers make a short trip out of their visit, sticking mostly to the short nature trail, a visit to the stream, and a stop at the Iao Needle observation deck.

DRAGON'S TEETH AT MAKALUAPUNA POINT
These "Dragon's Teeth" look like they come from inside the mouth of a fire-breathing beast, and in a way, they did. The West Maui volcano, during one of the last lava flows on Maui, poured into the ocean near present-day Kapalua, but the winds howled the lava back toward the volcano, creating jagged outcroppings that stretch toward the sky.

WAIMOKU FALLS AND THE PIPIWAI TRAIL

This 1.8-mile hiking trail inside Haleakala National Park takes you to Waimoku Falls, a 400-foot sheer cliff that showers water into a rocky pool below. You'll walk through lush rain forests, peaceful, enveloping bamboo groves, and another waterfall along the way, Makahiku Falls.

WAIANAPANAPA STATE PARK

There are many natural delights packed into the oceanside section of this 120-acre park. Visit the black sands of Pailoa Beach and linger to take a swim and visit the ocean cave. Camping and cabins are available, and a longer visit allows for exploring freshwater caves, a *heiau* (sacred site), and more.

HALEAKALA

Ascending the 10,023 feet to the summit of Haleakala to watch the sunrise is one of the most memorable activities Maui has to offer. Trek down one of the trails into the national park's massive bowl and see how powerful the earth's exhalations can be at this dormant volcano.

POOLS OF OHEO

On the "back side" of Haleakala, not far past Hana, lies an incredible waterfall experience. The erroneously nicknamed Seven Sacred Pools is home to (as long as the river is flowing nicely) more than seven pools, and they aren't considered sacred. They are, however, considered "something special," which is what Oheo means in Hawaiian.

LAHAINA BANYAN TREE

Right in the middle of the hustle and bustle of Lahaina's harbor and visitor-filled Front Street stands a 137-year-old banyan tree, the largest in the United States, offering shade to those who want to take in its majesty. Be sure to save some time to linger beneath this beauty; maybe enjoy a shave ice on the bench and see how many chickens you can count roosting in the lower branches.

Flora and Fauna in Hawaii

KUKUI
The *kukui*, or candlenut, is Hawaii's state tree, and Hawaiians have had many uses for it. Oil was extracted from its nuts and burned as a light source and also rubbed on fishing nets to preserve them. The juice from the husk's fruit was used as a dye. The small kukui blossoms and nuts also have medicinal purposes.

PLUMERIA
Also known as frangipani, this fragrant flower is named after Charles Plumier, the noted French botanist who discovered it in Central America in the late 1600s. Plumeria come in shades of white, yellow, pink, red, and orange. The hearty, plentiful blossoms are frequently used in lei.

GARDENIA
The gardenia is a favorite for lei makers because of its sweet smell. The plant is native to tropical regions throughout China and Africa, but there are also endemic gardenias in Hawaii. The nanu gardenia is found only in the Islands and has petite white blossoms.

HONU
The *honu*, or Hawaiian green sea turtle, is a magical sight. The graceful reptile is an endangered and protected species in Hawaii. It's easier to encounter *honu* during a snorkeling or scuba-diving excursion, but they occasionally can be spotted basking on beaches.

HUMPBACK WHALES
Each year, North Pacific humpback whales make the long journey to Hawaii from Alaska. With its warm, protected waters, Hawaii provides the ideal place for the marine mammals to mate and to birth, and to nurse their young. They arrive between November and May, and their presence is an anticipated event. You can see them up close during whale-watching boat tours.

MONK SEAL

Known as the *ilio holo i ka uaua*, meaning "dog that runs in rough water," monk seals are endemic to Hawaii and critically endangered. The majority of these mammals, which can grow to more than seven feet long, live in the remote, uninhabited Northwestern Hawaiian Islands.

TROPICAL FISH

Approximately 25% of the fish species in the Islands are endemic. Snorkeling in Hawaii is a unique, fun opportunity to see colorful fish found nowhere else on Earth. Interestingly, Hawaii's state fish, the *humuhumunukunukuapuaa*, or reef trigger, is not endemic to the state.

NENE GOOSE

Pronounced *nay-nay*, the endemic nene goose (Hawaii's state bird) is one of the world's rarest. A descendant of the Canada goose, it has been bred back from the edge of extinction and reintroduced into the wild. Use caution driving in national and state parks, which they frequent.

HIBISCUS

In 1923, the Territory of Hawaii passed a law designating hibiscus as Hawaii's official flower. While there are more than 30 introduced species of the large, colorful flowers throughout the Islands, there are five endemic types. The endemic hibiscus has yellow blossoms and is known in Hawaiian as *mao hau hele*, which means the "traveling green tree."

PIKAKE

These small, delicate blossoms are known for their hypnotic, sweet scent. The jasmine flower was introduced from India and was a favorite of Princess Kaiulani. *Pikake*, which is the Hawaiian word for the blossom as well as for a peacock—another favorite of the princess—is the subject of many *mele*, or Hawaiian songs.

What to Eat and Drink in Hawaii

SHAVE ICE

Shave ice is simple in its composition—fluffy ice drizzled in Technicolor syrups. Shave ice traces its roots to Hawaii's plantation past. Japanese laborers would use the machetes from their field work to finely shave ice from large frozen blocks and then pour fruit juice over it.

MUSUBI

Musubi are Hawaii's answer to the perfect snack. Portable, handheld, and salty, *musubi* are a great go-to any time of day. The local comfort food is a slice of fried Spam encased in packed white rice and snugly wrapped with nori, or dried seaweed. Available everywhere, *musubi* are usually just a few dollars.

MAI TAI

When people think of a Hawaiian cocktail, the colorful mai tai often comes to mind. It's the unofficial drink to imbibe at a luau and refreshingly tropical. This potent concoction has a rum base and is traditionally made with orange curaçao, orgeat, fresh-squeezed lime juice, and simple syrup.

HAWAIIAN PLATE

The Hawaiian plate comprises the delicious, traditional foods of Hawaii, all on one heaping plate. You can find these combo meals anywhere, from roadside lunch wagons to five-star restaurants. Get yours with the melt-in-your-mouth shredded kalua pig, pork, or chicken *laulau* (cooked in ti leaves) with *lomi* salmon (diced salmon with tomatoes and onions) on the side and the coconut-milk *haupia* for dessert. Most Hawaiian plates come with the requisite two scoops of white rice. Don't forget to try *poi*, or pounded and cooked taro.

POKE

In Hawaiian, *poke* is a verb that means to slice and cut into pieces. It perfectly describes the technique Hawaiians have used for centuries to prepare poke the dish. The cubed raw fish, most commonly *ahi* (yellowfin tuna), is traditionally tossed with Hawaiian sea salt, *limu kohu* (red seaweed), or *inamona* (crushed kukui nuts). Today, countless varieties of this must-try dish are served in all kinds of restaurants across the Islands. Poke shacks offer no-frills, made-to-order poke.

SAIMIN

This only-in-Hawaii noodle dish is the culinary innovation of Hawaii plantation workers in the late 1800s who created a new comfort food with ingredients and traditions from their home countries.

Poke

MANAPUA

When *kamaaina*, or Hawaii residents, are invited to a potluck, business meeting, or even an impromptu party, you'll inevitably see a box filled with *manapua*. Inside these airy white buns are pockets of sweet *char siu* pork. Head to cities and towns around the Islands, and you'll find restaurants with manapua on their menus, as well as manapua takeout places serving a variety of fillings. There's sweet potato, curry chicken, *lap cheong* (or Chinese sausage)—and even sweet flavors, such as custard and *ube*, a purple yam popular in Filipino desserts.

MALASADA

Malasadas are a beloved treat in Hawaii. The Portuguese pastries are about the size of a baseball and are airy, deep-fried, and dusted with sugar. They are best enjoyed hot and filled with custard; fillings are a Hawaiian variation on the original.

LOCO MOCO

The traditional version of one of Hawaii's classic comfort-food dishes consists of white rice topped with a hamburger patty and fried eggs and generously blanketed in rich, brown gravy. Cafe 100 in Hilo on the Big Island is renowned as the home of the *loco moco*, but you'll find this popular staple everywhere. It can be eaten any time of day.

KONA COFFEE

In Kona, on the Big Island, coffee reigns supreme. There are roughly 600 coffee farms dotting the west side of the island, each producing flavorful (and quite expensive) coffee grown in the rich, volcanic soil. Kona coffee is typically hand-harvested from August through December.

What to Buy in Hawaii

MACADAMIA NUT CANDY

Macadamia nuts are native to Australia, but the gumball-sized nut remains an important crop in Hawaii. It was first introduced in the late 1880s as a windbreak for sugarcane crops. Today, mac nuts are a popular local snack and are especially good baked in cookies or other desserts.

LEI

As a visitor to Hawaii, you may well receive a lei, either a shell, kukui nut, or fragrant flower variety, as a welcome to the Islands. *Kamaaina* (Hawaii residents) mark special occasions by gifting lei.

ALOHA WEAR

Aloha wear in Hawaii has come a long way from the polyester fabrics with too-bright, kitschy patterns (although those still exist). Local designers have been creating dressy, modern aloha attire with softer prints that evoke Island botanicals, heritage, and traditional patterns. Hawaii residents don aloha wear for everything from work to weddings.

LAUHALA

The hala tree is most known for its long, thin leaves and the masterful crafts that are created from them. Lauhala weavers make baskets, hats, mats, jewelry, and more, using intricate traditional patterns and techniques.

JEWELRY

Island-inspired jewelry comes in many styles. Tahitian pearl pendants and earrings are a local favorite, as are delicate, inexpensive shell pieces. The most coveted are Hawaiian heirloom bracelets in gold or silver with one's name enameled in Old English script.

HAWAIIAN COFFEE
Reminisce about your Hawaii getaway each time you brew a cup of aromatic, full-bodied coffee, whether it's from Kona or Kauai. All the main islands grow distinctive coffee. Stores and cafés sell bags of varying sizes, and in some places you can buy direct from a farmer.

HAWAIIAN HONEY
With its temperate climate and bountiful foliage, Hawaii is ideal for honeybees. The Islands' ecosystem contributes to honeys with robust flavors and textures, including elixirs extracted from the blossoms of the macadamia nut tree, the lehua flower, and the invasive Christmasberry shrub.

KOA WOOD
If you're looking for an heirloom keepsake from the Islands, consider a koa wood product. Grown only in Hawaii, the valuable koa is some of the world's rarest and hardest wood. Hawaiians traditionally made surfboards and canoes from these trees, which today grow only in upland forests.

HAWAIIAN SEA SALT
A long tradition of harvesting salt beds by hand continues today on all the Islands. The salt comes in various colors, including inky black and brick red—the result of the salt reacting and mixing with activated charcoal and *alaea* (volcanic clay). It is renowned by chefs around the state.

UKULELE
In Hawaiian, *ukulele* means "the jumping flea." The small instrument made its way to the Islands in the 1880s via Portuguese immigrants who brought with them the four-string, guitar-like *machete de braga*. It is famous as a solo instrument today, with virtuoso artists like Jake Shimabukuro and Taimane Gardner popularizing the ukulele's versatile sound.

Maui for Kids and Families

With dozens of adventures to take, discoveries to make, and loads of kid-friendly beaches, Maui is a blast for families.

CHOOSING A PLACE TO STAY

Resorts. On the South Shore, your best bet is the all-suites Fairmont Kea Lani; the Grand Wailea Resort and Marriott's Wailea Beach Resort have spectacular water complexes. In West Maui, all of the Westin resorts have fun water features and excellent full- and half-day programs for *keiki* (children).

Condos. You'll be able to cook your own meals with condos and vacation rentals, and prime beaches are usually a short walk away. Plus, you'll get twice the space of a hotel room for about a quarter of the price.

OCEAN ACTIVITIES

Hawaii is all about getting your kids outside—away from screens. And who could resist the turquoise water, the promise of spotting dolphins or whales, and the fun of bodyboarding or surfing?

On the beach. Maui's leeward South Shore has many calm beaches. Keawakapu, Ulua/Mokapu, Wailea, and the Kamaole parks are some of the Island's best for swimming, snorkeling, bodyboarding, and building sandcastles. In West Maui, Napili Bay and D. T. Fleming are your best bets.

On the waves. Launiupoko outside Lahaina town and Cove Park in Kihei are best for beginners. For lessons, contact Royal Hawaiian Surf Academy or Maui Surfer Girls on the west side, and Big Kahuna Adventures on the south side.

The underwater world. Rent snorkeling gear and head to Olowalu or Puu Kekaa (Black Rock) in front of the Sheraton Maui in West Maui, or any of the beaches in Kihei or Wailea. Trilogy Excursions offers full- and half-day snorkeling cruises to Molokini and other prime spots, leaving from Maalaea and Lahaina.

Whales ahoy. A close encounter with a humpback whale could be the experience your kids remember most about their Maui vacation. Pacific Whale Foundation's two-hour whale-watch trips out of Maalaea and Lahaina provide onboard naturalists and are just long enough to be out on the water.

LAND ACTIVITIES

Maui Tropical Plantation in Central Maui hosts Maui Zipline's introductory course, ideal for older kids. Flyin Hawaiian Zipline's mountainside tours will satisfy thrill-seeking teens with the state's longest, highest, and fastest zips.

See reef fish, sea turtles, manta rays, and sharks swim behind glass at the excellent Maui Ocean Center in Maalaea. It's expensive, but kids (and adults) will learn a lot from the exhibits.

When exploring the Upcountry farm region, stop by Surfing Goat Dairy, where kids can milk a goat and learn how cheese is made, or treasure hunt at Alii Kula Lavender farm.

AFTER DARK

A luau's heart-stopping Samoan fire-knife dances and gyrating Tahitian numbers will impress even the most jaded teens. One of the best is the nightly Old Lahaina Luau, which needs to be booked well in advance.

HAWAIIAN CULTURAL TRADITIONS HULA, LEI, AND LUAU

HULA: MORE THAN A FOLK DANCE

Hula has been called "the heartbeat of the Hawaiian people" and also "the world's best-known, most misunderstood dance." Both are true. Hula isn't just dance. It is storytelling.

Chanter Edith McKinzie calls it "an extension of a piece of poetry." In its adornments, implements, and customs, hula integrates every important Hawaiian cultural practice: poetry, history, genealogy, craft, plant cultivation, martial arts, religion, protocol. So when 19th-century Christian missionaries sought to eradicate a practice they considered depraved, they threatened more than just a folk dance.

With public performance outlawed and private hula practice discouraged, hula went underground for a generation. The fragile verbal link by which culture was transmitted from teacher to student hung by a thread. Even increasing literacy did not help because hula's practitioners were a secretive and protected circle.

As if that weren't bad enough, vaudeville, Broadway, and Hollywood got hold of the hula, giving it the glitz treatment in an unbroken line from "Oh, How She Could Wicky Wacky Woo" to "Rock-A-Hula Baby." Hula became shorthand for paradise: fragrant flowers, lazy hours. Ironically, this development assured that hundreds of Hawaiians could make a living performing and teaching hula. Many danced 'auana (modern form) in performance; but taught kahiko (traditional), quietly, at home or in hula schools.

Today, decades after the cultural revival known as the Hawaiian Renaissance, language immersion programs have assured a new generation of proficient chanters, songwriters, and translators. Visitors can see more—and more authentic—traditional hula now than at any other time in the last 200 years.

Like the culture of which it is the beating heart, hula has survived.

Lei poo. Head lei. In *kahiko,* greenery only. In auana, flowers.

Face emotes appropriate expression. Dancer should not be a smiling automaton.

Shoulders remain relaxed and still, never hunched, even with arms raised. No bouncing.

Eyes always follow leading hand.

Lei. Hula is rarely performed without a shoulder lei.

Arms and hands remain loose, relaxed, below shoulder level—except as required by interpretive movements.

Traditional hula skirt is loose fabric, smocked and gathered at the waist.

Hip is canted over weight-bearing foot.

Knees are always slightly bent, accentuating hip sway.

Kupee. Ankle bracelet of flowers, shells, or foliage.

In *kahiko*, feet are flat. In *auana*, they may be more arched, but not tiptoes or bouncing.

BASIC MOTIONS

Speak or sing

Moon or sun

Grass shack or house

Mountains or heights

Love or caress

At backyard parties, hula is performed in bare feet and street clothes, but in performance, adornments play a key role, as do rhythm-keeping implements such as the *pahu* drum and the *ipu* (gourd).

In hula *kahiko* (traditional style), the usual dress is multiple layers of stiff fabric (often with a pellom lining, which most closely resembles *kapa*, the paperlike bark cloth of the Hawaiians). These wrap tightly around the bosom but flare below the waist to form a skirt. In pre-contact times, dancers wore only kapa skirts. Men traditionally wear loincloths.

Monarchy-period hula is performed in voluminous muumuu or high-necked muslin blouses and gathered skirts. Men wear white or gingham shirts and black pants.

In hula *auana* (modern), dress for women can range from grass skirts and strapless tops to contemporary tea-length dresses. Men generally wear aloha shirts, but sometimes grass skirts over pants or even everyday gear.

SURPRISING HULA FACTS

■ Grass skirts are not traditional; workers from Kiribati (the Gilbert Islands) brought this custom to Hawaii.

■ In olden-day Hawaii, *mele* (songs) for hula were composed for every occasion—name songs for babies, dirges for funerals, welcome songs for visitors, celebrations of favorite pursuits.

■ Hula *mai* is a traditional hula form in praise of a noble's genitals; the power of the *alii* (royalty) to procreate gave mana (spiritual power) to the entire culture.

■ Hula students in old Hawaii adhered to high standards: scrupulous cleanliness, no sex, daily cleansing rituals, certain food prohibitions, and no contact with the dead. They were fined if they broke the rules.

WHERE TO WATCH

If you're interested in "the real thing," there are annual hula festivals on each island. Check the individual island visitors' bureaus websites at ⊕ *www.gohawaii.com*.

If you can't make it to a festival, there are plenty of other hula shows—at most resorts, many lounges, and even at certain shopping centers. Ask your hotel concierge for performance information.

ALL ABOUT LEI

Lei brighten every occasion in Hawaii, from birthdays to bar mitz-vahs to baptisms. Creative artisans weave nature's bounty—flowers, ferns, vines, and seeds—into gorgeous creations that convey an array of heartfelt messages: "Welcome," "Congratulations," "Good luck," "Farewell," "Thank you," "I love you." When it's difficult to find the right words, a lei expresses exactly the right sentiment.

WHERE TO BUY THE BEST LEI

Most airports in Hawaii have lei stands where you can buy a fragrant garland upon arrival. Every florist shop in the Islands sells lei; you can also treat yourself to a lei while shopping for provisions at any supermarket or box store. And you'll always find lei sellers at crafts fairs and outdoor festivals.

LEI ETIQUETTE

■ To wear a closed lei, drape it over your shoulders, half in front and half in back. Open lei are worn around the neck, with the ends draped over the front in equal lengths.

■ Pikake, ginger, and other sweet, delicate blossoms are "feminine" lei. Men opt for cigar, crown flower, and ti leaf lei, which are sturdier and don't emit as much fragrance.

■ Lei are always presented with a kiss, a custom that supposedly dates back to World War II when a hula dancer fancied an officer at a U.S.O. show. Taking a dare from members of her troupe, she took off her lei, placed it around his neck, and kissed him on the cheek.

■ You shouldn't wear a lei before you give it to someone else. Hawaiians believe the lei absorbs your mana (spirit); if you give your lei away, you'll be giving away part of your essence.

ORCHID

Growing wild on every continent except Antarctica, orchids—which range in color from yellow to green to purple—comprise the largest family of plants in the world. There are more than 20,000 species of orchids, but only three are native to Hawaii—and they are very rare. The pretty lavender vanda you see hanging by the dozens at local lei stands has probably been imported from Thailand.

MAILE

Maile, an endemic twining vine with a heady aroma, is sacred to Laka, goddess of the hula. In ancient times, dancers wore maile and decorated hula altars with it to honor Laka. Today, "open" maile lei usually are given to men. Instead of ribbon, interwoven lengths of maile are used at dedications of new businesses. The maile is untied, never snipped, for doing so would symbolically "cut" the company's success.

ILIMA

Designated by Hawaii's Territorial Legislature in 1923 as the official flower of the island of Oahu, the golden ilima is so delicate it lasts for just a day. Five to seven hundred blossoms are needed to make one garland. Queen Emma, wife of King Kamehameha IV, preferred ilima over all other lei, which may have led to the incorrect belief that they were reserved only for royalty.

PLUMERIA

This ubiquitous flower is named after Charles Plumier, the noted French botanist who discovered it in Central America in the late 1600s. Plumeria ranks among the most popular lei in Hawaii because it's fragrant, hardy, plentiful, inexpensive, and requires very little care. Although yellow is the most common color, you'll also find plumeria lei in shades of pink, red, orange, and "rainbow" blends.

PIKAKE

Favored for its fragile beauty and sweet scent, pikake was introduced from India. In lieu of pearls, many brides in Hawaii adorn themselves with long, multiple strands of white pikake. Princess Kaiulani enjoyed showing guests her beloved pikake and peacocks at Ainahau, her Waikiki home. Interestingly, pikake is the Hawaiian word for both the bird and the blossom.

KUKUI

The kukui (candlenut) is Hawaii's state tree. Early Hawaiians strung kukui nuts (which are quite oily) together and burned them for light; mixed burned nuts with oil to make an indelible dye; and mashed roasted nuts to consume as a laxative. Kukui nut lei may not have been made until after Western contact, when the Hawaiians saw black beads from Europe and wanted to imitate them.

LUAU: A TASTE OF HAWAII

The best place to sample Hawaiian food is at a backyard luau. Aunts and uncles are cooking, the pig is from a cousin's farm, and the fish is from a brother's boat.

But even locals have to angle for invitations to those rare occasions. So your choice is most likely between a commercial luau and a Hawaiian restaurant.

Some commercial luau are less authentic; they offer little of the traditional diet and are more about umbrella drinks, spectacle, and fun.

For greater culinary authenticity, folksy experiences, and rock-bottom prices, visit a Hawaiian restaurant (most are in anonymous storefronts in residential neighborhoods). Expect rough edges and some effort negotiating the menu.

In either case, much of what is known today as Hawaiian food would be as foreign to a 16th-century Hawaiian as risotto or chow mien. The pre-contact diet was simple and healthy—mainly raw and steamed seafood and vegetables. Early Hawaiians used earth ovens and heated stones to cook seafood, taro, sweet potatoes, and breadfruit and seasoned their food with sea salt and ground kukui nuts. Seaweed, fern shoots, sweet potato vines, coconut, banana, sugarcane, and select greens and roots rounded out the diet.

Successive waves of immigrants added their favorites to the ti leaf–lined table. So it is that foods as disparate as salt salmon and chicken long rice are now Hawaiian—even though there is no salmon in Hawaiian waters and long rice (cellophane noodles) is Chinese.

AT THE LUAU: KALUA PORK

The heart of any luau is the *imu*, the earth oven in which a whole pig is roasted. The preparation of an imu is an arduous affair for most families, who tackle it only once a year or so, for a baby's first birthday or at Thanksgiving, when many Islanders prefer to imu their turkeys. Commercial luau operations have it down to a science, however.

THE ART OF THE STONE

The key to a proper imu is the *pohaku*, the stones. Imu cook by means of long, slow, moist heat released by special stones that can withstand a hot fire without exploding. Many Hawaiian families treasure their imu stones, keeping them in a pile in the backyard and passing them on through generations.

PIT COOKING

The imu makers first dig a pit about the size of a refrigerator, then lay down *kiawe* (mesquite) wood and stones, and build a white-hot fire that is allowed to burn itself out. The ashes are raked away, and the hot stones covered with banana and ti leaves. Well-wrapped in ti or banana leaves and a net of chicken wire, the pig is lowered onto the leaf-covered stones. *Laulau* (leaf-wrapped bundles of meats, fish, and taro leaves) may also be placed inside. Leaves—ti, banana, even ginger—cover the pig followed by wet burlap sacks (to create steam). The whole is topped with a canvas tarp and left to steam for the better part of a day.

OPENING THE IMU

This is the moment everyone waits for: The imu is unwrapped like a giant present and the imu keepers gingerly wrestle out the steaming pig. When it's unwrapped, the meat falls moist and smoky-flavored from the bone, looking just like Southern-style pulled pork, but without the barbecue sauce.

WHICH LUAU?

Most resort hotels have luau on their grounds that include hula, music, and, of course, lots of food and drink. Each island also has at least one "authentic" luau. For lists of the best luau on each island, visit the Hawaii Visitors and Convention Bureau website at ⊕ *www. gohawaii.com.*

MEA AI ONO: GOOD THINGS TO EAT.

LAULAU
Steamed meats, fish, and taro leaf in ti-leaf bundles: fork-tender, a medley of flavors; the taro resembles spinach.

Laulau

LOMI LOMI SALMON
Salt salmon in a piquant salad or relish with onions and tomatoes.

POI
Poi, a paste made of pounded taro root, may be an acquired taste, but it's a must-try during your visit.

Consider: The Hawaiian Adam is descended from *kalo* (taro). Young taro plants are called "keiki" (children). Poi is the first food after mother's milk for many Islanders. *Ai*, the word for food, is synonymous with poi in many contexts.

Lomi lomi salmon

Not only that, locals love it. "There is no meat that doesn't taste good with poi," the old Hawaiians said.

But you have to know how to eat it: with something rich or powerfully flavored. "It is salt that makes the poi go in," is another adage. When you're served poi, try it with a mouthful of smoky kalua pork or salty *lomi lomi* salmon. Its slightly sour blandness cleanses the palate. And if you don't like it, smile and say something polite. (And slide that bowl over to a local.)

Poi

E HELE MAI AI! COME AND EAT!

Local-style Hawaiian restaurants tend to be inconveniently located in well-worn storefronts with little or no parking, outfitted with battered tables and clattering Melmac dishes, but they personify aloha, invariably run by local families who welcome tourists who take the trouble to find them.

Many are cash-only operations and combination plates, known as "plate lunch," are a standard feature: one or two entrées, two scoops of steamed rice, one scoop of macaroni salad, and—if the place is really old-style—a tiny portion of coarse Hawaiian salt and some raw onions for relish.

Most serve some foods that aren't, strictly speaking, Hawaiian, but are beloved of *kamaaina* (locals), such as salt meat with watercress (preserved meat in a tasty broth), or *akubone* (skipjack tuna fried in a tangy vinegar sauce).

What to Read and Watch

HAWAIIAN MYTHOLOGY BY MARTHA BECKWITH

This exhaustive work of ethnology and folklore was researched and collected by Martha Beckwith over decades and published when she was 69. *Hawaiian Mythology* is a comprehensive look at the Hawaiian ancestral deities and their importance throughout history.

HAWAII'S STORY BY HAWAII'S QUEEN, BY LILIUOKALANI

This poignant book by Queen Liliuokalani chronicles the 1893 overthrow of the Hawaiian monarchy and her plea for her people. It's an essential read to understand the political undercurrent and the push for sovereignty that exists in the Islands more than 125 years later.

LETTERS FROM HAWAII BY MARK TWAIN

In 1866, when Samuel Clemens was 31, he sailed from California and spent four months in Hawaii. He eventually mailed 25 letters to the *Sacramento Union* newspaper about his experiences. Along the way, Twain sheds some cultural biases as he visits Kilauea Volcano, meets with Hawaii's newly formed legislators, and examines the sugar trade.

SHOAL OF TIME: A HISTORY OF THE HAWAIIAN ISLANDS BY GAVAN DAWS

Perhaps the most popular book by this best-selling Honolulu author is *Shoal of Time*. Published in 1974, the account of modern Hawaiian history details the colonization of Hawaii and everything that was lost in the process.

MOLOKAI BY ALAN BRENNERT

The writer's debut novel, set in the 1890s, follows a Hawaiian woman who contracts leprosy as a child and is sent to the remote, quarantined community of Kalaupapa on the island of Molokai, where she then lives. The Southern California–based author was inspired to write the book during his visits to Hawaii.

HAWAII SAYS "ALOHA" BY DON BLANDING

First published in 1928, this volume of enchanting, rhyming verse about Hawaii evokes the rich details about the Islands that mesmerized the author in the 1920s and for the rest of his life. Blanding also illustrated this and many other books and was later named Hawaii's poet laureate.

THE DESCENDANTS

Based on the book by local author Kaui Hart Hemmings, the film adaptation starring George Clooney and directed by Alexander Payne was filmed on Oahu and Kauai. It spotlights a contemporary, upper-class family in Hawaii as they deal with family grief and landholdings in flux.

BLUE HAWAII

The 1961 musical features the hip-shaking songs and moves of Elvis Presley, who plays tour guide Chadwick Gates. Elvis famously sings "Ke Kali Nei Au," or "The Hawaiian Wedding Song," at the iconic and now-shuttered Coco Palms Resort on Kauai. (The resort has remained closed since 1992 following Hurricane Iniki.)

MOANA

The release of *Moana* in 2016 was celebrated by many in Hawaii and the Pacific for showcasing Polynesian culture. The now-beloved animated movie, which tells the story of the demigod Maui, features the voice talents of Aulii Cravalho and Dwayne Johnson. In 2018, *Moana* was re-recorded and distributed in Olelo Hawaii, or the Hawaiian language, with Cravalho reprising her role. It marked the first time a Disney movie was available in Hawaiian.

Chapter 2

TRAVEL SMART

Updated by
Syndi Texeira

★ **CAPITAL:**
Honolulu (Capital of Hawaii)

POPULATION:
169,000

LANGUAGE:
Hawaiian and English

$ CURRENCY:
USD

⚠ **EMERGENCIES:**
911

🚗 **DRIVING:**
On the right

⚡ **ELECTRICITY:**
120v/60 cycles; electrical
plugs have two round prongs

🕐 **TIME:**
Six hours behind New York
(depending on daylight
savings)

🌐 **WEB RESOURCES:**
gohawaii.org
hvcb.org
mauicounty.gov

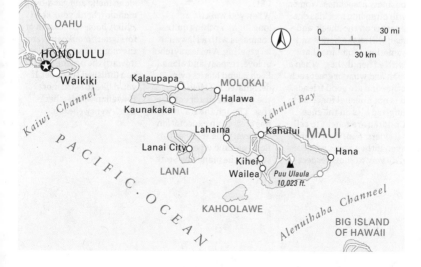

Know Before You Go

Do they really hand you a lei when you arrive? What are some common Hawaiian phrases? How can I help protect the coral? Traveling to Maui is an easy adventure, but we've got tips to make your trip seamless and more meaningful. Below are all the answers to FAQs about Maui and Hawaii.

DON'T CALL IT "THE STATES"

Hawaii was admitted to the Union in 1959, so residents can be somewhat sensitive when visitors refer to their hometowns as "back in the States." Instead, refer to the contiguous 48 states as "the continent." You won't appear to be such a *malihini* (newcomer) when you do.

WELCOME ISLAND-STYLE GREETINGS

Hawaii is a friendly place, which is reflected in the day-to-day encounters with friends, family, and even business associates. Women will often hug and kiss one another on the cheek, and men will shake hands and sometimes combine that with a friendly hug. When a man and woman greet each other and are good friends, it is not unusual for them to hug and kiss on the cheek. Children are taught to call all elders "auntie" or "uncle," even if they aren't related; it's a way to show respect.

LOOK, BUT DON'T TOUCH

Help protect Hawaii's wildlife by loving it from a distance. Stay at least 10 feet away from turtles on land and in the water, and 50 feet from monk seals, wherever you encounter them. Though they may not look it, corals are alive and fragile; harming them also harms the habitat for reef fish and other marine life. Avoid touching or stepping on coral, and take extra care when entering and exiting the water.

ENJOY A FRESH FLOWER LEI

When you walk off a long flight, nothing quite compares with a Hawaiian lei greeting. A lei is a symbol of love, respect, and aloha. Each Island has its own designated lei; Maui has the pink *lokelani* or cottage rose. Though the tradition has created an expectation that everyone receives this floral garland when they step off the plane, the State of Hawaii cannot greet each of its more than 8 million annual visitors. If you've booked a vacation with a wholesaler or tour company, a lei greeting might be included in your package. If not, it's easy to arrange a lei greeting before you arrive at Kahului Airport with Alii Greeting Service (☎ 808/877–7088 ⊕ *aliigreetingservice.com*). An orchid lei is considered standard and costs about $29 per person. You can tuck a single flower behind your ear; a flower behind the left ear means you are in a relationship or unavailable, while the right ear indicates you are looking for love.

APPRECIATE THE HAWAIIAN LANGUAGE

Hawaiian and English are both official state languages, the latter being more prominent. However, making an effort to learn some Hawaiian words can be rewarding. Hawaiian words you are most likely to encounter during your visit to the Islands are *aloha* (hello and good-bye), *mahalo* (thank you), *keiki* (child), *haole* (Caucasian or foreigner), *mauka* (toward the mountains), *makai* (toward the ocean), and *pau* (finished, all done). If you'd like to learn more Hawaiian words, check out ⊕ *wehewehe.org*.

LISTEN FOR HAWAII'S OTHER LANGUAGE

Besides Hawaiian and English, there's a third language spoken here. Hawaiian history includes waves of immigrants, each bringing their native language. To communicate, they developed a dialect known as Hawaiian Pidgin English, or "Pidgin" for short. In 2015, the U.S. Census added Hawaiian Pidgin to the list of official languages in Hawaii. If you listen closely, you will know what is said by the inflections and body language. For an informative and sometimes hilarious view of Pidgin, check out *Pidgin to da Max* by Douglas Simonson and *Fax to da Max* by Jerry Hopkins. Both are available at most local bookstores in the Hawaiiana sections and various stores. While it's nice to appreciate this unique language, it's not wise to emulate it, as it can be considered disrespectful.

BE MINDFUL OF LOCAL CUSTOMS

If you're invited to the home of friends living in Hawaii (an ultimate compliment), bring an *omiyage* (small gift) and take off your shoes when you enter their house. Try to participate in a cultural festival during your stay in the Islands; there is no better way to get a glimpse of Hawaii's ethnic mosaic.

MIND YOUR (ROAD) MANNERS

In Hawaii, they drive with aloha. Merging is freely allowed and residents expect to be let into lanes of traffic. When someone allows you to merge, don't forget to *shaka*; it's the local way to say thank you. Honking your horn is frowned upon unless you're in an emergency or an accident is imminent. Sudden roadside attractions like rainbows or a breaching whale are relatively common, and it's easy to become distracted behind the wheel. Just remember that people live and work here, so it's best to keep traffic moving. If there's a lineup of cars behind you, especially on the winding Road to Hana (one of the most popular attractions on Maui and known all over the world), pull over and let them pass.

CHECK THE WEATHER

On Maui, it seems there's a natural wonder around every corner. But don't be caught off guard by the pretty vistas—the environment can change in an instant, and with little or no warning. Strong ocean currents, flash flooding, and rockslides are a real threat, especially during extreme weather events. If you're hiking somewhere like Haleakala National Park, you'll want to check the wind, rain, and snow conditions, as all three elements are common. The County of Maui offers safety tips for visitors (⊕ *co. maui.hi.us/oceansafety*), and it's a good idea to familiarize yourself with local conditions before heading out on any adventure.

USE REEF-SAFE SUNSCREEN

In 2021, Maui lawmakers passed a bill banning the sale, distribution, or use of non-mineral sunscreens. Non-mineral sunscreens can harm coral reefs and marine ecosystems. Zinc oxide and titanium dioxide are mineral sunscreens deemed safe by the United States Food and Drug Administration. Protect the environment by using a product that's marine safe; you'll feel good about the product you're buying and more confident when heading out for a day in the sun. Or avoid the need for added sunscreen by wearing a long-sleeved rash guard.

Getting Here

Air

Flying time to Maui is about 10 hours from New York, 8 hours from Chicago, and 5 hours from Los Angeles.

Hawaii is the primary destination link for flights between the U.S. mainland, Asia, Australia, New Zealand, and the South Pacific. Island-hopping is easy, with more than 170 daily interisland flights connecting all the major islands. International travelers also have options: Oahu and Hawaii Island are gateways to the United States.

Although Maui's airports are smaller and more casual than Oahu's Daniel K. Inouye International Airport, they can also be quite busy during peak times. Allow extra travel time to either airport during morning and afternoon rush-hour traffic periods, and allow time if you are returning a rental car. Plan to arrive at the airport at least two hours before departure for interisland flights and three hours for transpacific flights.

Plants and plant products are subject to regulation by the Department of Agriculture, both when entering and leaving Hawaii. Upon leaving the Islands, your bags are X-rayed and tagged at one of the airport's agricultural-inspection stations before you proceed to check in. Pineapples and coconuts with the packer's agricultural-inspection stamp pass freely; papayas must be treated, inspected, and stamped. All other fresh fruits are banned for export to the U.S. mainland. Flowers are allowed except for jade vine and mauna loa. Also forbidden are insects, snails, soil, cotton, cacti, sugarcane, and berry plants, including fresh coffee berries.

Dogs and other pets must be left at home: a quarantine of up to 30 days is imposed to keep out rabies, which is nonexistent in Hawaii. However, if specific pre- and post-arrival requirements are satisfied, animals may qualify for five-day-or-less quarantine.

The Transportation Security Administration has answers for almost every question that might come up.

AIRPORTS

Hawaii's major islands have their own airports, but Oahu's Daniel K. Inouye International Airport is the main stopover for most U.S. mainland and international flights. From Honolulu, daily flights to Maui leave from early morning until late evening. You can depart from the interisland or commuter terminals in two structures adjacent to the overseas terminal building. The Wiki Wiki Shuttle, a free bus service, can transport you between terminals. Flights from Honolulu into Lanai and Molokai are offered several times a day. In addition, several carriers offer nonstop service directly from the U.S. mainland to Maui.

Maui has two major airports. Kahului Airport handles major airlines and interisland flights; it's the only airport on Maui with direct service from the mainland. Kapalua–West Maui Airport is served by Hawaiian and Mokulele airlines. If you're staying in West Maui and flying in from another island, you can avoid the hour drive from the Kahului Airport by flying into Kapalua–West Maui Airport. Hana Airport in East Maui is small; Mokulele Airlines offers daily flights between Kahului and Hana.

Molokai's Hoolehua Airport and Lanai Airport are small and centrally located. Both rural airports handle a limited number of flights per day. There's a small airfield at Kalaupapa on Molokai and required visitor permits are available via tour companies listed on the National Park Service website ⊕ *nps.gov*. Visitors coming from the U.S. mainland to these islands must first stop on Oahu or Maui and change to an interisland flight. Lanai Airport has a federal agricultural inspection station, so guests departing to the mainland can check luggage directly.

GROUND TRANSPORTATION

If you're not renting a car, you'll need to take a taxi, rideshare, or SpeediShuttle if your hotel is along its route. Maui Airport Taxi & Shuttle serves the Kahului Airport. Cab fares for up to five passengers to locations around the island are estimated as follows: Kaanapali $79, Kahului $15, Kapalua $99, Kihei $45, Lahaina $69, Maalaea $35, Makena $59, Wailea $49, and Wailuku $20. It will cost more, but the shuttles can accommodate up to 12 passengers.

SpeediShuttle offers transportation between the Kahului Airport and hotels, resorts, and condominium complexes throughout Maui. There is an online reservation and fare-quote system for information and bookings. You can expect to pay around $78 per couple to Kaanapali and $55 to Wailea.

FLIGHTS

Service to Maui changes regularly, so it's best to check when you are ready to book. Southwest is the newest airline to arrive on Maui, with direct flights from Sacramento, Oakland, San Jose, and San Diego. Alaska Airlines offers nonstop flights from Anchorage, Los Angeles, Oakland, Sacramento, San Diego, San Francisco, San Jose, Seattle, and Portland. American Airlines flies from Dallas, Los Angeles, and Phoenix. Hawaiian Airlines has nonstop service from Los Angeles, Oakland, San Jose, San Diego, Portland, San Francisco, Seattle, and New York City. United's nonstop flights leave from Chicago, Denver, Los Angeles, and San Francisco. Delta has flights from Los Angeles, Salt Lake City, and Seattle. Virgin Atlantic flies nonstop from Los Angeles and San Francisco. In addition to offering competitive rates and online specials, all have frequent-flyer programs that will entitle you to rewards and upgrades the more you fly.

CHARTER FLIGHTS

George's Aviation offers on-demand private air charters and cargo service between all the major Hawaiian Islands. Should you want to explore Maui, Kauai, Oahu, and Hawaii Island from the air and ground, you can book tours through Discover Hawaii Tours.

INTERISLAND FLIGHTS

Hawaii's interisland airline market can be volatile, and many smaller carriers have come and gone over the years. The exception is Hawaiian Airlines, which has a long history of safe, reliable flying. It offers regular interisland service to Maui's Kahului and Kapalua airports. Southwest Airlines brought some competition and lower fares when they entered the market in 2019. Southwest flies from Kahului Airport to the major Hawaiian Islands. Mokulele Airlines provides interisland service between Maui (Kahului), Lanai, Molokai (Hoolehua), Oahu, and Hawaii Island. Mokulele also services Maui's Kapalua and Hana airports. Mokulele departs from the commuter terminals, which means you can arrive a minimum of 30 minutes before departure time and skip the TSA lines.

Be sure to compare prices offered by all interisland carriers. Plan and be flexible with your dates and times if you're looking for an affordable flight.

Getting Here

Bus

Maui Bus, operated by the tour company Roberts Hawaii, offers 12 routes in and between various Central, South, and West Maui communities. You can travel in and around Wailuku, Kahului, Lahaina, Kaanapali, Kapalua, Kihei, Wailea, Maalaea, the North Shore (Paia), and Upcountry (including Kula, Pukalani, Makawao, Haliimaile, and Haiku). The Upcountry and Haiku Islander routes include a stop at Kahului Airport. All routes cost $2 per boarding; children five and under ride free.

Car

Should you plan to do any sightseeing on Maui, it's best to rent a car. Even if all you want to do is relax at your resort, you may want to hop in the car to check out one of the Island's popular restaurants.

Many of Maui's roads are two lanes, so allow plenty of time to your next destination. Check the local traffic reports and Google Maps for delays. During morning and afternoon rush hours, traffic can be awful. Morning (6:30–9:30 am) and afternoon (3:30–6:30 pm) rush-hour traffic around Kahului, Paia, Kihei, and Lahaina can cause significant delays, so use caution. When returning your rental car, give yourself about 3½ to 4 hours before your transpacific flight departure time due to traffic and long airport security lines. Remember to drive with aloha.

On Molokai and Lanai, four-wheel-drive vehicles are recommended for exploring off the beaten path. Many of the roads are poorly paved or unpaved.

Make sure you've got a GPS or a good map. You can find free visitor publications containing high-quality road maps at airports, hotels, and shops. Don't depend on your mobile phone as service is spotty or nonexistent in some areas.

Asking for directions will almost always produce a helpful explanation from the locals, but you should be prepared for an island term or two. Hawaii residents refer to places as either *mauka* (toward the mountains) or *makai* (toward the ocean).

Hawaii has a strict seatbelt law. All passengers, regardless of age, in the front and back seat must wear a seat belt. The fine for not wearing a seat belt is $102. Jaywalking is also common, so pay careful attention to pedestrians. Turning right on a red light is legal in the state, except where noted. Your valid mainland driver's license is suitable for rental cars for up to 90 days.

GASOLINE

Gas costs more on Maui than on the U.S. mainland, up to $1–$1.50 more per gallon. Expect to pay more (sometimes significantly more) on Lanai and Molokai. The only gas station on Lanai is Lanai City Service.

In rural areas, it's not unusual for gas stations to close early. If you see that your tank is getting low, don't take any chances; fill up at the nearest station.

PARKING

With a population of more than 169,000 and around 60,000 visitors on any given day, Maui has parking challenges. Parking lots sprinkled throughout West Maui charge by the hour. There are about 700 parking spaces at the Outlets of Maui in Lahaina; shoppers can get validated parking here, as well as Whalers Village. Parking along many streets is curtailed during rush hours, and towing is widely practiced. Read curbside parking signs before leaving your vehicle.

Car Rental Resources

LOCAL AGENCIES

AA Aloha Cars-R-Us	800/655–7989	hawaiicarrental.com
Mobettah Car Rentals (Molokai)	808/308-9566	mobettahcarrentals.com
Lanai Cheap Jeep Rentals (Lanai)	808/469–2296	lanaicheapjeeps.com
Maui Camper & Van Rentals	855/671–1122	mauicamperrental.com
Bio-Beetle Eco Rental Cars	808/873–6121	bio-beetle.com
Discount Hawaii Car Rental	888/292–1930	discounthawaiicarrental.com
North Shore Maui Rent A Car	623/850–3087	northshoremauirentacar.com
Hawaii Harley Rental	808/877–1859	rentaharleyhawaii.com

RENTALS

While on Maui, you can rent anything from a subcompact to a Ferrari. Rates are usually better if you reserve through a rental agency's website. All the big national rental-car agencies have locations on Maui, but Alamo (⊕ alamo.com) is the only one on Molokai. There are also local rental-car companies, so be sure to compare prices before you book. It's wise to make reservations far in advance, especially if you're visiting during peak seasons or for major conventions or sporting events, as car rental companies often sell out entirely during these times.

For more specifics about renting on Molokai and Lanai, see the Planning sections of Chapters 11 and 12.

Rates begin at around $30-$45 a day for an economy car with air-conditioning, automatic transmission, and unlimited mileage, depending on your pickup location. This cost does not include the airport concession fee, general excise tax, rental-vehicle surcharge, or vehicle license fee. Before you reserve a car, ask about cancellation penalties and drop-off charges should you plan to pick up the vehicle in one location and return it to another. Many rental companies offer money-saving coupons for local attractions.

In Hawaii, you must be 21 to rent a car and have a valid driver's license and a major credit card. You can use a debit card at most rental agencies, but they will put a $500 hold on your account for the rental duration. Those under 25 will pay a daily surcharge of $10–$25. Request car seats and extras such as a GPS when making your reservation. Hawaii's Child Restraint Law requires that all children under age four be in an approved child-safety seat in the backseat of a vehicle. Children ages four to seven, who are less than 4 feet 9 inches tall and weigh less than 80 pounds, must be seated in a rear booster seat or child restraint such as a lap and shoulder belt. Car seats and boosters run $7–$12 per day; some companies have a maximum charge per rental period.

Maui has some unusual rental options. Maui Campers & Van Rentals rents older VW Westfalia campers and newer Honda Elements and Chrysler Town & Country minivans for $99–$149 per day, depending upon the season, with a three-day minimum. And if exploring the Island on two wheels is more your speed, Hawaii

Getting Here

Harley Rental rents motorcycles. Hawaiian Riders also rent luxury cars. Prefer an earth-friendly automobile that gets 35–50 miles to the gallon? Bio-Beetle Eco Rental Cars run on clean-burning diesel fuel from renewable sources like recycled vegetable oil.

RENTALS ON LANAI

Renting a four-wheel-drive vehicle is expensive but almost essential to get beyond the resorts. There are only 30 miles of paved road on the Island. The rest of your driving takes place on bumpy, sometimes muddy, secondary roads. Make reservations far in advance, because Lanai's fleet of vehicles is limited.

ROAD CONDITIONS

Getting around Maui is relatively easy, as only a few major roads hit the must-see sights. Honoapiilani Highway will get you from the central Maui towns of Wailuku and Kahului to the leeward coast and Lahaina, Kaanapali, Kahana, and Kapalua. Those gorgeous mountains that hug Honoapiilani Highway are the West Maui Mountains. Depending on traffic, it should take about 30–45 minutes to travel this route. The other road connecting West Maui with the rest of the Island is a less-traveled (and sometimes treacherous) back road, so if there's an accident or other traffic jam, the drive can take hours.

North and South Kihei Road will take you to the town of Kihei and the resort area of Wailea on the South Shore. The drive from the airport in Kahului to Wailea should take about 30 minutes, and the drive from Kaanapali in West Maui to Wailea on the South Shore will take about 45–60 minutes.

Your vacation to Maui must include a visit to Haleakala National Park, and you should plan on 2–2½ hours' driving time from Kaanapali or Wailea. The drive from Kaanapali or Wailea to the charming towns of Makawao and Kula will take about 45–60 minutes. And you must not miss the Road to Hana, a 55-mile stretch with one-lane bridges, hairpin turns, and breathtaking views. The Hawaii Visitors and Convention Bureau's red-caped King Kamehameha signs mark significant attractions and scenic spots.

All major roads on Maui are passable with two-wheel-drive vehicles. It would be best to exercise caution on Kahekili Highway between Waihee Point and Keawalua, which is somewhat treacherous due to sheer drop-offs and the southern stretch of Piilani Highway between Ulupalakua and Kipahulu, which has sections of extraordinarily rough and unpaved roadway. Both roads are remote, have no gas stations, and provide minimal cell phone service, so plan accordingly.

In rural areas, it's not unusual for gas stations to close early. Use caution during heavy downpours, especially if you see signs warning of falling rocks. If you enjoy the views or need to study a map, pull over to the side. Remember the aloha spirit: allow other cars to merge, don't honk (it's considered rude), and use your headlights and turn signals.

Essentials

📍 Dining and Lodging on Maui

Hawaii is a melting pot of cultures, and nowhere is this more apparent than in its cuisines. There's no shortage of exciting flavors and presentations, from luau and plate lunches to sushi and teriyaki steak. The restaurant atmosphere varies from casual local spots to elegantly decorated resort restaurants.

Whether you're looking for a quick snack or a multicourse meal, we can help you find the best eating experiences the island has to offer. *Hele mai* (come) and enjoy!

Choosing where to lodge is a tough decision, but fret not: our expert writers and editors have done most of the legwork.

To help narrow your choices, consider what type of property you'd like to stay at (big resort, quiet bed-and-breakfast, or condo rental) and what kind of Island climate you're looking for (beachfront or remote rain forest). We give you all the details you need to book a place that suits your style.

■TIP→ **Reserve your room well in advance, and ask about discounts and packages. Hotel websites often have Internet-only deals.**

WHAT IT COSTS in U.S. Dollars			
$	$$	$$$	$$$$
RESTAURANTS			
Under $18	$18–$26	$27–$35	over $35
HOTELS			
Under $181	$181–$260	$261–$340	over $340

🌐 Communications

INTERNET

If you've brought your laptop or tablet with you to Maui, you should have no problem checking email or connecting to the Internet. Most major hotels and resorts offer high-speed access in rooms or public areas. If you're staying at a small inn or B&B without Internet access, ask the proprietor for the nearest café or coffee shop with wireless access.

Most Maui hotels, restaurants, and tour companies have mobile-friendly websites. Reliable Internet access from your smartphone is available throughout Maui, but can be challenging in some rural areas.

PHONES

The area code for the State of Hawaii is 808. For local calls on Maui, dial the 10-digit number, including the area code. If you call a neighbor island or long-distance while on Maui, you need to dial 1 followed by the 10-digit number.

➕ Health

Hawaii is known as the Health State. The life expectancy here is 81.3 years, the longest in the nation. Tropical weather makes it easy to remain active year-round, and the low-stress aloha attitude contributes to the general well-being. When visiting the Islands, however, there are a few health issues to keep in mind.

The Hawaii State Department of Health recommends that you drink 16 ounces of water per hour to avoid dehydration when hiking or spending time in the sun. Use mineral sunblock, wear UV-reflective sunglasses, and protect your head with a

Essentials

visor or hat. If you're not used to warm, humid weather, allow plenty of time for rest stops and refreshments.

When visiting freshwater streams, be aware of the relatively rare tropical disease leptospirosis, which is spread by animal urine. Symptoms include fever, headache, nausea, and red eyes. To avoid leptospirosis, don't swim or wade in freshwater streams or ponds if you have open sores, and don't drink from any freshwater streams or ponds. If you do exhibit symptoms after exposure to freshwater streams, seek immediate medical attention.

On the Islands, fog is a rare occurrence, but there can often be "vog," an airborne haze of gases released from volcanic vents on Hawaii Island. During certain weather conditions such as "Kona Winds," the vog can settle over the Island and wreak havoc with respiratory conditions, especially asthma or emphysema. If susceptible, stay indoors and get emergency assistance if needed.

The Islands have their share of insects. Most are harmless but annoying. When planning to spend time outdoors in hiking areas, wear long-sleeved clothing and long pants and use mosquito repellent containing DEET. In damp places, you may encounter the dreaded local centipedes, which are brown or blue and measure up to twelve inches long. Their painful sting is similar to those of bees and wasps. When camping, shake out your sleeping bag and check your shoes, as the centipedes like cozy places. When hiking in remote areas, always carry a first-aid kit.

◉ Hours of Operation

Even people in paradise have to work. Generally, local business hours are weekdays 8–5 except on holidays. Hawaii has state and county holidays that differ from the mainland. Banks are usually open Monday through Thursday 8:30–4 and until 6 pm on Friday. Some banks have weekend hours.

Many self-serve gas stations stay open around the clock, with full-service stations usually open 7 am–9 pm; stations in rural spots may close earlier. U.S. post offices generally open between 8:30 and 9:30 am on weekdays and close between 3:30 and 4:30 pm. Saturday hours are usually short and vary from office to office.

Most museums open their doors between 9 and 10 am and stay open until 4 or 4:30 pm. Many museums close on Sunday and Monday. Visitor-attraction hours vary throughout the state, but most sights are open daily except for major holidays.

Stores in resort areas sometimes open as early as 8 am, with shopping center opening hours varying from 9:30 to 10 am on weekdays and Saturdays, a bit later on Sunday. Larger malls stay open until 9 pm weekdays and Saturday and close at 5 pm on Sunday. Boutiques in resort areas may stay open even later.

ⓢ Money

Prices in listings are for adults. Substantially reduced fees are almost always available for children, students, seniors, veterans, and active U.S. military.

ⓞ Packing

An essential item to pack is mineral sunscreen. However, you can purchase reef-safe sunscreen just about anywhere on the Island. In 2021, Maui banned the sale, distribution, and use of nonmineral sunscreen harmful to coral reefs and marine life. There are many tanning oils on the market in Hawaii, including coconut and *kukui* (candlenut) oils, but they can cause severe burns. Hats, sunglasses, and rash guards offer sun protection, too.

Hawaii is casual: sandals, bathing suits, and comfortable, informal cotton clothing are the norm. In the summer, synthetic slacks and shirts can be uncomfortably warm. The aloha shirt is an accepted attire in Hawaii for business and most social occasions.

Shorts are acceptable daytime attire, along with a T-shirt or polo shirt. There's no need to buy expensive sandals on the mainland—here, you can get flip-flops for a few dollars and off-brand sandals for $20 or less. Many golf courses have dress codes requiring a collared shirt. If you're visiting in winter or planning to visit a high-altitude area, bring a sweater, a light- to medium-weight jacket, or a fleece pullover.

If your vacation plans include an exploration of Maui's northeastern coast, including Hana and Upcountry Maui, pack a light rain jacket. And if you'll be exploring Haleakala National Park, make sure you pack appropriately, as weather at the summit can be very cold and windy. Bring good boots for hiking at Haleakala Crater; sneakers will suffice for most other trails on Maui.

⊕ Safety

Hawaii is generally a safe tourist destination, but it's still wise to follow common-sense safety precautions. Don't leave any valuables inside your rental car, not even in a locked trunk. Avoid poorly lit areas, beach parks, and isolated areas after dark. When hiking, stay on marked trails, no matter how alluring the temptation might be to stray. Weather conditions can cause landscapes to become muddy, slippery, and tenuous, so staying on marked trails will lessen the possibility of a fall or getting lost.

Always follow the safety precautions you would use in any major destination. Stay away from isolated areas after dark; camping and hiking solo is not advised.

ⓢ Taxes

There's a 4.5% state sales tax on all purchases, including food. A hotel room tax of 10.25%, combined with the sales tax of 4.5%, equals a 14.75% rate added to your hotel bill. A $5-per-day road tax is added to rental vehicles.

Essentials

Tipping Guidelines for Maui

Bartender	15%–20%; 20% being the norm at restaurants and bars.
Bellhop	$3–$5 per bag, depending on the level of the hotel and whether you have bulky items like heavy luggage, golf clubs, surf-boards, etc.
Hotel concierge	$5 or more, depending on the service.
Hotel doorman	$3–$5 if he helps you get a cab or helps with bags, golf clubs, etc.
Hotel cleaning person	$5–$10 per day depending on the level of the hotel and how much cleaning is needed (preferred daily, in cash, as the personnel may change).
Hotel room-service server	$3–$5 per delivery, even if there's a service charge.
Airport porter	$3-$5 per bag.
Airport skycap	$3–$5 per bag checked.
Spa personnel	15%–20% of the cost of your service.
Taxi driver	15%–20%, but round up the fare to the next dollar amount.
Tour guide	10%-15% of the cost of the tour.
Valet-parking attendant	$3–$5 each time your car is brought to you or parked.
Server	15%–20%, with 20% being the norm at restaurants; nothing additional if a service charge has been added to the bill.

🧭 Time

Hawaii is on Hawaiian Standard Time, 5 hours behind New York, 2 hours behind Los Angeles, and 10 hours behind London.

When the U.S. mainland is on daylight savings time, Hawaii is not, so add an extra hour of the time difference between the Islands and U.S. mainland destinations. You may find that things generally move more slowly here. That has nothing to do with your watch—it's the laid-back way of life called Hawaiian time.

💲 Tipping

Tipping is not only common but expect-ed: Hawaii is a major vacation destina-tion, and many of the people who work at the hotels, resorts, and restaurants rely on tips to supplement their wages.

📍 Visitor Information

The Hawaii Visitors and Convention Bureau (HVCB) has a lot of general and vacation-planning information for Maui and all the Islands. HVCB also offers a free official vacation planner

Tours

Guided tours are a good option when you don't want to do it yourself. You travel along with a group (sometimes large, sometimes small), stay in prebooked hotels, eat with your fellow travelers (the cost of meals is not always included in the price of your tour), and follow a schedule.

Tours can be just the thing for first-time travelers to Maui or those who enjoy the group-traveling experience. None of the companies offering general-interest tours in Hawaii include Molokai or Lanai. When you book a guided tour, find out what's included and what isn't. A "land-only" tour includes all your ground transportation but not your flights. Most prices in tour brochures don't include fees, taxes, or tips.

TOUR COMPANIES

Atlas Cruises & Tours

GUIDED TOURS | This escorted-tour operator, in business for more than 30 years, partners with major companies such as Collette, Globus, Tauck, and Trafalgar to offer a wide variety of travel experiences. Tours run 7–12 nights. ⊠ *8409 N. Military Trl. #106, Palm Beach Gardens* ☏ *800/942–3301* ⊕ *atlastravelweb.com* ⊠ *From $2,846.*

Globus

GUIDED TOURS | Founded in 1928 by a man who transported visitors across Lake Lugano, Switzerland, in a rowboat, this family-owned company grew to become the largest guided vacation operator in the world. Globus offers four Hawaii itineraries, running 9–12 nights; two include a 7-night cruise on Norwegian Cruise Lines. ⊠ *5301 South Federal Circle, Littleton* ☏ *866/755–8581* ⊕ *globusjourneys. com* ⊠ *From $3,515.*

Trafalgar

GUIDED TOURS | This company prides itself on its "Insider Experiences," defined as visiting hidden places, meeting local people, and sharing traditions you may not discover on your own. Trafalgar offers several itineraries, running 7–12 nights. ⊠ *555 Theodore Fremd Ave. Suite C204, Rye* ☏ *866/513–1995* ⊕ *trafalgar.com* ⊠ *From $3,350.*

Great Itineraries

Maui in 1 Week

Lounging beside the pool or napping on a sandy beach may fulfill your initial fantasy of a tropical Hawaiian vacation, but Maui has much more to offer: underwater encounters with rainbow-colored fish, an icy dip in a jungle waterfall, or a trek across the moonlike landscape of a dormant volcano.

⚠ **As a tropical island, Maui is susceptible to dangerous surf, flash flooding, and other natural hazards. Always check road, ocean, and wilderness advisories before venturing out.**

DAY 1: GETTING SETTLED

On your way out of Kahului Airport, stop at Costco, Target, or Walmart to pick up beach gear, sunscreen, food, and drink.

Once ensconced at your hotel or condo, unwind from your long flight by exploring the grounds, dozing by the pool, or splashing in the ocean—isn't it why you came to Maui?

Logistics: Road signs will point you to the two main resort areas: Highway 311 (Maui Veterans Highway) to 31 (Piilani), south to Kihei and Wailea, and Highway 380 (Kuihelani) to 30 (Honoapiilani) west to Lahaina and Kapalua.

DAY 2: SURF, SAND AND ... FORE!

Head to the nearest beach for snorkeling, swimming, sunbathing, or surfing in the gentle waves of Cove Park in Kihei or Launiupoko in West Maui. If golf's more your game, hit the tournament-quality golf links in the resort areas. You can find more affordable rates at the scenic Waiehu, Waikapu, and Maui Lani courses in Central Maui. Spend the evening (when it's cooler) visiting Lahaina town, filled with shops, restaurants, and art galleries.

Logistics: Many hotels and condos offer complimentary shuttle service to golfing, shopping, and dining. Driving to Lahaina from South Maui, take Highway 310 (North Kihei Road) and turn left on Highway 30 (Honoapiilani).

DAY 3: ADVENTURE ON LAND AND SEA

Get a different view of the island—and discover what's beneath the surface—on a full- or half-day boat excursion to Molokini, a crescent-shaped islet that sits 3 miles off South Maui, or snorkeling, scuba diving, or dolphin- and whale-watching trip. If you prefer dry land, head to Maui Tropical Plantation in Waikapu, which offers tram tours and a country store; it's also the home base for Flyin Hawaiian Zipline and Maui Zipline's introductory course. Plan to be back early enough for a sunset luau at your resort or at Old Lahaina Luau.

Logistics: Boat tours leave from Maalaea Harbor in South Maui and Lahaina Harbor in West Maui. To get to the Maui Tropical Plantation from West Maui, follow Highway 30 (Honoapiilani) south to Waikapu; from South Maui, take Highway 310 (North Kihei Road) and turn right onto Highway 30.

DAY 4: HALEAKALA AND UPCOUNTRY

At the 10,000-foot summit of this dormant volcano, sunrise is so popular that the National Park Service now requires reservations (make yours as early as possible, up to 60 days in advance of your visit). To avoid the crowd, consider planning your day in reverse. Start with some terrific bodysurfing at Baldwin Beach Park on the North Shore, followed by lunch in the former plantation town of Paa, home to charming boutiques and cafés. Once Upcountry, tour Surfing Goat

Dairy, Alii Kula Lavender, or MauiWine, before heading to the Haleakala summit in the afternoon when the park is uncrowded. It's not sunrise, but the spectacular sunset vista encompasses at least three islands and the broad expanse separating Maui's two mountains.

Logistics: To reach Haleakala from South Maui, take Highway 311 (Maui Veterans Highway) out of Kihei to connect with Highway 36 (Hana) and then Highway 37 (Haleakala). From West Maui, follow Highway 30 (Honoapiilani) to 380 (Kuihelani), connecting to Highway 36.

DAY 5: THE ROAD TO HANA

Today's the day to tackle the 600 curves of the Road to Hana (Highway 36/360). There aren't a lot of dining options in Hana, but many hotels offer picnic baskets for the road, or fill your cooler and gas tank in Paia, the last chance for provisions. Pause to stretch your legs at the Keanae Arboretum, picturesque Keanae Landing, or any of the roadside waterfalls. Approaching Hana town, turn into Waianapanapa State Park, with its rugged lava outcroppings, black-sand beach, trails, and caves with freshwater pools. There isn't much reason to stop in Hana town, except for lunch at the food trucks if you didn't bring your own, so continue on to the Kipahulu District of Haleakala National Park, site of the Pools of Oheo (nicknamed Seven Sacred Pools) and 400-foot Waimoku Falls. (Check for updates on closures due to flash flooding and landslides.) Don't leave Kipahulu without visiting the gravesite of famed aviator Charles Lindbergh, who is buried at 19th-century Palapala Hoomau Congregational Church.

Logistics: Follow directions to Haleakala, but stay on Highway 36/360 (Hana).

DAY 6: BACK TO THE BEACH

A full day is needed to recover from a trek to Hana, so take it easy with a visit to the Maui Ocean Center, where you'll be mesmerized by the sharks, rays, and tuna circling the 750,000-gallon open-ocean tank. Then spend the rest of the day relaxing in the water or at the spa with lunch beside the pool.

Logistics: From South Maui, take Highway 31 (Piilani) to 310 (North Kihei Road), then head a short distance left on Highway 30 (Honoapiilani). From West Maui, head south on Highway 30 to Maalaea/Maui Ocean Center.

DAY 7: CENTRAL MAUI

Squeeze in a final session at the beach or pool before checking out of your hotel and heading to Central Maui to be closer to the airport. If you like history, Hale Hoikeike at the Bailey House features the Island's largest collection of Hawaiian artifacts. Just five minutes up the road is Iao Valley State Park and one of the most photographed landmarks in Hawaii: Iao Needle. Eat like a local with lunch or an early dinner at Umi Maui, Miko's Cuisine, Ichiban Okazuya, or A Saigon Cafe in Wailuku or 808 on Main, Cafe O'Lei at the Dunes, or Tin Roof in Kahului. If there's still time, visit Kanaha Beach Park by Kahului Airport to watch world-class wind- and kitesurfers or shop for gifts and souvenirs at the many malls.

Logistics: From South Maui, take Highway 311 (Maui Veterans Highway) all the way to 32 (Kaahumanu) in Kahului, then turn left toward Wailuku; from West Maui, Highway 30 (Honoapiilani) leads right into Wailuku town. Kahului Airport is a 10-minute drive from here.

Contacts

✈ Air

AIR-TRAVEL RESOURCES IN MAUI State of Hawaii Airports Division Offices. ✉ *300 Rodgers Blvd. #6, Honolulu* ☎ *808/836–6413* ⊕ *hidot.hawaii.gov.*

AIRPORT INFORMATION Daniel K. Inouye International Airport (HNL). ✉ *300 Rodgers Blvd., Airport Area* ☎ *808/836–6411* ⊕ *airports.hawaii.gov/hnl.* **Hana Airport (HNM).** ✉ *700 Alalele Rd., Hana* ☎ *808/872–3830* ⊕ *airports.hawaii.gov/hnm.* **Kalaupapa Airfield (LUP).** ✉ *Kalaupapa* ☎ *808/838–8701* ⊕ *airports.hawaii.gov/lup.* **Kapalua–West Maui Airport (JHM).** ✉ *4050 HI-30, 4050 Honoapiilani Hwy, Lahaina* ☎ *808/665–6108* ⊕ *airports.hawaii.gov/jhm.* **Molokai Airport.** (*MKK*). ✉ *3980 Airport Loop, Hoolehua* ☎ *808/567–9660* ⊕ *airports.hawaii.gov/mkk.* **Lanai Airport.** (*LNY*). ✉ *Lanai Avenue, Lanai City* ☎ *808/565–7942* ⊕ *airports.hawaii.gov/lny.* **Kahului Airport.** (*OGG*). ✉ *1 Keolani Pl., Kahului* ☎ *808/872–3830* ⊕ *airports.hawaii.gov/ogg.*

GROUND TRANSPORTATION Maui Airport Taxi & Shuttle. ✉ *2145 Kaohu Street, Kahului* ☎ *808/877–2002* ⊕ *mauiairporttaxi-shuttle.com.* **SpeediShuttle.** ✉ *150 Paahana Street, Kahului* ☎ *808/242–5777* ⊕ *speedishuttle.com.*

CHARTER COMPANIES Discover Hawaii Tours. ✉ *1039 11th Ave., Honolulu* ☎ *808/824–3995* ⊕ *discoverhawaiitours.com.* **George's Aviation.** ✉ *18 Lagoon Dr., Honolulu* ☎ *808/834–2120* ⊕ *georgesaviation.com.*

AIRLINE CONTACTS Hawaiian Airlines. ✉ *3375 Koapaka Street, G-350, Honolulu* ☎ *800/367–5320* ⊕ *hawaiianairlines.com.* **Mokulele Airlines.** ✉ *355 Hukilike Street, Suite 103, Kahului* ☎ *808/495–4188 local, 866/260–7070 toll free* ⊕ *mokuleleairlines.com.* **Southwest Airlines.** ✉ *2702 Love Field Drive, Dallas, TX* ☎ *800/435–9792* ⊕ *southwest.com.*

⊖ Boat and Ferry

FERRY CONTACTS Expeditions Lana'i Ferry. ✉ *658 Front St., Suite 127, Lahaina* ☎ *800/695–2624 toll free, 808/661–3756 local* ⊕ *go-lanai.com.*

🚌 Bus

BUS CONTACT Maui Bus. ✉ *Kahului* ☎ *808/871–4838* ⊕ *mauicounty.gov/bus.*

◉ Visitor Information

CONTACTS Maui Visitors Bureau. ✉ *427 Ala Makani Street, Kahului* ⊕ *gohawaii.com/islands/maui.*

WEST MAUI

3

Updated by
Laurie Lyons-Makaimoku

⊙ Sights	🍽 Restaurants	🛏 Hotels	🛍 Shopping	🍸 Nightlife
★★★★★	★★★★★	★★★★★	★★★★★	★★★☆☆

WELCOME TO WEST MAUI

TOP REASONS TO GO

★ **Seek the sun.** West Maui enjoys clear days throughout the year, and each evening is punctuated with rich sunsets that dip into the Pacific Ocean, offering a daily dose of relaxation and reflection.

★ **Live the ocean lifestyle.** Aquatic activities are just a paddle away. The area's gentle shores are ideal for learning to surf or heading out for a leisurely stand-up paddle excursion.

★ **Stroll world-famous Front Street.** Located at the ocean's edge, this street is home to great shopping, art galleries, and dining options ranging from burger joints to fine dining.

★ **Step back in time.** Once the capital of the Kingdom of Hawaii, by the 1800s the area became an epicenter of the Pacific whaling industry. Walking tours and historic sites bring this heritage to life.

★ **Vacation your way.** West Maui includes several distinctive towns, each with its own personality. From happening Lahaina town, to family-friendly Kaanapali, there's a home away from home for you.

Separated from the remainder of the island by steep *pali* (cliffs), West Maui is sometimes considered an island within an island, as many visitors and residents can find everything they need right here. The towns in this area have much in common: prime oceanfront accommodations, epic sunsets, and a wealth of activity and dining options. Beyond that, they boast their own charm and can range from budget-friendly to luxe. Traveling north on Honoapiilani Highway, you'll first encounter sleepy Olowalu, which despite its sparse population is worth a stop for its impressive reef and famous pie shop. Drive farther until you reach eclectic Lahaina, home to bustling Front Street and action-packed Lahaina Harbor. Just outside of Lahaina is the resort town of Kaanapali, where you'll find massive beachfront hotels and condos, and a host of ocean activities. As you travel north to Napili-Honokowai, mega-resorts give way

to cozy condos and a slower pace. Just a few miles away in Kapalua, fine dining, spas, and world-class golf courses cater to a more glamorous clientele.

1 Olowalu. This blink-and-you'll-miss-it town entices with incredible snorkeling and a beloved restaurant.

2 Lahaina. Rich history and modern comforts converge at this harbor town, home to fantastic dining options, activities, and entertainment.

3 Kaanapali. Maui's first planned resort still shines with manicured mega-hotels, a renowned beach, and a host of activities for all ages.

4 Napili. Offering a more laid-back version of paradise, this quaint seaside community is a mix of residential neighborhoods and low-rise condos.

5 Kapalua. Home to prestigious golf courses and exclusive accommodations, this tony resort is an enclave for affluent travelers.

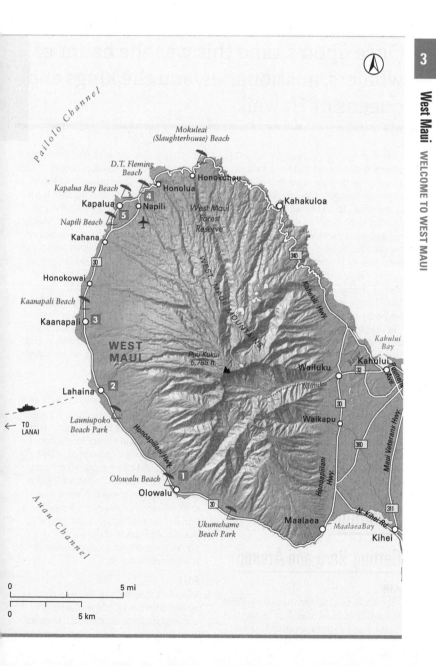

Pailolo Channel

Mokuleai
(Slaughterhouse) Beach

D.T. Fleming
Beach

Honokohau

Kapalua Bay Beach

Honolua

Kapalua

Napili

Kahakuloa

Napili Beach

West Maui
Forest
Reserve

Kahana

WEST MAUI MOUNTAINS

Honokowai

Kahekili Hwy.

Kaanapali Beach

Kaanapali

340

WEST
MAUI

Puu Kukui
5,788 ft.

Wailuku

Kahului
Bay

Kahului

Lahaina

Waikapu

TO
LANAI

Launiupoko
Beach Park

Honoapiilani Hwy.

Waiinee

Iao

32

Keawe

Puunene Ave.

30

Maui Veterans Hwy.

380

Honoapiilani Hwy.

Auau Channel

Olowalu Beach

Olowalu

30

Ukumehame
Beach Park

Maalaea

MaalaeaBay

N. Kihei Rd.

311

Kihei

0				5 mi
0				5 km

Separated from the remainder of the Island by steep *pali* (cliffs), West Maui has a reputation for attitude and action. Once upon a time this was the haunt of whalers, missionaries, and the kings and queens of Hawaii.

Today the main drag, Front Street, is crowded with T-shirt and trinket shops, art galleries, and restaurants. Farther north is Kaanapali, Maui's first planned resort area. Its first hotel, the Sheraton, opened in 1963. Since then, massive resorts, luxury condos, and a shopping center have sprung up along the white-sand beaches, with championship golf courses across the road. A few miles farther up the coast is the ultimate in West Maui luxury, the resort area of Kapalua. In between, dozens of strip malls line both the *makai* (toward the sea) and *mauka* (toward the mountains) sides of the highway. There are gems here, too, like Napili Bay and its jaw-dropping crescent of sand.

In addition to Mele Mei musical events during May, Maui also plays host to some exciting culinary, cultural, and eco-driven festivals. Residents and visitors gather to partake in great food and drink, as well as family-friendly cultural festivities that usually span multiple days.

Planning

Getting Here and Around

AIR
Kapalua Airport, sometimes called West Maui Airport, is located 6 miles north of Lahaina and 4 miles south of Kapalua.

This tiny facility includes just one runway and is served by smaller propeller and commuter-style planes that travel between islands, so arriving here from the mainland isn't an option. Mokulele Airlines operates flights during daylight hours only, as the airport closes before dusk. Services and amenities are limited, so you'll need to plan ahead for ground transportation. There are no car rental facilities here, though you can arrange for an airport pickup from some of the national companies, like Avis or Budget, which have offices in West Maui. Many nearby hotels offer free shuttles to and from the airport, and taxis or ride-shares are also an option.

BOAT
If you plan to travel to neighboring Lanai by ferry, there's only one option. Expeditions' ferry departs from Lahaina Harbor to Lanai's Manele Harbor four times a day. The 9-mile crossing costs $60 round trip and takes about 45 minutes, depending on ocean conditions (which can sometimes make this trip a rough one). Advance reservations are highly recommended, though a harborside ticket booth opens about 45 minutes before each departure, and tickets can be purchased on the spot.

BUS
Maui Bus, operated by the tour company Roberts Hawaii, is the island's only public transportation system. There are

14 routes in and between various Maui communities, including several loops serving West Maui. All routes cost $2 per boarding.

CAR

Should you plan to do any sightseeing on Maui, it's best to rent a car. Many points of interest and natural wonders are off the beaten path, making them nearly impossible to reach without one. Most visitors arrive at Kahului Airport, and you're best off arranging in advance to pick one up there. All the national rental companies have locations on Maui, and it's wise to make reservations far in advance, especially if you're visiting during peak seasons, as cars are sometimes completely sold out during these times.

Beaches

The beaches in West Maui are legendary for their glittering aquamarine waters backed by long stretches of golden sand. Reef fronts much of the western shore, making the underwater panorama something to behold. A few tips: parking can be challenging in resort areas; look for the blue "Shoreline Access" signs to find limited parking and a public path to the beach; and watch out for *kiawe* thorns when you park off-road, because they can puncture tires—and feet.

Events

★ Celebration of the Arts Festival, the Ritz-Carlton, Kapalua

CULTURAL FESTIVALS | In April, cultural practitioners, community artisans, artists, and activists gather at the Ritz-Carlton, Kapalua, for a series of events that celebrate Hawaiian tradition and explore current societal topics. Visitors can partake in an *awa* (kava) ritual, observe *lauhala* (pandan or hala leaves) weaving, watch locally produced films, and listen to cultural panels. The festival concludes with a celebration luau. ⊠ *The Ritz-Carlton, Kapalua, 1*

Ritz-Carlton Dr., Kapalua ☎ *808/669–6200* ⊕ *kapaluacelebrationofthehearts.com.*

Kapalua Wine and Food Festival

FESTIVALS | Kapalua Resort kicks off the summer in June with the Kapalua Wine and Food Festival. Events are held at various resorts and restaurants in Kapalua and draw celebrated chefs, sommeliers, industry insiders, and foodies for themed tastings, wine seminars, and evening galas. Guests may book tickets to individual events or a festival package; tickets can be purchased online or, as the date of the event nears, at specific venues. ⊠ *Kapalua* ⊕ *kapaluawineandfoodfestival. com.*

Hotels

From basic condos to charming bed-and-breakfasts to mega-resorts, West Maui offers just about any kind of accommodation, ranging from moderately priced to ultra-luxury. While Lahaina is a hub of visitor action, accommodation options are mostly in the form of boutique hotels and private rentals. Kaanapali Resort is lined with sprawling hotels that feature high-rise buildings, meandering pools and waterways, multiple dining options, and a host of activities. Most resorts charge parking and facility fees, aka a "resort fee." For those seeking more budget-friendly options, condos in Napili and Honokowai remain a smart choice. Many are oceanfront and offer the amenities of a hotel without the cost. High-end condo developments in Kaanapali and Kapalua mean you no longer have to compromise on luxury to get the comfort and convenience of a condo rental.

Restaurants

You'll find a rainbow of cuisines in just about every price category in West Maui, and exploring this area through your taste buds is always a good idea. You'll find the most diversity, both in cuisine and prices,

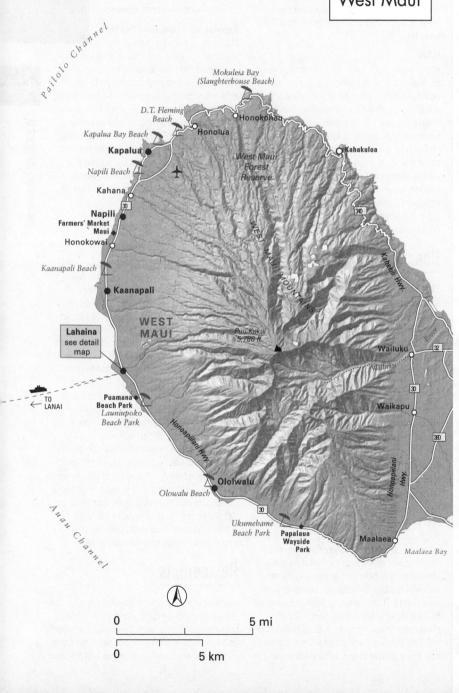

West Maui

Pailolo Channel

Mokuleia Bay
(Slaughterhouse Beach)

D.T. Fleming
Beach

Honokohau

Kapalua Bay Beach

Honolua

Kahakuloa

Kapalua

West Maui
Forest
Reserve

Napili Beach

Kahana

340

30

Napili

**Farmers'
Market
Maui**

Honokowai

WEST MAUI MOUNTAINS

Kaanapali Beach

Kahekili Hwy.

Kaanapali

**WEST
MAUI**

Puu Kukui
5,788 ft.

Wailuku

River

Lahaina
see detail
map

32

Wailuku

TO
← LANAI

30

**Puamana
Beach Park**

Waikapu

Launiupoko
Beach Park

Honoapiilani Hwy.

380

Auau Channel

Ololwalu

Honoapiilani Hwy.

Olowalu Beach

30

Ukumehame
Beach Park

**Papalaua
Wayside
Park**

Maalaea

Maalaea Bay

0   5 mi

0   5 km

surrounding Front Street in Lahaina. Many of the large hotels in Kaanapali boast a signature restaurant, plus more casual dining options throughout the property. Farther north, Honokowai and Napili offer more casual dining options and take-out spots, while Kapalua offers several high-end options.

HOTEL AND RESTAURANT PRICES

Hotel prices in the reviews are the lowest cost of a standard double room in high season. Restaurant prices in the reviews are the average cost of a main course at dinner, or if dinner is not served, at lunch.

WHAT IT COSTS in U.S. Dollars			
$	$$	$$$	$$$$
RESTAURANTS			
under $18	$18–$26	$27–$35	over $35
HOTELS			
under $181	$181–$260	$261–$340	over $340

Nightlife

Your best bet when it comes to bars on Maui? If you walk by and it sounds lively, go in. If you want to scope out your options in advance, check the free *Maui Time Weekly,* available at most stores and restaurants, to find out who's playing where. The resorts and their bars and restaurants often have a good scene, too. The *Maui News* also publishes an entertainment schedule in its Thursday edition of the "Maui Scene." With an open mind (and a little luck), you can find some fun.

Shopping

One of Maui's top resort areas, West Maui supports abundant shopping options both cheap and high-end, from weekend crafts fairs under Lahaina's

historical banyan tree to golf apparel at Kapalua and the art galleries on Front Street. Souvenir tchotchkes can be found in local swap meets, and Hawaiian confectionery items are available in most grocery stores.

Visitor Information

History buffs will want to stop at the Old Lahaina Courthouse, home to the Lahaina Visitor Center and Lahaina Heritage Museum. Conveniently located in the heart of town between Lahaina Harbor and the famous banyan tree, Lahaina Visitor Center is a great place to start your exploration. Lahaina Restoration Foundation maintains several museums and sites within the historic district, and the knowledgeable staff can offer tips and a walking-tour brochure. For details, visit ⊕ *lahainarestoration.org.*

Olowalu

6 miles south of Lahaina.

Olowalu is a dot on the map, and if you aren't paying attention, you might drive through it without even noticing. There are a handful of oceanfront mansions and a popular restaurant, but not much else. Most visitors come here for its ocean attractions, which include a popular surf break and fantastic snorkeling spot.

⊕ Beaches

Olowalu

BEACH | More an offshore snorkel and stand-up paddling spot than a beach, Olowalu is also a great place to watch for turtles and whales in season. The beach is literally a pullover from the road, which can make for some unwelcome noise if you're looking for quiet. The entrance can be rocky (reef shoes help), but if you've got your snorkel gear it's a 200-yard swim to an extensive and diverse reef.

Shoreline visibility can vary depending on the swell and time of day; late morning is best. Except for during a south swell, the waters are usually calm. You can find this rocky surf break a half mile north of mile marker 14. Snorkeling here is along pathways that wind among coral heads. Note: this is a local hangout and can be unfriendly at times. **Amenities:** none. **Best for:** snorkeling. ✉ *Rte. 30, Olowalu* ⊹ *Look for mile marker 14, south of Olowalu General Store.*

Papalaua Wayside Park

BEACH | This popular park is also known as Thousand Peaks because there's barely a break between each wave. Beginner to intermediate surfers say it's a good spot to longboard or bodyboard. It's easy entry into the water, and you don't have to paddle out far. The beach itself leaves something to be desired, but there is some shade, mostly from thorny kiawe trees; footwear is a good idea. Camping is allowed by county permit and with only roadside parking the beach park is often crowded. Portable toilets are available. **Amenities:** toilets. **Best for:** surfing. ✉ *Rte. 30, Olowalu* ⊹ *Near mile marker 11/12* ⊕ *mauicounty.gov.*

🍴 Restaurants

★ Leoda's Kitchen and Pie Shop

$ | **AMERICAN** | Slow down as you drive through the little roadside village of Olowalu, about 15 minutes before Lahaina town if you're coming from the airport, so you don't miss this adorable farmhouse-chic restaurant and pie shop, where everything is prepared with care. All the breads are house-made and excellent, and most ingredients are sourced locally; try a sandwich or a burger with Kula onions for lunch, or comfort food like pot pies for an early dinner. **Known for:** out-of-this-world banana cream pie; delicious spicy tuna sandwiches; can order online to beat long lines. $ *Average main: $14* ✉ *820 Olowalu Village Rd., Olowalu* ☎ *808/662–3600* ⊕ *leodas.com.*

Lahaina

27 miles west of Kahului; 4 miles south of Kaanapali.

Lahaina is a bustling waterfront town packed with visitors from around the globe. Some may describe the area as tacky, with too many T-shirt vendors and not enough mom-and-pop shops, but this historic town houses some of Hawaii's best restaurants, boutiques, cafés, and galleries.

■ **TIP→ If you spend Friday afternoon exploring Front Street, hang around for Friday Night Is Art Night, when the galleries stay open late and offer entertainment, including artists demonstrating their work.**

Sunset cruises and other excursions depart from Lahaina Harbor. At the southern end of town is an important archaeological site known as Mokuula, which was once a spiritual and political center, as well as home to Maui's chiefs.

The town has been welcoming visitors for more than 200 years. In 1798, after waging war to unite the Hawaiian Islands, Kamehameha the Great chose Lahaina, then called *Lele*, as the seat of his monarchy. Warriors from Kamehameha's 800 canoes, stretched along the coast from Olowalu to Honokowai, turned inland and filled the lush valleys with networks of stream-fed *loi kalo*, or taro patches. For nearly 50 years Lahaina remained the capital of the Hawaiian Kingdom. During this period, the scent of Hawaiian sandalwood brought those who traded with China to these waters. Whaling ships followed, chasing sperm whales from Japan to the Arctic. Lahaina became known around the world for its rough-and-tumble ways.

Then, almost as quickly as it had come, the tide of foreign trade receded. The Hawaiian capital was moved to Honolulu in 1845, and by 1860 the sandalwood forests were empty and sperm whales nearly extinct. Luckily, Lahaina had already grown into an international, sophisticated (if sometimes rowdy) town, laying claim to the first printing press and high school west of the Rockies. Sugar interests kept the town afloat until tourism stepped in.

GETTING HERE AND AROUND

It's about a 45-minute drive from Kahului Airport to Lahaina (take Route 380 to Route 30), depending on the traffic on this heavily traveled route. Traffic can be slow around Lahaina, especially from 4 to 6 pm. Shuttles and taxis are available from Kahului Airport. The Maui Bus Lahaina Islander route runs from Queen Kaahumanu Center in Kahului to the Wharf Cinema Center on Front Street, Lahaina's main thoroughfare.

CRUISE TRAVEL TO LAHAINA

Visitors arriving by sea at Lahaina Harbor are greeted by the version of Hawaii seen in postcards. A former whaling port, Lahaina has a rich history, several informative museums, and flashy shops, art galleries, and restaurants. Lahaina Visitor Center in the Old Lahaina Courthouse is a good place to start your exploration, and any one of the staff members there can answer your questions or provide information on the best sites to visit.

Lahaina is relatively compact, with sandy beaches and creature comforts within walking distance. Taxi fares run $10–$20 in and around Lahaina. Famed Kaanapali Beach is just 4½ miles away.

 Sights

Baldwin Home Museum

HISTORIC HOME | If you want some insight into 19th-century life in Hawaii, this informative museum is an excellent place to start. Begun in 1834 and completed the following year, the coral-and-stone house was originally home to missionary Dr. Dwight Baldwin and his family. The building has been carefully restored to reflect the period, and many of the

Walking Tours 👁

Lahaina's side streets are best explored on foot. Both the Baldwin Home Museum and the Lahaina Visitor Center offer self-guided walking-tour brochures with a map for $2 each. The historic trail map is easy to follow; it details three short but enjoyable loops of the town.

original furnishings remain: you can view the family's grand piano, carved four-poster bed, and most interestingly, Dr. Baldwin's dispensary. Also on display is the "thunderpot"—learn how the doctor single-handedly inoculated 10,000 Maui residents against smallpox. ■TIP➔ **Self-guided tours run Tues.-Sun. from 10am-4pm, or come Friday at dusk for a special candlelight tour every half hour from 5–8pm.** ✉ *120 Dickenson St., Lahaina* ☎ *808/661–3262* ⊕ *lahainarestoration.org* 💵 *$7* ⊗ *Closed Mon.*

★ Banyan Tree

CITY PARK | Planted in 1873, this massive tree is the largest of its kind in the United States and provides a welcome retreat and playground for visitors and locals, who rest and play music under its awesome branches.

■TIP➔ **The Banyan Tree is a popular and hard-to-miss meeting place if your party splits up for independent exploring.**

It's also a terrific place to be when the sun sets—mynah birds settle in here for a screeching symphony, which is an event in itself. During the day it's a respite for a variety of chickens. ✉ *Front St. between Hotel St. and Canal St., Lahaina* ⊕ *lahainarestoration.org.*

Hale Paahao (Old Prison)

JAIL/PRISON | Lahaina's jailhouse is a reminder of rowdy whaling days. Its name literally means "stuck-in-irons house," referring to the wall shackles and

Lahaina

KEY
- ① Sights
- ① Restaurants
- ① Quick Bites
- ① Hotels

Anau Channel

Kahoma Stream

Honoapiilani Hwy.

Ala Moana St.
Mala Wharf Rd.
Front St.
Puunoa Pl.
Kapanukea St.
Keawe St. Ext.
Kenui St.
Baker St.
Wainee St.
Mill St.
Papalaua St.
Lahainaluna Rd.
Panaewa St.
Mill St.
Dickenson St.
Market St.
Luakini St.
Hale St.
Canal St.
Prison St.
Mokuhinia St.
Shaw St.
Iliikahi St.
Ailo St.
Wainee St.
Kuhua St.
Panoa St.

Cruise-ship/ Ferry dock
Hotel St.
Wharf St.

TO KAANAPALI, KAPALUA & KAHAKULOA

TO LAUNIUPOKO BEACH PARK

0　　　　　　　1/2 mi

0　　　　　　　1/2 km

Kupuohi St.

Paunau St.

Lahaina Bypass

ball-and-chain restraints. The compound was built in the 1850s by convict laborers out of blocks of coral that had been salvaged from the demolished waterfront fort. Most prisoners were sent here for desertion, drunkenness, or reckless horse riding. Today, a figure representing an imprisoned old sailor tells his recorded tale of woe. There are also interpretive signs for the botanical garden and whale boat in the yard. ⊠ *187 Prison St., Lahaina ⊕ lahainarestoration.org ☑ Free, donation suggested.*

Hauola Stone

OTHER ATTRACTION | Just visible above the tide is a gigantic stone, perfectly molded into the shape of a low-back chair and believed by Hawaiians to hold healing powers. It sits in the harbor, just off the land, where the sea and the underground freshwater meet. ⊠ *Wharf and Papelekane Sts., behind Lahaina Public Library, Lahaina.*

Holy Innocents Episcopal Church

CHURCH | Built in 1927, this beautiful open-air church is decorated with paintings depicting Hawaiian versions of Christian symbols (including a Hawaiian Madonna and child), rare or extinct birds, and native plants. At Sunday services, the congregation is typically dressed in traditional clothing from Samoa and Tonga. Anyone is welcome to slip into one of the pews, carved from native woods. Queen Liliuokalani, Hawaii's last reigning monarch, lived in a large grass house on this site as a child. ⊠ *561 Front St., near Mokuhina St., Lahaina ☎ 808/661–4202 ⊕ holyimaui.org ☑ Free.*

Lahaina Harbor

MARINA/PIER | For centuries, Lahaina has drawn ships of all sizes to its calm harbor: King Kamehameha's conquering fleet of 800 carved *koa* canoes gave way to Chinese trading ships, Boston whalers, United States Navy frigates, and, finally, a slew of pleasure craft. The picturesque harbor is the departure point for ferries headed to nearby islands,

Fun Things to Do in West Maui

- Get into the Hawaiian swing of things at the Old Lahaina Luau.

- Take a late-afternoon stroll on the beach fronting the Lahaina Jodo Mission.

- Make an offering at the Taoist altar in the Wo Hing Museum.

- Sail into the sunset from Lahaina Harbor.

- Attend the mynah birds' symphony beneath the Banyan Tree.

sailing charters, deep-sea fishing trips, and snorkeling excursions. It's also a port of call for cruise ships from around the world. ⊠ *Wharf St., Lahaina ☑ Free.*

Lahaina Jodo Mission

TEMPLE | Established at the turn of the 20th century by Japanese contract workers, this Buddhist mission is one of Lahaina's most popular sites thanks to its idyllic setting and spectacular views across the channel. Although the buildings are not open to the public, you can stroll the grounds and enjoy glimpses of a 90-foot-high pagoda, as well as a great 3.5-ton copper and bronze statue of the Amida Buddha (erected in 1968, it's one of the largest Buddha statues outside of Asia). If you're in the vicinity at 8 on any evening, you may be able to hear the temple bell toll 11 times; the first three peals signifying Buddhist creeds, and the following representing the Noble Eightfold Path. ⊠ *12 Ala Moana St., near Lahaina Cannery Mall, Lahaina ☎ 808/661–4304 ☑ Free.*

★ Old Lahaina Courthouse

GOVERNMENT BUILDING | The Lahaina Arts Society, Lahaina Visitor Center,

Once a whaling center, Lahaina Harbor bustles with tour boats, fishing vessels, and pleasure craft.

and Lahaina Heritage Museum occupy this charming old government building in the center of town. Wander among the terrific displays and engage with an interactive exhibit about Lahaina's history, pump the knowledgeable visitor center staff for tips—be sure to ask for the walking-tour brochure covering historic Lahaina sites—and stop at the theater with a rotating array of films about everything from whales to canoes. Erected in 1859 and restored in 1999, the building has served as a customs and court house, governor's office, post office, vault and collector's office, and police station. On August 12, 1898, its postmaster witnessed the lowering of the Hawaiian flag when Hawaii became a U.S. territory. The flag now hangs above the stairway. ■TIP➔ **There's a public restroom in the building.** ⊠ *648 Wharf St., Lahaina* ☎ *808/667–9193 for Lahaina Visitor Center, 808/661–3262 for Lahaina Heritage Museum* ⊕ *lahainarestoration. org* ☎ *Free.*

Pioneer Mill Smokestack & Locomotives
HISTORIC SIGHT | The former Pioneer Mill Company used this site to mill sugar back when Lahaina's main moneymaker was sugarcane. In 2010, the Lahaina Restoration Foundation restored the original smokestack—the tallest structure in Lahaina—and created a place for visitors to learn about the rich plantation history of West Maui. Take an interpretive walk around the smokestack along the landscaped grounds, then check out the old mill and field equipment, and refurbished locomotives that used to cart sugar between the fields and the mill. ⊠ *275 Lahainaluna Rd., Lahaina* ☎ *808/661– 3262* ⊕ *lahainarestoration.org* ☎ *Free.*

★ **Waiola Church and Wainee Cemetery**
CEMETERY | Immortalized in James Michener's *Hawaii*, the original church from the early 1800s was destroyed once by fire and twice by fierce windstorms. Repositioned and rebuilt in 1954, the church was renamed Waiola ("water of life") and has been standing proudly ever since. The adjacent cemetery was the

region's first Christian cemetery and is the final resting place of many of Hawaii's most important monarchs, including Kamehameha the Great's wife, Queen Keopuolani, who was baptized during her final illness. ⊠ *535 Wainee St., Lahaina* ☎ *808/661–4349* ⊕ *waiolachurch.org* ⊠ *Free.*

★ Wo Hing Museum

HISTORY MUSEUM | Smack-dab in the center of Front Street, this eye-catching Chinese temple reflects the importance of early Chinese immigrants to Lahaina. Built by the Wo Hing Society in 1912, the museum contains beautiful artifacts, historic photo displays of Dr. Sun Yat-sen, and a Taoist altar. Don't miss the films playing in the rustic cookhouse next door—some of Thomas Edison's first films, shot in Hawaii circa 1898, show Hawaiian wranglers herding steer onto ships. Ask the docent for some star fruit from the tree outside, for an offering or for yourself. ■ **TIP→ If you're in town in late January or early February, this museum hosts a nice Chinese New Year festival.** ⊠ *858 Front St., Lahaina* ☎ *808/661–5553* ⊕ *lahainarestoration.org* ⊠ *$7.*

Beaches

Launiupoko Beach Park

BEACH | FAMILY | This is the beach park of all beach parks: both a surf break and a beach, it offers a little something for everyone with its inviting stretch of lawn, soft white sand, and gentle waves. The shoreline reef creates a protected wading pool, perfect for small children. Outside the reef, beginner surfers will find good longboard rides. From the long sliver of beach, you can enjoy superb views of neighboring islands, and, landside, of deep valleys cutting through West Maui's mountain. Because of its endless sunshine and serenity—not to mention such amenities as picnic tables and grills—Launiupoko draws a crowd on the weekends, but there's space for everyone (and overflow parking across

the street). **Amenities:** parking (no fee); showers; toilets. **Best for:** partiers; sunset; surfing; swimming. ⊠ *Rte. 30, Lahaina* ✛ *At mile marker 18* ⊕ *maui-county.gov.*

Puamana Beach Park

BEACH | This is both a friendly beach park and a surf spot for mellow longboard rides. With a narrow sandy beach and a grassy area with plenty of shade, it offers mostly calm swimming conditions and a good view of neighboring Lanai. Smaller than Launiupoko, this beach park tends to attract locals looking to surf and barbecue; it has picnic tables and grills. **Amenities:** parking (no fee); showers; toilets. **Best for:** sunset; surfing; picnics. ⊠ *Rte. 30, Lahaina* ✛ *About ¼ mile south of Lahaina.*

🍽 Restaurants

Alchemy Maui

$$ | ECLECTIC | This cute, casual café by Valley Isle Kombucha is part kombucha tasting room, part eatery. Try one of the many kombucha flavors on tap, which is crafted in small batches using local ingredients, and comes in flavors like guava pineapple and Kula strawberry. **Known for:** fresh and local ingredients; vegetarian and vegan options; friendly staff. ⑤ *Average main: $19* ⊠ *157 Kupuohi St., Lahaina* ☎ *808/793–2115* ⊕ *alchemymauibistro.com* ◷ *Closed Sat. and Sun.*

Cheeseburger in Paradise

$$ | BURGER | A chain joint on Front Street, this place is known for—what else?—big beefy cheeseburgers, not to mention a great turkey burger, as well as healthier options such as smoothies and hearty salads. The second-floor balcony gives you a bird's-eye view of Lahaina's Front Street action. **Known for:** Island Style Burger with avocado, pineapple, and teriyaki glaze; great cocktails and local beers; generous portions. ⑤ *Average main: $18* ⊠ *811 Front St., Lahaina* ☎ *808/661–4855* ⊕ *cheeseburgernation.com.*

Maui's Food Trucks: Movable Feasts

As in so many other places, food-truck culture has taken hold on Maui, but don't expect to find well-equipped, customized trucks like the ones you see on the Food Network. Most have no websites, Instagram accounts, or Facebook pages; some don't even have phones. Many have irregular days and hours of operation.

A group of trucks has formed a food court across from the Costco parking lot, just minutes from Kahului Airport. In Kihei, look for the food truck park behind the Azeka Mauka Center. Honokowai has developed a park of its own, which is located along Lower Honoapiilani Highway.

★ Down the Hatch

$$ | **AMERICAN** | **FAMILY** | Located steps from Lahaina Harbor, this casual restaurant serves top-notch seafood with Southern flair. The shrimp po'boy, seared *ahi* (yellowfin tuna) tacos, and fish-and-chips are perennial favorites. **Known for:** daily happy hour from 2 to 5 pm; fun and lively atmosphere; expansive seafood menu. $ *Average main: $21* ⊠ *Wharf Cinema Center, 658 Front St., Lahaina* ☎ *808/661–4900* ⊕ *dthmaui.com.*

Frida's Mexican Beach House

$$$ | **MEXICAN FUSION** | No matter the cuisine, serial restaurateur Mark Ellman always delivers, as he does yet again with this oceanfront eatery along Front Street. The setting is reason enough to dine here, but the food—specializing in Latin-inspired dishes—attracts diners all on its own and 40 varieties of tequila dominate the bar. **Known for:** live music on Mon. and Tues. evenings; plenty of tasty vegetarian options; grilled Spanish octopus. $ *Average main: $32* ⊠ *1287 Front St., Lahaina* ☎ *808/661-1287* ⊕ *fridasmaui.com* ☽ *Closed Sun.*

Honu Seafood & Pizza

$$$$ | **ECLECTIC** | This oceanfront fish house and pizza restaurant began as a way to showcase the work of celebrity chef Mark Ellman before recently changing ownership. Guests can expect a lot of their favorite dishes to remain on the menu, with some fun food and cocktail additions to come. **Known for:** fantastic selection of craft beers and cocktails; gluten-free options; unparalleled ocean views with sea turtle sightings. $ *Average main: $36* ⊠ *1295 Front St., Lahaina* ☎ *808/667–9390* ⊕ *honumaui.com* ☽ *Closed Sun.*

Lahaina Grill

$$$$ | **AMERICAN** | At the top of many "best restaurants" lists, this expensive upscale bistro is about as fashionably chic as it gets on Maui, and the interior is as pretty as the patrons. Wagyu beef ravioli, bufala salad with locally grown tomatoes, and Kona-coffee–roasted rack of lamb are a few of the classics customers demand; the full menu—including dessert—is available at the bar. **Known for:** downtown location; extensive dessert menu; romantic ambience. $ *Average main: $60* ⊠ *127 Lahainaluna Rd., Lahaina* ☎ *808/667–5117* ⊕ *lahainagrill. com* ☽ *No lunch.*

★ Mala Ocean Tavern

$$$$ | **MODERN HAWAIIAN** | The menu at this oceanfront standout features interesting local-style Hawaiian food fusions. There's a focus on ingredients that promote local sustainability, and the cocktails and wine list are great, too. **Known for:** seafood brodo; friendly and attentive staff; seared

ahi (yellowfin tuna) bruschetta. $ *Average main: $38* ⊠ *1307 Front St., Lahaina* ☎ *808/667–9394* ⊕ *malaoceantavern. com.*

PacificO

$$$$ | MODERN HAWAIIAN | Sophisticated outdoor dining on the beach (yes, truly *on* the beach) and creative Island cuisine using local, fresh-caught fish and greens and veggies grown in the restaurant's own Upcountry Oo Farm (and, quite possibly, picked that very morning)—this is the Maui dining experience you've been dreaming about. Start with a variety of fresh vegetable dishes on the appetizer menu, move on to any of the fantastic fresh fish dishes, and for dessert, finish with the banana bread ice cream sandwich. **Known for:** Hamakua mushroom risotto; exceptional wine list; lemongrass curry with tiger prawns. $ *Average main: $45* ⊠ *505 Front St., Lahaina* ☎ *808/667– 4341* ⊕ *pacificomaui.com* ☉ *Closed Sun. and Mon.*

Penne Pasta Cafe

$ | ITALIAN | A couple of blocks off Front Street in Lahaina, this small restaurant packs a powerhouse of a menu with reasonably priced pizzas, pastas, salads, and sandwiches. The name can be found on the menu in four dishes; two can easily split a salad and entrée and leave completely sated. **Known for:** fast and friendly service; fantastic desserts; gluten-free and vegan options. $ *Average main: $12* ⊠ *180 Dickenson St., Lahaina* ☎ *808/661–6633* ⊕ *pennepastacafe.net.*

Sale Pepe

$$ | ITALIAN | Aromas from a wood-fired oven lure you into this cozy Italian restaurant set just off of Front Street, and the wine list tempts you to stay awhile. Quality is paramount here—many of the ingredients are imported directly from Italy, while farm-fresh produce and meats come from Maui. **Known for:** salumi and house-made focaccia; brick-oven pizzas; packaged handmade pasta and sauces

to-go. $ *Average main: $24* ⊠ *878 Front St., Units 7 and 8, Lahaina* ☎ *808/667– 7667* ⊕ *salepepemaui.com* ☉ *Closed Sun.*

★ Star Noodle

$ | ASIAN | This local favorite, one of Maui's most popular restaurants, recently moved to an oceanside locale. The expanse of the Pacific sets the scene for an eclectic Asian menu with must-try items like the *ahi* (yellowfin tuna) avo, tempura shrimp, and noodle dishes like the Lahaina fried soup that's served with fat chow fun, pork, and bean sprouts. **Known for:** shared, small-plate dining; house-made noodles; steamed pork buns. $ *Average main: $16* ⊠ *1285 Front St., Lahaina* ☎ *808/667–5400* ⊕ *starnoodle.com.*

💻 Coffee and Quick Bites

★ Ululani's Hawaiian Shave Ice

$ | CAFÉ | Ululani's has elevated this simple Hawaiian treat to gourmet proportions with superfine ice shavings and homemade syrups in exotic flavors— guava, *li hing mui* (a savory-sweet plum flavor), and mango—and fun add-ons like sweet adzuki beans and mochi balls to complete the frosty experience. The original location is in Lahaina, but there are also branches in Kihei, Wailuku, Kahului, and at the Hyatt Regency Maui in Kaanapali, so satisfying that sweet tooth is a short drive away from wherever you are. **Known for:** long lines on most days; locations across the island; classic shave ice with gourmet twists. $ *Average main: $6* ⊠ *790 Front St., Lahaina* ☎ *808/877-3700* ⊕ *ululanisshaveice.com.*

🛏 Hotels

Lahaina doesn't have a huge range of accommodations, but it does make a great headquarters for active families or those who want to avoid spending a bundle on resorts. One major advantage is the proximity of restaurants, shops, and activities—everything is within walking distance. It's a business district, however, and won't provide the same peace and quiet as resorts or secluded vacation rentals. Still, Lahaina has a nostalgic charm, especially early in the morning before the streets have filled with visitors and vendors.

Best Western Pioneer Inn

$$$ | HOTEL | This small hotel, built in 1901 when Lahaina was the bawdy heart of the Pacific's whaling industry, has been substantially remodeled and updated to offer clean and basic rooms, all on the second floor and each with a lanai equipped with rocking chairs. **Pros:** convenient location for the harbor, shops, and restaurants; children under 12 stay free; free parking and Wi-Fi. **Cons:** no elevator; off-site parking; can be noisy, sandwiched between Front Street and the harbor. ⑤ *Rooms from: $307* ⊠ *658 Wharf St., Lahaina* ☎ *808/661–3636, 800/457–5457* ⊕ *pioneerinnmaui.com* ⇨ *34 rooms* ⑩ *No Meals.*

★ Hooilo House

$$$$ | B&B/INN | A luxurious intimate getaway without resort facilities, this stunning, 2-acre B&B in the foothills of West Maui's mountain, just south of Lahaina town, exemplifies quiet perfection. **Pros:** friendly, on-site hosts; beautiful furnishings; gazebo for special events. **Cons:** three-night minimum; far from shops and restaurants; not good for families with younger children. ⑤ *Rooms from: $499* ⊠ *138 Awaiku St., Lahaina* ☎ *808/667–6669* ⊕ *hooilohouse.com* ⇨ *6 rooms* ⑩ *Free Breakfast.*

Lahaina Shores Beach Resort

$$ | APARTMENT | You really can't get any closer to the beach than this seven-story rental property that offers panoramic ocean and mountain views, and fully equipped kitchens. **Pros:** right on the beach; historical sites, attractions, and activities are a short walk away; free

parking, no additional costs and no resort fee. **Cons:** no posh, resort-type amenities; no restaurant on-site; older property. ⑤ *Rooms from: $250* ⊠ *475 Front St., Lahaina* ☎ *866/934–9176* ⊕ *lahainashores.com* ⇨ *199 rooms* ⑩ *No Meals.*

Maui Garden Oasis

$$ | B&B/INN | In an older neighborhood just outside of busy Lahaina town lies a quiet place that welcomes you with light and clean rooms featuring pleasant island furnishings and private entrances. **Pros:** free use of chairs, coolers, boogie boards, and other beach toys; knowledgeable hosts; maid service. **Cons:** one-time $40 cleaning fee; no stores within safe, easy walking distance; not secluded. ⑤ *Rooms from: $199* ⊠ *67 Kaniau Rd., Lahaina* ☎ *808/661–8800* ⊕ *mauigardenoasis.com* ⇨ *6 rooms* ⑩ *No Meals.*

The Plantation Inn

$$$ | B&B/INN | Ten minutes from the beach, this adults-only, tropical plantation-era inn with stained-glass windows and historic photographs of Lahaina is a fine value for those who want easy access to shops, sights, and restaurants. **Pros:** guests have full privileges at the sister Kaanapali Beach Hotel, 3 miles north; free parking; 24-hour access to pool and hot tub. **Cons:** two-story inn has no elevator or bellhop; no children allowed; older property. ⑤ *Rooms from: $263* ⊠ *174 Lahainaluna Rd., Lahaina* ☎ *808/667–9225, 800/433–6815* ⊕ *theplantationinn.com* ⇨ *18 rooms* ⑩ *Free Breakfast.*

Puunoa Beach Estates

$$$$ | APARTMENT | High-end travelers tired of sharing their slice of vacation paradise with the noisy hordes will find privacy and luxury at this 10-unit, beachfront enclave located in a residential neighborhood; guests have access to the banana and citrus trees in the garden. **Pros:** gated driveway for security; no resort fee; free parking. **Cons:** a bit far to walk to Lahaina

stores and tourist center; borders busy public beach; stairs may pose an obstacle for some. $ *Rooms from: $1100* ⊠ *45 Kai Pali Pl., Lahaina* ☎ *877/657–7909* ⊕ *puunoabeachestates.com* ⤳ *10 units* ⊙⏐ *No Meals.*

Nightlife

Cool Cat Café

LIVE MUSIC | You could easily miss this casual 1950s-style diner while strolling through Lahaina. Tucked in the second floor of the Wharf Cinema Center, its semi-outdoor area plays host to rockin' local music Thursday through Sunday nights. The entertainment lineup covers reggae, light rock, contemporary Hawaiian, and traditional island rhythms. It doesn't hurt that the kitchen dishes out specialty burgers, fish that's fresh from the harbor, and delicious homemade sauces from the owner's family recipes. ⊠ *658 Front St., Lahaina* ☎ *808/667–0908* ⊕ *coolcatcafe.com.*

Down the Hatch

BARS | This lively spot in the middle of Front Street is great for food, drinks, and sports by day, and a variety of activities at night. Happy hour runs from 2–5 pm and the bar stays open until 1 am, which is considered pretty late for Maui. A rotating calendar of nightly activities includes live band karaoke, open dance floor, live music, silent discos, and trivia nights on Sundays. ⊠ *658 Front Street, Lahaina* ☎ *808/661–4900* ⊕ *dthmaui.com.*

Performing Arts

★ Feast at Lele

THEMED ENTERTAINMENT | This place redefines the luau by crossing it with Islands-style fine dining in an intimate beach setting. Each course of this succulent sit-down meal represents the Pacific Island cultures—Hawaiian, Samoan, Maori, Tahitian—featured onstage. Wine, spirits, and cocktail options are

What's a Lava Flow?

Can't decide between a piña colada and a strawberry daiquiri? Go with a Lava Flow—a mix of light rum, coconut and pineapple juice, and a banana, with a swirl of strawberry purée. It's served with a wedge of fresh pineapple and a paper umbrella.

copious and go beyond the usual tropical concoctions. Lahaina's gorgeous sunset serves as the backdrop to the show, which forgoes gimmicks and pageantry for an authentic expression of Polynesian chants and dances. Lele, by the way, is the traditional name for Lahaina. ⊠ *505 Front St., Lahaina* ☎ *808/667–5353* ⊕ *feastatlele.com.*

★ Old Lahaina Luau

THEMED ENTERTAINMENT | **FAMILY** | Considered the best luau on Maui, it's certainly the most traditional. Sitting either at a table or on a *lauhala* (mat made of leaves), you can dine on Hawaiian cuisine such as pork *laulau* (wrapped with taro sprouts in ti leaves), *ahi* poke (raw yellowfin tuna salad), *lomi lomi* salmon (traditional Hawaiian diced side dish), and *haupia* (coconut pudding). At sunset, the historical journey touches on the arrival of the Polynesians, the influence of missionaries and, later, the advent of tourism. Talented performers will charm you with beautiful music, powerful chanting, and a variety of hula styles, from *kahiko,* the ancient way of communicating with the gods, to *auana,* the modern hula. You won't see fire dancers here, as they aren't considered traditional. ■ **TIP→ This luau sells out regularly, so make reservations before your trip to Maui.** ⊠ *1251 Front St., near Lahaina Cannery Mall, Lahaina* ☎ *808/667–1998* ⊕ *oldlahainaluau.com.*

Scotch Mist Charters

SAILING | Sailing is at its best on this two-hour champagne cruise. The 50-foot *Scotch Mist,* which holds just 22 passengers, gives you an intimate and exhilarating ride, with champagne, chocolate, juice, beer, and white wine included in the price. Private charters are available. ⊠ *Lahaina Harbor, Front St., Lahaina* ☎ *808/661–0386* ⊕ *scotchmistsailingcharters.com* ⊠ *$84.*

Warren & Annabelle's

THEATER | This is a hearty comedy with amazing sleight of hand. Founder Warren Gibson, or a rotating lineup of magicians, entice guests into a swank nightclub with a gleaming mahogany bar, a grand piano, and a resident ghost named Annabelle who tickles the ivories. Servers efficiently ply you with à la carte appetizers, desserts, and cocktails (or purchase the Royal Flush package for a larger meal), while obliging a few impromptu song requests. Then, guests are ushered into a small theater where magic hilariously ensues. Because this is a nightclub act, no one under 21 is allowed. ⊠ *The Outlets of Maui, 900 Front St., Lahaina* ☎ *808/667–6244* ⊕ *warrenandannabelles. com* ⊠ *$92.*

🛍 Shopping

BOOKSTORES

★ Maui Friends of the Library

BOOKS | This nonprofit bookstore is run by volunteers who are happy to let you spend a few minutes (or hours) browsing shelves filled with mystery, sci-fi, fiction, military history, and "oddball" volumes. There's a nice section reserved for new Hawaiiana books. If you've finished with your vacation reading, donate it to benefit the Island's public libraries. There are also locations at Queen Kaahumanu Center and behind the former Puunene School in Kahului. ⊠ *Outlets of Maui, 900 Front St., H4, Lahaina* ☎ *808/667–2696* ⊕ *mfol.org.*

Maui Midnight 🍸

If you want to see any action on Maui, head out early. Otherwise, you might be out past what locals call "Maui Midnight," where as early as 9 pm the restaurants close and the streets empty. What can you expect, though, when most people wake up with the sun? After a long salty day of sea and surf, you might be ready for some shut-eye yourself.

CLOTHING

Hilo Hattie

MIXED CLOTHING | FAMILY | Hawaii's largest manufacturer of aloha shirts also carries brightly colored blouses, skirts, and children's clothing. You can pick up many trinkets and gifts here, but be aware that many are not made locally. ⊠ *The Outlets of Maui, 900 Front St., Lahaina* ☎ *808/667–7911* ⊕ *hilohattie.com.*

Honolua Surf Company

MIXED CLOTHING | If you're in the market for colorful print shirts and sundresses, check out this surf shop. It's popular with young women and men for surf trunks, casual clothing, and accessories. There are two locations on Front Street, plus branches in Whalers Village, The Shops at Wailea, and Paia. ⊠ *845 Front St., Lahaina* ☎ *808/661–8848* ⊕ *honoluasurf.com.*

Mahina

WOMEN'S CLOTHING | At this boutique you can snap up the latest styles without breaking the bank. A friendly staff, easy-breezy dresses, resort-perfect rompers, and loads of accessories await the smart shopper. There are branches in Kihei, The Shops at Wailea, Whalers Village, Lahaina Gateway Center, and Paia. ⊠ *335 Keawe St., #208, Lahaina* ☎ *808/661–0383* ⊕ *shopmahina.com.*

GALLERIES

★ Lahaina Printsellers Ltd

ART GALLERIES | Available here are Hawaii's largest selection of original antique maps and prints of Hawaii and the Pacific. You can also buy museum-quality reproductions, plus paintings and photographs, many from local artists. Visit their production gallery at 1013 Limahana Place in Lahaina for an even greater selection. ✉ 764 Front St., Lahaina ☎ 808/667–7843 ⊕ printsellers.com.

LIK Fine Art Lahaina

ART GALLERIES | Fine art photographer Peter Lik is known all over the world. It's easy to understand why when you see his exquisite and hyper-real pictures of vast Maui landscapes displayed in this Lahaina gallery. ✉ 712 Front St., Lahaina ☎ 808/661–6623 ⊕ lik.com.

Martin Lawrence Galleries

ART GALLERIES | In business since 1975, Martin Lawrence displays and sells the works of such world-renowned artists as Picasso, Erté, and Chagall in a bright and friendly gallery. There are also modern and pop art pieces by Keith Haring, Andy Warhol, and Japanese creative icon Takashi Murakami. ✉ 790 Front St., at Lahainaluna Rd., Lahaina ☎ 808/661–1788 ⊕ martinlawrence.com.

Village Galleries Maui

ART GALLERIES | The oldest art gallery in the state, this gallery houses the landscape paintings of popular local artists Betty Hay Freeland, George Allan, Joseph Fletcher, Pamela Andelin, Fred KenKnight, and Macario Pascual. ✉ 120 Dickenson St., Lahaina ☎ 808/661–4402 ⊕ villagegalleriesmaui.com.

HOME DECOR

Hale Zen

HOUSEWARES | If you're shopping for gifts in West Maui, don't miss this store packed with beautiful island-inspired pieces for the home. Most of the teak furniture and home accessories are imported from Bali, but local purveyors supply the inventory of clothing, jewelry, beauty products, kitchenware, and food. ✉ 180 Dickenson St., Suite 111, Lahaina ☎ 808/661–4802 ⊕ halezen.com.

JEWELRY

Maui Divers Jewelry

JEWELRY & WATCHES | This company has been crafting pearls, coral, and traditional gemstones into jewelry for more than 60 years. There are branches at Whalers Village in Kaapanali, inside Pioneer Inn in Lahaina, and at the Kahului Airport. ✉ 658 Wharf St., Lahaina ☎ 808/662–8666 ⊕ mauidivers.com.

MARKETS

Maui Gift and Craft Fair

MARKET | An eclectic mix of vendors and artists set up shop at this outdoor market on Sundays, offering fine art, jewelry, and clothing with an island vibe. ✉ Lahaina Gateway, 305 Keawe St., Lahaina ⊕ mauigiftandcraftfair.com ⊘ Closed Mon.–Sat.

SHOPPING CENTERS

Lahaina Cannery Mall

MALL | FAMILY | This mall, housed inside an old pineapple cannery, hosts free events year-round including Hawaiian crafts, hula lessons, and a weekly hula show on Sundays. Stop at Na Hoku, a purveyor of striking Hawaiian heirloom-quality jewelry and pearls. Whether you're searching for surf and skate threads or tropical resort wear, Crazy Shirts, Hawaiian Island Creations, Serendipity, and other retailers give you ample selections, and Banana Wind carries ocean-inspired home decor. ✉ 1221 Honoapiilani Hwy., Lahaina ☎ 808/661–5304 ⊕ lahainacannerymall.com.

🏃 Activities

SPAS

★ Kamahao Marilyn Monroe Spas, Hyatt Regency Maui

SPAS | The spa's oceanfront salon has a million-dollar view and is a convenient beach stroll away from its adjacent parking lot. The facility is spacious and well-appointed, with a relaxation room that looks out over the Pacific. Offerings include traditional Hawaiian lomilomi and hot stone massage both in the spa and oceanside, in addition to refreshing treatments like the after sun revitalizing treatment. Facial treatments use the Pure Fiji skin care line. ✉ *Hyatt Regency Maui, 200 Nohea Kai Dr., Lahaina* ☎ *808/667–4500* 🌐 *marilynmonroespas.com* 💳 *$165 for 50-min massage, $250 spa packages.*

Kaanapali

4 miles north of Lahaina.

As you drive north from Lahaina, the first resort community you reach is Kaanapali, a cluster of high-rise hotels framing a world-class white-sand beach. This is part of West Maui's famous resort strip and is a perfect destination for families and romance seekers wanting to be in the center of the action.

The theatrical look of Hawaii tourism—planned resort communities where luxury homes mix with high-rise hotels, fantasy swimming pools, and a theme-park landscape—began right here in the 1960s, when clever marketers built this sunny shoreline into a playground for the world's vacationers. Three miles of uninterrupted white-sand beach and placid water form the front yard of this artificial utopia, with its many tennis courts and two championship golf courses.

In ancient times, the area near Sheraton Maui was known for its bountiful fishing (especially lobster) and its seaside cliffs. The sleepy fishing village was washed away by the wave of Hawaii's new economy: tourism. Puu Kekaa (today incorrectly referred to as Black Rock) was a *leina a ka uhane,* a place in ancient Hawaii believed to be where souls leaped into the afterlife.

A little farther up the road lie the condo-filled beach towns of Honokowai and Napili, followed by Kapalua. Each boasts its own style and flavor, though most rely on a low-key beach vibe for people wanting upscale vacation rentals.

GETTING HERE AND AROUND

Shuttles and taxis are available from Kahului and Kapalua (West Maui) airports. Resorts offer free shuttles between properties, and some hotels also provide complimentary shuttles into Lahaina. In the Maui Bus system, the West Maui Islander begins and ends at Wharf Cinema Center in Lahaina and stops at most condos along the coastal road as far north as Napili Bay.

Beaches

★ Kaanapali Beach

BEACH | If you're looking for quiet and seclusion, this is not the beach for you. But if you want lots of action, spread out your towel here. Stretching from the northernmost end of the Sheraton Maui Resort & Spa to the Hyatt Regency Maui Resort & Spa at its southern tip, Kaanapali Beach is lined with resorts, condominiums, restaurants, and shops. Ocean activity companies launch from the shoreline fronting Whalers Village, making it one of Maui's best people-watching spots. A concrete pathway weaves along the length of this 3-mile-long beach, leading from one astounding resort to the next.

The drop-off from Kaanapali's soft sugary sand is steep, but waves hit the shore with barely a rippling slap outside of winter months. The landmark promontory known as Puu Kekaa (nicknamed "Black Rock") was traditionally considered a *leina a ka uhane*, or jumping-off place for spirits. It's easy to get into the water from the beach to enjoy the prime snorkeling among the lava-rock outcroppings.

■TIP→ Strong rip currents are often present near Puu Kekaa; always snorkel with a companion.

Throughout the resort, blue "Shoreline Access" signs point the way to a few free-parking stalls and public rights-of-way to the beach. Kaanapali Resort public beach parking can be found between the Hyatt and the Marriott, between the Marriott and the Kaanapali Alii, next to Whalers Village, and at the Sheraton. You can park for a fee at most of the large hotels and at Whalers Village. The merchants in the shopping village will validate your parking ticket if you make a purchase. **Amenities:** parking (no fee); showers; toilets. **Best for:** snorkeling; sunset; swimming; walking. ⌧ *Honoapiilani Hwy., Kaanapali* ⊹ *Follow any of the 3 Kaanapali exits.*

🍴 Restaurants

Kaanapali's dining scene is centered around the mega-resorts that line Kaanapali Beach which offer everything from take-out to fine dining. Oceanfront Whalers Village and nearby Fairway Shops add some good options to the mix.

Honokowai Okazuya & Deli

$ | ECLECTIC | Located within a nondescript mini strip mall, this small place has only a few stools and a couple of tables outside, but it's fast and the food is consistently good—all it takes to keep the place filled with locals. The beef and black bean chow fun and the *mahimahi* (dolphinfish) with lemon capers are the top-selling favorites, but there are vegetarian options and lighter fare such as Grandma's spicy tofu, egg foo yung, and even a veggie burger. **Known for:** local-style flavors; quality food at a reasonable price; huge portions. ⑤ *Average main: $12* ⌧ *3600-D Lower Honoapiilani Hwy., Honokowai* ☎ *808/665–0512* ▭ *No credit cards* ⊘ *Closed Sun. Closed daily 2:30–4:30 pm.*

Huihui

$$$$ | HAWAIIAN | The 5,000 square-foot venue Huihui, meaning "constellation," is a new shining star in the culinary scene in Hawaii. Executive Chef Tom Muromoto created a menu featuring unique Hawaiian dishes using fresh local ingredients, showcasing the Island's diversity. **Known for:** happy hour from 2–4 pm; live music in the evenings; fabulous desserts. ⑤ *Average main: $37* ⌧ *2525 Kaanapali Pkwy, Kaanapali* ☎ *808/667–0124* ⊕ *huihuirestaurant.com.*

★ Japengo

$$$$ | ASIAN | Located inside the Hyatt Regency, this spot sits atop a man-made pool grotto and offers stunning ocean views and a gorgeous glassed-in sushi bar. The views aside, it's the food that makes Japengo worth a visit; the fresh local fish is well prepared—as are the sushi and hand rolls—and the desserts are amazing. **Known for:** outstanding chef's specials; nice sake menu with flight options; live Hawaiian and acoustic entertainment. ⑤ *Average main: $42* ⌧ *Hyatt Regency Maui Resort & Spa, 200 Nohea Kai Dr., Kaanapali* ☎ *808/667–4909* ⊕ *hyatt.com/en-US/hotel/hawaii/hyatt-regency-maui-resort-and-spa/oggrm/dining* ⊘ *No lunch.*

Pizza Paradiso

$ | ITALIAN | When it opened in 1995 this was an over-the-counter pizza place, but it's evolved over the years into a local favorite, serving Mediterranean-style pizza and comfort food including pitas, gyros, and kabobs. **Known for:** gelato and Dole Whip for dessert; pizzas with local Maui produce; fresh, homemade pesto. ⑤ *Average main: $15* ⌧ *Honokowai Marketplace, 3350 Lower Honoapiilani Hwy., Honokowai* ☎ *808/667–2929* ⊕ *pizzaparadiso.com.*

★ Son'z Steakhouse

$$$$ | STEAKHOUSE | To enter the only steak house in West Maui, you descend a grand staircase into an amber-lighted dining room with soaring ceilings and a

massive artificial lagoon complete with swans, ducks, waterfalls, and tropical gardens. Chef Amy Mayers' classic menu features favorites like the bone-in rib eye and Tomahawk steaks with accompaniments including five house-made sauces and a variety of sides and seafood add-ons, as well as lighter plates like shrimp cocktail and the must-try black and blue *ahi* starter. **Known for:** astounding wine cellar; private, lagoon-front setting; 100% USDA-certified-prime steaks. $ *Average main: $40 ⌧ Hyatt Regency Maui, 200 Nohea Kai Dr., Kaanapali ☎ 808/667–4506 ⊕ sonzsteakhouse.com ⊘ No lunch.*

🛏 Hotels

With its long stretch of beach lined with luxury resorts, shops, and restaurants, Kaanapali is a vacationers' playground. Expect top-class service here and everything you could want a few steps from your room, including the calm waters of sun-kissed Kaanapali Beach. Wandering along the beach path between resorts is a recreational activity unto itself. Weather is dependably warm, and for that reason as well as all the others, Kaanapali is a popular—at times, downright crowded—destination.

★ Hyatt Regency Maui Resort & Spa
$$$$ | RESORT | FAMILY | Splashing waterfalls, swim-through grottos, a lagoon-like swimming pool, and a 150-foot waterslide "wow" guests of all ages at this bustling Kaanapali resort; spacious standard rooms are another draw. **Pros:** Drums of the Pacific luau and the must-see rooftop astronomy Tour of the Stars; Hawaiian cultural programs and wildlife education; water wonderland will thrill families. **Cons:** might not offer the most peaceful escape; daily resort and parking fees; can be difficult to find a space in self-parking. $ *Rooms from: $733 ⌧ 200 Nohea Kai Dr., Kaanapali ☎ 808/661–1234 ⊕ hyattregencymaui.com ⇌ 810 rooms ⫯◎⫯ No Meals.*

Kaanapali Alii
$$$$ | APARTMENT | FAMILY | Amenities like maid service, an activities desk, a small store with complimentary DVDs for guests to borrow, and a 24-hour front-desk service—and no pesky resort fees—make this a winning choice for families and those wanting to play house on Maui's most stunning shores. **Pros:** large comfortable units on the beach; quiet compared to other hotels in the resort; free parking. **Cons:** no on-site restaurant; small pools can get crowded; parking can be crowded during high season. $ *Rooms from: $534 ⌧ 50 Nohea Kai Dr., Kaanapali ☎ 866/644–6410 ⊕ kaanapalialii.com ⇌ 264 units ⫯◎⫯ No Meals.*

★ Kaanapali Beach Hotel
$$$$ | HOTEL | This charming beachfront hotel is full of aloha—locals say it's one of the few resorts on the Island where you can get a true Hawaiian experience as the entire staff takes part in the hotel's Pookela program, which teaches guests about the history, traditions, and values of Hawaiian culture. **Pros:** no resort fee; friendly staff; diverse array of cultural activities. **Cons:** fewer amenities than other places along this beach; daily parking fee; property is older than neighboring modern resorts. $ *Rooms from: $350 ⌧ 2525 Kaanapali Pkwy., Kaanapali ☎ 808/661–0011, 800/262–8450 ⊕ kbhmaui.com ⇌ 432 rooms ⫯◎⫯ No Meals.*

★ Maui Eldorado Kaanapali
$$$ | APARTMENT | The Kaanapali Golf Course's fairways wrap around this fine, well-priced, two-story condo complex that boasts spacious studios, one- and two-bedroom units with fully equipped kitchens, and access to a stocked beach cabana on a semiprivate beach. **Pros:** privileges at the Kaanapali Golf Courses; Wi-Fi in all units; friendly staff. **Cons:** some distance from attractions of the Kaanapali Resort; no housekeeping but checkout cleaning fee; not right on beach. $ *Rooms from: $300 ⌧ 2661 Kekaa Dr., Kaanapali ☎ 808/633-8331*

⊕ *mauikaanapalivacationrentals.com*
🛏 *204 units* ⦿I *No Meals.*

Royal Lahaina Resort

$$$$ | **RESORT** | Built in 1962, this grand property on the uncrowded, sandy shore in North Kaanapali has hosted million-aires and Hollywood stars, and today it pleases families and budget seekers as well as luxury travelers with a variety of lodging styles. **Pros:** on-site luau; variety of lodgings and rates; tennis ranch with 11 courts and a pro shop. **Cons:** daily self-parking fee; evening luau noise can be loud; older property. ⑤ *Rooms from: $420* ✉ *2780 Kekaa Dr., Kaanapali* ☎ *800/447–6925* ⊕ *royallahaina.com* 🛏 *447 units* ⦿I *No Meals.*

★ Sheraton Maui Resort & Spa

$$$$ | **RESORT** | Set among dense gardens on Kaanapali's best stretch of beach, the Sheraton offers a quieter, more low-key atmosphere than its neighboring resorts, and sits next to and on top of Puu Kekaa, the site of a nightly torch-lighting and cliff-diving ritual. **Pros:** free shuttle to Lahaina and shopping malls; great snorkeling right off the beach; Maui Nui luau three times a week. **Cons:** daily resort and parking fees; beach subject to seasonal erosion; extensive property can mean a long walk from your room to lobby, restaurants, and beach. ⑤ *Rooms from: $759* ✉ *2605 Kaanapali Pkwy., Kaanapali* ☎ *808/661–0031* ⊕ *marriott.com/hnmsi* 🛏 *508 units* ⦿I *No Meals.*

The Westin Maui Resort & Spa

$$$$ | **RESORT** | **FAMILY** | This 12-acre beachfront paradise offers a setting that is both beautiful and calming. **Pros:** free shuttle to Lahaina town; excellent concierge desk; one adults-only pool. **Cons:** a lot going on; crowded pool and common areas; daily resort and parking fees. ⑤ *Rooms from: $797* ✉ *2365 Kaanapali Pkwy., Kaanapali* ☎ *808/667–2525* ⊕ *westinmaui.com* 🛏 *770 rooms* ⦿I *No Meals.*

Westin Nanea Ocean Villas

$$$$ | **RESORT** | **FAMILY** | It's rare to find a resort that so thoroughly incorporates authentic Hawaiian cultural symbols and traditions into its design, but this deluxe beachfront property in North Kaanapali carries this commitment into its native landscaping and the Puuhonua O Nanea cultural center that hosts artifacts, displays, activities, and talks. **Pros:** "zero-entry" family pool with sandy bottom and water slide; great location for snorkeling and water sports; free shuttle to Lahaina town and other Westin resorts. **Cons:** outside main Kaanapali resort; limited dining options; may be pitched to join time-share club. ⑤ *Rooms from: $891* ✉ *45 Kai Malina Pkwy., Kaanapali* ☎ *808/662–6300* ⊕ *marriott.com* 🛏 *390 units* ⦿I *No Meals.*

🎭 Performing Arts

Drums of the Pacific Luau

THEMED ENTERTAINMENT | **FAMILY** | By Kaanapali Beach, this luau shines in every category—convenient parking, well-made food, and a nicely paced program that touches on Hawaiian, Samoan, Tahitian, Fijian, Tongan, and Maori cultures. Some guests get tickled by the onstage audience hula tutorial. The finale features three fire-knife dancers. You'll feast on delicious Hawaiian delicacies like teriyaki steak, oven-roasted *mahimahi* (dolphinfish), and Pacific *ahi* poke (pickled raw yellowfin tuna, tossed with herbs and seasonings). The dessert spread consists of chocolate and coconut indulgences. An open bar offers beer, seltzer, wine, and standard tropical mixes. ✉ *Hyatt Regency Maui, 200 Nohea Kai Dr., Kaanapali* ☎ *808/667–4727* ⊕ *drumsofthepacificmaui.com.*

★ Hula Girl

SAILING | **FAMILY** | This custom catamaran is one of the slickest and best-equipped boats on the Island, complete with a VIP lounge by the captain's fly bridge.

The initial cost doesn't include the cooked-to-order meals, but guests can choose from a relatively extensive menu that includes filet mignon, daily fish specials, and crème brûlée. If you're willing to splurge a little for live music, an onboard chef, and upscale service, this is your best bet. From mid-December to early April the cruise focuses on whale-watching. Check-in is in front of Leilani's restaurant at Whalers Village. ⊠ *Whalers Village, 2435 Kaanapali Pkwy., Kaanapali* ☎ *808/665–0344, 808/667–5980* ⊕ *sailingmaui.com* ⌁ *$90.*

Tour of the Stars
READINGS/LECTURES | FAMILY | For nightlife of the celestial sort, children and astronomy buffs can try Tour of the Stars, a one-hour stargazing program on the roof of the Hyatt Regency Maui held Thursday through Monday nights on the hour from 8–11 pm. Check in at the hotel lobby 15 minutes prior to starting time; program availability dependent on weather. ⊠ *Hyatt Regency Maui Resort & Spa, 200 Nohea Kai Dr., Kaanapali* ☎ *808/667–4727* ⊕ *hyattregencymaui. com* ⌁ *$40–$50.*

Wailele Polynesian Luau
THEMED ENTERTAINMENT | The oceanfront Aloha Pavilion at the Westin provides a picturesque setting for this Polynesian feast. Seating is family style, and on a first-come basis, although premium tickets get reserved seating and slightly better views. A buffet of traditional dishes such as kalua pork and *ahi* poke (pickled raw yellowfin tuna salad) precede the dessert spread. The performance showcases stories of the demi-god Maui, traditional costumes, hula *kahiko,* and a pulse-raising fire-knife dance finale. ⊠ *Westin Maui Resort & Spa, 2365 Kaanapali Pkwy., Kaanapali* ☎ *808/661– 2992* ⊕ *westinmauiluau.com* ☉ *Closed Mon.—also closed Wed. and Fri. except for summer and holidays.*

Mai Tai 🍸

Don't let your sweet tooth fool you. Maui's favorite drink—the mai tai— can be as lethal as it is sweet. The Original Trader Vic's recipe calls for two ounces of aged dark rum, mixed with almond syrup, orange curaçao, the juice of one lime, and (wouldn't you know it) rock-candy syrup.

🛍 Shopping

SHOPPING CENTERS
★ **Whalers Village**
MALL | FAMILY | Chic Whalers Village boasts wonderful oceanfront restaurants and shops in the heart of Kaanapali. Upscale haunts include Louis Vuitton and Tourneau, and beautyphiles can get their fix at Sephora. Elegant home accessories at Martin and MacArthur and Totally Hawaiian Gift Gallery are perfect Hawaii-made souvenirs, while the many great surf and swimwear shops will prepare you for a day at the beach. Kids will fall in love with the whimsical two-story climbing structure at the lower courtyard. The outdoor mall also offers free weekly entertainment, lei-making classes, and hula lessons; check their website for a complete schedule. ⊠ *2435 Kaana-pali Pkwy., Kaanapali* ☎ *808/661–4567* ⊕ *whalersvillage.com.*

Napili

Situated between Kahana and Kapalua, Napili is a peaceful community with a mix of residential neighborhoods and modest but comfortable condominiums and resorts. Here it's possible to find reasonably priced accommodations and dining options, while still being close to many attractions and world-class beaches.

With a central location almost midway between the Hyatt and Sheraton resorts in Kaanapali, Whaler's Village offers a mix of upscale shopping, dining, and even live entertainment.

Beaches

★ Napili Beach

BEACH | FAMILY | Surrounded by sleepy condos, this round bay is a turtle-filled pool lined with a sparkling white crescent of sand. Sunbathers love this beach, which is also a terrific sunset spot. The shore break is steep but gentle, so it's great for bodyboarding and bodysurfing. It's easy to keep an eye on kids here as the entire bay is visible from everywhere. The beach is right outside the Napili Kai Beach Resort, a popular local-style resort for honeymooners and families, only a few miles south of Kapalua. **Amenities:** showers; toilets. **Best for:** sunset; surfing; swimming; snorkeling. ⊠ *5900 Lower Honoapiilani Hwy., Napili* ✛ *Look for Napili Pl. or Hui Dr.*

Restaurants

Aa Roots

$ | **VEGETARIAN** | The meals at this charming vegan restaurant are almost too gorgeous to eat; don't be surprised to find edible flowers or a rainbow of fruit adorning your meal. Choose from hearty soups, salads, sandwiches, and smoothies, plus rice bowls piled high with healthy ingredients. **Known for:** hearty burritos; locally sourced ingredients; dragon fruit açaí bowl. ⑤ *Average main: $14* ⊠ *Napili Plaza Shopping Center, 5095 Napilihau St., Napili* ☎ *808/298–2499* ⊕ *aarootsmaui.com* ⊗ *Closed Wed.*

Duke's Beachhouse

$$$$ | **HAWAIIAN** | Though it may seem like a tourist trap, this oceanside restaurant does not disappoint in the quality of its food, paired with an ambience steeped in Hawaiian history. The restaurant is named for famed surfer Duke Kahanamoku, and guests can learn about his life through memorabilia throughout. **Known for:** incredible seafood risotto; imported cold water lobster; warm and friendly service. ⑤ *Average main: $38* ⊠ *130 Kai Malina Parkway, Napili* ☎ *808/662–2900* ⊕ *dukesmaui.com.*

The Gazebo Restaurant

$ | DINER | Breakfast is the reason to seek out this restaurant located poolside at the Napili Shores Resort. The food is standard diner fare, but the portions are big, the prices are low, and many folks think the pancakes—with bananas, macadamia nuts, or white chocolate chips—are the best in West Maui. **Known for:** create-your-own pancakes; enormous omelets; long but fast-moving lines. ⑤ *Average main: $13* ✉ *Napili Shores Maui, 5315 Lower Honoapiilani Hwy., Napili* ☎ *808/669–5621* ☻ *No dinner.*

★ Joey's Kitchen

$$ | FILIPINO | Chef-owner Joey Macadangdang, who has been at the helm of fine-dining kitchens for most of his career, brings his good taste to the masses with this unfussy restaurant featuring Filipino, Asian, and American fusion dishes. A longtime champion of local producers, many of his recipes highlight ingredients grown on Maui. **Known for:** local ingredients; excellent value; Filipino cuisine. ⑤ *Average main: $20* ✉ *Napili Plaza Shopping Center, 5095 Napilihau St., Napili* ☎ *808/214–5590* ⊕ *joeyskitchenhimaui.com.*

★ Sea House Restaurant

$$$$ | SEAFOOD | Built in the 1960s at the Napili Kai Beach Resort, before there were laws forbidding construction so close to the beach, this restaurant is literally footsteps away from gorgeous Napili Bay. Wear your beach wrap to breakfast and enjoy the signature oven-baked pancakes or the beautifully delicious Molokai sweet potato egg frittata; the menu also offers fish from Hawaiian waters and fresh local produce. **Known for:** sunset views from the lanai; affordable breakfast and lunch; daily happy hour from 2 to 4:30 pm. ⑤ *Average main: $36* ✉ *Napili Kai Beach Resort, 5900 Lower Honoapiilani Rd., Napili* ☎ *808/669–1500* ⊕ *napilikai.com/dining.*

🛏 Hotels

Aston Mahana at Kaanapali

$$$$ | HOTEL | FAMILY | Though the name claims Kaanapali, this older, 12-story oceanfront condominium complex, where all units have unobstructed panoramic views of the ocean and nearby islands, is actually in quiet, neighboring Honokowai. **Pros:** private lanai and massive windows great for sunsets and whale-watching; tennis, shuffleboard, and pickleball courts; shell lei and children's gift on check-in. **Cons:** no shops or restaurants on property; lacks resort amenities; furnishings in some units may need updating. ⑤ *Rooms from: $519* ✉ *110 Kaanapali Shores Pl., Honokowai* ☎ *808/661–8751, 866/945–4046* ⊕ *aquaaston.com* ⤳ *215 units* ❍ *No Meals.*

Honua Kai Resort & Spa

$$$$ | APARTMENT | FAMILY | Two high-rise towers contain these individually owned, eco-friendly (and family-friendly) units combining the conveniences of a condo with the full service of a hotel. **Pros:** large spacious rooms with full kitchens; upscale appliances and furnishings; beautiful, well-maintained grounds. **Cons:** housekeeping every other day; beach is small and rocky, not good for swimming; sometimes windy. ⑤ *Rooms from: $700* ✉ *130 Kai Malina Pkwy., Honokowai* ☎ *808/662–2800, 855/718–5789* ⊕ *honuakai.com* ⤳ *628 units* ❍ *No Meals.*

Mahina Surf

$$$ | APARTMENT | Of the many condo complexes lining the ocean-side stretch of Honoapiilani Highway, this one offers friendly service, a saline oceanfront pool, and affordable units—some with million-dollar views. **Pros:** oceanfront barbecues; resident turtles hang out on the rocks below; no hidden fees. **Cons:** no housekeeping (and cleaning fee for stays fewer than seven nights); minimum three-night stay; rocky shoreline rather than a beach. ⑤ *Rooms from:*

$272 ✉ 4057 Lower Honoapiilani Hwy. ☎ 808/669–6068, 800/544–0300 ⊕ mahinasurf.com ⇆ 56 units ⦿ No Meals.

The Mauian on Napili Bay

$$$ | APARTMENT | If you're looking for a low-key place with a friendly staff, this small, delightful beachfront property on Napili Bay may be for you. **Pros:** reasonable rates; located on one of Maui's top swimming and snorkeling beaches; free parking and no resort fees. **Cons:** some may find motel-like design reduces privacy; few amenities; small units. ⑤ Rooms from: $299 ✉ 5441 Lower Honoapiilani Hwy., Napili ☎ 808/669–6205 ⊕ mauian.com ⇆ 44 rooms ⦿ No Meals.

★ Napili Kai Beach Resort

$$$$ | RESORT | FAMILY | Spread across 10 beautiful acres along one of the best beaches on Maui, the family-friendly Napili Kai with its "old Hawaii" feel draws a loyal following to its island-style rooms that open onto private lanai. **Pros:** weekly kids' hula performances and Hawaiian slack-key guitar concert; fantastic swimming and sunning beach; no resort fees. **Cons:** beach subject to periodic erosion; parking spaces tight for some; not as modern as other resorts in West Maui. ⑤ Rooms from: $355 ✉ 5900 Lower Honoapi'ilani Hwy., Napili ☎ 808/669–6271 ⊕ napilikai.com ⇆ 163 units ⦿ No Meals.

Papakea Resort

$$$$ | APARTMENT | FAMILY | All studios and one- and two-bedroom units at this casual, oceanfront condominium complex face the ocean and, because the units are spread out among 11 low-rise buildings on about 13 acres of land, there is built-in privacy and easy parking. **Pros:** large rooms; lovely garden landscaping; weekly mai tai party. **Cons:** pool can get crowded; busy, family-oriented property; no beach in front of property. ⑤ Rooms from: $365 ✉ 3543 Lower Honoapiilani Hwy., Honokowai ☎ 808/665–0880, 855/945–4047 ⊕ astonatpapakea.com ⇆ 364 units ⦿ No Meals.

Sands of Kahana

$$$$ | APARTMENT | Meandering gardens, spacious rooms, and an on-site restaurant distinguish this large condominium complex—units on the upper floors benefit from the height, with unrivaled ocean views stretching away from private lanais. **Pros:** restaurant on premises; fitness center, tennis courts, and sand volleyball court; one-, two-, and three-bedroom units available. **Cons:** street-facing units can get a bit noisy; property a bit dated; may be approached about buying a time-share unit. ⑤ Rooms from: $494 ✉ 4299 Lower Honoapiilani Hwy., Kahana ☎ 808/669–0400 property phone, 855/386–4658 ⊕ sandsofkahanaresort.com ⇆ 196 units ⦿ No Meals.

ⓨ Nightlife

★ Slack Key Show: Masters of Hawaiian Music

LIVE MUSIC | Grammy-winning musician George Kahumoku Jr. hosts this program on Wednesday, as well as some Saturdays, which features a rotating lineup of the Island's finest slack-key artists as well as other traditional forms of Hawaiian music. The setup at Aloha Pavilion is humble, but you'll enjoy these beloved musicians in an intimate setting. ✉ Napili Kai Beach Resort, 5900 Lower Honoapiilani Rd., Lahaina ☎ 808/249–2125 ⊕ slackkeyshow.com.

ⓢ Shopping

Farmer's Market Maui

MARKET | From pineapples to papayas, the produce at this West Maui market is local and flavorful. Prices are good, too. The deli offers hot and cold food items, and colorful tropical flowers and handcrafted items are also available. ✉ 3636 Honoapiilani Hwy., across from Honokowai Park, Honokowai ☎ 808/669–7004 ⊕ farmersmarketmaui.com ◔ Closed Sun.

Kapalua

Kapalua is 10 miles north of Kaanapali; 36 miles west of Kahului.

Beautiful and secluded, Kapalua is West Maui's northernmost resort community. First developed in the late 1970s, the resort now includes the Ritz-Carlton, posh residential complexes, two golf courses, and the surrounding former pineapple fields. The area's distinctive shops and restaurants cater to dedicated golfers, celebrities who want to be left alone, and some of the world's richest folks. In addition to golf, recreational activities include hiking and snorkeling. Mists regularly envelop the landscape of tall Cook pines and rolling fairways in Kapalua, which is cooler and quieter than its southern neighbors. The beaches here, including Kapalua and D. T. Fleming, are among Maui's finest.

GETTING HERE AND AROUND

Shuttles and taxis are available from Kahului and West Maui airports. The Ritz-Carlton, Kapalua, has a resort shuttle within the Kapalua Resort.

🌞 Beaches

D. T. Fleming Beach

BEACH | FAMILY | Because the current can be quite strong, this charming, mile-long sandy cove is better for sunbathing than for swimming or water sports. Still, it's one of the Island's most popular beaches. It's a perfect spot to watch the spectacular Maui sunsets, and there are picnic tables and grills. Part of the beach runs along the front of the Ritz-Carlton, Kapalua—a good place to grab a cocktail and enjoy the view. **Amenities:** lifeguards; parking (no fee); showers; toilets. **Best for:** sunset; walking. ⊠ *Rte. 30, Kapalua* ✛ *About 1 mile north of Kapalua.*

★ Kapalua Bay Beach

BEACH | FAMILY | Over the years, Kapalua has been recognized as one of the world's best beaches, and for good reason: it fronts a pristine bay that is good for snorkeling, swimming, and general lazing. Just north of Napili Bay, this lovely sheltered shore often remains calm late into the afternoon, although currents may be strong offshore. Snorkeling is easy here, and there are lots of colorful reef fish. This popular area is bordered by the Kapalua Resort, so don't expect to have the beach to yourself. Walk through the tunnel from the parking lot at the end of Kapalua Place to get here. **Amenities:** parking (no fee); showers; toilets. **Best for:** snorkeling; sunset; swimming. ⊠ *Rte. 30, Kapalua* ✛ *Turn onto Kapalua Pl.*

Mokuleia Bay (Slaughterhouse Beach)

BEACH | The Island's northernmost beach is part of the Honolua-Mokuleia Marine Life Conservation District. "Slaughterhouse" is the surfers' nickname for what is officially Mokuleia. Weather permitting, this is a great place for bodysurfing and sunbathing. Concrete steps and a railing help you get down the cliff to the sand, but it's generally a difficult area to access for younger children. The next bay over, Honolua, has no beach but offers one of the best surf breaks in Hawaii. Competitions are sometimes held there; telltale signs are cars pulled off the road and parked in the old pineapple field. **Amenities:** none. **Best for:** sunset; surfing; snorkeling. ⊠ *Rte. 30, Kapalua* ✛ *At mile marker 32.*

🍴 Restaurants

Kapalua is where the wealthy come to stay and play, so it's no surprise that area restaurants cater to an affluent clientele. Dining here is more than filling your belly; it's a culinary exploration featuring innovative menus, local ingredients, and island flare.

Banyan Tree

$$$$ | ECLECTIC | This eclectic farm-to-table dinner spot is an open-air, ocean-view restaurant and lounge. Classic Hawaiian

Beach Safety on Maui

Hawaii's beautiful beaches can be dangerous at times due to large waves and strong currents. Look for posted black and yellow hazard signs warning of high surf, jellyfish, sharks, and other dangers. Be especially cautious at beaches without lifeguards.

Generally, North Shore beaches (including Mokuleia and D. T. Fleming on the west side of the Island) can be rough in the winter and not good for swimming or beginner-level water sports. On the south side, large summer swells and Kona storms (which usually occur in winter) can cause strong rip currents and powerful shore breaks.

Swim only when there's a normal caution rating, never swim alone, and don't dive into unknown water or shallow breaking waves. If you're unable to swim out of a rip current, tread water and wave your arms in the air to signal for help.

Even in calm conditions, there are other dangerous things in the water to be aware of, including razor-sharp coral, jellyfish, eels, and the occasional shark. Jellyfish cause the most ocean injuries, and signs are posted along beaches when they're present. Box jellyfish swarm to Hawaii's leeward shores 9–10 days after a full moon. Portuguese man-of-war jellyfish are usually found when winds blow from the ocean onto land. Reactions to a sting are usually mild (burning sensation, redness); however, in some cases they can be severe (breathing difficulties). If you are stung, pick off the tentacles, rinse the affected area with water, and apply ice. Seek first aid from a lifeguard if you experience severe reactions.

According to state sources, the chances of getting bitten by a shark in Hawaiian waters are low. To reduce your shark-attack risk:

■ Swim, surf, or dive with others at beaches patrolled by lifeguards.

■ Avoid swimming at dawn, dusk, and night.

■ Don't enter the water if you have open wounds or are bleeding.

■ Avoid murky waters, harbor entrances, areas near stream mouths, channels, or steep drop-offs.

■ Don't wear high-contrast swimwear or shiny jewelry.

■ Leave the water quickly and calmly if you spot a shark.

recipes combined with Mediterranean cooking techniques result in unique, fresh, coastal cuisine. **Known for:** creative presentation; island cuisine; local ingredients. ⑤ *Average main: $45 ⊠ The Ritz-Carlton, Kapalua, 1 Ritz-Carlton Drive, Kapalua* ☎ *808/669–6200* ⊕ *banyantreekapalua.com.*

★ **Merriman's Maui**

$$$$ | MODERN HAWAIIAN | Perched above the postcard-perfect Kapalua Bay, this is the place to impress your date, as Chef Peter Merriman highlights the Islands' bounty by using fresh seafood and ingredients from local farms. A nightly changing prix-fixe menu ($120) features stunning dishes that represent land and sea options and a vegetarian option that abounds with local produce. **Known for:** exceptional wine list; fire pit on the outdoor lanai; panoramic ocean views. ⑤ *Average main: $120 ⊠ 1 Bay Club Pl.,*

Kapalua ☎ 808/669–6400 ⊕ merriman-shawaii.com ⊗ No lunch.

★ Sansei Seafood Restaurant & Sushi Bar

$$$$ | ASIAN | With locations on three islands, Sansei takes sushi, sashimi, and contemporary Japanese food to a new level. If you're a fish or shellfish lover, this is the place for you. **Known for:** panko-crusted ahi (yellowfin tuna) sashimi; inventive rolls and sushi appetizers; award-winning Shrimp Dynamite (tempura shrimp with a garlic masago aioli). ⑤ Average main: $36 ⊠ 600 Office Rd., Kapalua ☎ 808/669–6286 ⊕ sanseihawaii.com ⊗ No lunch.

Taverna

$$$ | ITALIAN | Acclaimed chef Roger Stettler leans on his Italian heritage to create this award-winning menu. This rustic, open-air restaurant dishes hearty soups, salads, and sandwiches at lunchtime, and the house-made pastas are the highlight of the more upscale dinner service. **Known for:** house-made pastas; amazing house lasagna; Italian comfort food. ⑤ Average main: $34 ⊠ 2000 Village Road, Kapalua ☎ 808/667–2426 ⊕ tavernamaui.com.

🛌 Hotels

The neighborhoods north of Kaanapali—Honokowai, Mahinahina, Kahana, Napili, and finally, Kapalua—blend almost seamlessly into one another along Lower Honoapiilani Highway. Each has a few shops and restaurants and a secluded bay or two to call its own. Many visitors have found a second home here, at one of the condominiums nestled between beach-access roads and groves of mango trees. You won't get the stellar service of a resort (except at Kapalua), but you'll be among the locals here, in a relatively quiet part of the island. Be prepared for a long commute, though, if you're planning to do much exploring elsewhere on the island. Kapalua is the area farthest north, but well worth all the driving to stay at the elegant Ritz-Carlton, which is surrounded by misty greenery and overlooks beautiful D. T. Fleming Beach.

The Kapalua Villas Maui

$$$$ | APARTMENT | Set among the 22,000 sprawling acres of the Kapalua Resort, these posh condominiums are named for their locations: the Golf Villas line the fairways of Kapalua's Bay Golf Course; the Ridge Villas are perched along a cliff overlooking the ocean; the Bay Villas are at the water's edge; and the Gold Villas are ultra-luxe. **Pros:** Individual Unit Choice program allows you to see the actual unit before booking; amazing views; network of walking and running trails. **Cons:** sometimes windy; small pools; stores, beaches, and restaurants not within walking distance. ⑤ Rooms from: $458 ⊠ 300 Kapalua Dr., Kapalua ☎ 808/665–9170, 800/545–0018 ⊕ kapaluavillas.com ⇄ 120 villas ⦿ No Meals.

★ Montage Kapalua Bay

$$$$ | RESORT | FAMILY | This luxury resort caters to well-heeled travelers who want the comfort and privacy of a residential-style suite combined with resort service and amenities—elegantly furnished one- to four-bedroom units with gourmet kitchens, in-unit washers/dryers, and the largest lanai to be found. **Pros:** prime snorkeling; great kids clubs for children and teens; large, well-appointed rooms. **Cons:** large property means lots of walking; far from other Maui attractions; pricey daily parking and resort fees. ⑤ Rooms from: $1200 ⊠ 1 Bay Dr., Kapalua ☎ 808/662–6600 ⊕ montagehotels.com/kapaluabay ⇄ 50 units ⦿ No Meals.

★ The Ritz-Carlton, Kapalua

$$$$ | RESORT | This notable hillside property features luxurious service and upscale accommodations along with an enhanced Hawaiian sense of place. **Pros:** spa, golf, walking trails, and many other activities; AAA 4-Diamond Banyan Tree restaurant will please locavores; many cultural and recreational programs. **Cons:** far from major attractions such as Haleakala; daily

parking and resort fees; can be windy on grounds and at pool. ⑤ *Rooms from: $1665* ✉ *1 Ritz-Carlton Dr., Kapalua* ☎ *808/669–6200* ⊕ *ritzcarlton.com/kapalua* ↻ *466 units* ⦿ *No Meals.*

Nightlife

Alaloa Lounge

LIVE MUSIC | When ambience weighs heavy on the priority list, this spot at the Ritz-Carlton, Kapalua, might just be the ticket. Live performances range from jazz to island rhythms on Tuesday through Saturday nights (6–9 pm), and the menu includes locally inspired cocktails and a fresh sushi station from 5–9 pm. Step onto the lanai for that plumeria-tinged tropical air and gaze at the deep blue of the Pacific.

You'll find an extensive menu of specialty cocktails, domestic and imported beers, premium spirits, and signature appetizers, including a fresh sushi station, open daily from 5–9 pm. The best sunsets can be viewed from here and, from December to April, enjoy whale-watching while having lunch. As the sun sets, relax and enjoy live entertainment Tuesday to Saturday from 6–9 pm. ✉ *The Ritz-Carlton, Kapalua, 1 Ritz-Carlton Dr., Kapalua* ☎ *808/669–6200* ⊕ *ritzcarlton.com.*

🛍 Shopping

FOOD

Honolua Store

FOOD | In contrast to Kapalua's many high-end retailers, the old Honolua Store still plies the groceries and household goods it did in plantation times. Hefty plates of *ono* (delicious) local foods are served at the deli until 3 pm and best enjoyed on the wraparound porch. The plate lunches are the quintessential local meal. The coffee bar is welcoming and includes air-conditioning and free Wi-Fi daily until 5 pm. ✉ *502 Office Rd., Kapalua* ☎ *808/665–9105* ⊕ *honoluastore.com.*

🏃 Activities

SPAS

Spa Montage Kapalua Bay

SPAS | FAMILY | This spa's grand entrance opens onto an airy, modern beach house with panoramic island and ocean views. With amenities including a movement studio, fitness center, and coed infinity pool you can easily spend a day meandering about the spa's expansive layout without feeling cooped up. The spa menu includes therapies that incorporate local ingredients and calming ingredients from the sea. This spa is for the whole family, with treatments available for kids as young as four. ✉ *1 Bay Dr., Kapalua* ☎ *808/665–8282* ⊕ *montagehotels. com/kapaluabay/spa* 🔁 *$215 for 60-min massage.*

The Ritz-Carlton Spa, Kapalua

SPAS | At this gorgeous 17,500-square-foot spa, you enter a blissful maze where floor-to-ceiling riverbed stones lead to serene treatment rooms, couples' *hales* (cabanas), and a rain forest–like grotto with a Jacuzzi, dry cedar sauna, and eucalyptus steam rooms. Hang out in the coed waiting area, where sliding-glass doors open to a whirlpool overlooking a taro-patch garden. Exfoliate any rough spots with an alaea salt (Hawaiian red sea salt) scrub, then wash off in a private outdoor shower garden before indulging in a lomilomi massage. High-end beauty treatments include advanced oxygen technology to tighten and nourish mature skin. The boutique has a highly coveted collection of organic, local, and high-end beauty products, fitness wear, and Maui-made Nina Kuna jewelry and natural skin-care lines. ✉ *The Ritz-Carlton, Kapalua, 1 Ritz-Carlton Dr., Kapalua* ☎ *808/665–7079* ⊕ *ritzcarlton.com* 🔁 *$190 for 50-min massage, $350 spa packages.*

Chapter 4

SOUTH SHORE

4

Updated by
Laurie Lyons-Makaimoku

👁 **Sights**
★★★★★

🍴 **Restaurants**
★★★★★

🛏 **Hotels**
★★★★★

🛍 **Shopping**
★★★☆☆

🍸 **Nightlife**
★★★☆☆

WELCOME TO SOUTH SHORE

TOP REASONS TO GO

★ **Enjoy a variety of activities.** The Island's most energetic and action-packed region, South Maui offers a bit of everything.

★ **Soak up beach culture.** South Maui's coastal culture means that, whatever your plans, sun and sand are always within reach.

★ **Party on.** Once the sun sets, night owls and partygoers keep the action pumping at local bars and lounges concentrated at Kihei Kalama Village on South Kihei Road, aptly nicknamed "the Triangle" or "the Bar-muda Triangle."

★ **See how Maui's other half lives.** Whether you're looking to view Maui's underwater inhabitants from the ocean depths or from the comfort of dry land, Maalaea is the place to be.

★ **Take a walk on the wild side.** Bird's the word at the Kealia Coastal Boardwalk, where you can spot the area's feathered residents, including two of Hawaii's endangered waterbirds: the Hawaiian coot and Hawaiian stilt.

The area known as South Maui is comprised of several seaside towns, from Maalaea in the north to La Peruse Bay in the south. There are two main roads connecting the area: the coast-hugging South Kihei Road, and Piilani Highway (Highway 31), which sits about half a mile *mauka* (toward the mountains) and runs parallel. If you're not in a rush, cruise scenic South Kihei Road to get the lay of the land and see the action. Note that while South Maui appears just a stone's throw from Upcountry, there are no public roads that connect these two regions, and driving times can be 45 minutes or more.

1 Maalaea. This small-but-mighty town is home to a busy harbor, aquarium, shops, and several oceanfront condos. Tour boats depart from Maalaea Harbor daily, en route to deep-sea fishing excursions, snorkeling trips, whale-watches and more. The harborfront Maui Ocean Center aquarium is home to one of the largest collections of live Pacific corals in the world. Marine experts share their knowledge during daily interactive talks, including the popular Ocean Exhibit dive, when a mic-equipped diver answers questions from inside the 750,000-gallon tank. Steps away is the 54-foot tunnel through waters that teem with charismatic sharks, stingrays, and tropical fish.

2 Kihei. With miles of sandy shoreline, a host of ocean activities and reliably sunny days, there's no wonder Kihei is synonymous with beaches. Add to that a bounty of dining options and entertainment for all ages, and you've got a place where rest and relaxation is practically sport.

3 Wailea. Maui's posh seaside enclave is the place to see and be seen. Home to million-dollar mansions, luxury resorts, and fine dining restaurants, this is as fancy as it gets on Maui.

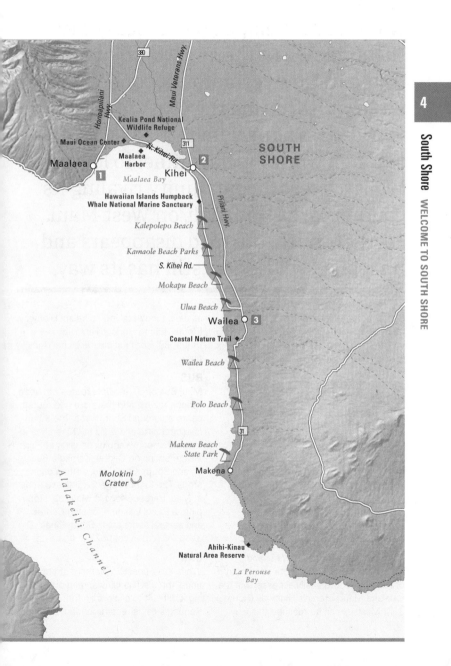

Blessed by more than its fair share of sun, the southern shore of Haleakala was an undeveloped wilderness until the 1970s, when the sun worshippers found it. Now restaurants, condos, and luxury resorts line the coast from the world-class aquarium at Maalaea Harbor through working-class Kihei to lovely Wailea, a resort community rivaling its counterpart, Kaanapali, on West Maui. Farther south, the road disappears and unspoiled wilderness still has its way.

Because the South Shore includes so many fine beach choices, a trip here—if you're staying elsewhere on the Island—is an all-day excursion, especially if you include a visit to the aquarium. Get active in the morning with exploring and snorkeling, then shower in a beach park, dress up a little, and enjoy the cool luxury of the Wailea resorts. At sunset, settle in for dinner at one of the area's many fine restaurants.

Planning

Getting Here and Around

The South Maui towns of Kihei and Wailea are a quick 25-minute ride south of Kahului Airport, easily accessed via the four-lane Maui Veteran's Highway (Route 311). Maalaea can be reached this way

as well, though taking Kuihelani Highway (Route 380) to Honoapiilani Highway (Route 30) from Kahului takes half the time.

BUS

Maui Bus offers multiple routes between various towns, and there are two routes centered around South Maui. The Kihei Islander starts and ends at Queen Kaahumanu Center in Kahului, pausing at Piilani Village Shopping Center, Kamaole Beach III, and South Kihei Road, among other stops. The Kihei Villager begins and ends at Maui Harbor Shops in Maalaea, stopping at Piilani Village Shopping Center and several spots along South Kihei Road. All routes cost $2 per boarding.

CAR

While Kihei boasts a plethora of attractions, the town is fairly spread out, making it difficult to explore on foot alone. Renting a car is recommended, even for just a few days, to explore all that the South Shore—and Maui—has to offer.

Hotels

The South Shore has two main communities: down-to-earth Kihei and resort-filled Wailea. In general, the farther south you go, the fancier the accommodations get. As you travel down South Kihei Road, you can find condos both fronting and across the street from inviting beach parks and close to shops and restaurants. Once you hit Wailea, the opulence quotient takes a giant leap; this is the land of perfectly groomed resorts.

Restaurants

South Maui's dining scene begins at Maalaea Harbor and wends its way through the beach towns of Kihei and Wailea. There are plenty of casual, relatively inexpensive eateries along the way—until you reach Wailea, where most of the dining is pricey.

HOTEL AND RESTAURANT PRICES

Hotel prices in the reviews are the lowest cost of a standard double room in high season. Restaurant prices in the reviews are the average cost of a main course at dinner, or if dinner is not served, at lunch.

WHAT IT COSTS in U.S. Dollars			
$	$$	$$$	$$$$
RESTAURANTS			
under $18	$18–$26	$27–$35	over $35
HOTELS			
under $181	$181–$260	$261–$340	over $340

Kihei

9 miles south of Kahului; 20 miles east of Lahaina.

Traffic lights and shopping malls may not fit your notion of paradise, but Kihei offers dependably warm sun, excellent beaches, and a front-row seat to marine life of all sorts. Besides all the sun and sand, the town's relatively inexpensive condos and excellent restaurants make this a home base for many Maui visitors.

County beach parks, such as Kamaole I, II, and III, have lawns, showers, and picnic tables.

■ TIP→ **Remember: beach park or no beach park, the public has a right to the entire coastal strand, but not to cross private property to get to it.**

GETTING HERE AND AROUND

Kihei is an easy 25-minute ride south of Kahului Airport, easily accessed via the four-lane Maui Veteran's Highway (Route 311). Once there, if you plan to plant yourself at the water's edge for most of your vacation, a car may not be necessary, especially if you're staying at a hotel or condo within walking distance of Kihei's fabulous beaches. For those wanting to explore beyond the beach, renting a car is a good idea.

◉ Sights

Farmers' Market of Maui–Kihei

MARKET | Tropical flowers, tempting produce, massive avocados, and locally made preserves, banana bread, and crafts are among the bargains at this South Shore market in the west end of Kihei, next to the ABC Store. ⊠ *61 S. Kihei Rd., Kihei* ☎ *808/875–0949* ⊕ *farmersmarketsmaui.com/kihei* ⊗ *Closed Wed., Sat., Sun.*

★ Hawaiian Islands Humpback Whale National Marine Sanctuary

COLLEGE | FAMILY | This nature center sits in prime humpback-viewing territory beside a restored ancient Hawaiian fishpond. Whether the whales are here or not, the education center is a great stop for youngsters curious to know more about underwater life, and for anyone eager to gain insight into the cultural connection between Hawaii and its whale residents. Interactive displays and informative naturalists explain it all, including the sanctuary that acts as a breeding ground for humpbacks. Throughout the year, the center hosts activities that include talks, labs, and volunteer opportunities. The sanctuary itself includes virtually all the waters surrounding the archipelago. ■TIP→ **Just outside the visitor center is the ancient Koieie fishpond; it is a popular place for locals to bring their children to wade in the water.** ✉ *726 S. Kihei Rd., Kihei* ☎ *808/879–2818, 800/831–4888* ⊕ *hawaiihumpbackwhale. noaa.gov* 🖾 *Free* ☉ *Closed weekends.*

Kealia Pond National Wildlife Refuge

TRAIL | FAMILY | Natural wetlands have become rare in the Islands, so the 700 acres of this reserve attract migratory birds, such as Hawaiian coots and long-legged Hawaiian stilts that casually dip their beaks into the shallow waters as traffic shuttles by; it's also home to other wildlife. The visitor center provides a good introduction, and interpretive signs on the half-mile elevated boardwalk, which stretches along the coast by North Kihei Road, explain the journey of the endangered hawksbill turtles and how they return to the sandy dunes year after year. The boardwalk includes ramps that lead to the adjacent beach so visitors can explore tidal pools. Note that there's no restroom at the boardwalk. ✉ *Mokulele Hwy., mile marker 6, Kihei* ✢ *Main entrance on Mokulele Hwy.*

☎ *808/875–1582* ⊕ *fws.gov/refuge/kealia- pond* 🖾 *Free* ☉ *Visitor center closed weekends.*

🕸 Beaches

Sandy beaches front nearly the entire southern coastline of Maui. The farther south, the better the beaches get. Kihei has excellent beach parks in town, with white sand, plenty of amenities, and paved parking lots. There are a great number of options for picnicking with food truck fare, and good snorkeling can be found along the beaches' rocky borders. As good as Kihei is, Wailea is better. The beaches are cleaner, and the views more impressive. You can take a mile-long walk on a shore path from Ulua to near Polo Beach. Look for blue "Shoreline Access" signs for parking along the main thoroughfare, Wailea Alanui Drive.

■TIP→ **Break-ins have been reported at many parking lots, so don't leave valuables in the car.**

As you head to Makena, the terrain gets wilder; bring lunch, water, and lots of reef-safe sunscreen.

Charley Young Beach

BEACH | FAMILY | This secluded 3-acre park sits off the main drag in a residential area. The sand is soft and smooth, with a gentle slope into the ocean. A cloister of lava rocks shelters the beach from heavy afternoon winds, creating a mellow spot in which to laze around. The usually gentle waves make for good swimming, and you can find interesting snorkeling along the rocks on the north end. From South Kihei Road, turn onto Kaiau Street, just north of Kamaole I. **Amenities:** parking (no fee); showers; toilets. **Best for:** snorkeling; swimming. ✉ *2200 South Kihei Rd, Kihei.*

Cove Beach Park

BEACH | Go to the Cove if you want to learn to surf or stand-up paddle. All the surf schools are here in the morning, pushing longboard beginners onto the bunny-slope waves. For spectators there's a grassy area with some shade—and a tiny blink of a beach. If you aren't here to learn to surf, don't bother. The shallow water is sketchy at best and plenty of other beaches are better. **Amenities:** parking (no fee); showers; toilets. **Best for:** stand-up paddling; surfing. ⊠ *S. Kihei Rd., Kihei* ✛ *Turn onto Iliili Rd.*

Kalama Park

BEACH | FAMILY | Stocked with grills and picnic pavilions, this 36-acre beach park with plenty of shade is great for families and sports lovers. With its extensive lawns and sports fields, the park welcomes volleyball, basketball, baseball, and tennis players, and even has a playground, skateboard park, and a roller hockey rink. The beach itself is all but nonexistent, but swimming is fair—though you must brave the rocky steps down to the water. If you aren't completely comfortable with this entrance, stick to the burgers and bocce ball. **Amenities:** parking (no fee); showers; toilets. **Best for:** partiers. ⊠ *1900 S. Kihei Road, Kihei* ✛ *Across from Kihei Kalama Village.*

Kalepolepo Beach Park

BEACH | This tiny beach is the site of the ancient Kalepolepo Village, the prized property of King Kamehameha III in the 1850s. Here the *makaainana* (commoners) farmed, fished, and raised taro. Today, community stewards work to restore the ancient pond. The park has lots of shady trees and stays pretty quiet; however, the beach is only a sprinkling of sand, and swimming in the often-murky waters isn't recommended. Kaleopolepo is just south of Hawaiian Islands Humpback Whale National Marine Sanctuary. A portable toilet is available, and there are picnic tables and grills. **Amenities:** parking (no fee); showers; toilets. **Best for:** solitude. ⊠ *726 S. Kihei Rd., Kihei.*

Fun Things to Do on the South Shore 👁

- Witness the hammerheads feeding at the Maui Ocean Center.

- Spike a volleyball at Kalama Park.

- Observe the green sea turtles while snorkeling at Ulua Beach.

- Take a surf lesson.

- Decipher whale song at the Hawaiian Islands Humpback Whale National Marine Sanctuary.

- Sink into Makena's soft sand.

Kamaole I, II, and III

BEACH | FAMILY | Three steps from South Kihei Road are three golden stretches of sand separated by outcroppings of dark, jagged lava rocks. You can walk the length of all three beaches if you're willing to get your feet wet. The northernmost of the trio, Kamaole I (across from the ABC Store—important to know if you forget your sunscreen) offers perfect swimming and an active volleyball court. There's also a great lawn, where you can spread out at the south end of the beach. Kamaole II is nearly identical except for the lawn, but there is no parking lot. The last beach, the one with all the people on it, is 10-acre Kamaole III, perfect for throwing a disk or throwing down a blanket. This is a great family beach, complete with a playground, barbecue grills, kite flying, and, frequently, rented inflatable castles—a must at birthday parties for cool kids. All three beach parks offer wheelchair ramps to the beach;

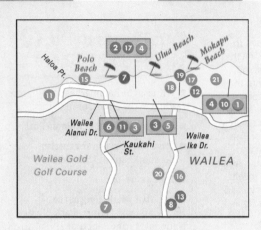

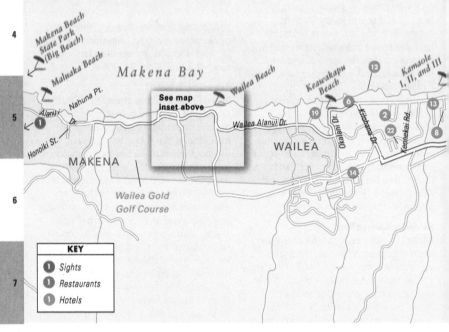

KEY
- **1** Sights
- **1** Restaurants
- **1** Hotels

Sights ▼

1 Ahihi-Kinau Natural Area Reserve............ **A5**

2 Farmers' Market Of Maui-Kihei................. **J4**

3 Hawaiian Islands Humpback Whale National Marine Sanctuary................. **H4**

4 Kealia Pond National Wildlife Refuge.......... **J3**

5 Maalaea Harbor **J2**

6 Maui Ocean Center..... **J2**

7 Wailea Beach Path..... **B1**

Restaurants ▼

1 Cuatro.................... **F4**

2 Ferraro's Bar e Ristorante................. **B2**

3 Humuhumunukunu-kuapuaa................. **B2**

4 Kaana Kitchen **C1**

5 Kihei Caffe............... **G4**

6 Ko........................ **B2**

7 Maui Brewing Company................. **H5**

8 Monkeypod Kitchen.... **C3**

9 Monsoon India.......... **H4**

10 Morimoto Maui **C1**

11 Nick's Fish Market Maui..................... **B2**

12 The Pint & Cork **C2**

13 Pita Paradise Mediterranean Bistro .. **C3**

14 Roasted Chiles **H4**

15 Seascape Restaurant................ **J2**

16 South Shore Tiki Lounge **G4**

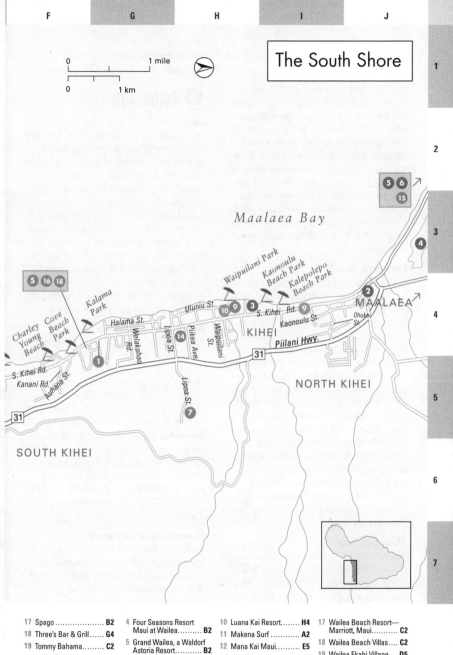

The South Shore

0   1 mile

0   1 km

Maalaea Bay

Waipuilani Park

Kaonoulu Beach Park

Kalepolepo Beach Park

Charley Young Beach

Cove Beach Park

Kalama Park

Kalama Park

Halama St.

Uluniu St.

S. Kihei Rd.

Kaonoulu St.

Ohukai St.

MAALAEA

Welakahao Rd.

Lipoa St.

Piikea Ave.

Waipuilani St.

KIHEI

Piilani Hwy.

S. Kihei Rd.

Kanani Rd.

Auhana St.

Lipoa St.

31

31

NORTH KIHEI

SOUTH KIHEI

Kamaole I is the only beach on Maui with a beach access chair.

Locally—and quite disrespectfully, according to Native Hawaiians—known as "Kam" I, II, and III, all three beaches have great swimming and lifeguards. In the morning the water can be as still as a lap pool. Kamaole III offers terrific breaks for beginning bodysurfers. **Amenities:** lifeguards; parking (no fee); showers; toilets. **Best for:** sunsets, surfing; swimming; walking. ✉ *S. Kihei Rd., between Alii Ke Alanui and Hale Kamaole Condominiums, Kihei* ☎ *808/270–6136 for beach wheelchair availability.*

Keawakapu Beach

BEACH | FAMILY | Everyone loves Keawakapu, with its long stretch of golden sand, near-perfect swimming, and views of Puu Olai cinder cone. It's great fun to walk or jog this beach south into Wailea, as it's lined with over-the-top residences. It's best here in the morning—the winds pick up in the afternoon (beware of sandstorms). Keawakapu has three entrances: one is at the Mana Kai Maui resort (look for the blue "Shoreline Access" sign); the second is directly across from the parking lot on Kilohana Street (the entrance is unmarked); and the third is at the dead end of Kihei Road. Toilets are portable. **Amenities:** parking (no fee); showers; toilets. **Best for:** sunset; swimming; walking. ✉ *S. Kihei Rd., near Kilohana St., Kihei.*

Waipuilani Park

BEACH | FAMILY | Fronting the Maui Sunset Resort, Waipuilani Park is a spectacular place to sunbathe, relax, or picnic on golf course–grade grass. You can swim here, but the water can be murky. A small beach hides behind the dunes, although it's usually speckled with seaweed and shells. This park often hosts local activities, such as volleyball and croquet, and it attracts many dog lovers. There are tennis courts, too. Although the park can be crowded, it's still a perfect place to watch the sunset. **Amenities:** parking (no fee);

toilets. **Best for:** partiers; sunset. ✉ *W. Waipuilani Rd., Kihei* ✛ *Off S. Kihei Rd.*

🍴 Restaurants

Cuatro

$$$ | ECLECTIC | Chef-owner Eric Arbogast has admirably turned this tiny space tucked into a corner of a strip mall into a comfortable restaurant serving well-prepared, delicious food. Signature dishes include spicy tuna nachos, fresh local fish, Asian-style marinated grilled steak, and south-of-the-border-style marinated pork. **Known for:** Asian Latin fusion; warm and friendly atmosphere; BYOB with a corkage fee of $10. ⑤ *Average main: $32* ✉ *Kihei Town Center, 1881 S. Kihei Rd., Kihei* ☎ *808/879–1110* ⊕ *cuatro808.com* ⊗ *No lunch, closed Mon. and Tues.*

Ferraro's Bar e Ristorante

$$$$ | ITALIAN | Overlooking the ocean from a bluff above Wailea Beach, this outdoor Italian restaurant at Four Seasons Resort Maui is Wailea's only oceanfront restaurant. For lunch, indulge in the catch of the day, artisanal sandwiches, or one of a variety of stone-baked pizzas. **Known for:** excellent selection of Italian wines; classical music in the moonlight; romantic ambience. ⑤ *Average main: $47* ✉ *Four Seasons Resort Maui at Wailea, 3900 Wailea Alanui Dr., Wailea* ☎ *808/874–8000* ⊕ *fourseasons.com/ maui.*

Humuhumunukunukuapuaa

$$$$ | MODERN HAWAIIAN | This Polynesian-style thatch-roof, open-air restaurant "floats" atop a saltwater lagoon, which gives it an exotic romantic feel that's suited for special occasions. Daily breakfast features hearty, yet elegant options. **Known for:** nightly live music; seasonal, farm-to-table dishes; macadamia-crusted catch of the day. ⑤ *Average main: $52* ✉ *Grand Wailea, 3850 Wailea Alanui Dr., Wailea* ☎ *808/875–1234* ⊕ *grandwailea. com/humuhumunukunukuapuaa* ⊗ *No lunch, closed for dinner Mon. and Tues.*

The Plate Lunch Tradition

To experience Island history first-hand, take a seat at one of Hawaii's ubiquitous "plate lunch" eateries, where you'll be served a segmented plate piled with a protein—usually in an Asian-style preparation, like beef teriyaki—two scoops of rice, a scoop of macaroni salad, and maybe a pickled vegetable condiment. On the sugar plantations, immigrant workers from many different countries ate together in the fields, sharing food from their *kaukau* tins, the utilitarian version of the Japanese *bento* (a divided box filled with savory items). From this stir-fry of people came the vibrant pidgin language and its equivalent in food: the plate lunch.

At beaches and public parks you will probably see locals eating plate lunches from nearby restaurants, stands, or trucks. Favorite combos include deep-fried chicken *katsu* (rolled in Japanese panko flour and spices), marinated beef teriyaki, and miso butterfish. *Saimin*, a noodle soup with Japanese fish stock and Chinese red-tinted barbecue pork, is a distinctly local medley. Koreans have contributed spicy barbecue *kalbi* ribs, often served with chili-laden *kimchi* (pickled cabbage or, sometimes, cucumber). Portuguese bean soup and tangy Filipino *pinakbet* (a mixed-vegetable dish with eggplant, okra, and bitter melons in fish sauce) are also favorites. The most popular contribution to this genre is the Hawaiian plate, featuring *laulau*, a mix of meat and fish and young taro leaves, wrapped in ti leaves and steamed, *kalua* pork and cabbage, *lomi lomi* salmon, and chicken long rice, along with *haupia* (coconut pudding) for dessert.

★ Kaana Kitchen

$$$$ | MODERN HAWAIIAN | This signature restaurant at Maui's most stylish luxury resort, Andaz Maui at Wailea, has it all: ingredients sourced within the Islands, marvelous wine list, stellar service, and spectacular views from every table. The whole space has been masterfully designed with the gorgeous exhibition kitchen as the focal point of the restaurant and both indoor and outdoor seating wrapping around the space. **Known for:** most ingredients locally sourced; plantation flavors with a modern twist; romantic setting for sunset dining. Ⓢ *Average main: $44* ✉ *Andaz Maui at Wailea, 3550 Wailea Alanui Dr., Wailea* ☎ *808/879–1234* ⊕ *andazmaui.com* ⊗ *No lunch.*

★ Kihei Caffe

$ | AMERICAN | This unassuming popular spot across the street from Kalama Beach Park has a breakfast menu that runs the gamut from healthy yogurt-filled papaya to the local classic *loco moco*—two eggs, ground beef patty, rice, and brown gravy—and everything in between. Unique menu items include corned beef hash and catfish at breakfast and a calamari sandwich at lunch. **Known for:** enormous portions; breakfast served all day; killer cinnamon rolls. Ⓢ *Average main: $15* ✉ *1945 S. Kihei Rd., Kihei* ☎ *808/879–2230* ⊕ *kiheicaffe.com* ⊗ *No dinner.*

Ko

$$$$ | MODERN HAWAIIAN | The menu at Ko—which means "sugarcane" in Hawaiian—features dishes from the many cultures of the plantation era, some of which are local family recipes. Executive Chef Emeritus Tylun Pang created a menu featuring modern, innovative twists to Hawaiian, Chinese, Filipino, Portuguese, Korean, and Japanese dishes. **Known for:** delicious lobster tempura; zarzuela seafood dish, simmered in saffron; must-order dish: seafood laulau. ⑤ *Average main: $45 ⊠ Fairmont Kea Lani, 4100 Wailea Alanui Dr., Wailea ☎ 808/875–2210 ⊕ korestaurant.com.*

★ Maui Brewing Company

$ | **AMERICAN** | You don't need to be a beer lover to appreciate a visit to Maui Brewing Company's flagship location. Spanning more than five acres, the Kihei compound includes a restaurant, brewery, and tasting room. **Known for:** spacious venue with open-air setting; lively bar scene separate from the dining area; boozy "sloshies" from MBC's Kupu Spirits. ⑤ *Average main: $17 ⊠ 605 Lipoa Parkway, Kihei ☎ 808/201–2337 ⊕ maui-brewingco.com.*

Monkeypod Kitchen

$$ | **ECLECTIC** | The wooden surfboards hanging above the bar and surf videos playing in the background set a decidedly chill vibe at this buzzing restaurant, the creation of local celebrity-chef Peter Merriman. He offers a menu that highlights local bounty, with such standout dishes as poke tacos, coconut corn chowder, and wood-fired pizzas. **Known for:** live music twice daily; pecan-crusted *mahimahi* (dolphinfish); fun cocktails such as Monkeypod mai tai. ⑤ *Average main: $26 ⊠ 10 Wailea Gateway Pl., Wailea ☎ 808/891–2322 ⊕ monkeypodkitchen.com.*

Monsoon India

$$ | **INDIAN** | This authentic Indian restaurant offers stunning ocean views and appetizers like *papadum* chips and samosas served with homemade chutneys. There are 10+ breads—naan and more, including a gluten-free option—that come

hot from the tandoori oven, along with mix-and-match curries, lots of vegetarian selections, kebabs, and biryanis. **Known for:** covered, open-air setting; full bar with ocean view; vegetarian-friendly options. ⑤ *Average main: $21 ⊠ Menehune Shores, 760 S. Kihei Rd., Kihei ☎ 808/875–6666 ⊕ monsoonindiakiheihi.com* ⊘ *No lunch Mon.*

★ Morimoto Maui

$$$$ | **ASIAN** | "Iron Chef" Masaharu Morimoto's eponymous restaurant, located at the Andaz Maui resort, has some of Maui's most creative presentations and, arguably, some of its best food. Poolside outdoor tables that sit directly under the stars, a bustling dining room, and a sushi bar all make it a lively choice, but the food is ultimately the reason to go. **Known for:** signature Morimoto dishes; excellent ambience; fantastic levels of service. ⑤ *Average main: $64 ⊠ Andaz Maui at Wailea, 3550 Wailea Alanui Dr., Wailea ☎ 808/243–4766 ⊕ morimotomaui.com.*

★ Nick's Fishmarket Maui

$$$$ | **SEAFOOD** | Find some of the best seafood on the Island at this elegant eatery inside the Fairmont Kea Lani. This dinner-only restaurant sources the freshest fish possible, and often has beautifully prepared offerings, like *opakapaka* (pink snapper), that other fish restaurants don't. **Known for:** outstanding levels of service; strawberries panzini dessert (flambéed with Grand Marnier); good selection of gluten-free options. ⑤ *Average main: $55 ⊠ 4100 Wailea Alanui Dr., Wailea ⊕ nicksfishmarketmaui.com.*

The Pint & Cork

$$ | **AMERICAN** | For a little break from the Maui sun and fruity cocktails, spend an afternoon digging into elegant pub fare backed by an excellent, expert cocktail program with a focus on whiskey. It's the perfect spot to recover from a sunburn or catch a game while still being social and enjoying what Maui has to offer. **Known**

Shave Ice and Ice Cream

The two most critical components in the making of the Islands' favorite frosty treat—shave ice—are the fineness of the shave and the quality of the syrup. The shave should be almost powdery, like snow. Top that ice with tropical flavors like mango, *lilikoi* (Hawaiian passion fruit), or guava. For a multipart taste sensation, start with a scoop of vanilla ice cream in the bottom (and maybe some Japanese adzuki beans), add shave ice and flavoring, and then top it with a drizzle of cream or a sprinkle of *li hing mui* (Chinese plum) powder for a salty-pungent kick. A great pick is **Ululani's Hawaiian Shave Ice**, which makes "gourmet" shave ice and has

locations all over Maui. The Kihei location includes sister company Sugar Beach Bake Shop (✉ 61 S. Kihei Road ☎ 808/757–8285).

Prefer ice cream on its own? Maui's own Roselani has been made from scratch in Wailuku since 1932. Look for the brand's line of Tropics flavors, available at all Maui supermarkets. *Haupia* (coconut pudding) is the best-selling flavor. Some of the best ice cream parlors in South Maui are **Hula Cookies & Ice Cream** (✉ 300 Maalaea Road, Maalaea ☎ 808/243–2271), **Maui Gelato and Waffles** (✉ 2395 S. Kihei Rd., No. 120, Kihei ☎ 808/419–6213), and **Maui Sweet Shoppe** (✉ 1819 S. Kihei Road, Kihei ☎ 808/214–5151).

4

South Shore KIHEI

for: unique menu items such as deviled eggs and "Irish" tacos; warm and friendly locals' favorite; fantastic burgers. $ *Average main: $20* ✉ *3750 Wailea Alanui Dr., inside Shops at Wailea, Wailea* ⊕ *thepintandcork.com.*

★ Pita Paradise Mediterranean Bistro
$$ | **MEDITERRANEAN** | Don't be fooled by its playful name; this place serves high-quality food that befits its chic surroundings. This restaurant's owner is a fisherman himself, so you know the fish here is the freshest available. **Known for:** baklava ice-cream cake with Roselani ice cream; lamb gnocchi, made in-house; Mediterranean chicken pita. $ *Average main: $24* ✉ *Wailea Gateway Center, 34 Wailea Gateway Pl., A-108, Wailea* ☎ *808/879–7177* ⊕ *pitaparadisehawaii. com.*

Roasted Chiles
$$ | **MEXICAN** | This family-run restaurant serves authentic flavors from Mexico City and just about everything—from the furniture to the artisanal plates on

the wall—has been brought directly from Mexico. All menu items are made in-house; try Grandma's classic chicken mole recipe, which packs in more than 25 ingredients. **Known for:** creamy langostino enchiladas; welcoming atmosphere; 40-plus tequila options. $ *Average main: $18* ✉ *1279 S. Kihei Rd., Suite 122, Kihei* ☎ *808/868–4357* ⊕ *roastedchileshawaii. com* ☉ *Closed Sun.*

South Shore Tiki Lounge
$ | **AMERICAN** | This tiki bar—tucked into Kihei Kalama Village—serves burgers, sandwiches, and delicious specialty pizzas that are crafted from scratch with sauces made from fresh Roma tomatoes and Maui herbs. **Known for:** all-day happy hour; late-night dancing under the gaze of the lounge's namesake tiki; kitchen open until 10 pm. $ *Average main: $18* ✉ *Kihei Kalama Village, 1913-J S. Kihei Rd., Kihei* ☎ *808/874–6444* ⊕ *southshoretikilounge. com.*

Spago

$$$$ | MODERN HAWAIIAN | It's a marriage made in Hawaii heaven: the California cuisine of celebrity-chef Wolfgang Puck combined with Maui flavors and served lobby-level and oceanfront at the luxurious Four Seasons Resort Maui. Try the spicy *ahi* (yellowfin tuna) poke in sesame-miso cones to start and then see what the chef can do with some of Maui's fantastic local fish. **Known for:** show-stopping desserts; sunset views from the patio; exceptional wine list. ⑤ *Average main: $79 ☒ Four Seasons Resort Maui at Wailea, 3900 Wailea Alanui Dr., Wailea* ☎ *808/879–2999* ⊕ *wolfgangpuck.com/dining/spago-maui* ⊙ *No lunch.*

Three's Bar & Grill

$$ | ECLECTIC | The name of the restaurant comes from the three young chefs who each have a distinctive culinary style (Hawaiian, Southwestern, and Pacific Rim), but somehow it all works. The space is as big as the menu—there are salads, burgers, steaks, and fresh fish, as well as a raw bar with sushi and hand rolls—with three separate dining areas, plus an outdoor patio. **Known for:** daily happy hour with some killer deals; hurricane fries tossed in sriracha aioli; kalua pork quesadilla. ⑤ *Average main: $25 ☒ 1945-G S. Kihei Rd., Kihei* ☎ *808/879–3133* ⊕ *threesbarandgrill.com.*

★ Tommy Bahama

$$$$ | MODERN AMERICAN | It's more "Island-style" than Hawaii-style—and yes, it's a chain—but the food is consistently great, the service is filled with aloha, and the ambience is Island refined. The cocktails are among the best and most creative on the Island and include well-priced non-alcoholic options. **Known for:** filet mignon in a variety of preparations; festive bar scene; miso-glazed King Salmon. ⑤ *Average main: $40 ☒ The Shops at Wailea, 3750 Wailea Alanui Dr., Wailea* ☎ *808/875–9983* ⊕ *tommybahama.com* ⊙ *Closed Mon.*

🛌 Hotels

If you're a beach lover, you won't find many disadvantages to staying in Kihei. A string of welcoming beaches stretches from tip to tip. Snorkeling, bodyboarding, and barbecuing find their ultimate expression here. Affordable condos line South Kihei Road; however, some find the busy traffic and the strip-mall shopping distinctly un-Maui and prefer quieter hideaways.

Aston Maui Hill

$$$$ | APARTMENT | FAMILY | Take in sweeping views of the ocean and Haleakala from the large lanai of the one- to three-bedroom units on this sprawling, well-maintained property just outside the swanky Wailea Resort. **Pros:** great option for large groups needing multiple units; no resort or parking fees; spacious layout makes property seem less crowded. **Cons:** units are not handicapped-accessible; stairs and walking distances may be challenging to guests with mobility issues; decor may seem dated. ⑤ *Rooms from: $399 ☒ 2881 South Kihei Rd., Kihei* ☎ *808/879–6321, 855/945–4044* ⊕ *aquaaston.com* ↰ *140 units* ⦿ *No Meals.*

Hale Hui Kai

$$$$ | APARTMENT | FAMILY | This modest three-story condo complex of mostly two-bedroom units is just steps away from the beach. **Pros:** far enough from noise and tumult of "central" Kihei; well-maintained grounds; free street parking. **Cons:** some units are dated; no daily housekeeping; most units have one-week minimum stays. ⑤ *Rooms from: $350 ☒ 2994 S. Kihei Rd., Kihei* ☎ *808/879–1219* ⊕ *bookings-bellorealty.escapia.com* ↰ *40 units* ⦿ *No Meals.*

Kamaole Sands

$$$ | APARTMENT | FAMILY | This South Kihei property sits across the street from Kamaole III beach and is perfect for active families. **Pros:** pleasant grounds and well-maintained units; elevators,

Food Shopping for Renters

Condo renters in search of food and takeout meals should try these great places around Maui.

West Maui

Foodland Farms. This large supermarket combines the best of gourmet selections and local products with all the familiar staples you need to stock your vacation kitchen. It also makes an excellent *poke* (diced raw fish). ⊠ *Lahaina Gateway Shopping Center, 345 Keawe St., Lahaina* ☎ *808/662–7088* ⊕ *foodland.com.*

South Shore

Safeway. Find everything you could possibly need at this 24-hour supermarket, located in the Piilani Village Shopping Center. There's also a deli, prepared-foods and seafood section, and bakery. ⊠ *277 Piikea Ave., Kihei* ☎ *808/891–9120* ⊕ *www.safeway.com.*

Times Supermarket. This locally owned and -operated grocery store chain is a community staple on Maui, with an outstanding seafood counter, locally made products, bakery, and a full grocery selection. ⊠ *1310 S. Kihei Rd., Kihei* ⊕ *timessupermarkets.com.*

Central Maui

Safeway. Located a minute from Kahului Airport, this gigantic 24-hour supermarket has all the essentials, and then some. The deli, prepared foods, and seafood sections, and bakery are all fantastic. There's a good wine selection, tons of produce, and a flower shop where you can treat yourself to a fresh lei. ⊠ *1090 Hookele St., Kahului* ☎ *808/359–2970* ⊕ *safeway. com.*

Whole Foods Market. This busy supermarket carries local organic produce, and the seafood, bakery, beer and wine, and meat offerings are exceptional. The pricey prepared foods—including pizza, sushi, a salad bar, Asian bowls, and Mexican fare—attract crowds. ⊠ *70 E. Kaahumanu Ave., Kahului* ☎ *808/872–3310* ⊕ *wholefoodsmarket.com.*

Upcountry

Foodland. This branch of the local supermarket chain at the Pukalani Terrace Center is a full-service store with prepared foods, a deli, fresh sushi, local produce, and a good seafood section in addition to the usual fare. Sign up for a Maikai Rewards card for deep (and necessary) savings. ⊠ *55 Pukalani St., Pukalani* ☎ *808/572–0674* ⊕ *foodland.com.*

Pukalani Superette. Stop at this family-owned store on your way up or down Haleakala for fresh Maui-grown produce and meat, flowers, and a variety of made-in-Maui products. ⊠ *15 Makawao Ave., Pukalani* ☎ *808/572–7616* ⊕ *pukalanisuperette.com.*

---

unlike many low-rise condos; free assigned parking. **Cons:** lack of diversity among building facades; older property; large cleaning fee. $ *Rooms from: $269* ⊠ *2695 S. Kihei Rd., Kihei* ☎ *808/270–1200, 877/367–1912* ⊕ *castleresorts. com/maui/kamaole-sands* ⤳ *400 units* ⦿ *No Meals.*

Kohea Kai Resort Maui

$$$ | HOTEL | Located across the beach and in the quieter north end of Kihei, this relaxed, family-friendly property has 26 units—some with kitchens and kitchenettes—that range from standard rooms to three-bedroom, two-bath penthouses. **Pros:** no resort or parking fees; no

minimum stay; free Wi-Fi and beach toy use. **Cons:** located next to busy South Kihei Road; most rooms lack views; small pool. $ *Rooms from: $298* ✉ *551 S. Kihei Rd., Kihei* ☎ *808/879–1261* ⊕ *koheakai. com* ⌖ *26 units* ⦿ *No Meals.*

★ Luana Kai Resort

$$ | **APARTMENT** | If you don't need everything to be totally modern, consider setting up house at this great value condominium-by-the-sea. **Pros:** meticulously landscaped grounds; excellent management team; free parking. **Cons:** no maid service; air-conditioning only available in some units for an additional fee; no elevators. $ *Rooms from: $229* ✉ *940 S. Kihei Rd., Kihei* ☎ *808/879–1268* ⊕ *luanakai.com* ⌖ *113 units* ⦿ *No Meals.*

Mana Kai Maui

$$$$ | **APARTMENT** | **FAMILY** | You simply cannot get any closer to gorgeous Keawakapu Beach than this unsung hero of South Shore hotels, offering both renovated hotel rooms and condos that may be older than its competitors but are well priced and have marvelous ocean views, especially during the winter humpback whale season; one- and two-bedroom condos have private lanai and kitchens. **Pros:** arguably the best beach on the South Shore; good for families; free reserved parking. **Cons:** interior design might not appeal to discerning travelers; some rooms are small; older property. $ *Rooms from: $485* ✉ *2960 S. Kihei Rd., Kihei* ☎ *808/879–1561, 800/525–2025* ⊕ *manakaimaui.com* ⌖ *98 units* ⦿ *No Meals.*

Maui Kamaole

$$$$ | **APARTMENT** | These one- and two-bedroom condos—some with ocean views—lie across the street from one of Maui's best beach parks, Kamaole III, and the property has tropical gardens, two tennis courts, a grotto pool with a waterfall, a Jacuzzi spa, another pool, and barbecue grills. **Pros:** great location in sunny Kihei; no resort fee; free parking.

Cons: four-night minimum; high cleaning fee; no elevators in two-story buildings. $ *Rooms from: $420* ✉ *2777 S. Kihei Rd, Kihei* ☎ *808/879–2778, 800/844-0606* ⊕ *mauikamaole.com* ⌖ *316 condos* ⦿ *No Meals.*

Pineapple Inn

$$ | **B&B/INN** | Entry to the property, which is in a residential area, is through a courtyard overflowing with colorful flowers and a koi pond. **Pros:** no resort fees; resort-quality furnishings; well-stocked mini-refrigerator. **Cons:** short drive to the beach; some traffic noise from nearby highway; rest of neighborhood not as well maintained. $ *Rooms from: $249* ✉ *3170 Akala Dr., Kihei* ☎ *808/298–4403* ⊕ *pineappleinnmaui.com* ⌖ *5 units* ⦿ *Free Breakfast.*

What a Wonderful World B&B

$$ | **B&B/INN** | Convenient, comfortable, and affordable, this Polynesian-style pole house provides a good base for exploring the Island, as it's only a half-mile from beaches, five minutes from golf courses, and close to restaurants and shopping. **Pros:** no minimum night stays outside of high season; everything needed to have fun is here, from books and beach toys to blankets for sunrise at Haleakala; no cleaning fees. **Cons:** slightly hard to find in the neighborhood; no resort amenities; owner's dogs on premises. $ *Rooms from: $215* ✉ *2828 Umalu Pl., Kihei* ☎ *808/870–2191* ⊕ *amauibedandbreakfast.com* ⌖ *4 units* ⦿ *Free Breakfast.*

ⓨ Nightlife

Kahale's Beach Club

BARS | If you're looking for a genuine dive bar among the more tropical, touristy spots, this is the place. The bartenders are friendly, and you'll find plenty of locals to talk story with; just be sure to mind your manners—the classic dive bar fistfights can also frequently be found here. ✉ *36 Keala Pl., Kihei* ☎ *808/215–9939* ⊕ *kahales.com.*

Life's a Beach

BARS | This dive bar brings in a young bunch looking to par-tay. A lively rotation of entertainment keeps the good times rolling, including live island-style music, guest bands, karaoke, and open-mic nights. A casual Mexican-food menu with great prices keeps the munchies away. ☒ *1913 S. Kihei Rd., Kihei* ☎ *808/891–8010* ⊕ *mauibars.com.*

South Shore Tiki Lounge

COCKTAIL LOUNGES | Good eats are paired with cool tunes in this breezy tropical tavern. Local acts and DJs are featured from 4 to 6 pm most evenings, and DJs get the dance floor shaking at 10 pm Thursday through Saturday. Happy hour specials run from 11 am to 6 pm. This is the bar where locals hang out, so if you'd like to mix with the local scene, this is the spot. ☒ *Kihei Kalama Village, 1913-J S. Kihei Rd., Kihei* ☎ *808/874–6444* ⊕ *southshoretikilounge.com.*

Vibe Bar Maui

COCKTAIL LOUNGES | This speakeasy-style bar is smack dab in the middle of Kihei's nightlife scene, and it stands out for its lineup of specialty cocktails. It's the size of a living room, but mixology is given more consideration here than at other venues. ☒ *1913 S. Kihei Rd., Kihei* ☎ *808/891–1011.*

🛍 Shopping

The South Shore resort area is best known for expensive designer shopping in the Wailea area, but you can find cheaper, more local options in Kihei. Browse ornate beaded accessories while listening to island rhythms at Kihei Kalama Village, or splurge on high-end labels at The Shops at Wailea.

SHOPPING CENTERS

Azeka Shopping Center

SHOPPING CENTER | Spread across two complexes on either side of South Kihei Road, this no-frills shopping center is in the heart of Kihei. The mall is comprised of more than 50 stores, including a scuba shop for rentals and dive bookings, a gas station, several great takeout and dine-in restaurants, a coffee shop, and a post office. Ample free parking makes this an easy stop to fulfill your basic needs. ☒ *1279 and 1280 S. Kihei Rd., Kihei* ☎ *808/879–5000* ⊕ *azekashoppingcenter. com.*

Kihei Kalama Village

MALL | Encompassing more than 40 specialty shops and restaurants, this area known as "the Triangle" attracts visitors and locals alike. In addition to the brick-and-mortar establishments, there are shaded outdoor stalls selling everything from printed and hand-painted T-shirts and sundresses to jewelry, pottery, wood carvings, fruit, and gaudily painted coconut husks—some, but not all, made by local craftspeople. ☒ *1941 S. Kihei Rd., Kihei* ☎ *808/879–6610* ⊕ *kiheikalamavillage.com.*

Rainbow Mall

SHOPPING CENTER | Condo guests can do some one-stop shopping at this mall—it offers salon treatments, Hawaiian gifts, local art, plate lunches, snorkel rental, and a liquor store. ☒ *2439 S. Kihei Rd., Kihei* ☎ *808/879–1145* ⊕ *rainbow-mall-maui.com.*

Maalaea

13 miles south of Kahului; 6 miles west of Kihei; 14 miles southeast of Lahaina.

Pronounced "Mah-*ah*-lye-*ah*," this spot is not much more than a few condos, an aquarium, and a wind-blasted harbor (where there are tour boats)—but that's more than enough for some visitors. Humpback whales seem to think Maalaea is tops for meeting mates, and green sea turtles treat it like their own personal spa, regularly seeking appointments with cleaner wrasses in

At Maui Ocean Center you'll see turtles, rays, and sharks.

the harbor. Surfers revere this spot for "freight trains," reportedly one of the world's fastest waves.

A small Shinto shrine stands at the shore here, dedicated to the fishing god Ebisu Sama; it's the only Shinto fishing shrine remaining in the world, other than in Japan. Across the street, a giant hook often swings heavy with the sea's bounty, proving the worth of the shrine. At the end of Hauoli Street (the town's sole road), a small community garden is sometimes privy to traditional Hawaiian ceremonies. There's not much else, but the few residents here like it that way.

◉ Sights

Maalaea Harbor
MARINA/PIER | With so many good reasons to head out onto the water, this active little harbor is quite busy. Many snorkeling and whale-watching excursions depart from here. There was a plan to expand the facility, but surfers argued

that would have destroyed the world-renowned surf breaks. The elusive spot to the left of the harbor, called "freight train," rarely breaks, but when it does, it's said to be the fastest anywhere. Shops, restaurants, and the Maui Ocean Center aquarium front the harbor. ⊠ *101 Maalaea Boat Harbor Rd., off Honoapiilani Hwy., Maalaea.*

★ Maui Ocean Center
AQUARIUM | **FAMILY** | You'll feel as though you're walking from the seashore down to the bottom of the reef at this aquarium, which focuses on creatures of the Pacific. Vibrant exhibits let you get close to turtles, rays, sharks, and the unusual creatures of the tide pools; allow two hours or so to explore it all. A whale exhibit includes interactive learning stations and a dome theater that uses 3-D technology to give viewers a whale's-eye-view. There's also a moving exhibit highlighting the history of Kahoolawe, a neighboring island that can be seen just across the Alalakeiki Channel. It's not

an enormous facility, but it does provide an excellent introduction to the sea life that makes Hawaii special. The center is part of a complex of retail shops and restaurants overlooking the harbor. Enter from Honoapiilani Highway as it curves past Maalaea Harbor. ■ TIP→ **The Ocean Center's gift shop is one of the best on Maui for artsy souvenirs and toys.** ⊠ *192 Maalaea Rd., off Honoapiilani Hwy., Maalaea* ☎ *808/270–7000* ⊕ *mauioceancenter.com* ☜ *$45.*

🍴 Restaurants

Seascape Restaurant

$$ | **SEAFOOD** | **FAMILY** | Maui Ocean Center's signature restaurant is a great choice for seafood (aquarium admission is not required to dine here) and offers harbor and ocean views from its open-air perch. The restaurant promotes heart-healthy cuisine, using sustainable seafood and trans fat–free items, but still allows for indulgence in their well-priced cocktail menu. **Known for:** friendly service; excellent vegan options; certified "ocean-friendly restaurant". ⑤ *Average main: $23* ⊠ *Maui Ocean Center, 192 Maalaea Rd., Maalaea* ☎ *808/270–7000* ⊕ *mauioceancenter.com/dine* ⊙ *Lunch only.*

🎭 Performing Arts

Pacific Whale Foundation

FOLK/TRADITIONAL DANCE | The nonprofit Pacific Whale Foundation helps protect the ocean through education and advocacy. They also happen to host a fabulous sunset dinner cruise, with live island-style music and delectable fare from Three's Catering, including freshly grilled shrimp with *lilikoi* (passion fruit) butter sauce and coconut-whipped sweet potatoes. Wash it down with Maui Brewing Company craft beers, wine, or cocktails. ⊠ *Maalaea Harbor, 101 Maalaea Boat Harbor Rd., Maalaea* ☎ *808/249-8811* ⊕ *pacificwhale.org* ☜ *$100-$150.*

Pride of Maui

FOLK/TRADITIONAL DANCE | A 65-foot catamaran built specifically for Maui's waters, the *Pride of Maui* has a spacious cabin for live entertainment, a dance floor, and a large upper deck for unobstructed sightseeing. Evening cruises include Polynesian dance performances, top-shelf cocktails, and an impressive spread cooked onboard, including baby back ribs, stir-fried vegetables, and shoyu chicken, plus seasonal desserts. ⊠ *Maalaea Harbor, 101 Maalaea Boat Harbor Rd., Maalaea* ☎ *808/242-0955* ⊕ *prideofmaui.com* ☜ *$118.*

Wailea

15 miles south of Kahului, at the southern border of Kihei.

The South Shore's resort community, Wailea is slightly quieter and drier than its West Maui sister, Kaanapali. Many visitors cannot pick a favorite, so they stay at both. The luxury of the resorts and the simple grandeur of the coastal views make the otherwise stark landscape an outstanding destination. Take time to stroll the coastal beach path; a handful of perfect little beaches, all with public access, front the resorts.

The first two resorts were built here in the late 1970s. Soon a cluster of upscale properties sprang up, including the Four Seasons Resort Maui at Wailea and the Fairmont Kea Lani. Check out the Grand Wailea Resort's chapel, which tells a Hawaiian love story in stained glass.

GETTING HERE AND AROUND

From Kahului Airport, take Route 311 (Maui Veteran's Highway) to Route 31 (Piilani Highway) until it ends in Wailea. Shuttles and taxis are available at the airport.

◉ Sights

Sandy shorelines front nearly the entire southern coastline of Maui, and Wailea boasts some of the most impressive beaches along this stretch. You can take a mile-long walk on a shore path from Ulua to near Polo Beach. Look for blue "Shoreline Access" signs for parking along the main thoroughfare, Wailea Alanui Drive. This resort area is best known for luxury shopping, whether at one of the resort boutiques or The Shops at Wailea, an open-air mall that features designer brands such as Gucci, Louis Vuitton, and Tiffany & Co.

Ahihi-Kinau Natural Area Reserve

NATURE PRESERVE | South of Makena State Park, the road fades away into a vast territory of black-lava flows, the result of Haleakala's last eruption and now a place for exploration. The road passes through the Ahihi-Kinau Natural Area Reserve, an excellent place for morning snorkel adventures. All wildlife, vegetation, coral, lava rock formations, and archaeological sites are highly protected under state law, which means that removing or disturbing items is prohibited, as is fishing. Two miles of coastline and the interior of the reserve are closed so that endangered species have an undisturbed area. You can visit one mile of the reserve's coastline for a ½-mile hike or snorkeling, from 5:30 am to 7:30 pm. To snorkel Ahihi Bay, park at the reserve's main lot and follow signage. Be sure to wear mineral sunblocks instead of chemical sunscreens, which kill corals—other sunscreens are now banned in Hawaii. Adjacent to Ahihi-Kinau is the Keoneoio archaeological district, where the start of the Hoapili Trail can be found. ■ TIP→ Limited cell phone service exists at the reserve. ✉ *Just before end of Makena Alanui Rd., Wailea* ⊕ *dlnr.hawaii.gov.*

Wailea Beach Path

TRAIL | A 1.5-mile-long paved beach walk allows you to stroll among Wailea's prettiest properties, restaurants, and rocky coves. The trail, teeming with joggers in the morning and late afternoon, is landscaped with rare native plants like the silvery *hinahina,* named after the Hawaiian moon goddess. In winter, keep an eye out for whales. The trail is accessible from Polo Beach as well as from the many Wailea beachfront resorts. ✉ *Wailea Beach, Wailea Alanui Dr., south of Grand Wailea Resort, Wailea.*

◉ Beaches

Five crescent-shaped beaches stretch along Wailea, starting from Mokapu Beach and running down to Makena Beach State Park (Big Beach). Most of the beaches have amenities including (limited) free parking, though you'll pay parking and entrance fees at the state park. Many of the area resorts that are fronting the beaches take up some of the prime real estate but arriving early still allows for a great spot to plop your chair or towel on.

★ Makena Beach State Park (Big Beach)

BEACH | Locals successfully fought to turn Makena—one of Hawaii's most breathtaking beaches—into a state park. This stretch of deep golden sand abutting sparkling aquamarine water is 3,000 feet long and 100 feet wide. It's often mistakenly referred to as Big Beach, but natives prefer its Hawaiian name, Oneloa. The water is fine for swimming, but use caution.

■ TIP→ The shore drop-off is steep, and swells can get deceptively big.

Despite the infamous "Makena cloud," a blanket that rolls in during the early afternoon and obscures the sun, it seldom rains here. For a dramatic view of the beach, climb Puu Olai, the steep

Did You Know?

Maui's South Shore beaches, generally white and sandy, get better as you go south. Wailea's beaches have great views. For wider landscapes, keep heading south to Makena.

Sun Safety on Maui

Hawaii's weather—seemingly never-ending warm, sunny days with gentle trade winds—can be enjoyed year-round with good sun sense. Because of Hawaii's subtropical location, the length of daylight here changes little throughout the year. The sun is particularly strong, with a daily UV average over 11.

Follow these sun safety tips:

■ Plan your beach, golf, hiking, and other outdoor activities for the early morning or late afternoon, avoiding the sun between 10 am and 4 pm.

■ Apply a broad-spectrum sunscreen with a sun protection factor (SPF) of at least 15. Hawaii lifeguards use sunscreens with an SPF of 30. Cover areas that are most prone to burning like your nose, shoulders, tops of feet, and ears. Don't forget your lips.

■ Apply sunscreen at least 30 minutes before you plan to be outdoors, and reapply every two hours, even on cloudy days.

■ Wear light, protective clothing, such as a long-sleeve shirt and pants, broad-brimmed hat, and sunglasses.

■ Stay in the shade whenever possible—especially on the beach—by using an umbrella.

■ Apply sunscreen frequently and liberally on children and minimize their time in the sun; they need extra protection. Sunscreen is not recommended for children under the age of six months.

■ In 2018, Hawaii became the first state to ban the sale of sunscreen with oxybenzone and octinoxate due to their effects on coral reefs. To be the most mindful visitor, look for reef-*safe* (not reef-*friendly*) mineral sunscreens that have zinc oxide or titanium dioxide before hopping in the ocean.

cinder cone near the first entrance you pass if you're driving south. Continue over the cinder cone's side to discover "Little Beach"—clothing-optional by popular practice, although this is technically illegal. On Sunday, free spirits of all kinds crowd Little Beach's tiny shoreline for a drumming circle and bonfire. Little Beach has the Island's best bodysurfing (no pun intended). Skimboarders catch air at Makena's third entrance, which is a little tricky to find (it's just a dirt path with street parking). Access to all beaches now requires paid parking and an entrance fee for non-resident visitors. **Amenities:** lifeguards; parking ($10 fee for non-residents); toilets. **Best for:** surfing; swimming; walking. ⊠ *Makena* ✛ *Off Wailea Alanui Dr.* ⊕ *www.hawaiistateparks.org.*

Mokapu and Ulua
BEACH | FAMILY | Look for a little road and public parking lot near the Wailea Beach Resort if you are heading to Mokapu and Ulua beaches. Although there are no lifeguards, families love this place. Reef formations create tons of tide pools for kids to explore, and the beaches are protected from major swells. Snorkeling is excellent at Ulua, the beach to the left of the entrance. Mokapu, to the right, tends to be less crowded. **Amenities:** parking (no fee); showers; toilets. **Best for:** snorkeling; swimming. ⊠ *Halealii Pl., Wailea* ✛ *Before Shops of Wailea.*

Polo Beach
BEACH | FAMILY | Small and secluded, this crescent fronts the Fairmont Kea Lani. Swimming and snorkeling are great here,

The Four Seasons Maui in Wailea

and it's a good place for whale-watching. As at Wailea Beach, private umbrellas and chaise lounges occupy the choicest real estate, but there's plenty of room for you and your towel. There's a nice grass picnic area, although it's a considerable distance from the beach. The pathway connecting the two beaches is a great spot to jog or to take in awesome views of nearby Molokini and Kahoolawe. Rare native plants grow along the ocean, or *makai,* side of the path—the honey-sweet-smelling one is *naio,* or false sandalwood. **Amenities:** parking (no fee); showers; toilets. **Best for:** snorkeling; swimming. ⊠ *Kaukahi St., Wailea* ✛ *South of Fairmont Kea Lani entrance.*

Wailea Beach
BEACH | FAMILY | A road near the Grand Wailea Resort takes you to Wailea Beach, a wide, sandy stretch with snorkeling and swimming. If you're not a guest at the Grand Wailea or Four Seasons, the cluster of private umbrellas and chaise lounges can be a little annoying, but the calm unclouded waters and soft white sand more than make up for this. From the parking lot, walk to the right to get to the main beach; to the left is another, smaller section that fronts the Four Seasons Resort. There are picnic tables and grills away from the beach. **Amenities:** parking (no fee); showers; toilets. **Best for:** snorkeling; swimming. ⊠ *Wailea Alanui Dr., Wailea* ✛ *South of Grand Wailea Resort entrance.*

🛏 Hotels

Warm, serene, and luxurious, Wailea properties offer less "action" than West Maui resorts. The properties here tend to focus on ambience, thoughtful details, and natural scenery. Nightlife is pretty much nil, save for a few swanky bars. However, you have your choice of sandy beaches with good snorkeling. Farther south, Makena is a little less developed. Expect everything—even bottled water—to double in price when you cross the line from Kihei to Wailea.

★ Andaz Maui at Wailea Resort

$$$$ | **RESORT** | Sophisticated travelers and romance-seeking couples will swoon at the sleek luxury of this eco-friendly, beachfront resort. **Pros:** outstanding service and dining; one-of-a-kind resort on Maui; free shuttle service around Wailea. **Cons:** not the best resort for families; slick design style might feel cold to some; rooms on the small side. ⑤ *Rooms from: $1033* ✉ *3550 Wailea Alanui Dr., Wailea* ☎ *808/573–1234* ⊕ *andazmaui.com* ↬ *321 units* ⦿ *No Meals.*

Fairmont Kea Lani Maui

$$$$ | **RESORT** | **FAMILY** | Gleaming white spires and tiled archways are the hallmark of this stunning resort that's particularly good for families with its spacious suite and villa options. **Pros:** all rooms are suites; 22,000-square-foot water complex; located on almost-private Polo Beach. **Cons:** daily resort and parking fees; lounge chairs in high demand; noisy families at play may be a turnoff for some. ⑤ *Rooms from: $1089* ✉ *4100 Wailea Alanui Dr., Wailea* ☎ *808/875–4100, 866/540-4456* ⊕ *fairmont.com/kealani* ↬ *450 suites* ⦿ *No Meals.*

★ Four Seasons Resort Maui at Wailea

$$$$ | **RESORT** | "Impeccably stylish" and "extravagant" describe most Four Seasons properties, and this elegant one fronting Wailea Beach is no exception, with its beautiful courtyards and luxuries such as 24-hour room service, twice-daily housekeeping, excellent restaurants, on-site spa, and adults-only serenity pool with outstanding views. **Pros:** no resort fee; complimentary kids' club, snorkeling, tennis, and cultural activities; great shopping and local crafts and artwork market. **Cons:** a bit ostentatious for some; when fully booked facilities can seem crowded; adults-only pool chairs fill up fast. ⑤ *Rooms from: $1045* ✉ *3900 Wailea Alanui Dr., Wailea* ☎ *808/874–8000, 800/311–0630* ⊕ *fourseasons.com/maui* ↬ *383 rooms* ⦿ *No Meals.*

Grand Wailea, a Waldorf Astoria Resort

$$$$ | **RESORT** | **FAMILY** | "Grand" is no exaggeration for this opulent, sunny 40-acre resort that's wildly entertaining due to its elaborate water features such as the Wailea Activity Pool with enclosed "lava tube," slides, caves, a Tarzan swing, and the world's only water elevator. **Pros:** set on beautiful Wailea Beach; offers one of the largest varieties of cultural programs on Maui; many shops. **Cons:** sprawling property can be difficult to traverse; limited poolside chairs; daily resort and parking fees. ⑤ *Rooms from: $1222* ✉ *3850 Wailea Alanui Dr., Wailea* ☎ *808/875–1234, 800/888–6100* ⊕ *grandwailea.com* ↬ *776 rooms* ⦿ *No Meals.*

Hotel Wailea, Relais & Chateaux

$$$$ | **HOTEL** | This adults-only, luxury boutique hotel, perched on a quiet hillside above Wailea, delivers romance with spectacular views. **Pros:** beautiful grounds with running water throughout; secluded location away from resort row; small intimate setting. **Cons:** small pool area; no shops or beaches within easy walking distance; not on the beach. ⑤ *Rooms from: $749* ✉ *555 Kaukahi St., Wailea* ☎ *866/970–4167* ⊕ *hotelwailea.com* ↬ *72 suites* ⦿ *No Meals.*

Makena Surf

$$$$ | **APARTMENT** | For travelers who've done all there is to do on Maui and just want simple but luxurious relaxation at a condo that spills onto a private beach, this is the spot. **Pros:** away from it all, yet still close enough to "civilization"; great snorkeling right off the beach; laundry facilities in every unit and daily housekeeping. **Cons:** split-level units may be difficult for guests with mobility issues; check-in at a different location; too secluded and "locked-up" for some. ⑤ *Rooms from: $964* ✉ *4850 Makena Alanui, Makena* ☎ *808/891–6200 guest services, 800/367–5246 reservations* ⊕ *destinationresidenceswailea.com* ↬ *105 units* ⦿ *No Meals.*

Polo Beach Club

$$$$ | APARTMENT | Lording over a hidden section of Polo Beach, this wonderful, older eight-story rental property's charm somehow manages to stay under the radar. **Pros:** ocean-view grills and herb garden you can pick from; beautiful beach fronting the building; daily housekeeping. **Cons:** split-level units potentially challenging for those with impaired mobility; check-in at a different location; some may feel isolated. $ *Rooms from: $809 ⊠ 4400 Makena Alanui Rd., Makena ☎ 808/891–6200 guest services, 808/495-4491 reservations ⊕ destination-residencesmaui.com ⇨ 71 units* ○| *No Meals.*

Residence Inn by Marriott, Maui Wailea

$$$$ | HOTEL | Well-suited to business and leisure travelers, you'll pay less for the tastefully designed suites in this "condotel" than you would elsewhere in the luxury Wailea resort. **Pros:** on-site convenience store; great for extended stays; no resort fee. **Cons:** some rooms have unappealing views; daily parking fee; not on the beach. $ *Rooms from: $698 ⊠ 75 Wailea Ike Dr., Wailea ☎ 808/891–7460 ⊕ residenceinnmauiwailea.com ⇨ 200 units* ○| *Free Breakfast.*

★ Wailea Beach Resort—Marriott, Maui

$$$$ | RESORT | FAMILY | The Wailea Beach Resort, which sits closer to the crashing surf than most resorts, promises not only dramatic views but luxurious amenities and spacious accommodations. **Pros:** hosts the only Starbucks in Wailea; short walk to The Shops at Wailea; Te Au Moana Luau four nights a week. **Cons:** foot traffic on coastal beach walk; daily resort fee and daily self-parking fee (valet also available); rocky shore that is not quite beachfront. $ *Rooms from: $1175 ⊠ 3700 Wailea Alanui Dr., Wailea ☎ 808/879–1922 ⊕ waileamarriott.com ⇨ 547 units* ○| *No Meals.*

Wailea Beach Villas

$$$$ | APARTMENT | Wailea's hideaway for the rich and famous, these two- to three-bedroom villas are an immersion in luxury, with up to 3,100 square feet of living space, furnishings that inspire poetry, and gourmet kitchens fit for an Iron Chef. **Pros:** steps away from dining and luxury stores at The Shops at Wailea; solid security with gated driveway and guard station; no parking or resort fees. **Cons:** some units have limited views; decor in individually owned units may differ; not in most visitors' budgets. $ *Rooms from: $1450 ⊠ 3800 Wailea Alanui Dr., Wailea ☎ 808/891–4500 main, 866/384-1366 reservations ⊕ destinationresidenceshawaii.com ⇨ 98 units* ○| *No Meals.*

Wailea Ekahi Village

$$$$ | RESORT | Overlooking Keawakapu Beach, this family-friendly vacation resort features studios and one- and two-bedroom suites in low-rise buildings that span 34 acres of tropical gardens and won't cost your child's entire college fund. **Pros:** convenient access to a great beach; en-suite kitchen and laundry facilities; daily housekeeping. **Cons:** check-in at a different location; decor in individually owned units may differ; large complex can be tricky to find your way around. $ *Rooms from: $419 ⊠ 3300 Wailea Alanui Dr., Wailea ☎ 808/891–6200 guest services, 800/367–5246 reservations ⊕ destinationresidenceswailea.com ⇨ 289 units* ○| *No Meals.*

Wailea Ekolu Village

$$$$ | RESORT | These affordable Wailea condos are perched on a hillside and offer panoramic vistas of the resort, the ocean, and nearby islands. **Pros:** an affordable value in Wailea; good views; beautiful landscaping. **Cons:** confusing layout may make it difficult to find your unit; check-in at a different location; not on the beach. $ *Rooms from: $359 ⊠ 10 Wailea Ekolu Pl., Wailea ☎ 808/891–6200*

guest services, 800/367–5246 reservations ⊕ *destinationresidenceswailea.com* ➲ *148 units* ⦿ *No Meals.*

Wailea Elua Village

$$$$ | RESORT | Located on Ulua Beach, one of the Island's most beloved snorkeling spots, these upscale one-, two-, and three-bedroom condo suites have spectacular views and 24 acres of manicured lawns and gardens. **Pros:** easy access to the designer boutiques and upscale restaurants at The Shops at Wailea; daily housekeeping; on-site naturalist and organic herb garden. **Cons:** hard to find your way around; check-in at a different location; large complex. $ *Rooms from: $669* ⊠ *3600 Wailea Alanui Dr., Wailea* ☎ *808/891–6200, 800/367–5246* ⊕ *destinationresidenceswailea.com* ➲ *152 suites* ⦿ *No Meals.*

Nightlife

Most of Wailea's nightlife centers around dinner and drinks at some of the Island's most posh restaurants, including a few celebrity-driven eateries. Live music options range from raucous nights at an Irish pub to more Hawaiian-inspired entertainment at a high-end lobby lounge.

★ Lobby Lounge at Four Seasons Resort Maui

LIVE MUSIC | This lofty resort's lobby lounge is perfect when you want live Hawaiian music, a bit of hula, and freshly prepared sushi all in one sitting. If you're not in the mood for a ceremonious sit-down meal but still crave something out of the ordinary, the place is perfect for a quick bite. The artisanal cocktails are well done and highlight locally distilled spirits. The contemporary beachfront space, which boasts a stunning view of the Pacific, west Maui, and neighboring island of Lanai, is beautifully appointed with natural tones and textiles inspired by the destination, rare ivory cane palms, and locally made art. Food is served 5–10 pm; cocktails 5–11 pm. ⊠ *Four Seasons Resort Maui at Wailea, 3900 Wailea Alanui Dr., Wailea* ☎ *808/874–8000* ⊕ *fourseasons.com/maui.*

Mulligan's on the Blue

PUBS | Frothy pints of Guinness and late-night fish-and-chips—who could ask for more? Live music happens every night of the week, often featuring foot-stomping Irish jams that will have you dancing a jig, and singing something about "a whiskey for me-Johnny." In addition to the daily music, the venue hosts larger monthly events and concerts. ⊠ *Wailea Blue Golf Course, 100 Kaukahi St., Wailea* ☎ *808/874–1131* ⊕ *mulligansontheblue. com.*

Performing Arts

Luau—Grand Wailea

THEMED ENTERTAINMENT | FAMILY | Grand Wailea's spectacular luau features traditional ceremonies, music, and dishes such as poi, kalua pig, poke, and haupia. Guests can sit at their own private table overlooking Wailea Beach for an unforgettable evening filled with interactive entertainment, hula lessons, and amazing performances that showcase the myths and legends of Maui all in their colorful, fiery glory. Seating includes standard and Alii premium seating. ⊠ *Grand Wailea Resort & Spa, 3850 Wailea Alanui Dr., Wailea* ☎ *808/875–1234* ⊕ *grandwailea. com* ⦿ *Closed select days.*

Te Au Moana

THEMED ENTERTAINMENT | Te Au Moana means "ocean tide," which is all you need to know about the simply breathtaking backdrop for this South Maui luau at Wailea Beach Resort. The tasty family-style dinner serves a three-course dinner that includes variety of local staples and desserts, as well as an open bar. Longtime local entertainment company Tihati Productions seamlessly intertwines ancient Hawaiian stories and contemporary songs with traditional hula and Polynesian dances, concluding with a jaw-dropping solo fire-knife dance. ⊠ *Wailea Beach Resort—Marriott, Maui, 3700 Wailea Alanui, Wailea* ☎ *877/827–2740* ⊕ *teaumoana.com* ⊗ *Closed Sun.*

🛍 Shopping

Some of Maui's best shopping can be done in Wailea with shops ranging from essentials at the ubiquitous ABC Store and Island Gourmet Market to high-end splurges like Gucci and Tiffany & Co. Two of the main shopping centers are in the heart of the Wailea resorts, making them within walking distance if you don't want to get your car from the valet.

SHOPPING CENTERS

The Shops at Wailea

MALL | Stylish, upscale, and close to most of the resorts, this mall brings high-fashion to Wailea. Luxury boutiques such as Gucci, Cos Bar, and Tiffany & Co. are represented, as are less expensive chains like Billabong, Lululemon, and Tommy Bahama. Daily events include lei making, ukulele lessons, hula performances, and more. Dining options include elevated pub food at Pint & Cork, along with the hip and trendy Lineage. Island Gourmet Markets offers everything from grocery essentials to locally made food products, plus a wide selection of takeaway food options. ⊠ *3750 Wailea Alanui Dr., Wailea* ☎ *808/891–6770* ⊕ *shopsatwailea.com.*

Wailea Gateway Center

MALL | Located at the top of tony Wailea, this center is comprised of commercial offices and a handful of fantastic dining options. Although lunch at chef Peter Merriman's Monkeypod is reason enough to venture here, you might also be enticed by eateries including Pita Paradise, Sprout Vegan Cafe, and the Market Maui. ⊠ *34 Wailea Gateway Pl., Wailea.*

The Wailea Village

SHOPPING CENTER | This new open-air shopping center is mere steps from the area's more established mall, The Shops at Wailea, making it a convenient stop for anyone already in the neighborhood. Retailers include home-decor favorite Hue, Bikini Market, and a pair of art galleries, among others. Akamai Coffee will put some pep in your step, Manoli's Pizza is a great spot to grab a pie and a cocktail, while Wailea Urgent Care is open from 8 am to 8 pm daily, and accepts walk-in patients. The shopping center offers the Sunset Market featuring outdoor vendors, music, and other fun every first and third Thursday evening. ⊠ *The Wailea Village, 100 Wailea Ike Dr., Wailea* ☎ *949/760–9150* ⊕ *thewaileavillage.com.*

🏃 Activities

SPAS

Awili Spa and Salon, Andaz Maui at Wailea Resort

SPAS | At Awili Spa and Salon's apothecary or blending bar (*awili* means "to mix"), consultants assist in creating your personalized body products made from local ingredients. Set aside an extra hour to fully indulge in the blending bar, or opt for ready-made concoctions. The cool, soothing interior of this spa is an extension of the minimalist, monochromatic style of the Andaz Maui at Wailea Resort. Relaxation lounges are stocked with thoughtful amenities and the full salon takes care of pampering your hair and nails. ⊠ *Andaz Maui at Wailea Resort, 3550 Wailea Alanui Dr., Wailea* ☎ *808/573–1234* ⊕ *andazmaui.com* ⊟ *$200 for 60-min massage.*

★ Spa & Wellness Center at Four Seasons Resort Maui

SPAS | A wide array of beauty and health and wellness services are offered here including Hawaiian traditional massage, innovative facials, and a full hair and nail salon with barber, along with some services you won't find anywhere else on Maui. For the ultimate indulgence, reserve one of the seaside open-air *hale hau* (traditional thatch-roof houses), one of the best outdoor massage experiences on the Island. Recently added to the Health & Wellness lineup is California-based Next/Health, providing IV and Ozone Therapy services, as well as biomarker testing, in a lounge near the spa. ⊠ *Four Seasons Resort Maui at Wailea, 3900 Wailea Alanui Dr., Wailea* ☎ *808/874–2925* ⊕ *fourseasons.com/ maui* ✉ *$205 for 50-minute massage.*

Willow Stream Spa, Fairmont Kea Lani

SPAS | This spa makes meticulous use of Hawaii's natural elements to replenish your Zen. Give a full hour to enjoy the fascinating amenities, two if you plan to work out. Upon arrival, rinse off in a high-tech shower that combines color, sound, and hydrotherapy to mimic different types of Hawaiian rain. A heated stone bench and foot bed awaits to deepen the relaxation before the treatment. The spa has 17 indoor treatment rooms with a poolside and oceanside option for outdoor treatments. ⊠ *4100 Wailea Alanui, Wailea* ☎ *808/875–2229* ⊕ *fairmont-kea-lani.com* ✉ *$200 for 60-min massage.*

Chapter 5

CENTRAL MAUI

Updated by
Syndi Texeira

⊙ **Sights**
★★★★★

🍽 **Restaurants**
★★★☆☆

🛏 **Hotels**
★★★☆☆

🛍 **Shopping**
★★★☆☆

🍸 **Nightlife**
★★☆☆☆

WELCOME TO CENTRAL MAUI

TOP REASONS TO GO

★ **Learn to windsurf or kitesurf.** At Kahana Beach, windsurfers and kiteboarders from around the world play in the waters.

★ **See a show at the Maui Arts & Cultural Center.** Featuring two indoor theaters, multiple outdoor venues, an art gallery, dance studios, and classrooms, there's always something exciting happening at "the MACC."

★ **Explore historic Wailuku.** From landmark battles between ancient chiefs to serving as the current seat of Maui County government, what happens in Wailuku has long influenced the rest of the Island.

★ **Experience local flavor.** Don't miss Native Intelligence, a cultural resource center disguised as a store that offers handcrafted items by local artisans and practitioners.

★ **Discover the history and splendor of Iao Valley.** Head *mauka* (toward the mountains) to the wildly lush Iao Valley—or as Mark Twain dubbed it, the "Yosemite of the Pacific."

Bookended between Haleakala and West Maui's mountain is the appropriately named Central Maui, which includes the bustling towns of Kahului and Wailuku. Most visitors will arrive at Kahului Airport, perhaps stock up on essentials, and then make a beeline for their resort or condo. While Central Maui isn't exactly a tourist destination, there's still plenty to see here, and chances are you'll pass through this area on your way to other parts of the island. Iao Valley holds much of Maui's history: In 1790, Kamehameha I, chief of Hawaii Island, defeated Maui ruler Kalanikupule in a battle so bloody that warriors' bodies dammed the river. No trace remains of that long-ago bloodshed. Instead, the valley's Kepaniwai Park invites you to roam through Maui's more recent history: at the colorful Heritage Gardens, life-size structures honor cultures that contribute to Maui's diversity, including a Japanese tea house and a Filipino farmer's hut. This charming spot is picnic-perfect, complete with ample cabanas. Farther up the road is Iao Valley State Monument, where a paved trail leads to Kukaemoku, nicknamed Iao Needle, a towering 1,200-foot monolith carved by centuries of erosion.

1 Kahului. Kahului is the industrial and commercial center of Maui, and where you will likely land first when you come to visit. This residential area is home to Maui's main airport, a bustling commercial harbor and cruise ship port, and the island's largest shopping center. Just beyond Central Maui's industrial district and next to Kahului Airport lies one of the world's greatest water sports destinations— Kanaha Beach. Kahului's main drag is Kaahumanu Avenue, just 3 miles from the Kahului Airport, which you can get to from the airport if you take Route 36, aka Hana Highway. The Kahului Loop is accessible by bus and goes by the big chain stores.

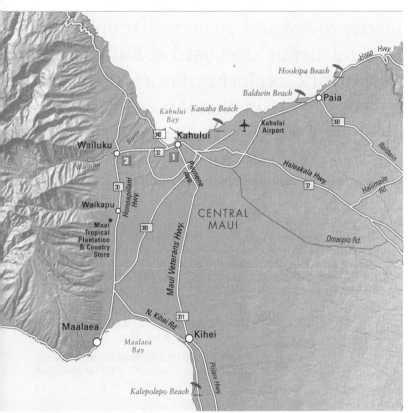

2 Wailuku. Wailuku is to the west of Kahului and is known as one of the most charming towns in Central Maui. Cradled at the base of West Maui's mountain, overlooking the Central Valley, Wailuku is a charismatic town packed with Hawaiian history and local flavor. Wailuku has one of the Island's main attractions, the Iao Valley State Monument and the Iao Valley Needle, which rises up 2,000 feet skyward. Wailuku sets the tone for the rest of the island. The storied Hale Hoikeike at the Bailey House contains a trove of Hawaiian artifacts and is historic in its own right. Wailuku Town, which centers around Market Street, is in the midst of a resurgence, and today you'll find a host of unique eateries, one-of-a-kind shops, and historical buildings. Wailuku was the political seat of the Island until the 1960s when the sugar industry declined and made way for tourism. Wailuku houses the county government.

Some visitors bypass Central Maui in favor of towns that cater to fun-in-the-sun activities. However, there's still plenty to see and do here—from learning to windsurf or kiteboard at Kanaha Beach Park, exploring nature and taking an ice-cold dip in lush Iao Valley, and catching a world-class concert at the Maui Arts & Cultural Center.

Kahului, where you most likely landed when you arrived on Maui, is the industrial and commercial center of the island. West of Kahului is Wailuku, the county seat since 1950 and the most charming town in Central Maui, with some good inexpensive restaurants. Outside these towns are attractions ranging from museums and historical sites to gardens.

You can combine sightseeing in Central Maui with shopping at the Queen Kaahumanu Center, Maui Mall, and Wailuku's Market Street. This is one of the best areas on the island to stock up on groceries and supplies, thanks to major retailers, including Safeway, Target, and Costco. Note that grocery prices are much higher than on the mainland.

Planning

Getting Here and Around

In most cases, it's wise to rent a car to see Maui's attractions, and Central Maui is no exception. National car rental agencies are located at and near Kahului Airport, and it's wise to make a reservation far in advance, especially during peak season or for major sporting events, as inventory is limited. Local car rentals are another excellent option; they usually deliver cars to the airport.

AIR

Kahului Airport handles major airlines and international flights, and it is the only airport on Maui that has direct service from the mainland.

CONTACTS Kahului Airport. ⊠ 1 Keolani Place, Kahului ☎ 808/872–3830 ⊕ airports.hawaii.gov/ogg.

BUS

Maui Bus offers four Central Maui routes that begin and end at Queen Kaahumanu Center; cost is $2 per boarding.

CONTACTS Maui Bus. ⊠ 2145 Kaohu St., Wailuku ☎ 808/871–4838 ⊕ mauibus.org.

CAR

There are eight national rental car companies at Kahului Airport, including familiar names like Avis, Budget, and Thrifty. Local rental-car companies can offer a better deal, though they are off-site and sometimes have older model vehicles. For maximum convenience and reliability, renting a car at or having it delivered to the airport is your best bet. It's wise to make reservations far in advance, especially if you're visiting during peak seasons or for major conventions or sporting events, as car rental companies can sell out during these times.

TAXI

If you're not renting a car, you'll need to take a taxi, rideshare, or shuttle to your accommodations. It's best to plan transportation ahead of time, though a taxi dispatcher can be found fronting the airport's baggage claim area.

CONTACTS Maui Airport Taxi Service.
✉ 101 Airport Rd., Kahului ☎ 808/877–0907 ⊕ airports.hawaii.gov/ogg/getting-to-from/ground-transportation/taxicab.

Hotels

Central Maui is where many residents live and work, so there aren't many attractions here that specifically cater to tourists. Accommodation options are limited, but it's a good base for exploring, especially for those who want to escape the more touristy sides of the island.

Restaurants

Central Maui is where the locals live and where you can find just about every ethnic cuisine on the Islands. Savory noodle shops and small joints dishing up *loco moco*—fried egg, on a hamburger patty set on top of two scoops of rice with rich brown gravy—are plentiful. Kahului offers more variety because it's the main traffic corridor and near the big-box stores you can even find potatoes instead of rice on a few menus. Take a chance on a mom-and-pop eatery in Wailuku, or walk along historic Market Street, where you can shop for souvenirs between bites. If you want to eat like a local and, more importantly, at local prices, don't miss Central Maui.

HOTEL AND RESTAURANT PRICES

Hotel prices in the reviews are the lowest cost of a standard double room in high season. Restaurant prices in the reviews are the average cost of a main course at dinner, or if dinner is not served, at lunch.

WHAT IT COSTS in U.S. Dollars			
$	$$	$$$	$$$$
RESTAURANTS			
under $18	$18–$26	$27–$35	over $35
HOTELS			
under $181	$181–$260	$261–$340	over $340

Kahului

3 miles west of Kahului Airport; 9 miles north of Kihei; 31 miles east of Kaanapali; 51 miles west of Hana.

With the Island's largest airport and commercial harbor, Kahului is Maui's commercial hub. But it also offers plenty of natural and cultural attractions. The town was developed in the early 1950s to meet the housing needs of the large sugarcane interests here, specifically those of Alexander & Baldwin. The company was tired of playing landlord to its many plantation workers and sold land to a developer who promised to create affordable housing. The scheme worked, and "Dream City," the first planned city in Hawaii, was born.

GETTING HERE AND AROUND

From the airport, take Keolani Place to Route 36 (Hana Highway), which becomes Kaahumanu Avenue, Kahului's main drag. Run by Maui Bus, the Kahului Loop route traverses all of the town's major shopping centers; the fare is $2.

⊙ Sights

Alexander & Baldwin Sugar Museum

HISTORY MUSEUM | Maui's largest landowner, A&B was one of the "Big Five" companies that spearheaded the planting, harvesting, and processing of sugarcane. At this museum, historic photos, artifacts, and documents explain the introduction of sugarcane to Hawaii. Exhibits reveal how plantations brought in laborers from other countries, forever changing the Islands' ethnic mix. Although sugarcane is no longer being grown on Maui, the crop was for many years the mainstay of the local economy. You can find the museum in a small, restored plantation manager's house across the street from the post office and the still-operating sugar refinery, where smoke billows up when the cane is being processed. Their gift shop sells plantation-themed memorabilia, coffee, and a selection of history books. ⊠ 3957 Hansen Rd., Puunene ☎ 808/871–8058 ⊕ sugarmuseum.com ⊠ $7 ⊙ Closed Fri., Sat., Sun.

Maui Fresh Farmers' Market

MARKET | Local purveyors showcase their fruits, vegetables, flowers, and crafts near the center stage at the Queen Kaahumanu Center. If local products are important to you, it's a good idea to ask about the particular product or flowers or whatever you want to purchase. ⊠ Queen Kaahumanu Center, 275 W. Kaahumanu Ave., Kahului ☎ 808/877–4325 ⊙ Closed Mon., Thurs., and weekends.

Maui Nui Botanical Gardens

GARDEN | FAMILY | Hawaiian and Polynesian species are cultivated at this fascinating 7-acre garden, including Hawaiian bananas; local varieties of sweet potatoes and sugarcane; and native poppies, hibiscus, and anapanapa, a plant that makes a natural shampoo when rubbed between your hands. Reserve ahead for the weekly ethnobotany tours. Self-guided tour booklets and an audio tour wand are included with admission (docent tours must be arranged online in advance). ⊠ 150 Kanaloa Ave., Kahului ☎ 808/249–2798 ⊕ mnbg.org ⊠ $10 admission; docent tour $10 ⊙ Closed Sun. and Mon.

Maui Swap Meet

MARKET | Even locals get up early on a Saturday to go to the Maui Swap Meet for fresh produce and floral bouquets. Each Saturday, hundreds of stalls sell everything from quilts to hammocks, plus island-themed souvenirs. Enter the parking lot from the traffic light at Kahului Beach Road. ⊠ University of Hawaii Maui College, 310 W Kaahumanu Ave., Kahului ☎ 808/244–3100 ⊠ 50 cents ⊙ Closed Sun.–Fri.

⊕ Beaches

Kanaha Beach

BEACH | Windsurfers, kiteboarders, joggers, and picnicking families like this long, golden strip of sand bordered by

---

Fun Things to ⊙ Do in Central Maui

■ Unwind to slack-key guitar at a Maui Arts & Cultural Center concert.

■ Marvel at indigenous plant life at Maui Nui Botanical Gardens.

■ Pick your way through Iao Valley's guava and ginger forest.

■ Imagine mastering the ancient weapons at Hale Hoikeike at the Bailey House.

■ Explore the charming boutiques and locally owned shops on Market Street.

The Maui Nui Botanical Gardens have acres of fascinating plant species from Hawaii and Polynesia.

a wide grassy area with lots of shade that is within walking distance of Kahului Airport. The winds pick up in the early afternoon, making for the best kiteboarding and windsurfing conditions—if you know what you're doing, that is. The best spot for watching kiteboarders is at the far left end of the beach. A picnic paired with surf-watching makes a great option for a farewell activity before getting on a departing flight. **Amenities:** lifeguard; parking (no fee); showers; toilets. **Best for:** walking; windsurfing. ⊠ *Amala Pl., Kahului* ✛ *From Kaahumanu Ave., turn makai onto Hobron St., then right onto Amala Pl. Drive just over a mile through an industrial area and take any of three entrances into Kanaha.*

🍴 Restaurants

Bistro Casanova
$$ | MEDITERRANEAN | The location of this Mediterranean restaurant is smack-dab in the middle of Kahului, making it a convenient choice for lunch or dinner. The menu features everything from salads to pasta, and the tapas menu (available from 4-9 pm) changes weekly and always has an excellent selection of dishes. **Known for:** beautiful desserts; perfect place for dinner before heading to the airport; paella with saffron rice, scallop linguine. ⑤ *Average main: $26* ⊠ *33 Lono Ave., Kahului* ☎ *808/873–3650* ⊕ *bistrocasanova.com* 🕐 *Closed Sun.*

Fork & Salad
$ | MODERN AMERICAN | Healthy, fresh, fast. This busy eatery is the second restaurant for chef-owners Jaron Blosser, Cody Christopher, and Travis Morrin, the first being Three's Bar and Grill in Kihei. **Known for:** locally sourced ingredients; kombucha on tap; healthy grab-and-go. ⑤ *Average main: $10* ⊠ *Puunene Shopping Center, 120 Hookele St., Kahului* ☎ *808/793–3256* ⊕ *forkandsaladmaui. com.*

Marco's Grill & Deli

$$ | **ITALIAN** | One of the go-to places for airport comers and goers, this popular Italian restaurant also draws a steady crowd of local residents, mostly for business lunches. Meatballs, sausages, and sauces are all made in-house, there's a long list of sandwiches that are available all day, and the affordable salads are big enough to share; substitutions or special requests are not recommended. **Known for:** chicken Parmesan; great selection of breakfasts; gluten-free options. $ *Average main: $18 ☒ 444 Hana Hwy., Kahului ☎ 808/877–4446 ⊕ marcosgrillanddeli. com.*

★ Tin Roof

$ | **MODERN HAWAIIAN** | Celebrity chef Sheldon Simeon has taken the fame he earned on *Top Chef* and opened this trendy lunch counter in a small Kahului warehouse. You can't miss this spot; look for the line of people waiting in the parking lot. **Known for:** fresh poke bowl; plantation-inspired "kau kau tins"; decadent treats such as mochi birthday cake bites. $ *Average main: $10 ☒ 360 Papa Pl., Suite Y, Kahului ☎ 808/868–0753 ⊕ tinroofmaui.com ⊗ No dinner. Closed Sun.*

🛏 Hotels

Kahului and Wailuku, the commercial, residential, and government centers that make up Central Maui, are not known for their lavish accommodations, but some options meet travelers' needs perfectly.

Courtyard by Marriott Maui Kahului Airport

$$$ | **HOTEL** | At the entrance to Kahului Airport, this hotel offers many amenities for business travelers and tourists. **Pros:** great for business and pleasure; central location; conference and banquet rooms available. **Cons:** airport and city noise; daily parking fee; not on the beach. $ *Rooms from: $289 ☒ 532 Keolani Pl., Kahului ☎ 808/871–1800, 877/852–1880 ⊕ marriott.com ⇨ 138 rooms ⦿ No Meals.*

Maui Beach Hotel

$$ | **HOTEL** | Budget-friendly rates and a central location in the Island's civic, transportation, and commercial hubs make this two-story bayfront hotel a solid choice. **Pros:** shuttle to Kahului Airport and central area; great base for exploring all corners of the island; aloha-minded staff. **Cons:** parts of property may seem dated; located on busy intersection; beach-fronting hotel is uninspiring. $ *Rooms from: $240 ☒ 170 Kaahumanu Ave., Kahului ☎ 808/877–0051 ⊕ mauibeachhotel.com ⇨ 147 units ⦿ No Meals.*

🎭 Performing Arts

★ Maui Film Festival

FESTIVALS | **FAMILY** | Held annually between mid-June to early July, this international festival attracts big-name celebrities, who come to Maui for cinema and soirées under the stars around Wailea and at the Maui Arts & Cultural Center in Kahului. The not-to-be-missed outdoor Celestial Cinema in Wailea turns golf greens into a spectacular theater under the stars. ☒ *1 Cameron Way, Kahului ☎ 808/579–9244 for info, 808/242–7469 for Maui Arts & Cultural Center box office ⊕ mauifilmfestival.com.*

🛍 Shopping

Locals come here in droves for their monthly Costco run or catch the latest flick at Queen Kaahumanu Center or Maui Mall. Still, Central Maui can also be an ideal shopping destination for visiting families who are passing the time on their way to or from the airport.

CLOTHING
★ Hi-Tech

MIXED CLOTHING | This locally owned shop is a favorite among stylish surfers and landlubbers alike. Stop here immediately after deplaning to stock up on surf trunks, windsurfing gear, bikinis, or sundresses. You can also rent a surfboard or sign up for windsurfing or kiteboarding lessons while you're at it. You'll find additional branches in Kihei and Paia. ✉ *425 Koloa St., Kahului* ☎ *808/877–2111* ⊕ *surfmaui.com.*

FOOD
Maui Coffee Roasters

FOOD | It's the best stop in Kahului for 100% Kona, Kau, and Maui coffee from the best coffee farms in Hawaii. This café and roasting house is near Kahului Airport. Sales associates are very helpful and friendly, and they will ship items. You can get a free cup of joe in a signature to-go cup when you buy a pound of coffee. Order online or call in your food or drink order and the barista will meet you at the door or bring it to your car! ✉ *444 Hana Hwy., Kahului* ☎ *808/877–2877* ⊕ *mauicoffeeroasters.com* ⊗ *Closed Sun.*

Minit Stop Kahului

CONVENIENCE STORE | This convenience store/gas station is a Maui staple, the first stop before a day at the beach or road trip. In addition to convenience items and Hawaiian-made snacks, it boasts some of the best fast food on the Island featuring local-style plate lunches, deli items, and their famous fried chicken and potato wedges. There are eight locations across Maui. ✉ *333 Dairy Rd., Kahului* ☎ *808/871–7325* ⊕ *minitstop. com.*

MARKETS
Maui Swap Meet

MARKET | Crafts, T-shirts, fresh produce, flowers, souvenirs that range from authentic to average make this enormous flea market—operating since 1981—the Island's biggest bargain. Maui-made food product vendors and freshly cracked coconuts can be found next to the food trucks serving fresh, affordable, authentic local food. ✉ *310 W Kaahumanu Ave., Kahului* ⚲ *UH Maui College, rear parking lot.* ☎ *808/244–3100* ⊕ *mauihawaii.org/ maui-shopping/swap-meet* ⊗ *Closed Sun.-Fri.*

SHOPPING CENTERS
Maui Mall

MALL | FAMILY | Conveniently located five minutes from the airport and across from Kahului Harbor, and anchored by Longs Drugs and Whole Foods, the Maui Mall is a haven for locals and travelers alike. There are several casual eateries ranging from fast food, national chains, and local eateries to sushi. Local favorite Tasaka Guri Guri Shop is also here—it's been around for more than a hundred years, selling a Japanese-style sherbet confection called *guri guri.* The mall also has a whimsically designed 12-screen megaplex. ✉ *70 E. Kaahumanu Ave., Kahului* ☎ *808/877–8952* ⊕ *mauimall.com.*

Pu'unene Shopping Center

MALL | This newer shopping center is near Kahului Airport. It is anchored by a Target store that includes a supermarket, making it convenient to purchase necessities and groceries after landing on Maui. Other retailers include Planet Fitness, Ulta, Maui Tacos, Petco, Starbucks, and the popular farm-to-table takeout joint Fork & Salad. ✉ *100 Hookele St., Kahului.*

Queen Kaahumanu Center

MALL | Maui's largest shopping center has more than 100 stores and restaurants, a movie theater, and a food court. The mall's attractive rooftop is easily spotted, composed of a series of manta ray-like umbrella shades. Stop at Camellia Seeds for what locals call "crack seed," a snack made from dried fruits, or swing by 180 Boardshop for Hawaii-based streetwear like 808 All Day or In4mation. For surf-inspired gear, stop by The Foam Company and Shapers. Other stops include Macy's, PacSun, Bath & Body Works, and American Eagle Outfitters. Beyond retail therapy, the mall also hosts a creative lineup of events throughout the month, including a farmers' market, live music, and car shows. ✉ *275 W. Kaahumanu Ave., Kahului* ☎ *808/877–3369* ⊕ *queen-kaahumanucenter.com.*

Wailuku

4 miles west of Kahului; 12 miles north of Kihei; 21 miles east of Lahaina.

Wailuku is peaceful now, although it wasn't always. Its name means "Water of Destruction," after the fateful battle in Iao Valley that pitted King Kamehameha the Great against Maui warriors. Wailuku was a politically important town until the sugar industry declined in the 1960s and tourism took hold. Businesses left the cradle of the West Maui mountains and followed the new market (and tourists) to the shores. Wailuku houses the county government but has the feel of a town that's been asleep for several decades.

The shops and offices now inhabiting Market Street's plantation-style buildings serve as reminders of a bygone era, and continued attempts at gentrification, at the very least, open the way for unique eateries, shops, and galleries.

GETTING HERE AND AROUND
Heading to Wailuku from the airport, Hana Highway turns into Kaahumanu Avenue, the main thoroughfare between Kahului and Wailuku. Maui Bus system's Wailuku Loop stops at shopping centers, medical facilities, and government buildings; the fare is $2.

◉ Sights

★ Hale Hoikeike at the Bailey House
HISTORIC HOME | This repository of the largest and best collection of Hawaiian artifacts on Maui includes objects from the sacred island of Kahoolawe. Erected in 1833 on the site of the compound of Kahekili (the last ruling chief of Maui), the building was occupied by the family of missionary teachers Edward and Caroline Bailey until 1888. Edward Bailey was something of a Renaissance man: not only a missionary, but also a surveyor, a naturalist, and an excellent artist. The museum contains missionary-period furniture and displays a number of Bailey's landscape paintings, which provide a snapshot of the island during his time. The grounds include gardens with native Hawaiian plants and a fine example of a traditional canoe. The gift shop is one of the best sources on Maui for items that are actually made in Hawaii. Before visiting, check their website for current hours of operation. ⊠ *2375A Main St., Wailuku* ☎ *808/244–3326* ⊕ *mauimuseum.org* 🖆 *$10* 🕙 *Closed Sun.*

★ Iao Valley State Monument
NATURE SIGHT | When Mark Twain saw this park, he dubbed it the Yosemite of the Pacific. Yosemite, it's not, but it is a lovely deep valley with the curious Iao Needle, a spire that rises more than 2,000 feet from the valley floor. You can walk from the parking lot across Iao Stream and explore the thick, jungle-like topography. This park has some lovely short strolls on paved paths, where you can stop and meditate by the edge of a stream or marvel at the native plants. Mist often rises if there has been raining, making it even more magical. Be aware that this area is prone to flash flooding; stay out of the water if it's been raining. ⊠ *Western end of Rte. 32, Wailuku* ⊕ *hawaiistateparks.org* 🖆 *$5 per person; $10 parking per vehicle.*

Kepaniwai Park & Heritage Gardens
CITY PARK | **FAMILY** | Picnic facilities dot the landscape of this county park, a memorial to Maui's cultural roots. Among the interesting displays are an early-Hawaiian *hale* (house), a New England–style saltbox, a Portuguese-style villa with gardens, and dwellings from such other cultures as China and the Philippines.

The peacefulness here belies the history of the area. In 1790, King Kamehameha the Great from the Island of Hawaii waged a successful bloody battle against Kahekili, the son of Maui's

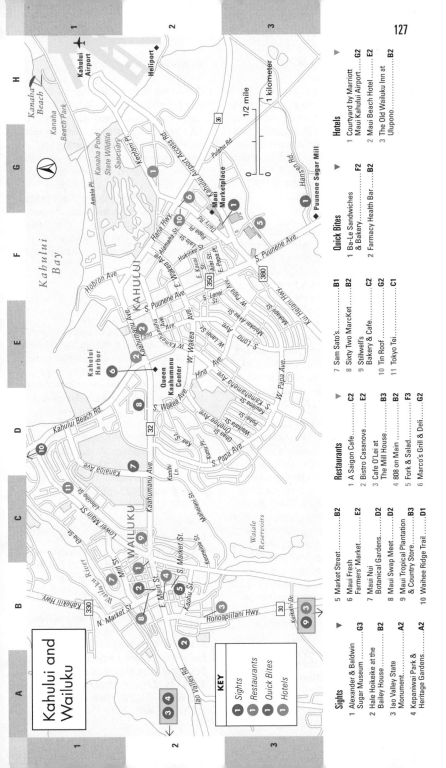

Kahului and Wailuku

KEY
- ① Sights
- ① Restaurants
- ① Quick Bites
- ① Hotels

chief. An earlier battle at the site had pitted Kahekili himself against an older Hawaii Island chief, Kalaniopuu. Kahekili prevailed, but the carnage was so great that the nearby stream became known as *Wailuku* (Water of Destruction), and the place where fallen warriors choked the stream's flow was called *Kepaniwai* (Damming of the Waters). ⊠ *870 Iao Valley Rd., Wailuku* ☎ *808/270–7980* ⊕ *mauicounty.gov* ⌨ *Free.*

Market Street

HISTORIC DISTRICT | A unique assortment of historic buildings, stylish boutiques, coffee shops, antique stores, and restaurants make Wailuku's Market Street a delightful place for a stroll. Brown-Kobayashi and the Bird of Paradise Unique Antiques are the best shops for interesting collectibles and furnishings. Brown Eyed Bella has stylish bikinis and island wear. Wailuku Coffee Company holds works by local artists and occasionally offers live entertainment in the evening. ⊠ *Market St., Wailuku* ⊕ *wailukulive.com* ⌨ *Free.*

Maui Tropical Plantation & Country Store

FARM/RANCH | **FAMILY** | When Maui's cash crops declined in importance, a group of visionaries opened an agricultural theme park on the site of this former sugar-cane field. The 60-acre preserve offers zip-lining courses, and a 40-minute tour and tram ride with informative narration that covers the growing process and plant types. Children will enjoy activities like coconut husking. You'll also find an art gallery, a restaurant, and a store specializing in "Made in Maui" products. Don't leave without checking out the new Kumu Cafe and Farm Bar, which offers coffee, tea, brewing supplies, seasonal organic produce, and some of the tastiest papayas around. ⊠ *1670 Honoapiilani Hwy., Waikapu* ☎ *808/244–7643* ⊕ *mauitropicalplantation.com* ⌨ *Free; Tour $25.*

Waihee Ridge Trail

HIKING & WALKING | Hiking with a view doesn't get much better than the 2.5-mile (round-trip) Waihee Ridge Trail. The catch: You'll have to work for it. This out-and-back trail is steep, climbing more than 1,500 feet before rewarding you with a panorama of the central valley and curtains of emerald vegetation. Smart hikers go early to take advantage of cooler temperatures. Don't forget to stop at the one-mile mark and enjoy the best view of Makamakaole Falls. Open 7 am to 7 pm daily. ⊠ *Maluhia Road, Wailuku* ⊕ *dlnr.hawaii.gov/recreation* ⌨ *Free.*

🍴 Restaurants

A Saigon Cafe

$$ | **VIETNAMESE** | Locals have been flocking to this off-the-beaten-path gem for years, lured in by the reliably delicious Vietnamese cuisine served family-style at decent prices. It's tucked behind a nondescript overpass—and only recently did they put a sign on its building—but you can't go wrong with the green papaya salad, mixed fondue, and the make-your-own Vietnamese burritos. **Known for:** authentic Com Tay Cam (rice in a clay pot); known locally as "Jennifer's"; strong cocktails well mixed. $ *Average main: $19* ⊠ *1792 Main St., Wailuku* ☎ *808/243–9560* ⊕ *asaigoncafe.com* 🏛 *Casual.*

Cafe O'Lei at the Mill House

$$$ | **FUSION** | The food is so fresh at this Waikapu standout that you can see the fields where the food was grown while seated at your mountain view table. This family-owned restaurant creates rich cuisine from *mauka* (mountain) to *makai* (ocean), boasting seasonal produce. **Known for:** bold flavors and farm-to-table freshness; ulu and sweet potato enchiladas; robust happy hour. $ *Average main: $27* ⊠ *1670 Honoapiilani Hwy., Waikapu* ☎ *808/270–0333* ⊕ *millhousemaui.com* ⊘ *Closed Mon.*

Did You Know?

The Waihee Ridge Trail in Maui offers views in all directions. You can see Haleakala, Makamakaole Falls, and the ocean.

★ Sam Sato's

$ | HAWAIIAN | Sam Sato's is a local favorite for noodles, *manju* (Japanese pastry filled with sweet bean paste), and plate lunches. Open for breakfast and lunch; the menu includes favorites like "dry noodles," beef tomato, omelets, and fried rice. **Known for:** huge portions of flavorful food; affordable local hideout; amazing spare ribs. ⑤ *Average main: $8 ⊠ The Millyard, 1750 Wili Pa Loop, Wailuku ☎ 808/244–7124 ▬ No credit cards ⊗ Closed Sun.*

SixtyTwo MarcKet

$$ | AMERICAN | Located in Wailuku on Market Street, serving breakfast and lunch crafted by chefs utilizing various cooking styles and techniques to showcase the seasonal bounty Maui has to offer. Rotating menus (every 62 days) are created using seasonally fresh farm ingredients. **Known for:** spam and egg bubble waffle breakfast; generous portions and good prices; amazing swordfish tacos. ⑤ *Average main: $18 ⊠ 62 N. Market. St, Wailuku ☎ 808/793 2277 ⊕ sixtytwomarcket.com ⊗ Closed Sat. ⋔ Casual.*

★ Stillwell's Bakery & Cafe

$ | BAKERY | Stillwell's is one of the best bakeries in Maui, so this is the place to come for coffee and an outrageously good strawberry florentine or a renowned cream horn. Their breakfast and lunch offerings are exceptional, from a fried egg sandwich to mouthwatering pancakes and gourmet sandwiches on house-made bread to their famous Chinese chicken salad. **Known for:** amazing pies (try the coconut cream); towering Rubens and BLTs; friendly staff who love to share local tips. ⑤ *Average main: $12 ⊠ 1740 Kaahumanu Ave., Wailuku ☎ 808/243–2243 ⊕ stillwellsbakery.com.*

Tokyo Tei

$ | JAPANESE | FAMILY | Tokyo Tei is worth seeking out for local-style Japanese food. At lunch, you can rub elbows with bankers and construction workers, and at dinner, three generations might be celebrating *tutu's* (grandma's) birthday at the next table. **Known for:** *misoyaki*-glazed fish; unlikeliest of locations for great food; local institution that's been around for more than eight decades. ⑤ *Average main: $12 ⊠ Puuone Plaza, 1063 Lower Main St., Wailuku ☎ 808/242–9630 ⊗ Closed Mon.–Sat. 1:30–5 pm; Sun. dinner only.*

★ 808 on Main

$ | AMERICAN | Delicious artisan sandwiches, classic burgers, and signature items make 808 on Main a local favorite. Their pupus, cocktails, and draft beers will make you wish they were open later (10-3 pm). **Known for:** fun and friendly atmosphere; tasty fish sandwiches; refreshing house-made strawberry lemonade. ⑤ *Average main: $16 ⊠ 2051 Main St., Wailuku ☎ 808/242–1111 ⊕ 808onmain. com ⊗ Closed Sun.*

☕ Coffee and Quick Bites

★ Ba-Le Sandwiches & Bakery

$ | VIETNAMESE | This popular spot began as a French-Vietnamese bakery on Oahu and has branched into popular small restaurants sprinkled throughout the Islands. Some are kiosks in malls; others are stand-alone with some picnic tables out front, as is the case at this location. **Known for:** boba teas in fun flavors like taro or pineapple; *opakapaka* (pink snapper) with garlic shrimp; affordable Vietnamese cuisine. ⑤ *Average main: $10 ⊠ 1824 Oihana St., Wailuku ☎ 808/249–8833 ⊕ balemaui.com ⊗ Closed Sun. ⋔ Casual.*

Farmacy Health Bar

$ | VEGETARIAN | Set in Wailuku's historic downtown, this casual stop is the place to check-in for an acai bowl, heaping kale salad, or tempeh and avocado sandwich. The smoothies are fresh and flavorful; take a sip of the "Maui Girl." It's a takeout spot so order to-go or have it delivered. **Known for:** delicious BBQ jackfruit sandwiches; green smoothies; *pono* (vegan and gluten-free soup). $ *Average main: $10* ⊠ *12 Market St., Wailuku* ☎ *808/866-4312* ⊕ *thefarmacymaui.com.*

Hotels

★ The Old Wailuku Inn at Ulupono

$$ | B&B/INN | Built in 1924 and listed on the State of Hawaii Register of Historic Places, this home with knowledgeable innkeepers offers the charm of old Hawaii, including authentic decor and architecture. **Pros:** walking distance to civic center, restaurants, historic Wailuku Town; lovely garden setting; immaculately maintained. **Cons:** traffic noise at certain times; parking can be tight; closest beach is a 15-minute drive away. $ *Rooms from: $185* ⊠ *2199 Kahookele St., Wailuku* ☎ *808/244–5897 local, 800/305–4899 toll free* ⊕ *mauiinn.com* ⤴ *10 rooms* ⦿❘ *Free Breakfast.*

Ⓨ Nightlife

Wai Bar

BARS | For the most part, Wailuku town goes quiet once the office workers clock out and the shops close for the day. Wai Bar is the exception, and to the delight of locals, this neighborhood hangout has become the go-to spot for late-night fun. There's a small dance floor, karaoke night, a patio out back, and an eclectic mix of live jazz, lounge music, and other funky tunes usually streaming. They don't serve food, but the craft cocktails and good vibes are the real draw. ⊠ *45 N. Market St., Unit B, Wailuku* ☎ *808/214–9829* ⊕ *waibarmaui.com* ⦿ *Closed Sun.*

🎭 Performing Arts

Maui Academy of Performing Arts

THEATER | FAMILY | Founded in 1974, this nonprofit performing arts group offers productions, as well as dance and drama classes for children and teens. Recent shows have included *Alice in Wonderland, Into the Woods, Nutcracker Sweets, Songs for a New World,* and *Disney's Frozen, Jr.* ⊠ *2050 Main St., Suite 3G, Wailuku* ☎ *808/244–6272* ⊕ *mauiacademy.org.*

Maui OnStage

THEATER | FAMILY | Located at the Historic Iao Theater in charming Wailuku Town, this nonprofit theater group stages several shows each season. Performances alternate between benefit concerts, plays, poetry slams, comedy nights, and more. The audience is mostly locals, but visitors are always welcome. Purchasing tickets in advance is recommended. ⊠ *Historic Iao Theater, 68 N. Market St., Wailuku* ☎ *808/242–6969* ⊕ *mauionstage.com.*

🛍 Shopping

ARTS AND CRAFTS

★ Mele Ukulele

MUSIC | For a professional-quality, authentic ukulele, skip the souvenir shops. Mele's handcrafted beauties are made of koa or mahogany and strung and finished by expert craftsmen on the Island. Owner Michael Rock has consciously observed the cultural significance and importance of the ukulele to the Hawaiian people and their music, by creating instruments for everyone from *kupuna* to *keiki* (grandparents to children). There is a location at The Shops at Wailea and in Paia. ⊠ *1750 Kaahumanu Ave., Wailuku* ☎ *808/244–3938* ⊕ *meleukulele.com* ⦿ *Closed Sun.*

★ Native Intelligence

OTHER SPECIALTY STORE | This store in the heart of Wailuku champions cultural traditions and craftsmanship. It has curated Hawaiian and Polynesian works of art that include traditional wear, jewelry, weaponry, photography, books, music, hula instruments, and even surfboards. ✉ *1980 Main St., Wailuku* ☎ *808/249–2421* ⊕ *native-intel.com* ☉ *Closed Sun.*

Sandell Artworks

ART GALLERIES | Cheeky celebrity portraits, trippy cartoons, and whimsical Maui scenes line the walls of this art gallery and studio run by the equally eclectic namesake artist. Sandell's affordable art comes in various sizes, and some designs are printed on T-shirts. ✉ *34 N. Market St., Wailuku* ☎ *808/249–2456* ⊕ *facebook.com/sandellartworks.*

CLOTHING

Ha Wahine

WOMEN'S CLOTHING | At this women's clothing store, statement Polynesian prints are redefined in vibrantly colored blouses, *pareos* (beach wraps), dresses, and aloha shirts. All clothing is designed and made locally, as is most of the jewelry. ✉ *53 N. Market St., Wailuku* ☎ *808/344–1642* ⊕ *facebook.com/hawahine* ☉ *Closed Sun.*

Chapter 6

UPCOUNTRY

Updated by
Syndi Texeira

👁 **Sights** 🍴 **Restaurants** 🛏 **Hotels** 🛍 **Shopping** 🍸 **Nightlife**
★★★★★   ★★★★★   ★★★★☆   ★★★☆☆   ★★☆☆☆

WELCOME TO UPCOUNTRY

TOP REASONS TO GO

★ **Discover a cozier side of paradise.** While Maui has become famous for its beaches, the majestic landscapes of Upcountry are equally enticing—be sure to pack a sweater.

★ **See a pineapple farm.** The former sugar plantation area of Haliimaile is an off-the-beaten-path locale lined with quiet streets and smaller homes that retains its rustic feel.

★ **Experience cowboy culture.** Makawao is synonymous with the *paniolo* (cowboy) lifestyle. The Makawao Rodeo and Parade is an annual tradition now more than sixty years in the making.

★ **Get a taste of farm country.** Kula sees primarily sunny days and crisp nights, a perfect environment for growing food.

★ **Sip wines made on Maui.** Once the haunt of Hawaiian royalty and other Island elites, MauiWine's picturesque estate is now home to tasting rooms where you can sample pineapple wines, sparkling wines, and exclusive bottlings.

Rolling pastures, romantic winding roads, and incredible panoramic vistas await you in this region of Maui, known for stunning views, the crown jewel Haleakala National Park, and its otherworldly crater, wine tastings, scenic farms, agriculture, and more. Most come here for a day trip as it is not too far from the South Shore and West Maui regions; it's also a quick drive from Kahului Airport. Comprised of several towns, "Upcountry" describes the areas that climb up the slope of Haleakala, including Haliimaile, Makawao, and Kula. Don't be fooled by the "Upcountry" moniker that groups these towns—each area offers a unique Maui lifestyle and community. Haliimaile was once a bustling plantation town. Today, it's home to a culinary gem, Haliimaile General Store. Haliimaile's agricultural heritage continues; you can visit a working pineapple farm and factory that's home to extra-sweet Maui Gold pineapples. For this chapter, we have divided up the regions: Haleakala National Park, the town of Kula and Kula Highway, and the town of Makawao.

1 Haleakala National Park. Haleakala National Park, which you can choose to view from above via helicopter or hike and explore up-close, is a true highlight of the entire island of Maui. The surreal wonders of Haleakala National Park can be experienced in several ways—from watching the sunrise atop the summit to daylong hikes and overnight wilderness camping. There are two sides of the park to explore. (*See the East Maui chapter for sights and destinations on the back side of Haleakala National Park.*) The focal point of the park, of course, is Mt. Haleakala. Culturally significant, Haleakala spans 34,000 acres from sea level to the 10,023-foot summit and offers numerous hiking trails, campsites, and unparalleled wilderness experiences.

2 Kula and Kula Highway. Nestled along the mountainside at about 3,000 feet, Kula sees primarily sunny days and crisp nights, a perfect

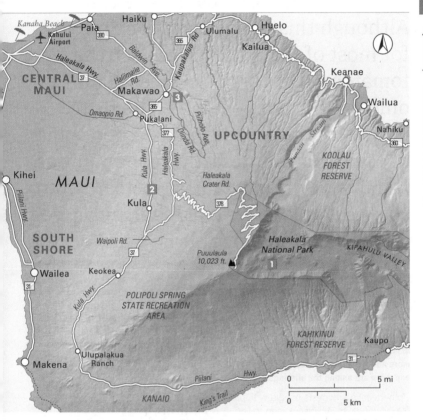

environment for growing food. This area has long been Maui's "breadbasket," producing a variety of fresh produce, including its world-famous onions and strawberries. Known for its rural scenery and rich agricultural heritage, the town of Kula is home to large-scale farmers, boutique growers, and agritourism operations that showcase locally grown produce. Route 37, also known as Haleakala Highway, runs into Route 377 (Kula Highway). Upper and Lower Kula highways are numbered 377 but join at two points.

3 Makawao. This distinctive town sits on the northwestern slope of Haleakala, surrounded by pastureland and forest. It's aptly named—Makawao translates to "eye of the forest." Makawao is also the heart and soul of Maui's *paniolo* (cowboy) heritage. The *paniolo* culture rose in the 19th century, influenced by vaqueros from California who were invited to the region by King Kamehameha III.

The west-facing upper slope of Haleakala is considered "Upcountry" by locals and is a hidden gem by most accounts. Although this region is responsible for most of Maui's produce—lettuce, tomatoes, strawberries, sweet Maui onions, and more—it is also home to innovators, renegades, artists, and some of Maui's most interesting communities. It may not be the Maui of postcards, but some say this is the real Maui and is well worth exploring for at least a day or two.

Upcountry is also fertile ranch land; *paniolo* (cowboys) still work the historic 18,000-acre Ulupalakua Ranch fields and the 30,000-acre Haleakala Ranch.

■ TIP→ **Take an agricultural tour and learn more about the Island's bounty. Lavender and wine are among the offerings.**

Up here cactus thickets mingle with purple jacaranda, wild hibiscus, and towering eucalyptus trees. Keep an eye out for *pueo*, Hawaii's native owl, which hunts these fields during daylight hours.

A drive to Upcountry Maui from Wailea (South Shore) or Kaanapali (West Maui) can be an all-day outing if you take the time to visit MauiWine and the tiny but entertaining town of Makawao. You may want to cut these side trips short and combine your Upcountry tour with a visit to Haleakala National Park (*see the Haleakala National Park feature in this chapter*)—it's a Maui must-see. Suppose you leave early enough to catch the sunrise from the summit of Haleakala. In that case, you should have plenty of time to explore the mountain, have lunch in Kula or at Ulupalakua Ranch, and end your day with dinner in Makawao.

Planning

Getting Here and Around

To get to this region, you can drive from Wailea (South Shore) or Kaanapali (West Maui). Wailea to the town of Kula is less than 27 miles via HI-37 and State Highway 31/Piilani Highway. Kaanapali is a bit farther: 40 miles from Kula via Honoapiilani Hwy and HI-37. You can also take a bus or shuttle from the Kahului airport (about 13 miles).

AIR

CONTACTS Kahului Airport (OGG). ✉ *1 Keolani Place, Kahului* ☎ *808/872–3830* ⊕ *airports.hawaii.gov/ogg.*

BUS

Maui Bus, operated by the tour company Roberts Hawaii, offers 12 routes in and between various Central, South, and West Maui communities. You can travel in and around Wailuku, Kahului, Lahaina, Kaanapali, Kapalua, Kihei, Wailea, Maalaea, the North Shore (Paia), and Upcountry (including Kula, Pukalani, Makawao, Haliimaile, and Haiku). The Upcountry and Haiku Islander routes include a stop at Kahului Airport. All routes cost $2 per boarding; children five and under ride free.

CONTACTS Maui Bus. ✉ *2145 Kaohu St., Suite 102, Wailuku* ☎ *808/871–4838* ⊕ *mauicounty.gov/bus.*

CAR

See the Travel Smart chapter for a list of car rental companies on Maui.

TAXI

CONTACTS Maui Airport Taxi & Shuttle. ✉ *576 Imi Drive, Wailuku* ☎ *808/877–2002* ⊕ *mauiairporttaxi-shuttle.com.* **SpeediShuttle.** ☎ *877/242–5777* ⊕ *speedishuttle.com.*

Hotels

B&Bs, inns, lodges, retreats, and private vacation homes offer spectacular views of the region.

Restaurants

From farm-to-table, Italian cuisine, food trucks, and general stores, there are plenty of standout dining options in Makawao, Haliimaile, and Kula.

HOTEL AND RESTAURANT PRICES

Hotel prices in the reviews are the lowest cost of a standard double room in high season. Restaurant prices in the reviews are the average cost of a main course at dinner, or if dinner is not served, at lunch.

WHAT IT COSTS in U.S. Dollars			
$	**$$**	**$$$**	**$$$$**
RESTAURANTS			
under $18	$18–$26	$27–$35	over $35
HOTELS			
under $181	$181–$260	$261–$340	over $340

Safety

Always call the National Weather Service to check the conditions before hiking Haleakala National Park. Winds, heavy rain, and snow may occur. ☎ *866/944–5025, option 4.*

Tours

Air Maui Helicopters

AIR EXCURSIONS | Priding itself on a perfect safety record, Air Maui provides 45-minute flights covering Haleakala Crater and Hana ($229). A deluxe package ($303) includes a cliffside landing. Discounts are available online. Charter flights are also available. ✉ *1 Kahului Airport Rd., Hangar 110, Kahului* ☎ *877/238–4942, 808/877–7005* ⊕ *airmaui.com.*

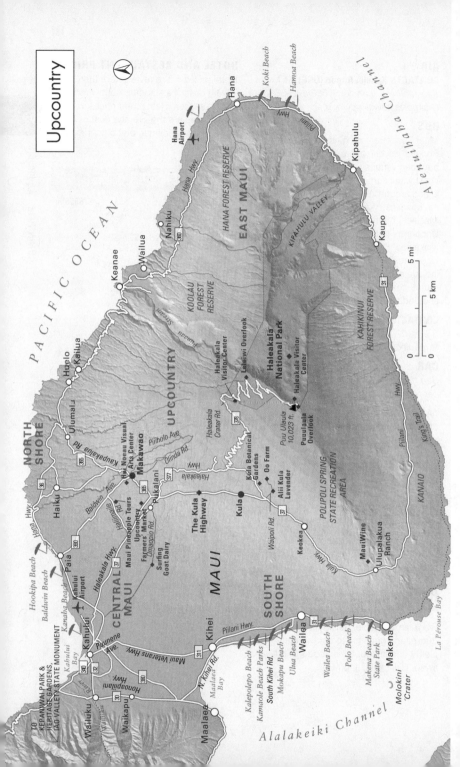

Upcountry

PACIFIC OCEAN

Alenuihaha Channel

Alalakeiki Channel

NORTH SHORE

CENTRAL MAUI

SOUTH SHORE

UPCOUNTRY

EAST MAUI

MAUI

HANA FOREST RESERVE

KOOLAU FOREST RESERVE

KIPAHULU VALLEY

KAHIKINUI FOREST RESERVE

KANAIO

POLIPOLI SPRING STATE RECREATION AREA

Haleakala National Park

Hana
Hana Airport
Hana Hwy
Koki Beach
Hamoa Beach
Kipahulu
Kaupo
Nahiku
Wailua
Keanae
Kailua
Huelo
Ulumalu
Haiku
Paia
Hookipa Beach
Baldwin Beach
Kanaha Beach
Kahului
Kahului Airport
Kahului Bay
Waikapu
Wailuku
Waihee
Maalaea
Maalaea Bay
Kihei
Wailea
Makena
Molokini Crater
La Perouse Bay

Pliholo Ave
Olinda Rd
Makawao
Hui Noeau Visual Arts Center
Kaupakalua Rd
Pukalani
Baldwin Ave
Haliimaile Rd
Maui Pineapple Tours
Upcountry Farmers' Market
Surfing Goat Dairy
Omaopio Rd
Haleakala Hwy
The Kula Highway
Kula
Kula Botanical Gardens
Oo Farm
Alii Kula Lavender
Keokea
Waipoli Rd
MauiWine
Ulupalakua Ranch
Kula Hwy

Haleakala Crater Rd
Haleakala Visitor Center
Leleiwi Overlook
Haleakala Visitor Center
Puu Ulaula 10,023 ft.
Puuulaula Overlook

King's Trail
Piilani
Pliani Hwy

Hana Hwy
Honoapiilani Hwy
Maui Veterans Hwy
Piilani Hwy
N. Kihei Rd.
S. Kihei Rd.
Piilani Ave
Puunene Ave

KEPANIWAI PARK & HERITAGE GARDENS, IAO VALLEY STATE MONUMENT

Kalepolepo Beach
Kamaole Beach Parks
South Kihei Rd.
Mokapu Beach
Ulua Beach
Wailea Beach
Polo Beach
Makena Beach State Park

36
360
365
390
37
377
378
31
311
30
32

5 mi
5 km
0
0

Waiehu Stream
Piinau Stream

Haleakala Visitor Center

Makawao

27 miles from Kahului.

Despite its easygoing pace and small-town feel, Makawao remains the center of Upcountry action. The area is synonymous with the rugged *paniolo* (cowboy) lifestyle, and cowboys and cowgirls still work the fields and care for the livestock as the generations before have. Festivities abound when the Makawao Rodeo and Parade trots into town, an annual tradition now more than 60 years in the making. Spend an afternoon in Makawao Town, centered at the crossroads of Makawao and Baldwin Avenues browsing upscale clothing boutiques and gift shops or talking to a local artist at one of the many galleries. Of course, no visit to Makawao is complete without a stop at Maui's infamous mom-and-pop landmark, T. Komoda Store and Bakery. Grab a cream puff or two and don't forget the butter rolls.

GETTING HERE AND AROUND

From Kahului, take Route 37 (Haleakala Highway) until you reach Makawao Avenue. Locate the center of Makawao Town by traveling along Makawao Avenue until you reach Baldwin Avenue.

◉ Sights

Hui Noeau Visual Arts Center

ARTS CENTER | The grande dame of Maui's visual arts scene, "the Hui," hosts exhibits that are always satisfying. Located just outside Makawao, the center's main building is an elegant two-story Mediterranean-style villa designed in 1917 by Hawaii's architect of the era, C. W. Dickey. Explore the grounds, see locally made products, and experience community enrichment through art. Crafts, drawing, photography, and glass blowing are some of the classes offered. ⌂ *2841 Baldwin Ave., Makawao*

☏ *808/572–6560* ⊕ *huinoeau.com* ✉ *Free to visit; self-guided tour booklets are $6* ◷ *Closed Sun., Mon., and Tues.*

Maui Pineapple Tours

FARM/RANCH | The quintessence of sun-blessed tropical flavor, pineapple exudes tropical happiness. It just so happens Maui boasts the only tour of a working pineapple plantation in the United States. You'll join a worker on a stroll through the sunny fields and hear all about the especially sweet Maui Gold pineapples (and sample its various stages of maturity along the way). The best part? Everyone gets a free pineapple at the end!

■ **TIP→ Maui Pineapple Tours partners with Haliimaile Distilling Company, inviting guests after the plantation tour to visit the distillery and taste such island treats as Pau Maui Vodka, the world's only pineapple vodka.**

For an additional cost, your tour can also include lunch at Haliimaile General Store just across the street. ⌂ *883 Haliimaile Rd., Makawao* ☏ *808/665–5491* ⊕ *mauipineappletour.com* ✉ *From $75.*

⑪ Restaurants

Casanova Italian Restaurant

$$$ | ITALIAN | An authentic Italian ristorante, Casanova is smack dab in the middle of Maui's *paniolo* (cowboy) town of Makawao. Imported from Italy, the brick wood-burning oven has turned out perfect pies and steaming-hot focaccia for more than 20 years. **Known for:** attentive staff and friendly atmosphere; decadent desserts; outstanding calamari. ⑤ *Average main: $30* ⌂ *1188 Makawao Ave., Makawao* ☏ *808/572–0220* ⊕ *casanovamaui.com.*

★ Freshies Maui

$ | ECLECTIC | While the rest of Makawao Town eases into the day, fuel up with a hearty breakfast at this garden café in the shade of a sprawling Argentinian coral tree. With options like huevos rancheros, French toast, and housemade biscuits and gravy, it feels like Sunday brunch every day. **Known for:** vegetarian and vegan options; local and organic ingredients; peaceful setting. $ *Average main: $13* ⊠ *3620 Baldwin Ave., Makawao* ☏ *808/868–2350* ⊕ *freshiesmaui.com* ⊘ *Closed Mon. and major holidays; no dinner.*

Polli's Mexican Restaurant

$ | MEXICAN | A Makawao staple since 1981, Polli's is set in the town's only intersection. Polli's is a lively Mexican restaurant that serves up the best fish tacos on the Island. **Known for:** huge dishes and family-style dining; tasty mango, strawberry, and *lilikoi* (Hawaiian passion fruit) margaritas; fun and friendly atmosphere. $ *Average main: $16* ⊠ *1202 Makawao Ave., Makawao* ☏ *808/572–7808* ⊕ *pollismexicanrestaurant.com* ⊘ *Closed Wed.*

★ T. Komoda Store and Bakery

$ | BAKERY | One of Makawao's landmarks is T. Komoda Store and Bakery, a mom-and-pop shop that has changed very little over the last century. **Known for:** amazing guava *malasadas* (Portuguese cream puffs); cool store with historic vibe; long but fast-moving lines. $ *Average main: $4* ⊠ *3674 Baldwin Ave., Makawao* ☏ *808/572–7261* ⊘ *Closed Wed. and Sun.* ☞ *Small parking lot to the right of building.*

⛾ Nightlife

Stopwatch Bar & Grill

BARS | This friendly dive bar hosts a popular karaoke night on Thursday from 7:30 to 10:30 pm. On tap, you'll find local Maui and Kona Brewing Company beers and happy hour from 3 to 6 pm daily. ⊠ *1127 Makawao Ave., Makawao* ☏ *808/572–1380* ⊕ *stopwatchbarandgrill.com.*

Maui's Best Omiyage 🍴

Omiyage is the Japanese term for souvenirs or small gifts you take home to family and friends.

- Lavender-salt seasoning from **Alii Kula Lavender**

- Peaberry beans from **Maui Coffee Company**

- Jeff's jams and jellies from **Paia Gelato**

- Hot sauces from **HI Spice**

🛍 Shopping

Beyond the resort areas and the airport retail strip, you can find some of Maui's most distinctive shops. Upcountry shopping centers around historic Makawao Town are home to art galleries, bohemian boutiques, and only-on-Maui gift shops. Upcountry is an ideal spot to find locally made creations and extra-special souvenirs.

ARTS AND CRAFTS

Hot Island Glass

GLASSWARE | With furnaces glowing bright orange and loads of mesmerizing sculptures on display, this glassworks is an exciting place to visit. The studio, set back from Makawao's main street in a little courtyard, is owned by a family of glassblowers. Open daily 9-5 pm. Call ahead for times the artists will be creating their masterpieces. ⊠ *3620 Baldwin Ave., #101-A, Makawao* ☏ *808/572–4527* ⊕ *hotislandglass.com.*

CLOTHING

Collections Maui

SOUVENIRS | This eclectic boutique is brimming with clothing, pretty jewelry, humorous gift cards, housewares, leather goods, yoga wear, and local beauty products. Collections Maui is a favorite among locals and visitors. ⊠ *3677 Baldwin Ave., Makawao* ☎ *808/572–0781.*

Designing Wahine Emporium and Hale Zen
HOUSEWARES | This Upcountry haven is a shopper's delight of beach luxe, wrapped in aloha, and sprinkled with zen. Featuring Hawaiian merchandise and Balinese imports, you'll find endless gift options like authentic aloha shirts, jams and jellies, children's clothes and books, bath and beauty products, and home decor. Find products from Capri Blue, Maka Sea, Velvet, Dolce Vita, and more. ⊠ *3640 Baldwin Ave., Makawao* ☎ *808/573–0990* ⊕ *halezen.com.*

Pink By Nature
MIXED CLOTHING | In 2004, Desiree Martinez established Pink By Nature in Makawao. She keeps her rustic store stocked with beautiful local jewelry and feminine pieces from brands such as Indah, Bella Dahl, and Novella Royale. Versatile plaid shirts from Rails are popular, along with stylish menswear and home decor. ⊠ *3663 Baldwin Ave., Makawao* ☎ *808/572–9576.*

GALLERIES
★ Sherri Reeve Gallery and Gifts
ART GALLERIES | Sherri Reeve is well-known for her watercolor pastel expressions of Maui's landscapes, flora, and fauna. Her origami-like sculpted works are sublime, and her designs have been applied to houseware goods that make for ideal gifts. The gallery is a family affair, and includes her niece Makana and her daughter Hailey. Stop in and marvel at the large paintings, clothes, matte prints, postcards, luggage tags, and more. ⊠ *3669 Baldwin Ave., Makawao* ☎ *808/572–8931* ⊕ *sreeve.com.*

Viewpoints Gallery
ART GALLERIES | This friendly gallery is co-owned by local artists and offers eclectic paintings, sculptures, photography, ceramics, and glass, along with locally made jewelry and quilts that celebrate Hawaii. Located in a cozy courtyard, the gallery's free monthly exhibits feature artists from various disciplines. ⊠ *3620 Baldwin Ave., Makawao* ☎ *808/280–2845* ⊕ *viewpointsgallery-maui.com.*

JEWELRY
Maui Master Jewelers
JEWELRY & WATCHES | The shop's exterior is as rustic as all the old buildings of Makawao and belies the elegance of the handcrafted jewelry displayed by more than 30 fine art jewelers. Each artist is unique, and expresses their designs using gold, silver, and platinum with colored gemstones, diamonds, and pearls. ⊠ *3655 Baldwin Ave., Makawao* ☎ *808/573–5400* ⊕ *mauimasterjewelers. com* ⊗ *Closed Sun. and Mon.*

Kula

15 miles east of Kahului; 44 miles east of Kaanapali; 28 miles east of Wailea.

Kula: most Mauians say it with a hint of a sigh. Why? It's just that much closer to heaven. On the broad shoulder of Haleakala, this is blessed country. From the Kula Highway most of Central Maui is visible—from the lava-scarred plains of Kanaio to the cruise ship–lighted waters of Kahului Harbor. Beyond the central valley's sugarcane fields, the plunging profile of the West Maui Mountains can be seen in its entirety, wreathed in ethereal mist. If this sounds too dramatic a description, you haven't been here yet. These views, coveted by many, continue to drive real-estate prices further skyward. Luckily, you can still have them for free—just pull over on the roadside and inhale the beauty. Explore it for yourself on some of the area's agricultural tours.

GETTING HERE AND AROUND

From Kahului, take Route 37 (Haleakala Highway), which runs into Route 377 (Kula Highway). Upper and Lower Kula highways are both numbered 377, but join each other at two points.

Sights

Alii Kula Lavender

FARM/RANCH | Created by Alii Chang, master horticulturist and visionary, Alii Kula Lavender farm has a falcon's view: it's *the* relaxing remedy for those suffering from too much sun, shopping, or golf. You can explore on your own or reserve a spot for the 30–40 minute tour that winds through paths of therapeutic lavender varieties, protea, and succulents. The gift shop has many locally made lavender products, such as honey, moisturizing lotions, and scone mixes. ⊠ *1100 Waipoli Rd., Kula* ☎ *808/878–3004* ⊕ *aklmaui. com* ✉ *$3, walking tours $12 (reservations recommended)* ⊗ *Closed Tues. to Thurs.*

Keokea

TOWN | More of a friendly gesture than a town, this tiny outpost is the last bit of civilization before Kula Highway becomes a winding back road. A coffee tree pushes through the sunny deck at Grandma's Coffee House, the morning watering hole for Maui's *paniolo* (cowboys) who work at Ulupalakua or Kaupo Ranch. Keokea Gallery next door sells cool, quirky artwork. And two tiny stores—Fong's and Ching's—are testament to the Chinese immigrants who settled the area in the late 19th century. ■**TIP**➜ **The only restroom for miles is in the public park, and the view makes stretching your legs worth it.** ⊠ *Kula.*

Kula Botanical Gardens

GARDEN | This picturesque garden has assimilated itself naturally into its precipitous 8-acre habitat. Over 2,500 plants

Fun Things to Do Upcountry

■ Nibble lavender scones with a view of the Valley Isle at Alii Kula Lavender Farm.

■ Taste pineapple wine at MauiWine.

■ Sit on the wraparound porch at Haliimaile General Store and dine on Hawaii regional cuisine.

and trees fill the enchanted garden, including native koa (prized by woodworkers) and *kukui* (the state tree, a symbol of enlightenment). A flowing stream feeds into a koi pond, where nene and ducks meander, and a paved pathway—stroller- and wheelchair-friendly—winds throughout the grounds. The new carved tiki exhibit, aviary, and Jackson chameleon exhibit entertain the *keiki* (children) ⊠ *638 Kekaulike Hwy., Kula* ☎ *808/878–1715* ⊕ *kulabotanicalgarden.com* ✉ *$10.*

★ MauiWine

WINERY | Maui's only winery in Ulupalakua is located on the former Rose Ranch on historical grounds. Stop by to learn about its history—which includes visits by monarchs, sugar production, and cattle ranching—and to sample its coveted wines. The King's Cottage was built in the late 1800s for frequent appearances from King Kalakaua, but today, tastings are held daily. A more intimate tasting held in the Old Jail building sometimes includes unreleased wines or special bottlings. Naturally, the winery's top seller is the pineapple wine Maui Blanc. ⊠ *Ulupalakua Vineyards, 14815 Piilani Hwy., Kula* ☎ *808/878–6058* ⊕ *mauiwine. com* ✉ *Free* ⊗ *Closed Mon.*

There are 2,500 species of plants and trees in Kula Botanical Garden.

★ Oo Farm

FARM/RANCH | About a mile from Alii Kula Lavender are 8 acres of organic salad greens, herbs, vegetables, coffee, cocoa, fruits, and berries—and the public is welcome to enjoy the bounty. Oo Farm is owned and operated by the restaurateurs responsible for one of Maui's finest dining establishments, PacificO, and more than 300 pounds of produce end up on diners' plates every week. Reserve a space for the breakfast or lunch tours that include an informational walk around the pastoral grounds and an alfresco meal prepared by an on-site chef. Cap off the experience with house-grown roasted and brewed coffee. Reservations are required. ⊠ *651 Waipoli Rd., Kula* ☎ *808/856–0965* ⊕ *oofarm.com* ✉ *Lunch tour from $125* ⊗ *Closed weekends.*

Surfing Goat Dairy

FARM/RANCH | FAMILY | It takes goats to make goat cheese, and they've got plenty of both at this 42-acre farm. The owners make more than two dozen kinds of goat cheese, from the plain, creamy "Udderly Delicious" to more exotic varieties that include tropical ingredients; all are available in the dairy store, along with gift baskets and even goat-milk soaps. Book your reservation online for the 30-minute walking tour of the dairy and farm, which run throughout the day. The Evening Chores and Milking Tour is educational and fun if you have the time; reservations are recommended. ⊠ *3651 Omaopio Rd., Kula* ☎ *808/878–2870* ⊕ *surfinggoatdairy.com* ✉ *Free, tours $12–$39* ⊗ *Closed Sun. and Mon.*

★ Upcountry Farmers' Market

MARKET | Most of Maui's produce is grown Upcountry, which is why everything is fresh at this outdoor market located next to Long's in the Kulamalu Town Center. Every Saturday from 7 to 11 am, vendors offer fruits, vegetables, flowers, jellies, bread, plus unique finds like venison, kimchi, and fresh caught fish. Prepared food offerings reflect the island's cultural melting pot, and there's an excellent selection of vegan and raw food. Go early, as nearly everything sells out. ⊠ 55 Kiopaa St., Pukalani ⊕ upcountryfarmersmarket.com 🖾 Free.

🍴 Restaurants

Take the drive up the slopes of magnificent Mt. Haleakala and you can find an abundance of restaurants catering to both locals and visitors. Haliimaile General Store is a landmark in the middle of rolling pineapple fields and the town of Haliimaile. In Makawao, you can sidle up to everything from an authentic Italian restaurant, landmark bakery, and a farm-to-table standout. Upcountry also encompasses Kula, with a few mom-and-pops, ranch stores, and grills. Many visitors opt to check out nearby farm tours between meals.

★ Haliimaile General Store
$$$$ | MODERN HAWAIIAN | Chef-restaurateur Beverly Gannon's first restaurant remains a culinary destination after more than 30 years, serving exquisite dishes like Bev's Famous Crab Pizza, sashimi napoleon, BBQ pork sandwich, and the macadamia nut–crusted fresh catch. There are daily and nightly specials, hand-crafted cocktails, and local beers as well. **Known for:** exquisite dining in an unlikely location; Hawaii regional cuisine; Bev Gannon's classic recipes. ⑤ Average main: $40 ⊠ 900 Haliimaile Rd., Haliimaile ⊹ Take exit on the left halfway up Haleakala Hwy. ☎ 808/572–2666 ⊕ hgsmaui.com ⊘ Closed Sun. and Mon.

Kula Bistro
$$ | ITALIAN | FAMILY | Nestled on the slopes of Haleakala, this bistro's atmosphere is reminiscent of trattorias in northern Italy. Serving up home-style food with a splash of Italian, this eatery makes the scenic drive worth it. **Known for:** family- and group-friendly; impressive desserts; BYOB. ⑤ Average main: $25 ⊠ 4566 Lower Kula Rd., Kula ☎ 808/871–2960 ⊕ kulabistro.com ⊘ No breakfast on Mon.

Nui's Garden Kitchen
$ | THAI | This roadside Thai food truck fronts the 40-acre Maui Nui Farm, owned by Nui and Kit. You can expect fresh produce and ingredients that change with the seasons. **Known for:** outdoor seating with views of Haleakala; excellent peanut sauce; farm-fresh ingredients. ⑤ Average main: $12 ⊠ 151 Pulehunui Rd., Kula ☎ 808/264–1103 ⊕ mauinuifarm.com.

☕ Coffee and Quick Bites

Grandma's Coffee House
$ | AMERICAN | FAMILY | If you're taking a drive through the gorgeous Upcountry, this is a great place to stop for a truly homegrown, organic cup of coffee. The Franco family has been perfecting their coffee since 1918, growing the beans, handpicking, drying them under the Maui sun, then roasting them at the coffeehouse. **Known for:** tasty, generously portioned breakfasts; idyllic country location best viewed from the back deck; fresh-pressed juices. ⑤ Average main: $12 ⊠ 9232 Kula Hwy., Keokea ☎ 808/878–2140 ⊕ grandmascoffeehousemaui.com 🏛 Casual.

Haleakala National Park

15 miles from Kula.

From the tropics to the moon! Two hours, 38 miles, 10,023 feet—those are the unlikely numbers involved in reaching Maui's highest point, the summit of the volcano Haleakala. Haleakala Crater is the park's centerpiece, though it's not actually a crater; technically, it's an erosional valley flushed out by water pouring from

Continued on page 151

HALEAKALA NATIONAL PARK

From the Tropics to the Moon! Two hours, 38 miles, 10,023 feet—those are the unlikely numbers involved in reaching Maui's highest point, the summit of the volcano Haleakala. Nowhere else on earth can you drive from sea level (Kahului) to 10,023 feet (the summit) in only 38 miles. And what's more shocking—in that short vertical ascent, you'll journey from lush, tropical-island landscape to the stark, moonlike basin of the volcano's enormous, otherworldly crater.

Established in 1916, Haleakala National Park covers an astonishing 33,222 acres. Haleakala "Crater" is the centerpiece of the park though it's not actually a crater. Technically, it's an erosional valley, flushed out by water pouring from the summit through two enormous gaps. The mountain has terrific camping and hiking, including a trail that loops through the crater, but the chance to witness this unearthly landscape is reason enough for a visit.

THE CLIMB TO THE SUMMIT

To reach Haleakala National Park and the mountain's breathtaking summit, take Route 36 east of Kahului to the Haleakala Highway (Route 37). Head east, up the mountain to the unlikely intersection of Haleakala Highway and Haleakala Highway. If you continue straight the road's name changes to Kula Highway (still Route 37). Instead, turn left onto Haleakala Highway—this is now Route 377. After about 6 miles, make a left onto

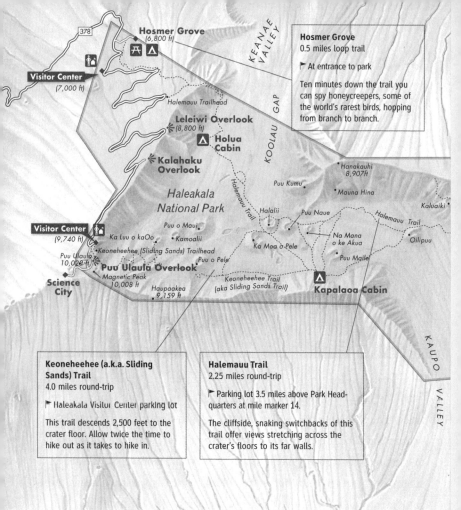

Hosmer Grove
(6,800 ft)

378

Visitor Center
(7,000 ft)

Halemauu Trailhead

Leleiwi Overlook
(8,800 ft)

Holua Cabin

Kalahaku Overlook

Haleakala National Park

K E A N A E   V A L L E Y

K O O L A U   G A P

Hanakauhi
8,907 ft

Puu Kumu

Mauna Hina

Kaluaiki

Halemauu Trail

Halalii

Puu Naue

Halemauu Trail

Oilipuu

Visitor Center
(9,740 ft)

Ka Luu o kaOo

Kamoali'i

Puu o Maui

Keoneheehee (Sliding Sands) Trailhead

Na Mana o ke Akua

Ka Moa o-Pele

Puu Mgile

Puu Ulaula
10,028 ft

Puu Ulaula Overlook

Puu o Pele

Magnetic Peak
10,008 ft

Haupaakea
9,159 ft

Keoneheehee Trail
(aka Sliding Sands Trail)

Kapalaoa Cabin

Science City

K A U P O   V A L L E Y

Hosmer Grove
0.5 miles loop trail

▶ At entrance to park

Ten minutes down the trail you can spy honeycreepers, some of the world's rarest birds, hopping from branch to branch.

Keoneheehee (a.k.a. Sliding Sands) Trail
4.0 miles round-trip

▶ Haleakala Visitor Center parking lot

This trail descends 2,500 feet to the crater floor. Allow twice the time to hike out as it takes to hike in.

Halemauu Trail
2.25 miles round-trip

▶ Parking lot 3.5 miles above Park Headquarters at mile marker 14.

The cliffside, snaking switchbacks of this trail offer views stretching across the crater's floors to its far walls.

Crater Road (Route 378). After several long switchbacks (look out for downhill bikers!) you'll come to the park entrance.

■ **TIP→ Before you head up Haleakala, call for the latest park weather conditions (☎ 866/944–5025). Extreme gusty winds, heavy rain, and even snow in winter are not uncommon. Because of the high altitude, the mountaintop temperature is often as much as 30 degrees cooler than that at sea level. Be sure to bring a jacket. Also make sure you have a full tank of gas. No service stations exist beyond Kula.**

There's a car fee to enter the park; but it's good for three days and can be used

at Oheo Gulch (Kipahulu), so save your receipt.

6,800 feet, Hosmer Grove. Just as you enter the park, Hosmer Grove has campsites and interpretive trails. Park rangers maintain a changing schedule of talks and hikes both here and at the top of the mountain. Call the park for current schedules.

7,000 feet, Park Headquarters/Visitor Center. Not far from Hosmer Grove, the Park Headquarters/Visitor Center has trail maps and displays about the volcano's origins and eruption history. Hikers and campers should check-in here before

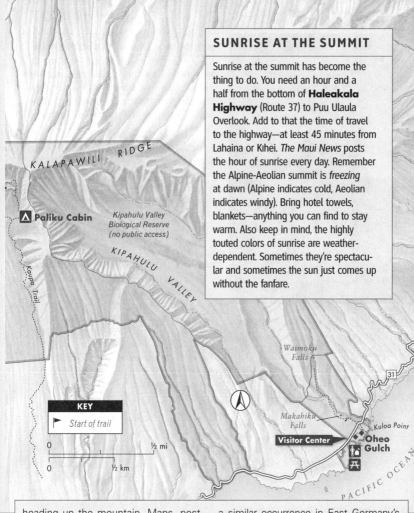

SUNRISE AT THE SUMMIT

Sunrise at the summit has become the thing to do. You need an hour and a half from the bottom of **Haleakala Highway** (Route 37) to Puu Ulaula Overlook. Add to that the time of travel to the highway—at least 45 minutes from Lahaina or Kihei. *The Maui News* posts the hour of sunrise every day. Remember the Alpine-Aeolian summit is *freezing* at dawn (Alpine indicates cold, Aeolian indicates windy). Bring hotel towels, blankets—anything you can find to stay warm. Also keep in mind, the highly touted colors of sunrise are weather-dependent. Sometimes they're spectacular and sometimes the sun just comes up without the fanfare.

KALAPAWILI RIDGE

KALAPAWILI

Paliku Cabin

Kipahulu Valley
Biological Reserve
(no public access)

KIPAHULU VALLEY

Kaupo Trail

Waimoku
Falls

31

KEY

Start of trail

Makahiku
Falls

Kuloa Point

Visitor Center

Oheo Gulch

0 ½ mi

0 ½ km

PACIFIC OCEAN

heading up the mountain. Maps, posters, and other memorabilia are available at the gift shop.

8,800 feet, Leleiwi Overlook. Continuing up the mountain, you come to Leleiwi Overlook. A short walk to the end of the parking lot reveals your first awe-inspiring view of the crater. The small hills in the basin are volcanic cinder cones (called *puu* in Hawaiian), each with a small crater at its top, and each the site of a former eruption.

If you're here in the late afternoon, it's possible you'll experience a phenomenon called the Brocken Specter. Named after a similar occurrence in East Germany's Harz Mountains, the "specter" allows you to see yourself reflected on the clouds and encircled by a rainbow. Don't wait all day for this because it's not a daily occurrence.

9,000 feet, Kalahaku Overlook. The next stopping point is Kalahaku Overlook. The view here offers a different perspective of the crater, and at this elevation the famous silversword plant grows amid the cinders. This odd, endangered beauty grows only here and at the same elevation on the Big Island's two peaks. It begins life as a silver, spiny-leaf rosette and is the sole home of a variety of native

■TIP➔The air is very thin at 10,000 feet. Don't be surprised if you feel a little breathless while walking around the summit. Take it easy and drink lots of water. Anyone who has been scuba diving within the last 24 hours should not make the trip up Haleakala.

On a small hill nearby, you can see **Science City**, an off-limits research and communications center straight out of an espionage thriller. The University of Hawaii maintains an observatory here, and the Department of Defense tracks satellites.

HIKING AND CAMPING

Exploring Haleakala Crater is one of the best hiking experiences on Maui. The volcanic terrain offers an impressive diversity of colors, textures, and shapes—almost as if the lava has been artfully sculpted. The barren landscape is home to many plants, insects, and birds that exist nowhere else on earth and have developed intriguing survival mechanisms, such as the sun-reflecting, hairy leaves of the silversword, which allow it to survive the intense climate.

Stop at park headquarters to register and pick up trail maps on your way into the park.

1-Hour Hike. Just as you enter Haleakala National Park, Hosmer Grove offers a short 10-minute hike and an hour-long, ½-mile loop trail that will give you insight into Hawaii's fragile ecology. Anyone can go on these hikes, whereas a longer trail through the Waikamoi Cloud Forest is accessible only with park ranger–guided hikes. Call park headquarters for the schedule. Facilities here include six campsites (no permit needed, available on a first-come, first-served basis), pit toilets, drinking water, and cooking shelters.

insects (it's the only shelter around). The silversword reaches maturity between 7 and 17 years, when it sends forth a 3- to 8-foot-tall stalk with several hundred tiny sunflowers. It blooms once, then dies.

9,740 feet, Haleakala Visitor Center. Another mile up is the Haleakala Visitor Center, open daily from sunrise to 3 pm except Christmas and New Year's. There are exhibits inside, and a trail from here leads to White Hill—a short easy walk that will give you an even better view of the valley.

10,023 feet, Puu Ulaula Overlook. The highest point on Maui is the Puu Ulaula Overlook, at the 10,023-foot summit. Here you find a glass-enclosed lookout with a 360-degree view. The building is open 24 hours a day, and this is where visitors gather for the best sunrise view. Dawn begins between 5:45 and 7, depending on the time of year. On a clear day you can see the islands of Molokai, Lanai, Kahoolawe, and Hawaii (the Big Island). On a *really* clear day you can even spot Oahu glimmering in the distance.

4-Hour Hikes. Two half-day hikes involve descending into the crater and returning the way you came. The first, Halemauu Trail (trailhead is between mile markers 14 and 15), is 2.25 miles round-trip. The cliffside, snaking switchbacks of this trail offer views stretching across the crater's puu-speckled floor to its far walls. On clear days you can peer through the Koolau Gap to Hana. Native flowers and shrubs grow along the trail, which is typically misty and cool (though still exposed to the sun). When you reach the gate at the bottom, head back up.

The other hike, which is 5 miles round-trip, descends down Keoneheehee (aka Sliding Sands) Trail (trailhead is at the Haleakala Visitor Center) into an alien landscape of reddish black cinders, lava bombs, and silverswords. It's easy to imagine life before humans in the solitude and silence of this place. Turn back when you hit the crater floor.

■ TIP→ **Bring water, sunscreen, and a reliable jacket. These are demanding hikes. Take it slowly to acclimate, and allow additional time for the uphill return trip.**

8-Hour Hike. The recommended way to explore the crater in a single, but full day is to go in two cars and ferry yourselves back and forth between the head of Halemauu Trail and the summit. This way, you can hike from the summit down Keoneheehee Trail, cross the crater's floor, investigate the Bottomless Pit and Pele's Paint Pot, then climb out on the switchback trail (Halemauu). When you emerge, the shelter of your waiting car will be very welcome (this is an 11.2-mile hike). If you don't have two cars, hitching a ride from Halemauu back to the summit should be relatively safe and easy.

■TIP→ **Take a backpack with lunch, water, sunscreen, and a reliable jacket for the beginning and end of the 8-hour hike. This is a demanding trip, but you will never regret or forget it.**

Overnight Hike. Staying overnight in one of Haleakala's three cabins or two wilderness campgrounds is an experience like no other. You'll feel like the only person on earth when you wake up inside this enchanted, strange landscape. The cabins, each tucked in a different corner of the crater's floor, are equipped with 12 bunk beds, wood-burning stoves, fake logs, and kitchen gear.

Holua cabin is the shortest hike, less than 4 hours (3.7 miles) from Halemauu Trail. *Kapalaoa* is about 5 hours (5.5 miles) down Keoneheehee Trail. The most cherished cabin is *Paliku*, an eight-hour (9.3-mile) hike starting from either trail. It's nestled against the cliffs above Kaupo Gap. Cabin reservations can be made up to 90 days in advance. Tent campsites at Holua and Paliku are free and easy to reserve on a first-come, first-served basis.

■TIP→ **Toilets and nonpotable water are available—bring iodine tablets to purify the water. Open fires are not allowed and packing out your trash is mandatory.**

For more information on hiking or camping, contact the National Park Service (✉ *Box 369, Makawao 96768* ☏ *808/572–4400* ⊕ *www.nps.gov/halo*).

OPTIONS FOR EXPLORING

If you're short on time you can drive to the summit, take a peek inside, and drive back down. But the "House of the Sun" is really worth a day, whether you explore by foot, horseback, or helicopter.

BIKING
At this writing, all guided bike tours inside park boundaries were suspended indefinitely. However, the tours continue but now start outside the boundary of the park. These can provide a speedy, satisfying downhill trip. The park is still open to individual bikes for a fee. There are no bike paths, however—just the same road that is used by vehicular traffic. Whether you're on your own or with a tour, be careful!

HELICOPTER TOURS
Viewing Haleakala from above can be a mind-altering experience, if you don't mind dropping $229+ per person for a few blissful moments above the crater. Most tours buzz Haleakala, where airspace is regulated, then head over to Hana in search of waterfalls.

HORSEBACK RIDING
Several companies offer half-day, full-day, and even overnight rides into the crater. On one half-day ride you descend into the crater on Keoneheehee Trail and have lunch before you head back.

the summit through two enormous gaps. The mountain has excellent camping and hiking, including a trail that loops through the crater, but the chance to witness this unearthly landscape is reason enough for a visit. Another section of the park, Oheo Gulch in Kipahulu, can be reached only via the Road to Hana.

Exploring Haleakala Crater is one of the best hiking experiences on Maui. The volcanic terrain offers an impressive diversity of colors, textures, and shapes—as if the lava has been artfully sculpted. The barren landscape is home to many plants, insects, and birds that exist nowhere else on earth and has developed intriguing survival mechanisms, such as the sun-reflecting, hairy leaves of the silversword, which allow it to survive the intense climate.

GETTING HERE AND AROUND

To reach Haleakala National Park and the mountain's breathtaking summit, take Route 36 east of Kahului to the Haleakala Highway (Route 37). Head east, up the mountain to the unlikely intersection of Haleakala Highway and Haleakala Highway. If you continue straight the road's name changes from Kula Highway (still Route 37). Instead, turn left onto Haleakala Highway—this is now Route 377. After about six miles, make a left onto Crater Road (Route 378). After several long switchbacks (look out for downhill bikers), you'll come to the park entrance.

VISITOR INFORMATION

Haleakala Visitor Center

VISITOR CENTER | Located at the crater summit, the visitor center has exhibits inside and a trail that leads to Pa Kaoao (White Hill)—a short, easy walk with even better views of the valley. Call ahead for hours of operation. ⊠ *Haleakala Hwy., Makawao* ☎ *808/572–4459* ⊕ *nps. gov/hale* ⊠ *Free; parking is $30 per vehicle.*

◉ Sights

★ Haleakala National Park

NATIONAL PARK | Nowhere else on Earth can you drive from sea level to 10,023 feet in only 38 miles. And what's more shocking: in that short vertical ascent to the summit of the volcano Haleakala you'll journey from lush, tropical island landscape to the stark, moon-like basin of the volcano's enormous, otherworldly crater.

Established in 1916, Haleakala National Park covers an astonishing 33,222 acres, with the Haleakala Crater as its centerpiece. There's terrific hiking, including trails for one-hour, four-hour, eight-hour, and overnight hikes, one of which goes through the Waikamoi Cloud Forest on Monday and Thursday only and requires reservations (call the park line no more than a week in advance). No other hikes require reservations. There is also on-site camping.

■ **TIP→ Before you head up Haleakala, call for the latest weather conditions. Extreme gusty winds, heavy rain, and even snow in winter are not uncommon. Because of the high altitude, the mountaintop temperature is often as much as 30°F cooler than that at sea level, so bring a jacket.**

There's a $30-per-car fee to enter the park, good for three days. Hold on to your receipt—it can also be used at Oheo Gulch in Kipahulu. Once inside the park, stop at the Park Headquarters to learn about the volcano's history, and pick up trail maps (and memorabilia, if you want) at the gift shop. Campers and hikers must check in here.

If you're planning to view the sunrise from the summit, you must make reservations (⊕ *recreation.gov*) up to 60 days before your visit. This allows you to enter the summit area between 3 and 7 am. A limited number of last-minute tickets are released online two days beforehand, but these can be difficult to secure. If you don't snag one of these coveted spots, consider visiting for sunset, which, on most days, offers equally stunning views. ■ TIP→ **The air is thin at 10,000 feet. Don't be surprised if you feel a little breathless while walking around the summit. Take it easy, and drink lots of water. Anyone who has been scuba diving within the last 24 hours should not make the trip up Haleakala.** ✉ *Haleakala Crater Rd., Makawao* ☎ *808/572–4400, 866/944–5025 for weather conditions* ⊕ *nps.gov/hale* 💲 *$30 per vehicle.*

Leleiwi Overlook

VIEWPOINT | Located at about the 8,800-foot level, the Leleiwi Overlook offers your first awe-inspiring view of the crater. The small hills in the basin are *puu* (cinder cones). If you're here in the late afternoon, it's possible you'll see yourself reflected on the clouds and encircled by a rainbow—a phenomenon called the Brocken Specter. Don't wait long for this, because it's not a daily occurrence. ✉ *Off Haleakala Hwy., Makawao.*

Puuulaula Overlook

VIEWPOINT | The highest point on Maui is this 10,023-foot summit, where a glass-enclosed lookout provides a 360-degree view. The building is open 24 hours a day, and this is where many visitors gather to view the sunrise. Bring jackets, warm layers, hats, and blankets to stay warm on the cold and windy summit. On a clear day, you can see the islands of Molokai, Lanai, Kahoolawe, and Hawaii Island; on a crystal clear day, you can even spot Oahu glimmering in the distance. ✉ *Makawao.*

Chapter 7

NORTH SHORE

Updated by
Laurie Lyons-Makaimoku

⦿ Sights	🍴 Restaurants	🛏 Hotels	🛍 Shopping	🍸 Nightlife
★★★★☆	★★★☆☆	★★★☆☆	★★★★☆	★☆☆☆☆

WELCOME TO NORTH SHORE

TOP REASONS TO GO

★ **Have a beach picnic.** There are lots of great places to eat in Paia, many of which make for great picnic provisions.

★ **Sleep in splendor.** Some of the most beautiful and unique accommodations on the island are found on the North Shore, including Mama's Fish House Inn, Paia Inn, and Mangolani Inn.

★ **Play in the sand.** With some of the softest sand on the island, North Shore beaches are excellent for relaxing, building sandcastles, and walking along expansive stretches of shore.

★ **Shop, shop, and shop some more.** Between the boutiques and galleries in Paia and the Cannery shops in Haiku, there are plenty of places to spend your money.

★ **Look for turtles.** Beaches here are frequented by sea turtles that are looking for a snack or nap, making it easy to spot at least one. Just be sure to keep your distance and absolutely no touching!

An area where parts of Upcountry, the Road to Hana, and Central Maui blend into one another, the North Shore is a draw mainly for its sparsely populated beaches. A destination for pro surfers for its waves in the winter, this region has a rugged shoreline yet to become a victim of overtourism. The North Shore region is a fairly small one but manages to contain some of the island's best shopping, beaches, and restaurants. This is the gateway to the Road to Hana, and even if it isn't a large part of your visit, this beautiful area deserves your attention. The North Shore is home to the biggest swells on the Island, making it an ideal spot to watch surfers and kiteboarders while enjoying a picnic on the soft sand of one of the area beaches.

1 Paia. Paia is a historic town located on the north coast of Maui, about 4 miles from Kahului if you are headed in the direction of Hana; it is divided into Lower Paia and Paia. The fish market and Hookipa Beach are top destinations for this town, once a plantation town and an epicenter of the sugar cane industry on Maui. You'll find a communal and welcoming atmosphere here. Surfers come to this region for its waves in the winter and to compete in tournaments. It goes without mentioning that only pros should attempt to ride these waves. Paia Bay is popular among bodysurfers and bodyboarders (again, don't attempt either unless you're experienced). Baldwin Beach Park is another popular destination in the area, both for water sports and relaxation. Shopping and dining are the most popular activities in this funky little surf town full of souvenir shops, galleries, and bikini boutiques. Grabbing a bite to eat typically involves fresh fish or interesting international fusions.

2 Haiku. Rural and surreal in its untamed beauty, Haiku is all at once a destination for weddings, foodies (try the sushi), and animal lovers (Leilani Farm Sanctuary is home to many rescued animals). Haiku is also home to Twin Falls, a must-see. Luscious jungles abound in Haiku, which connects the Upcountry region to the North Shore and Road to Hana. Its two defunct pineapple

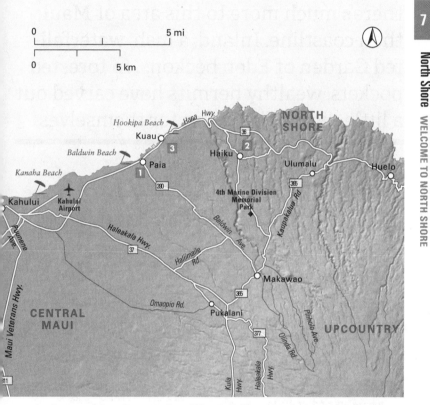

canneries turned shopping centers are focal points of the area, but there are also some hidden gems to look for, including surprisingly great dining.

3 Kuau. This blink-and-you'll-miss-it stretch of the road is anchored by two North Shore institutions, Mama's Fish House Restaurant and Inn, as well as Hookipa Beach and Lookout Point. Even if you don't dine or stay at Mama's, Kuau Cove next to the restaurant makes a great turtle-watching diversion. In fact, Kuau Cove is often referred to as "Mama's Fish House Beach," because of its proximity to the property. To add to the confusion, some locals even call it "Father Jules Papa," ("papa" meaning exposed reef; Father Jules was a well-known Kuau local). If anyone from your group is less interested in the epic waves of Paia's beaches, this cove is a good alternative for its much more manageable, yet still beautiful tidepools, flanked by a coconut grove.

Blasted by winter swells and wind, Maui's North Shore draws water-sports thrill seekers from around the world. But there's much more to this area of Maui than coastline. Inland, a lush, waterfall-fed Garden of Eden beckons. In forested pockets, wealthy hermits have carved out a little piece of paradise for themselves.

North Shore action centers on the colorful town of Paia and the windsurfing mecca of Hookipa Beach. It's a far cry from the more developed resort areas of West Maui and the South Shore. Paia is also a starting point for one of the most popular excursions in Maui, the Road to Hana. Waterfalls, phenomenal views of the coast and the ocean, and lush rainforest are all part of the spectacular 55-mile drive into East Maui.

Many of the people you see jaywalking in Paia sold everything they owned to come to Maui and live a beach bum's life. Beach culture abounds on the North Shore. But these folks aren't sunbathers; they're big-wave riders, windsurfers, or kiteboarders, and the North Shore is their challenging sports arena. Beaches here face the open ocean and tend to be rougher and windier than beaches elsewhere on Maui—but don't let that scare you off. On calm days the reef-speckled waters are truly beautiful and offer a quieter and less commercial beach-going experience than the leeward shore. Be sure to leave your locked car in a paved parking area so that it doesn't get stuck in soft sand.

Planning

Getting Here and Around

Traveling along the North Shore is mostly highway travel, thus walking from point to point is not easy (though once you arrive in the smaller towns, like Paia, you'll want to ditch your car for a while). Bus travel is available between Kahului, Paia, and Haiku, but if you're venturing past those points you'll need to rent a car. Budget travelers should search around for local outfitters, like North Shore Maui Rent-a-Car, that offer older vehicles at an affordable price (though some require minimum rentals, often around five days).

AIR

Kahului Airport (OGG) is a mere 8 miles from the North Shore, with easy access via car or the public bus system.

CONTACT Kahului Airport (OGG). ✉ *1 Keolani Pl., Kahului* ☎ *808/872–3830* ⊕ *airports.hawaii.gov/ogg.*

BUS

The Maui Public Bus services the North Shore via the Haiku Islander route, which includes a stop at Kahului Airport.

Maui Bus Public Transit System

BUS | The Maui county bus system provides access to the North Shore area with five stops, the last (and farthest east) of which is in Haiku. Roberts Hawaii operates the buses as a private contractor for the county. ⊠ *Maui County Offices, 200 S. High St., Wailuku* ☎ *808/871–4838 bus schedule line* ⊕ *mauicounty. gov/605/Bus-Service-Information.*

CAR

The majority of Maui's car rental facilities are located at or near Kahului Airport. For specialty vehicles like Jeeps or convertibles, you'll need to book early due to popularity. If you are looking for off-roading options you'll need to search for a peer-to-peer rental option, as rental car providers do not allow off-roading and most vehicles don't have four-wheel drive.

Maui Car Rentals

CAR RENTAL | This local car rental company offers weekly rental rates (minimum of seven days) on compact cars, vans, full-sized cars, and SUVs. Unlike most other rental companies, they will rent to drivers who are 21–24 years old for an additional daily fee. They also have car seats available for no extra charge. ⊠ *190D Papa Pl., Kahului* ☎ *808/877–3300 on Maui, 800/567–4659 toll free number* ⊕ *maui-carrentals.net.*

North Shore Maui Rent-a-Car

CAR RENTAL | Find everything from budget to luxury vehicles rented out from this local company owned by three champion windsurfers. Excellent rates combined with convenience and top-notch customer service make for a quick and easy rental car experience. A five-day minimum is required. ⊠ *1 Keolani Pl., Kahului* ☎ *623/850–3087* ⊕ *northshore-mauirentacar.com.*

TAXI

Taxi service is available on the North Shore from a variety of companies. Rates are standard and are set by Maui County.

CB Maui Taxi Service

TAXI | This family-owned and-operated taxi service is available 24/7, and can take you just about anywhere on the island. Complimentary car seats and booster seats are available upon request. Schedule your taxi ahead of time online or over the phone, or call them when you're ready for pick up. ⊠ *370 Molokai Hema St., Kahului* ☎ *808/243–8294* ⊕ *cbtaxi-maui.com.*

Hotels

You won't find any large resorts or condominium complexes along the North Shore, yet there's a variety of accommodations from the surf town of Paia, through tiny Kuau, and along the rain-forested Hana Highway through Haiku. Some are oceanfront but not necessarily beachfront (with sand); instead, look for tropical gardens overflowing with ginger, bananas, papayas, and nightly bug symphonies. Some have breathtaking views or the type of solitude that seeps in, easing your tension before you know it. You may encounter brief powerful downpours, but that's what makes this part of Maui green and lush. You'll need a car to enjoy staying on the North Shore.

Restaurants

The North Shore sets the dramatic stage for Maui's most famous restaurant, Mama's Fish House in Kuau. The area also encompasses the great food town of Paia and the up-and-coming restaurant town of Haiku. Be sure to bring your bathing suit for a dip in the ocean at one of the nearby beaches that make great locales for a picnic.

HOTEL AND RESTAURANT PRICES

Hotel prices in the reviews are the lowest cost of a standard double room in high season. Restaurant prices in the reviews are the average cost of a main course at dinner, or if dinner is not served, at lunch.

WHAT IT COSTS in U.S. Dollars

$	$$	$$$	$$$$
RESTAURANTS			
under $18	$18–$26	$27–$35	over $35
HOTELS			
under $181	$181–$260	$261–$340	over $340

Safety

When leaving your car be sure to hide property and lock doors. Try to avoid leaving phones, keys, and other personal belongings on the beach when you're in the water. Some of the beach pavilions in the area are occasionally host to some unsavory activities if they're not being used for gatherings, so it's best to avoid them.

Paia

9 miles east of Kahului; 4 miles west of Haiku.

At the intersection of Hana Highway and Baldwin Avenue, Paia has eclectic boutiques that supply everything from high fashion to hemp-oil candles. Some of Maui's best shops for surf trunks, Brazilian bikinis, and other beachwear are here. Restaurants provide excellent people-watching opportunities and an array of dining and takeout options, from flatbread to fresh fish. The abundance is helpful because Paia is the last place to snack before the pilgrimage to Hana and the first stop for the famished on the return trip. Its popularity has led to a bit of overcrowding, however, so bring your patience and be sure to leave plenty of time for parking (there are only a few public parking lots and they fill up quickly)

and for navigating crowds. Lunchtime is an especially busy time.

This little town on Maui's North Shore was once a sugarcane enclave, with a mill, plantation camps, and shops. The old sugar mill finally closed, but the town continues to thrive. In the 1970s Paia became a hippie town, as dropouts headed for Maui to open boutiques, galleries, and unusual eateries. In the 1980s, windsurfers—many of them European—discovered nearby Hookipa Beach and brought an international flavor to Paia. Today this historic town is hip and happening.

GETTING HERE AND AROUND
Route 36 (Hana Highway) runs directly though Paia; if you're journeying there from Upcountry, Route 37 can get you there, but not directly. You can take the Maui Bus from the airport and Queen Kaahumanu Shopping Center in Kahului to Paia.

🌀 Beaches

Those beautiful North Shore swells make the beaches in the area more likely to have water sports enthusiasts than swimmers on some days, but that doesn't mean that you can't enjoy a great beach day by lingering in the sand, soaking in the panoramic views, and taking walks along the surf.

Baldwin Beach
BEACH | FAMILY | A local favorite, this approximately 1-mile stretch of golden sand is a good place to stretch out, jog, or swim, although the waves can sometimes be choppy and the undertow strong. Don't be alarmed by those big brown blobs floating beneath the surface; they're just pieces of seaweed awash in the surf. You can find shade along the beach beneath the ironwood trees. Though there is a pavilion, it's not the safest place to hang out. Instead, take your picnics to the tree line and enjoy visits from friendly birds and dogs.

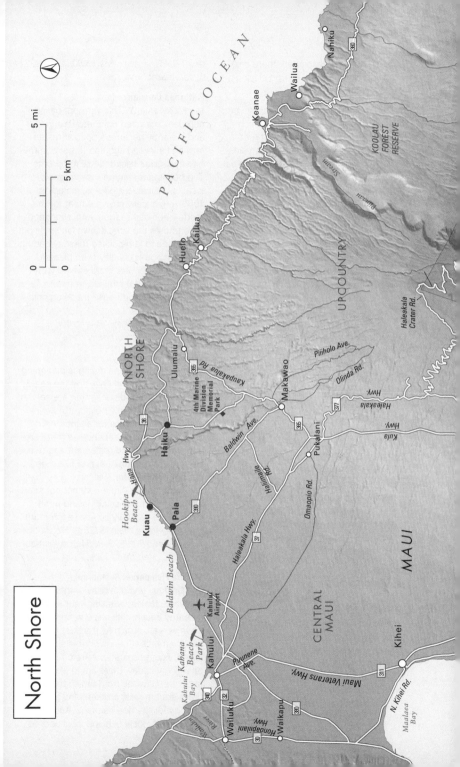

North Shore

Because this is a beach park there are picnic tables, grills, and a large playing field, as well.

The long, shallow pool at the Kahului end of the beach is known as Baby Beach. Separated from the surf by a flat reef wall, this is where ocean-loving families bring their kids (and sometimes puppies) to practice a few laps. Take a relaxing stroll along the water's edge from one end of Baldwin Beach to Baby Beach and enjoy the scenery. The view of the West Maui Mountains is hauntingly beautiful. **Amenities:** lifeguard; parking (no fee); showers; toilets. **Best for:** swimming; walking. ⊠ Hana Hwy., Paia ⊕ About 1 mile west of Baldwin Ave.

🍽 Restaurants

Restaurants in Paia cover a wide range of tastes, whether you've got a sweet tooth (Paia Gelato or Ululani's Hawaiian Shave Ice), or you're looking for a nice, sit-down meal (VANA or nyloS). For those who have dietary restrictions or crave something healthy, Mana Foods has a large selection of natural foods and a deli. There are also some fun options for beach picnic fare like fish tacos (or burgers or salads) at Paia Fish Market and interesting pizza combinations at Flatbread Company. Don't miss out on the unique fusions that happen in this town: here you can enjoy delicate French crepes or dig into a homey curry wrap, all from the same menu.

Cafe Mambo
$$ | ECLECTIC | Paia is one of Maui's most interesting food towns, and this colorful, airy, and brightly painted hangout is right in the thick of things. The menu features everything from burgers and fish to three different preparations of duck, and aside from the great food, the people-watching is fascinating. **Known for:** unique fajitas and salads; locally inspired tapas; fabulous breakfasts. ⑤ Average main: $19

⊠ 30 Baldwin Ave., Paia ☎ 808/579–8021 ⊕ cafemambomaui.com.

Flatbread Company
$$ | PIZZA | FAMILY | This Vermont-based company marched right into Paia in 2007 and instantly became a popular restaurant and a valued addition to the community as it gives back to local nonprofits. The bustling restaurant uses organic, local, sustainable products, including 100% organically grown wheat for the made-fresh-daily dough, and it's a good spot to take the kids. **Known for:** small but lively bar and jam-packed Tuesday benefit nights; wood-fired, clay-oven pizzas; Mopsy's Kalua Pork Pizza served with kiawe (mesquite)-smoked free-range pork shoulder and house-made organic mango barbecue sauce. ⑤ Average main: $22 ⊠ 89 Hana Hwy., Paia ☎ 808/579–8989 ⊕ flatbreadcompany.com.

nyloS
$$$$ | AMERICAN | Fine dining is beginning to take a foothold in Paia, and the seasonal, handcrafted plates that are served at nyloS are certainly helping. The chef's table concept makes for an intimate and memorable experience as there are only 14 seats in the restaurant and two seatings for the unique, prix fixe menu per night. **Known for:** welcoming husband-and-wife team; unique concept not seen elsewhere on the island; Island-fresh ingredients carefully curated each morning. ⑤ Average main: $175 ⊠ 115 Baldwin Ave., Paia ☎ 808/579–3354 ⊕ nylosmaui.com ⊘ Closed Sun.–Tues.

★ Paia Fishmarket Restaurant
$ | SEAFOOD | If you're okay with communal picnic tables, or taking your meal to a nearby beach, this place in funky Paia town serves, arguably, the best fresh fish for the best prices on this side of the island. Four preparations are offered and, on any given day, there are at least four to six fresh fishes from which to choose; there are burgers, chicken, and pasta options for the non-fish fans. **Known for:** grilled opah; local fish and local beer at

low, local prices; delectable side dishes. ⑤ *Average main: $15* ✉ *100 Hana Hwy., Paia* ☎ *808/579–8030* ⊕ *paiafishmarket. com.*

★ VANA
$$$ | JAPANESE FUSION | One of Paia's newest dining establishments, VANA brings a hip, fresh menu to an eclectic dinner food scene. Plates are full of Japanese-inspired fare with Hawaiian flair, with a rotating array of hot dishes served alongside lovely sushi options with seating that includes a main dining area and a bar area where the restaurant's mixologists serve up a variety of carefully crafted cocktails. **Known for:** ambience that encourages lingering and enjoying; vibrant mixology program for alcoholic and non-alcoholic drinks; stunning sushi options. ⑤ *Average main: $28* ✉ *93 Hana Hwy., Paia* ☎ *808/579–6002* ⊕ *www.vanapaia.com* ⊘ *Closed Sun. and Mon.*

Coffee and Quick Bites

Paia Bay Coffee Bar
$ | AMERICAN | The start to a lovely day in Paia begins at this popular coffee spot tucked away just behind the main buildings on Hana Highway. Grab a coffee or tea along with avocado toast or banana bread for breakfast or lunch. **Known for:** open early every day; inventive cocktail menu; weekly taco Tuesday menu. ⑤ *Average main: $12* ✉ *115 Hana Hwy., Paia* ☎ *808/579–3111* ⊕ *paiabaycoffee.com.*

★ Ululani's Hawaiian Shave Ice
$ | ICE CREAM | FAMILY | This Maui institution is a must-visit for interesting shave ice flavors featuring natural, hand-made syrups and a variety of toppings including Roselani's ice cream. The menu is extensive but features some popular combos to make your choice easier. **Known for:** decadent "snow cap" condensed milk or coconut cream topping; long but fast-moving lines to get served; unique and very delicious *ube* (purple yam)

syrup. ⑤ *Average main: $6* ✉ *115 Hana Hwy., Paia* ⊕ *ululanishawaiianshaveice. com.*

🛏 Hotels

Mangolani Inn
$$$$ | B&B/INN | This quaint, ocean view (but not oceanfront) inn sits next to the shops and restaurants among Paia, but is also secluded in its own little tropical world. **Pros:** early check-in time of 2 pm; one room is an actual treehouse; very hospitable hosts. **Cons:** closest beach is a mile walk; young children are not allowed in suites; $150 cleaning fee not included in room rate. ⑤ *Rooms from: $450* ✉ *325 Baldwin Ave., Paia* ☎ *808/579–3000* ⊕ *mauipaia.com* ⇆ *6 rooms* ❌ *No Meals.*

Paia Inn
$$$$ | B&B/INN | Located in the former plantation town of Paia, along Hana Highway, this chic inn with Southeast Asian influences is surprisingly quiet and includes oceanfront accommodations. **Pros:** unique and varied shops and dining just steps away in funky beach town; well-maintained property; excellent on-site restaurant. **Cons:** limited on- and

---

Fun Things to Do 👁 on the North Shore

- Buy a teeny-weeny Maui Girl bikini in Paia.

- Watch windsurfers somersault over waves at Hookipa.

- Dig into a fish sandwich and fries at the Paia Fish Market.

- Head out on the awesome Road to Hana, ending up in the tiny East Maui town.

- Hug a cow, kiss a pig, or cuddle a kitty at Leilani Farm Sanctuary.

off-site parking; lots of street action; some rooms are very small. $ *Rooms from: $429* ✉ *93 Hana Hwy., Paia* ☎ *808/579–6000* ⊕ *paiainn.com* ⇌ *15 units* ⦿ *No Meals.*

🛍 Shopping

Shopping and dining are the primary activities when visiting Paia, and there is no shortage of fun and funky boutiques along the main streets of Baldwin Avenue and Hana Highway. Whether you're looking to stock up on souvenirs, invest in some high-end, handcrafted home decor, or shop for bathing suits and jewelry, there's plenty to find in Paia. Stores don't typically open until late morning in this laid-back town, but don't wait to visit too close to lunch time or you'll be battling crowds.

CLOTHING

Biasa Rose

MIXED CLOTHING | The whole family can shop for stylish threads at this boutique. Charming items—including upcycled items, Hawaii-made products, pillows, shoes, and earth-friendly bags—are on display along with comfy cotton tees, airy tunics, and statement necklaces. The store has a great menswear selection that includes vintage aloha shirts. Repurposed kids' clothing and home accessories are locally made. At Rose's Closet, the women's consignment shop in the back, you can score designer pieces at great prices. ✉ *104 Hana Hwy., Paia* ☎ *808/579–8602* ⊕ *biasarose.com.*

★ Maui Girl Swimwear

WOMEN'S CLOTHING | This is *the* place on Maui for swimwear, cover-ups, beach hats, and sandals. Maui Girl designs its own suits, which have been spotted in *Sports Illustrated* fashion shoots and on celebrities. Tops and bottoms can be purchased separately, increasing your chances of finding the perfect fit. ✉ *12 Baldwin Ave., Paia* ☎ *808/579–9266* ⊕ *maui-girl.com.*

Nuage Bleu

MIXED CLOTHING | This boutique has been around for more than 30 years and is as popular as ever. Navigate the collections of top brands such as Frame, Spell, and Rhythm, or browse the shop's Nuage Bleu line for handmade leather bags and women's attire. The *keiki* (kids) section includes designer organic clothing, huggable stuffies, and a fantastic selection of books. ✉ *76 Hana Hwy., Paia* ☎ *808/579–9792* ⊕ *nuagebleu.com.*

FOOD

★ Mana Foods

FOOD | At this bustling health food store you can stock up on local fish and grass-fed beef for your barbecue. You'll find the best selection of organic produce on the Island, as well as a great bakery and deli. The health and beauty room has a dizzying selection of products that promise to keep you glowing. ✉ *49 Baldwin Ave., Paia* ☎ *808/579–8078* ⊕ *manafoodsmaui. com.*

Paia Pit Stop

WINE/SPIRITS | This is the only place to buy alcohol in Paia. This small but abundant store manages to squeeze in a huge selection of liquor, wine, and beer into an unassuming space. Be sure to try local products like Maui Brewing beers, Ocean Vodka, and spirits from nearby Haliimaile Distillery. Just remember that consuming alcohol on Maui beaches is prohibited. ✉ *181 Baldwin Ave., Paia* ☎ *808/579–8967.*

GALLERIES

Art Project Paia

ART GALLERIES | This multimedia gallery brings a stark and fresh perspective to the Maui art community with a well-curated selection of contemporary photography, sculptures, ceramics, and paintings. ✉ *77 Hana Hwy., Paia* ☎ *808/214–6949* ⊕ *artprojectpaia.com* ⊙ *Closed Tues. during low season.*

Above the rainforests of Haiku are views of the Pacific.

★ Maui Crafts Guild

ART GALLERIES | One of the Island's only artist cooperatives, Maui Crafts Guild is crammed with treasures. Resident artists produce lead-glazed pottery, basketry, glass and feather art, photography, ceramics, and woodwork pieces. The prices are surprisingly low, making this a great place to find gifts and one-of-a-kind items to take home. ⊠ *120 Hana Hwy., Paia* ☎ *808/579–9697* ⊕ *mauicraftsguild. com.*

★ Maui Hands

ART GALLERIES | This gallery shows work by more than 300 local artists: exquisite woodwork, lovely ceramics, authentic Niihau shell lei, wave metal etchings, and whimsical clay figures. There are locations in Lahaina, Makawao, and at The Shops at Wailea. At each location, the gallery offers a unique Artists in Residence program that connects the public to the artists at local "talk story" sessions each month. ⊠ *84 Hana Hwy., Paia* ☎ *808/579–9245* ⊕ *mauihands.com.*

Haiku

13 miles east of Kahului; 4 miles east of Paia.

At one time this area centered around a couple of enormous pineapple canneries, before they shuttered. Both have since been transformed into rustic warehouse malls. Because of the post office next door, Old Haiku Cannery earned the title of town center. Here you can try eateries offering everything from plate lunches to vegetarian dishes to juicy burgers and fantastic sushi. Follow windy Haiku Road to Pauwela Cannery, the other defunct factory-turned-hangout. This jungle hillside is a maze of flower-decked roads that seem to double back on themselves.

GETTING HERE AND AROUND

Route 36 (Hana Highway) runs directly through Paia; 4 miles east of town, follow the sign to Haiku, a short detour off the highway. You can take the Maui Bus from the airport and Queen Kaahumanu

Shopping Center in Kahului to Paia and on to Haiku.

Haiku is a short detour off Hana Highway (Route 36) just past Hookipa Beach Park on the way to Hana. Haiku Road turns into Kokomo Road at the post office.

TOURS

★ Leilani Farm Sanctuary

SPECIAL-INTEREST TOURS | For a chance to snuggle a sheep or hug a cow in paradise, an hour-long tour of Leilani Farm Sanctuary is just the thing. Visitors must make reservations and be at least seven years old to participate in these personalized, guided tours. While the tours are a crucial part of the sanctuary, visitors can really give back by volunteering during morning rounds on Monday and Wednesday (reservations preferred). ⊠ *260 East Kuiaha St., Haiku-Pauwela* ☎ *808/298–8544* ⊕ *leilanifarmsanctuary.org* ☞ *$50 tax-deductible donation* ☞ *Tours Mon., Wed., at 12 pm, Sat. at 10 am.*

Sights

There aren't too many sights in this little enclave, save for the park and the beautiful, jungly drives, but it's still a beautiful area to spend some time.

4th Marine Division Memorial Park

CITY PARK | **FAMILY** | Up Kokomo Road in Haiku you'll find a large *puu* (volcanic cinder cone) capped with a grove of columnar pines and the 4th Marine Division Memorial Park. During World War II, American GIs trained here for battles on Iwo Jima and Saipan. Locals nicknamed the cinder cone "Giggle Hill" because it was a popular hangout for Maui women and their favorite servicemen. The park includes an impressive playground, picnic tables, and lots of wide-open space. ⊠ *Mile 2, Kokomo Rd., Haiku-Pauwela* ⊕ *mauicounty.gov.*

🍴 Restaurants

There are some real standouts in contemporary cuisine in this little enclave, particularly at popular spots Colleen's at the Cannery and Nuka. But don't let these well-known spots steal all of the attention—this small area also offers vegetarian fast food, Mediterranean, tacos, local plates, and more, most of which can be found in a food truck park on Kokomo Road.

★ Colleen's at the Cannery

$$ | **AMERICAN** | You'd never guess what's inside by the nondescript exterior and the location in an old pineapple cannery-cum-strip-mall, but this is one of Maui's most overlooked and underrated restaurants. Popular with locals for breakfast, lunch, and a daily happy hour, at night during dinner is when the candles come out and it's time for martinis and fresh fish; you'll feel like you're at a hip urban eatery. **Known for:** specialty artisan pizzas and enormous salads; eggs Benedict (available every day) and Bloody Marys; excellent food featuring Upcountry's best produce. ⑤ *Average main: $24* ⊠ *Haiku Cannery Marketplace, 810 Haiku Rd., Haiku-Pauwela* ☎ *808/575–9211* ⊕ *colleensinhaiku.com.*

Nuka

$$ | **ASIAN FUSION** | This off-the-beaten-path izakaya-style Japanese eatery is worth the trek to sleepy Haiku. Diners flock here for the eclectic menu that includes everything from specialty French fries and fusion sushi rolls to sashimi and some of the best tempura around—all based on what's fresh from local farmers and fishermen. **Known for:** homemade green tea and black sesame ice cream; exceptional sushi and sashimi; hard to get a table (no reservations). ⑤ *Average main: $18* ⊠ *780 Haiku Rd., Haiku-Pauwela* ☎ *808/575–2939* ⊕ *nukamaui.com* ⊘ *Closed daily 2:30–4:30 pm. No lunch on weekends.*

Did You Know?

Many windsurfers in the 1980s came from Europe and "discovered" Hookipa Beach. Today you can see some of the finest windsurfing there.

📩 Shopping

The two former pineapple canneries, Haiku Cannery and Pauwela Cannery, offer an abundance of shopping options. Though a lot of what is offered here is more for locals, both shopping centers are worth spending a bit of time strolling about to find hidden gems.

Pauwela Cannery Center

NEIGHBORHOODS | The industrial-looking building that housed a pineapple cannery from the 1920s until 1961 is now home to over 40 local merchants that include art studios, health and beauty services, restaurants, tour operators, and more. ✉ 375 W. Kuiaha Rd., Haiku-Pauwela ☎ 808/877–7073 ⊕ pauwelacannery.com.

Kuau

Kuau is a small neighborhood just off the Road to Hana, home to a few standout spots for dining, swimming, grabbing a cup of coffee, and taking in the views. You may consider skipping this area in favor of getting an early start to Hana, but it's worth the extra time to visit.

🏝 Beaches

★ Hookipa Beach

BEACH | To see some of the world's finest windsurfers, hit this beach along the Hana Highway. It's also one of Maui's hottest surfing spots, with waves that can reach 20 feet. Hookipa is not necessarily a good swimming beach; however, there are a few spots that have protected reef areas that provide a shore break and places to play in the water, so getting wet isn't completely out of the question. It's also not the place to learn windsurfing, but it's great for hanging out and watching the pros. There are picnic tables and grills, though the pavilion area isn't particularly inviting. **Amenities:** lifeguard; parking (no fee); showers; toilets. **Best for:** surfing; windsurfing. ✉ Hana Hwy, Paia ⊕ At mile marker 9, about 2 miles east of Paia.

🍴 Restaurants

★ Mama's Fish House

$$$$ | HAWAIIAN | Few restaurants in Maui have the reputation of this North Shore eatery, tucked into a small cove just off the highway on the Road to Hana. You'll pay for the quality of your meal, but it's worth the splurge; the fish comes from as close as Maui's shores to as far away as the deep waters of Antarctica, and the daily menu often tells the story of that catch. **Known for:** Mama's Stuffed Fish, filled with lobster and crab then crusted in macadamia nuts; hard-to-come-by dinner reservations; incredibly fresh fish processed and served within 24 hours. $ Average main: $68 ✉ 799 Poho Pl., Paia ☎ 808/579–8488 ⊕ mamasfish-house.com/restaurant.

🛏 Hotels

★ The Inn at Mama's Fish House

$$$$ | B&B/INN | Nestled in gardens adjacent to one of Maui's most popular dining spots (Mama's Fish House) and fronting a small beach known as Kuau Cove, these well-maintained studios, suites, and one- and two-bedroom cottages have been recently renovated with high-end appliances and furnishings and decorated with local artwork to provide contemporary beach house luxury. **Pros:** easy access to Kuau Cove; free parking and Wi-Fi; near Hookipa Beach and Paia town shops and restaurants. **Cons:** limited swimming at beach; not a full-service hotel with concierge; restaurant can get crowded during the evening. $ Rooms from: $395 ✉ 799 Poho Pl., Kuau ☎ 808/579–9764 ⊕ innatmamas.com 🛏 12 rooms ⦿ No Meals.

Chapter 8

ROAD TO HANA

Updated by
Laurie Lyons-Makaimoku

◉ Sights	🍴 Restaurants	🏨 Hotels	🛍 Shopping	🍸 Nightlife
★★★★★	★★☆☆☆	★★★☆☆	★★☆☆☆	☆☆☆☆☆

WELCOME TO ROAD TO HANA

TOP REASONS TO GO

★ **Enjoy the drive.** The Road to Hana, flush with waterfalls, ocean vistas, and luscious greenery, is a road trip you'll never forget.

★ **Take a hike.** From gentle to more challenging, there are plenty of places to stretch your legs and enjoy unparalleled beauty. Just be prepared for mud and mosquitoes!

★ **Walk back in time.** Hawaii's religious history is well-represented in the various churches and *heiaus* (temples) along the way, including just past Hana Town.

★ **Commune with nature.** Besides the incredible flora that hugs the curves of the road, there are a few beautiful botanical gardens along the way for a fully immersive experience.

★ **Try the banana bread.** This local treat is found at many stops just off the road. Other sweet treats that can be found on the road include vegan ice cream and coconut candy.

It's not just about the destination, it's about the journey, and the Road to Hana is one of the most famed drives in the world. The entire road, believe it or not, extends beyond Hana, and is nearly 65 miles long. You can take a tour (luxury options are available) or venture out on your own with the right amount of preparation. If you do go out on your own, pay extra mind to being respectful to the people who call these communities home, and be sure to obey the No Parking signs recently added to some of the more popular spots along the highway. Some may choose to simply drive along and take in the views from behind the wheel, while others will want to truly explore via nature trails and gorgeous waterfalls. If you want to get to Hana but a long road trip isn't in the cards for you or someone in your party, you can get a quick flight to Hana from Kuhului Airport. Tiny towns and communities along the way give visitors a glimpse into the bucolic history

of this area with taro patches and small fruit farms throughout.

1 Huelo. This small community is still technically part of Haiku, making it the first community you come across after setting out along the road. The famous Twin Falls and Waikamoi Nature Trail will vie to be your first stop on the road.

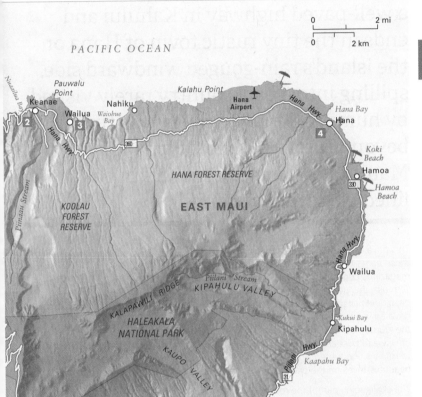

2 Keanae. The Keanae Peninsula is well worth the small diversion that it takes to drive down to the point just to take in the splendor of waves crashing along jagged lava rocks. The Keanae Congregational Church, the sole surviving building after a 1946 tsunami, also sits near the point.

3 Wailua. This sleepy little area is not much more than an old church, a few houses, and some taro patches, quilted together into a tiny town that is best experienced from the Wailua Overlook. If you do drive into town, you'll be treated to a view of Lower Waikani Falls that you can't see from the road.

4 Hana. The end of the road (though not literally; you really should keep going), Hana isn't home to much, but what is there is spectacular. A couple of beaches and swimming holes, some beautiful accommodations, and excellent food trucks beg you to stay the night in Hana, rather than just hopping back on the road.

The Road to Hana is a 55-mile journey into the unspoiled heart of Maui. Tracing a centuries-old path, the road begins as a well-paved highway in Kahului and ends in the tiny rustic town of Hana on the island's rain-gouged windward side, spilling into a backcountry rarely visited by humans. Many travelers venture beyond Hana to Oheo Gulch in East Maui, where one can cool off in basalt-lined pools and waterfalls.

This drive is a Hawaii pilgrimage for those eager to experience what glossy magazines consider the "real" Hawaii. To most, the lure of Hana is its timelessness, and paired with the spectacular drive (which brings to life the old adage: the journey *is* the destination), this is one of Hawaii's best experiences. The Road to Hana is undoubtedly one of the most beautiful drives on the planet.

The challenging part of the road takes only an hour and a half, but the drive begs to be taken at a leisurely pace. You'll want to slow the passage of time to take in foliage-hugged ribbons of road and roadside banana bread and food stands, to swim beneath a waterfall, and to inhale the lush Maui tropics in all their glory. You'll also want to stop often and let the driver enjoy the view, too.

Planning

Getting Here and Around

AIR
Though Kahului Airport is the primary airport for Maui, and likely where your journey will begin, there is a small commuter airport in Hana (HNM) that serves residents and visitors. All flights at HNM are serviced by Mokulele Airlines (⊕ *mokuleleairlines.com*). There is no car rental service available.

CAR
A rental car, which are available in Kahului, is the way to go on the Road to Hana. The alternative is to utilize a tour company, which allows you to relax and enjoy the view, while also providing additional information about the area. If you want to do the drive make sure you get a vehicle that can handle elevation

changes, but one that is also compact enough to handle the tight curves and narrow bridges. Also, be aware that this road is regularly traversed by locals—be sure to pull over and allow others to pass if you are lingering to enjoy the view.

CONTACTS Hana Airport (HNM). ✉ *700 Alalele Pl., Hana* ☎ *808/872–3808* ⊕ *airports.hawaii.gov/hnm.*

TAXI

While you could take a taxi along the road, you'd definitely be missing the point of the journey, and the cost would be prohibitive.

Beaches

East Maui's and Hana's beaches will literally stop you in your tracks—they're that beautiful. Black sand stands out against pewter skies and lush tropical foliage, creating picture-perfect scenes that seem too breathtaking to be real. Rough conditions often preclude swimming, but that doesn't mean you can't explore the shoreline.

Hotels

Lodging on the Road to Hana is typically found at the beginning and end of the journey. The primary options are nicely curated bed-and-breakfasts that offer their own brand of seaside splendor. Hana does offer one well-appointed resort, as well as a condo-hotel with a variety of housing options.

Restaurants

Food stands abound on the Road to Hana, with a surprising number of options popping up seemingly out of nowhere. Smoothies, plate lunches, huli huli chicken, and much more tempt travelers into pulling over for a bite. There is

also a growing number of food trucks in Hana, adding options to the dining scene that is dominated by Hana Ranch Restaurant. Banana bread is a must-grab treat along the highway, with Aunty Sandy's and Halfway to Hana (both in Keanae) as standouts.

HOTEL AND RESTAURANT PRICES

Hotel prices in the reviews are the lowest cost of a standard double room in high season. Restaurant prices in the reviews are the average cost of a main course at dinner, or if dinner is not served, at lunch.

WHAT IT COSTS in U.S. Dollars			
$	$$	$$$	$$$$
RESTAURANTS			
under $18	$18–$26	$27–$35	over $35
HOTELS			
under $181	$181–$260	$261–$340	over $340

Safety

This long stretch of road is full of twists, turns, and dramatic heights, which can be dangerous at times. If you're unfamiliar with the road be sure to travel during the day and take your time. That said, the locals have no time for lingering visitors, so be sure to pull off to the shoulder to allow residents to get where they need to go.

Shopping

Hana's shopping scene consists mainly of flower and fruit stands, but you won't want to miss the fine art collection at Hana Coast Gallery.

Huelo

10 miles east of Haiku.

As the Road to Hana begins its journey eastward, the slopes get steeper and the Pacific Ocean pops into view. The first waterfall you see, Twin Falls, is around mile marker 2, and farther up the road is the Koolau Forest Reserve. Embedded in the forest are two townships, Huelo and Kailua, both of which are great places to pull over and take in the dramatic landscape.

GETTING HERE AND AROUND

Just after Haiku, the mile markers on the Hana Highway change back to 0. The town of Huelo is at mile marker 4. To reach the township, follow the signs toward the *mauka* (ocean) side of the road.

Sights

Two spots full of natural splendor beckon travelers to get off of the road as their journey has just begun. Twin Falls has a small farm and snack stand that serves as entrance to the winding pathways that lead to waterfalls, while Waikamoi Nature Trail offers a little more of a challenging hike among ancient trees and sprawling ferns.

Twin Falls

WATERFALL | Keep an eye out for the Twin Falls Farm Stand just after mile marker 2 on the Hana Highway. Stop here and treat yourself to some fresh sugarcane juice. If you're feeling adventurous, follow the path beyond the stand to the paradisiacal waterfalls known as Twin Falls. Although it's still private property, the "no trespassing" signs have been replaced by colorfully painted arrows pointing toward the easily accessible falls. Several deep, emerald pools sparkle beneath waterfalls and offer excellent (and a little cold) swimming and photo opportunities. In recent years, this natural

attraction has become a tourist hot spot. Although the attention is well deserved, those who wish to avoid crowds may want to keep driving. The family who owns the property recently implemented a paid parking system to help manage the overcrowding; parking costs $10 per car and is available on a first-come, first-served basis. ⊠ *6300 Hana Hwy., past mile marker 2, Haiku-Pauwela* ⊕ *twinfalls-maui.net* ⊡ *$10.*

Huelo

TOWN | When you see the colorful mailboxes on the *makai* (toward the ocean) side of the road just past mile marker 4 on the Hana Highway, follow the windy road to the rural area of Huelo—a funky community that includes a mix of off-the-grid inhabitants and vacation rentals. The town features two picturesque churches, one of which is Kaulanapueo Church, constructed in 1853 out of coral blocks. If you linger a while, you may meet local residents and learn about a rural lifestyle you might not have expected to find on the Islands. The same can be said for nearby Kailua (mile marker 6). ■ TIP→ **When you're back up on Hana Highway, pull into the Huelo Lookout Fruit Stand for yummy smoothies and killer views of the Pacific below.** ⊠ *Hana Hwy., near mile marker 4, Huelo.*

Waikamoi Nature Trail

TRAIL | Slightly after the town of Huelo, the Hana Highway enters the Koolau Forest Reserve. Vines wrap around street signs, and waterfalls are so abundant that you don't know which direction to look. A good start is between mile markers 9 and 10, where the Waikamoi Nature Trail sign beckons you to stretch your car-weary limbs. A short (if muddy) trail leads through tall eucalyptus trees to a coastal vantage point with a picnic table. Signage reminds visitors: "Quiet, Trees at Work" and "Bamboo Picking Permit Required." *Awapuhi,* or Hawaiian shampoo ginger, sends up fragrant shoots along the trail. ■ TIP→ **The area**

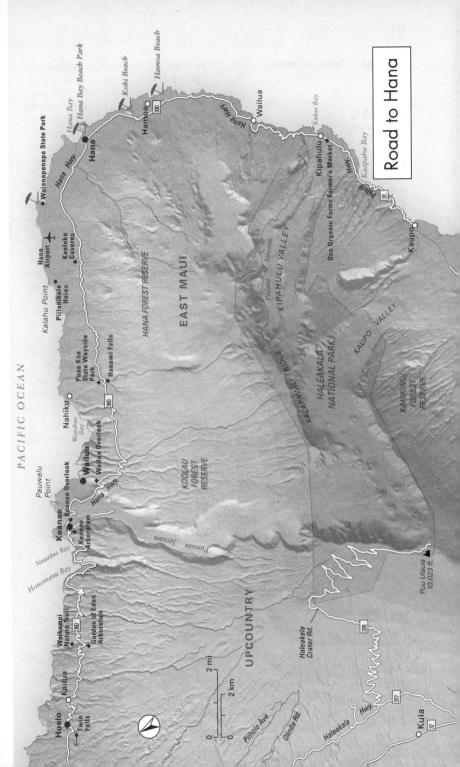

Road to Hana

has picnic tables and a restroom. ✉ *Hana Hwy., between mile markers 9 and 10.*

Keanae

13 miles east of Huelo.

Officially, Keanae is the halfway point to Hana, and for many, this is where the drive offers the most rewarding vistas. The greenery seems to envelop the skinny road, forcing drivers to slow to a crawl as they "ooh" and "aah" at the landscape. Around the village of Wailua, one of the most fiercely native Hawaiian regions on the Island, there seem to be waterfalls at every turn.

GETTING HERE AND AROUND

Just past mile marker 16, you'll find a roadway that takes you down to the peninsula where you'll pass plenty of cars heading back up the highway from the gorgeous diversion.

Sights

Visiting the rocky shores of the Keanae Peninsula can lead to sensory overload as ocean waves thunder to the shore, breaking on jagged volcanic outcroppings. That smell of the salt in the air, the pellets of spray, and the incredible sights of the mighty ocean doing its thing create a powerful experience worth making a stop for. The other big attractions in the area can be found at the two nearby arboretums.

★ Garden of Eden Arboretum

GARDEN | Just beyond mile marker 10 on the Hana Highway, the Garden of Eden Arboretum offers interpretive trails through 26 acres of manicured gardens. Anyone with a green thumb will appreciate the care and attention given to the more than 500 varieties of tropical plants—many of them native. Trails lead to views of the lovely Puohokamoa Falls and provide a glimpse into the botanical

wonders that thrive in this lush region. Be sure to stop by the gift shop on the way out for a wide variety of gifts made by local artisans and to hang out with the ducks and peacocks. To avoid lines and crowds, visit in the morning at opening time or in the afternoon after 2 pm. ✉ *10600 Hana Hwy., past mile marker 10, Haiku-Pauwela* ☎ *808/572–9899* ⊕ *mauigardenofeden.com* 🖃 *$20.*

Keanae Arboretum

GARDEN | Here you can add to your botanical education or enjoy a challenging hike into the forest. Signs help you learn the names of the many plants and trees now considered native to Hawaii. The meandering Piinaau Stream adds a graceful touch to the arboretum and provides a swimming pond when there is enough water. You can take a fairly rigorous hike from the arboretum if you can find the trail at one side of the large taro patch. Be careful not to lose the trail once you're on it. A lovely forest waits at the end of the 25-minute hike. ✉ *13385 Hana Hwy., past mile marker 16, Keanae* 🖃 *Free.*

Keanae Overlook

NATURE SIGHT | Near mile marker 17 along the Hana Highway, you can stop at the Keanae Overlook. From this observation point you can take in the patchwork effect the taro patches create against the dramatic backdrop of the ocean. In the other direction, there are awesome views of Haleakala through the foliage. This is a great spot for photos, but it is not recommended that you fly your drones over the inhabited areas. ✉ *Hana Hwy., near mile marker 17, Keanae.*

Puaa Kaa State Wayside Park

NATURE SIGHT | For a leg-stretching break, visitors will find a respite and real bathrooms at this small roadside park. This is one of the few places on the highway with plenty of parking, so take some time to linger and enjoy the short hike to a small waterfall and pool across the highway from the bathrooms. There are also

Photo Ops Along the Road to Hana ⊙

The entire Road to Hana features postcard-worthy views. You'll be craning your neck to take in the lush landscape that seems to swallow your car, and every turnoff offers another striking photo opportunity, each one seemingly better than the last. However, there are some pit stops you'll kick yourself for skipping.

For jaw-dropping views, pull into the Huelo Lookout near mile marker 5, order a smoothie, and drink in the expanse of the Pacific Ocean and the historic Huelo township below.

If you are a banana bread fan, be sure to stop in the small community of Keanae for some of the best loaves you're likely to try at Aunty Sandy's Banana Bread. Just be sure to arrive early since the stand sells out frequently.

At mile marker 24, Hanawi Falls is another picturesque spot. The best way to see the falls is from the bridge, and we advise against hiking beyond that point.

At mile marker 31, turn onto Ulaino Road to explore the vast cave network of Kaeleku Caverns. Afterward, make your way to nearby Piilanihale Heiau, a beautiful 16th-century temple. While there, you can also amble through the lovely Kahanu Garden.

Near mile marker 32 you should carve out time to hike the 3-mile trail from Waianapanapa State Park to Hana Bay. You'll scramble over lava rock and along a stunning coastline rarely seen by travelers.

After you arrive in Hana, motor straight to Hamoa Beach, one of Hawaii's most beautiful strands. But the road does not end in Hana. In fact, for many travelers, the payoff comes at Oheo Gulch's abundant hiking trails—don't miss the inland hike through the bamboo forest. After you're done, you can travel a mile past Oheo Gulch and pay your respects at the grave of Charles Lindbergh.

picnic tables and friendly cats to welcome you. ⊠ *Hana Hwy., Wailua (Maui County)* ✛ *½ mile past mile marker 22.*

Hanawi Falls

WATERFALL | At mile marker 24 of the Hana Highway, just as you approach the bridge, look toward the mountains to catch a glimpse of Hanawi Falls. This lush spring-fed stream travels 9 miles to the ocean, and the waterfalls are real crowd-pleasers, even when rains have been light. The best views are from the bridge. ⚠ **It is not safe to hike to the falls, and you must cross private property to get there. We strongly advise against this.** ⊠ *Hana Hwy., near mile marker 24, Keanae.*

🌀 Beaches

Though there are no swimming beaches along the Keanae Peninsula, this is definitely the place to stop and take in the epic splendor of the Pacific Ocean—no aerial views here; this jagged coastline practically tosses seawater into your mouth as you stand safely on land. This is definitely a place to have your camera ready.

Tropical Delights

The drive to Hana wouldn't be as enchanting without a stop or two at one of the countless fruit and flower (and banana bread) stands by the highway. Every so often a thatch hut tempts passersby with apple bananas (a smaller, firmer variety), *lilikoi* (passion fruit), avocados, or star fruit just plucked from the tree. Leave a few dollars in the can for the folks who live off the land. Huge bouquets of tropical flowers are available for a handful of change, and some farms will ship.

One standout is **Aunty Sandy's Banana Bread Stand**, in the blink-and-you'll-miss-it community of Keanae. This legendary banana-bread shop is just past the coral-and-lava-rock church. Aunty Sandy's sweet loaves lure locals and tourists alike, but be sure to arrive early, because once the stand runs out (it's also closed on Sundays), you'll have to scurry back up the main road to the **Halfway to Hana Fruit Stand** to find a tasty replacement.

Wailua

1 mile from Keanae.

This tiny town filled with one of the highest concentrations of Hawaiian blood in any island community (around 94% of the residents have at least partial Hawaiian blood) is best viewed from above at the overlook. The town below prefers not to have visitors, as tourists often trespass to get a better view. From above visitors will be able to enjoy the quilt of the taro patches and Saint Gabriel's Church. Just before the overlook, enjoy some time at the concrete arches of the beautiful Waikani Stream Bridge past mile marker 18.

◉ Sights

Wailua Overlook

SCENIC DRIVE | From the parking lot on the side of the Hana Highway near mile marker 20, you can see Wailua Canyon in one direction and Wailua Village in the other. Photos are spectacular in the morning light of the verdant expanse below. Also from your perch, you can see Wailua Village's landmark 1860 church, which was allegedly constructed of coral that washed up onto the shore during a storm. You'll want to take photos, but flying a drone over the populated area is strongly discouraged. ✉ *Hana Hwy., near mile marker 20, Wailua (Maui County).*

Hana

15 miles east of Keanae.

Even though Hana is a very small town with limited offerings, the relaxed pace of life that Hana residents enjoy will likely have you in its grasp. Hana is one of the few places where the slow pulse of the Island is still strong. The town centers on its lovely circular bay, dominated on the right-hand shore by a *puu* (volcanic cinder cone) called Kauiki. A short trail here leads to a cave, the birthplace of Queen Kaahumanu. Two miles beyond town, another puu presides over a loop road that passes Hana's two best beaches—Koki and Hamoa. The hill is called Ka Iwi O Pele (Pele's Bone). Offshore here, at tiny Alau Island, the demigod Maui supposedly fished up the Hawaiian Islands.

Upper Waikani Falls is considered "off-limits" by the Hana Community Organization, but you can view it from the road.

Although sugar was once the mainstay of Hana's economy, the last plantation shut down in the 1940s. In 1946 rancher Paul Fagan built the Hotel Hana-Maui and stocked the surrounding pastureland with cattle. The hotel became a Travaasa experiential resort in 2011, before changing hands in 2020. Now Hana-Maui Resort, the Mani Brothers Real Estate Group purchased the hotel and Hyatt was brought on in 2020 as the management company. The brothers also bought various other associated parcels of real estate in Hana. It's pleasant to stroll around this beautifully rustic property. The cross you can see on the hill above the hotel was put there in memory of Fagan.

GETTING HERE AND AROUND

Hana Town sits at mile marker 34. Once you've parked your car, the town is somewhat walkable (though there aren't many sidewalks).

Sights

Like most of the Road to Hana, Hana Town has sights that tell the tale of the Island's geological and cultural history. This side of Maui is great for history buffs, nature lovers, and adventurers who want to go below the surface (literally) of what the island has to offer.

Kaeleku Caverns

CAVE | FAMILY | If you're interested in spelunking, take the time to explore Kaeleku Caverns (aka Hana Lava Tube), just after mile marker 31 on the Hana Highway. The site is a mile down Ulaino Road. The friendly folks at the cave give a brief orientation and promptly send nature enthusiasts into Maui's largest lava tube, accented by colorful underworld formations. You can take a self-guided, 30- to 40-minute tour daily 10:30 am until 4 pm. LED flashlights are provided. For those who don't want to explore the caverns, this still makes for a great stop to check out the world's only red ti

Did You Know?

At Waianapanapa State Park, the tide pools turn red several times a year. Legend claims the color represents the blood of Popoalaea, said to have been murdered in one of the caves by her husband, Chief Kakae.

leaf maze on the grounds. ✉ *205 Ulaino Rd., off Hana Hwy., past mile marker 31, Hana* 🕿 *808/248–7308* ⊕ *mauicave.com* ✎ *$15.*

Ono Organic Farms Farmers' Market

MARKET | The family-owned Ono Farms offers certified organic produce at this roadside market at an old gas station. Depending on the season, you'll find such unusual delicacies as *rambutan* (resembling grapes), jackfruit (tastes like bananas), and *lilikoi* (passion fruit). Gordon Ramsay even gave the farm a visit while filming his show *Uncharted* for National Geographic. ■**TIP→ For a memorable on-farm experience, check out their Exotic Tropical Fruit Tasting Adventure, held on Tuesday by reservation.** ✉ *Hana Hwy., near Hasegawa General Store, Hana* 🕿 *808/248–7779* ⊕ *onofarms.com.*

Piilanihale Heiau

GARDEN | This temple, the largest *heiau* in Polynesia, was built for a great 16th-century Maui king named Piilani and his heirs. Hawaiian families continue to maintain and protect this sacred site as they have for centuries, and they have not been eager to turn it into a tourist attraction. However, there is now a brochure, so you can tour the property yourself. The *heiau* is situated within the 122-acre Kahanu Garden, a research center focusing on the ethnobotany of the Pacific. ✉ *650 Ulaino Rd., Hana* ♣ *To get here, turn left onto Ulaino Rd. at Hana Hwy. mile marker 31; the road turns to gravel; continue 1½ miles* 🕿 *808/248–8912* ⊕ *ntbg.org* ✎ *$16* ☾ *Closed Sat. and Sun.*

★ Waianapanapa State Park

BEACH | Home to one of Maui's few black-sand beaches and freshwater caves for adventurous swimmers to explore, this park is right on the ocean. It's a lovely spot to picnic, hike, or swim. To the left you'll find the volcanic sand beach, picnic tables, and cave pools; to the right is an ancient trail that snakes along the ocean

past blowholes, sea arches, and archaeological sites. Bird lovers could linger for hours watching the comings and goings of seabirds on the ocean outcroppings. The tide pools here turn red several times a year. Scientists say it's explained by the arrival of small shrimp, but legend claims the color represents the blood of Popoalaea, said to have been murdered in one of the caves by her husband, Chief Kakae. In either case, the dramatic landscape is bound to leave a lasting impression. There is a private cemetery on the grounds of the park, so be mindful to keep out of this area. ■**TIP→ With a permit, you can stay in a state-run cabin or campsite for a steal. It's wise to reserve as early as possible, as these spots book up quickly.** ✉ *Hana Hwy., near mile marker 32, Hana* 🕿 *808/984–8109* ⊕ *hawaii-istateparks.org* ✎ *Free.*

🌊 Beaches

Red, black, and salt-and-pepper colored beaches welcome visitors to some of the most visually stunning beaches you'll find. These aren't your white-sand resort beaches, rather ones where nature and civilization smash into one another to create truly memorable places.

★ Hamoa Beach

BEACH | FAMILY | Why did James Michener describe this stretch of salt-and-pepper sand as the most "South Pacific" beach he'd come across, even though it's in the North Pacific? Maybe it was the perfect half-moon shape, speckled with the shade of palm trees. Perhaps he was intrigued by the jutting black coastline, often outlined by rain showers out at sea, or the pervasive lack of hurry he felt here. Whatever it was, many still feel the lure. The beach can be crowded, yet it is nonetheless relaxing. Early mornings and late afternoons are best for swimming. At times the churning surf might intimidate swimmers, but the bodysurfing can be great. Though there are beach chairs and

Hamoa Beach is one of Maui's most beautiful stretches of sand.

a pavilion at the beach, they are strictly for the use of Travaasa Hana guests. Hamoa is half a mile past Koki Beach on Haneoo Loop Road, 2 miles south of Hana Town. **Amenities:** showers; toilets. **Best for:** surfing; swimming. ⊠ *Haneoo Loop Rd., Hana.*

Hana Bay Beach Park

CITY PARK | FAMILY | This family-friendly park situated around an old pier offers the calmest swimming opportunities in the area. The black-sand beach is a favorite among local families and canoe clubs, especially thanks to the picnic tables and showers available. Keep cash handy, as you can occasionally find craft vendors in the parking lot. Residents prefer that Sundays be left for local families to enjoy the facilities. **Amenities:** picnic tables, free parking. **Best for:** families. ⊠ *150 Keawa Pl., Hana* ☎ *808/248–7022* ⊕ *mauicounty. gov.*

Koki Beach

BEACH | You can tell from the trucks parked alongside the road that this is a favorite local surf spot.

■ TIP→ Swimming is not recommended here, as there are no lifeguards, and the rip currents are powerful.

Look for awesome views of the rugged coastline and a sea arch on the left end.

Iwa, or white-throated frigate birds, dart like pterodactyls over the offshore Alau Islet. Though it's not a swimming beach, the grassy area and picnic tables are cozy and allow visitors to watch the surfers navigate the waves, while the small red-sand beach is good for walks if the tide allows. **Amenities:** picnic tables. **Best for:** surfing. ⊠ *Haneoo Loop Rd., Hana* ✛ *About 2 miles south of Hana Town.*

🍴 Restaurants

Dining in Hana is limited to affordable food trucks and higher-end dining at the town's two main restaurants. The abundance of farm stands throughout the area also provide ingredients for creating your own hand-crafted meal. Keep an eye out for people fishing along some spots and you may even be able to purchase a fresh catch straight from the ocean.

★ **Hana Farms Bamboo Hale Grill & Pizzeria**
$$ | **AMERICAN** | Just outside of Hana is this small food truck that has been transformed into a permanent location with a large, covered patio, real restrooms, and beautiful wood-fired pizzas, calzones, and salads that highlight the vegetables from Hana Farms. While you wait for your food enjoy the free Wi-Fi (very rare in the area) and peruse the shelves of the farm stand for tropical fruits, banana bread, home and bath gifts, and more. **Known for:** farm-grown veggies included in every dish; a beautiful outdoor eatery; sides vibrantly flavored and colored with turmeric and curry powder. $ *Average main: $20* ⊠ *2910 Hana Hwy., Hana* ☎ *808/248–4047* ⊕ *hanafarms.com* ⊘ *No dinner Sun.–Thurs.*

★ **Hana Ranch Restaurant**
$$ | **AMERICAN** | The variety of abundance from local Hana farms is on display here with fresh produce highlighting plates with tasty American fare and a few local favorites like *loco moco* (white rice, burger patty, fried egg, and brown sauce) and *ahi* (yellowfin tuna) poke. The quality of meals and the prices are reflective of a more upscale restaurant, but customers can keep it casual here (no swimwear allowed, however). **Known for:** epic burgers and upscale plate lunches; generous portions; refreshing passion fruit lemonade. $ *Average main: $24* ⊠ *1752 Mill Pl., Hana* ☎ *808/270–5280* ⊕ *hanamauiresort.com/dining.*

🛏 Hotels

Why stay in Hana when it's so far from everything? In a world where everything moves at high speed, Hana still travels on horseback, ambling along slowly enough to smell the flowers. But old-fashioned and remote do not mean tame—this is a wild coast, known for heart-stopping scenery and frequent downpours. Leave city expectations behind. Be advised that dining and shopping options are slim but growing.

■ **TIP**→ **If you're staying for several days or at a vacation rental, stock up on groceries before you head out to Hana.**

Even with these inconveniences, Hana is a place you'll remember for a lifetime.

★ **Bamboo Inn on Hana Bay**
$$ | **B&B/INN** | A thatched-roof gate opens to the courtyard of this informal Balinese-inspired guesthouse with a sweeping view of Hana Bay. The ground-floor studio has a private outdoor shower and the other two units have private whirlpool hot tubs on their second-floor decks. **Pros:** fall asleep to the sound of waves lapping at the rocky coast; close to town center; large BBQ available for grilling. **Cons:** no air-conditioning; no nightlife in this early-to-bed, early-to-rise town; two-night minimum, though one-night fillers may be available. $ *Rooms from: $265* ⊠ *4869 Uakea Rd., Hana* ☎ *808/248–7718* ⊕ *bambooinn.com* ⌑ *3 rooms* ⊙ *No Meals.*

★ **Hana Kai Maui**
$$$$ | **HOTEL** | Perfectly situated on Hana Bay, this two-story "condotel" has an excellent reputation for cleanliness and visitor hospitality—and the ocean views are stunning. **Pros:** 10-minute walk to Hana Bay; one-night rentals are accepted, except oceanfront units; Wi-Fi available in all units. **Cons:** no elevator; no air-conditioning or TV; tight parking lot can be a little difficult to manage. $ *Rooms from: $465* ⊠ *4865 Uakea Rd., Hana* ☎ *808/248–8426, 800/346–2772* ⊕ *hanakaimaui.com* ⌑ *17 units* ⊙ *No Meals.*

Hana-Maui Resort
$$$$ | **RESORT** | After Travaasa-Hana resort was purchased by new owners in 2019, with Hyatt brought in to manage in 2020, Hana-Maui Resort began focusing on major renovations and updates to this

remote oceanside getaway that features bungalows and villas set on sprawling lawns with all of the resort amenities, including a focus on cultural experiences. Expect various closures during its first few years as the property gently incorporates modern touches and environmentally friendly upgrades. **Pros:** welcoming and attentive staff; romantic spot perfect for honeymooners; fun program of traditional activities. **Cons:** construction noise can be bothersome; some suites still in desperate need of an upgrade; disparity in quality of accommodations. $ *Rooms from: $749* ⊠ *5031 Hana Hwy., Hana* ☎ *808/400–1234* ⊕ *hanamauiresort.com* ⥯ *75 bungalows, villas* ⦿ *No Meals.*

🛍 Shopping

The majority of shopping in Hana centers around purchasing fresh foods, with plenty of small farm stands in the area. For take-home treasures, Hana Coast Gallery and Nahiku Marketplace are your best bets.

Hasegawa General Store

GENERAL STORE | Be sure to stop at Hana's charming, filled-to-the-rafters, one-stop shopping option. Built in 1910, the Hana institution isn't fancy, but it's one of Maui's oldest family-run businesses. Buy fishing tackle, beach towels, and a decent selection of groceries here. You also can buy the newspaper, although it may not always be delivered on time. Check out the bulletin board for local events. ⊠ *5165 Hana Hwy., Hana* ☎ *808/248–8231* ⊕ *hasegawastore.com.*

ARTS AND CRAFTS
Nahiku Marketplace

OTHER SPECIALTY STORE | Six miles before you reach Hana, the biggest collection of activity that you'll see along the highway can be found at mile marker 29. Here visitors can grab a cup of coffee at the café, snag a plate from a variety of cuisines, shop for a few bags of coconut candy to take home, and peruse the small gift shop with trinkets, jewelry, and more. There are also portable restrooms and a couple of cute "I survived the Road to Hana" cutouts for a quick family pic. ⊠ *Mile Marker 29, 1546 Hana Hwy., Hana.*

GALLERIES
★ Hana Coast Gallery

ART GALLERIES | One of the most well-curated galleries on the Island, this 3,000-square-foot facility has handcrafted koa furniture, marble sculptures, photography, and jewelry on consignment from local artists as well as artists from across Polynesia. The gallery makes a wonderful effort to give voice to the artists and to teach visitors about them. ⊠ *Hana-Maui Resort, 5031 Hana Hwy., Hana* ☎ *808/248–8636* ⊕ *hanacoast.com.*

🏃 Activities

SPAS
★ The Spa at Hana-Maui Resort

SPAS | A bamboo gate opens into an outdoor sanctuary with a lava-rock basking pool and hot tub. At first glimpse, this spa seems to have been organically grown, not built. Ferns still wet from Hana's frequent downpours nourish the spirit as you rest with a cup of Hawaiian herbal tea, take an invigorating dip in the cold plunge pool, or enjoy the views while enjoying a soak. Luxurious skincare treatments feature local products from Oshan and Malie Organics, and body treatments incorporate organic Maui-made Ala Lani Bath and Body products. ⊠ *Hana-Maui Resort, 5031 Hana Hwy., Hana* ☎ *808/400–1234* ⊕ *hanamauiresort.com* ⥯ *$180 for 60-minute massage.*

Chapter 9

EAST MAUI

Updated by
Laurie Lyons-Makaimoku

◉ **Sights**
★★★★★

🍴 **Restaurants**
☆☆☆☆☆

🛏 **Hotels**
★☆☆☆☆

🛍 **Shopping**
☆☆☆☆☆

🍸 **Nightlife**
☆☆☆☆☆

WELCOME TO EAST MAUI

TOP REASONS TO GO

★ **Get lost.** There's no reason that it can't be the Road Past Hana. For adventurous travelers, your journey will be much more memorable if you keep driving.

★ **Because, frankly, you can never have enough waterfalls.** Wailua Waterfall is incredibly beautiful and is right on the highway. Though you'll see plenty along the Road to Hana, this one is extra special.

★ **Go on some of the best hikes of your life.** If you're up for a challenge, the waterfalls and bamboo forest on the Pipiwai Trail are awe-inspiring. For an easier hike, Kuloa Point and Kahakai Trails also offer many of their own treasures.

★ **Get off the beaten path.** Literally. If you make it all the way around the east end and take Kaupo Road back to the Upcountry area, you'll be driving down roads that aren't nearly as frequented as others on the island.

One of the most remote areas on Maui, the eastern part of Maui is home to many ancient ruins, and is truly an off-the-beaten path destination to explore. It comprises the towns of Kipahulu, Mokulau, and Kaupo. After you pass Hana, the mile markers continue to climb until they reach mile marker 50 near Hamoa Beach, then count down from there. After visiting Hamoa and Koki Beach just south of Hana, your first stop will be Wailua Falls. From there you'll want to explore the attractions in Kipahulu, possibly staying overnight (camping seaside) for the chance to take in some of the less-visited areas of Haleakala National Park (*See the Upcountry chapter for more information on Haleakala National Park*). If you keep going past Kipahulu, you won't find too much more than ocean views, changing landscapes and climate zones, and challenging roads, but it's a journey worth taking if you like adventure. The highway becomes Highway 31 (also known as the Piilani Highway) around the

Kalepa Bridge. Along the way around the east end, you'll find three historical churches that are incredibly serene to visit and also offer expansive ocean views.

1 Kipahulu. Past Hana, Kipahulu is the biggest draw, with the grave of Charles Lindbergh at the Hoomau Church, as well as waterfalls, pools, and other features of Haleakala National Park. Kipahulu is very much an under-the-radar destination and a true escape from the mundane, yet with few things for visitors in terms of dining and lodging; but those who choose to visit will be met with unparalleled sights such as many ancient ruins, organic produce to buy, and most famously, views of the back side of stunning Haleakala National Park. Though the beaches here are beautiful, the surf is rough, making swimming off-limits.

2 Mokulau. For beautiful ocean vistas, take a quick turnoff of the highway to visit a small church and cemetery, as well as the southeast Maui coastline. Much like the other small communities along the Hana Highway, stopping to visit Mokulau means a good time to stretch your

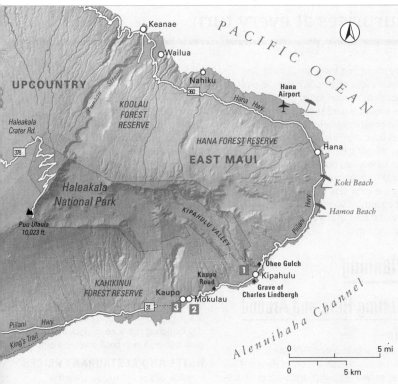

legs and get out your camera. Unlike the other small communities along the highway, you won't be fighting for space among other visitors.

3 Kaupo. Remote, peaceful Kaupo is mostly an area of grasslands where cattle graze (and occasionally wander onto the road), punctuated by the charming Kaupo General Store, which is one of the main reasons visitors come to this area. A sight of many ancient ruins, and where you will encounter some of the harshest winds, you might find it surprising that Kaupo was once the most populated area of all of Maui. Kaupo also provides visitors with a taste of what even the locals consider the "real Maui," with Kaupo Road, also known as Piilani Highway and Highway 31. Here you can see views of the desert and truly feel like you're in another world.

East Maui defies definition. Part hideaway for renegades, part escape for celebrities, this funky stretch of Maui surprises at every turn.

You might find a smoothie shop that powers your afternoon bike ride, or a hidden restaurant–artist gathering off a backcountry road serving organic cuisine that could have been dropped in from San Francisco. Farms are abundant, and the dramatic beauty seems to get better the farther you get from Hana. This route leads through stark ocean vistas rounding the back side of Haleakala and into Upcountry. If you plan to meander this way, be sure to check the weather and road conditions.

Planning

Getting Here and Around

AIR
For a quick drop into East Maui, there is a small commuter airport in Hana (HNM) that serves residents and visitors with service by Mokulele Airlines (⊕ *mokuleleairlines.com*). There is no car rental service available. For a trip to East Maui along the Road to Hana, fly into the main Maui airport in Kahului (OGG).

CAR
You will need a car, particularly one that can handle rougher roads, when venturing out to East Maui. Car rental companies can be a bit wary about customers venturing past Hana, particularly along Kaupo Road. If you have a rental car and you have an accident in East Maui, any help you need is likely yours to arrange and pay for.

Hotels

Though East Maui is likely a part of your journey, not your destination, there are a few bed-and-breakfast-style options for spending the night in remote Maui. Camping options can be found at Kipahulu Campground on the backside of Haleakala National Park. Be sure to stock up on provisions if you're staying overnight.

Restaurants

The closest thing you'll find to dining in East Maui is farm stands where you can grab juice, coffee, or some fresh produce at Kaupo Store. If you're spending the day exploring, be sure to pack a picnic or grab a to-go lunch before setting out.

HOTEL AND RESTAURANT PRICES
Hotel prices in the reviews are the lowest cost of a standard double room in high season. Restaurant prices in the reviews are the average cost of a main course at dinner, or if dinner is not served, at lunch.

WHAT IT COSTS in U.S. Dollars			
$	$$	$$$	$$$$
RESTAURANTS			
under $18	$18–$26	$27–$35	over $35
HOTELS			
under $181	$181–$260	$261–$340	over $340

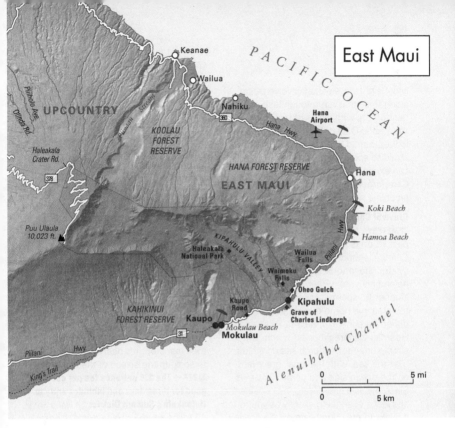

East Maui

Safety

The East Maui drive includes stretches where the road isn't paved and others where the road can be narrow and a little intimidating. Travel the road during the day and at a slow pace. The area is also prone to flash flooding and landslides, so use extra caution when the weather is rough, and be sure to obey all posted signs.

Kipahulu

11 miles east of Hana.

Most know Kipahulu as the resting place of Charles Lindbergh. Kipahulu devotes its energy to staying under the radar. There is not much for tourists, save an organic farm stand and astounding

natural landscapes, particularly those in the back side of Haleakala National Park. Beaches in the area are full of rough surf and strong currents, making them off-limits for swimming. This area was also home to many ancient Hawaiians, making it rife with ruins. Be sure not to touch them when you see them, but do take the time to learn more by talking with park rangers. Maui's wildest wilderness might not beg for your tourist dollars, but it is a tantalizing place to escape just about everything.

GETTING HERE AND AROUND

To access Kipahulu from Hana, continue on Hana Highway, also known as 360, for 11 miles southeast. You can also reach the area from Upcountry's Highway 37, which turns into Highway 31, although this route can take up to two hours and is a bit rough on your rental car.

⊙ Sights

Most sights in Kipahulu involve treks along trails that run through lush, green rain forests with views of waterfalls and the Pacific Ocean. Be prepared for hiking in wet, humid conditions, and don't be afraid to spend the night so that you can explore fully. Camping at Kipahulu Campground is now only offered through an online reservation system.

Grave of Charles Lindbergh

CEMETERY | Many people travel the mile past Oheo Gulch to see the grave of Charles Lindbergh. The world-renowned aviator chose to be buried here because he and his wife, writer Anne Morrow Lindbergh, spent a lot of time living in the area in a home they'd built. He was buried here in 1974, next to Palapala Hoomau Congregational Church. The simple one-room church sits on a bluff over the sea, with the small graveyard on the ocean side and gorgeous views. Since this is a churchyard, be considerate and leave everything exactly as you found it. Next to the churchyard on the ocean side is a small county park, a good place for a peaceful picnic. ⊠ *Palapala Hoomau Congregational Church, Piilani Hwy., Kipahulu* ⊕ *palapalahoomau.org.*

Haleakala National Park

VOLCANO | The Kipahulu section of Haleakala National Park, also known as the backside of Haleakala, is rich with greenery, waterfalls, ocean vistas, ancient archaeological sites, and a variety of hikes. Camping is also an option at the park via an online reservation system; just make sure to stock up on provisions. A single private vehicle costs $30 for a three-day park entrance permit; without a vehicle is $15 per person. Once in the park, the Pipiwai Trail to Waimoku Falls is a challenging 4-mile hike, while the Kuloa Point Trail and Kahakai Trails offer easier, 1/2-mile trails. ⊠ *Piilani Hwy., Kipahulu* ⊕ *12 miles past Hana* ☎ *808/572–4400*

⊕ *nps.gov/hale* ⚲ *Reservations required for camping and summit sunrise.*

Oheo Gulch

WATERFALL | One branch of Haleakala National Park runs down the mountain from the crater and reaches the sea here, 12 miles past Hana at mile marker 42 on the Hana Highway, where a basalt-lined stream cascades from one pool to the next. Some tour guides still incorrectly call this area Seven Sacred Pools, but in truth there are more than seven, and they've never been considered sacred.

⚠ **While you may be tempted to take a dip, know that the pools are often closed because of landslides and flash flooding. If you see a closure notice, take it seriously, as people have died here.**

The place gets crowded, as most people who drive the Hana Highway make this their last stop. It's best to get here early to soak up the solace of these waterfalls. ▪TIP➔ **The $30 entrance fee per car is good for three days and includes entry to Haleakala's Summit District.** ⊠ *Hana Hwy., 12 miles south of Hana, Hana* ⊕ *nps.gov/hale* ⊠ *$15–$30 National Park entry fee.*

★ Wailua Falls

WATERFALL | Once you've made it past Hana town, you're rewarded with views of what many consider to be the most beautiful and most photographed waterfall in Maui. The best part is that you don't even have to get off of the highway to see the stunning 80-foot falls that end in a gorgeous pool. Look for local food and gift vendors in the parking area. ⊠ *Piilani Hwy., Hana* ⊹ *Mile marker 45.*

★ Waimoku Falls

WATERFALL | If you enjoy hiking, go up the stream from the Pools of Oheo on the 2-mile hike to Waimoku Falls via Pipiwai Trail. The trail crosses a spectacular gorge, then turns into a boardwalk that takes you through an amazing bamboo forest. The hike also includes a giant banyan tree, views of Makahiku Falls, and forests of tropical plant life. After returning from your hike you can pitch a tent in the grassy campground down by the sea if you've made reservations in advance. ✉ *Piilani Hwy., Hana* ☎ *808/572–4400* 🌐 *nps.gov/hale* 🎫 *$15 per person on foot, $30 per vehicle.*

Hotels

This remote area of East Maui is limited to a secluded B&B and campgrounds along the backside of Haleakala. Staying overnight offers ample opportunity to explore Kipahulu's natural beauty, but it's imperative to plan in advance and bring in your own supplies.

Ala'aina Ocean Vista

$$$ | **B&B/INN** | This B&B on the grounds of an old banana plantation past Oheo Gulch (about a 40-minute drive past Hana town) is a simple, back-to-nature kind of spot that is "off the grid." Banana trees still populate the property, alongside mango, papaya, coconut, and avocado trees. **Pros:** quiet and secluded; no pesticides or chemicals used on property; gorgeous ocean views. **Cons:** remote location with no restaurants nearby; two-night minimum, four-night maximum stay; travel time from Kahului Airport is quite long. $ *Rooms from: $270* ✉ *184 Hana Hwy., 10 miles past Hana, Kipahulu* ☎ *808/248–7824* 🌐 *hanabedandbreakfast.com* 🛏 *1 room* 🍽 *Free Breakfast.*

Mokulau

16 miles from Hana, 5 miles from Kipahulu.

Mokulau means "many islets." This little diversion from the highway, beautiful from the road and down at the shoreline, is mostly visited for its stunning views and to check out the 19th-century Huialoha Church.

GETTING HERE AND AROUND

Continue along Route 360 from Kipahulu as the highway changes into Route 31, also known as the Piilani Highway, and approaches Mokulau. Around mile marker 37 is where the road changes to paved and graded dirt road for the next 10 miles. Look out for the turn to Mokulau, just before mile marker 35. You'll be heading toward the ocean on a dirt road, so be sure to take your time.

Sights

Huialoha Church

CHURCH | Originally constructed by Christian missionaries and their Hawaiian followers in 1859, the church has weathered earthquakes and storms, though it has needed major repair projects approximately every 30 years, beginning in the 1940s. The commitment to care for and restore the church, from both Kaupo residents and other visitors who fall in love with it, is just as beautiful as the two-foot-thick white rock walls that hold it up. The church is still used on occasions such as holidays, with one Sunday service per month, and the occasional wedding. Visitors often stop here for a picnic with gorgeous views, as the church sits oceanside. ✉ *Piilani Hwy., Hana* ✣ *just before mile marker 35* 🌐 *huialohachurchkaupo.org.*

Beaches

Mokulau Beach

BEACH | The shoreline on this little peninsula is full of black sand and stones, but the rough waters make this an unsafe place for swimming. Instead, enjoy the views, watch a few local fishermen fight for their catch, and try to spot one of the Hawaiian monk seals that occasionally bask here (be sure to keep your distance from them). **Amenities**: none. **Best for:** hiking. ✉ *Piilani Hwy., Hana* ✣ *just before mile marker 35.*

Kaupo

16 miles from Hana; 5 miles from Kipahulu.

This area, now home to cattle ranches and a small general store, was once the most populated area of Maui. There are pockets of ancient archaeological sites throughout, so be careful not to disturb them if you come across any while exploring. The winds here can be harsh, but there is something incredibly peaceful about just how remote it feels.

GETTING HERE AND AROUND

Just past the turnoff to Mokulau on Piilani Highway, you'll find the focal point of the area, the Kaupo General Store. Past Kaupo, as you continue along the highway, you'll have views of a number of bays, including Nuu Bay (mile marker 31) and Huakini Bay (mile marker 29.9).

⊙ Sights

Sights in the area are fairly limited, but the Kaupo General Store is worth a stop to get a feel for the people who live in this remote area.

Kaupo General Store

OTHER ATTRACTION | More than your run-of-the-mill general store, the Kaupo Store, opened in 1925, not only has the cold drinks and snacks that you'll be looking for this far into your drive, but it's also full of souvenirs, knickknacks, and a mini-museum housing vintage cameras, clocks, and more. In recent years the store has downsized to a small outdoor pop-up in the parking lot, with limited opening hours. This is a great place to linger and talk story with the owners and locals. ⊠ *34793 Piilani Hwy, Hana* ☎ *808/248–8054.*

Kaupo Road

SCENIC DRIVE | Also called Piilani Highway, this road winds through what locals say is one of the last parts of real Maui. It goes all the way around Haleakala's back side through Ulupalakua Ranch and into Kula. The desert-like area, with its grand vistas, is unlike anything else on the Island. This road has a reputation for being treacherous, and while narrow sections and steep cliffs can be intimidating for some drivers, recent road improvements have made this a much smoother ride.

⚠ **Some car-rental agencies call the area off-limits for their passenger cars, and they won't come to your rescue if you need emergency assistance. However, four-wheel drive isn't necessary.**

The small communities around East Maui cling tenuously to the old ways—please be respectful of that if you do pass this way. Between Kipahulu and Kula may be a mere 38 miles, but the twisty road makes the drive take up to two hours. If you must drive this road at night, keep an eye out for free-range cattle crossing your path.

■ TIP→ **Fill up on gas and food before departing, as the only stop out here is Kaupo General Store, which hawks a few pricey necessities.**

Chapter 10

MAUI ACTIVITIES

Updated by
Syndi Texeira

Getting into (or onto) the water may well be the highlight of your Maui trip. The Valley Isle is an aquatic wonderland where you can learn to surf, stand-up paddle, or scuba dive. Vibrant snorkel sites can be explored right off the shore or easily accessed aboard a kayak, motorized raft, or power catamaran. From November through April (peak season January–March), whale-watching adventures are a top draw as humpbacks escaping Alaska's frigid winter arrive in Maui's warm, protected waters to frolic, mate, and give birth.

Along Maui's leeward coastline, from Kaanapali on the West Shore to Ahi-hi Cove on the South Shore, you can discover great spots for snorkeling and swimming, some more crowded than others. On a good day, you might encounter dozens of green sea turtles at an underwater cleaning station, a pod of dolphins riding by the catamaran's bow, and an abundance of colorful fish hovering by bright cauliflower coral reefs.

When your preferred sport calls for calm glassy waters, get an early start when visibility is best; plus, the trade winds begin to roll through the valleys in the late morning and pick up speed in the afternoon. For those thrill-seekers who flock to Hawaii for the wind, it's best to head out to the North Shore's Hookipa, where consistent winds keep

kiteboarders flying and windsurfers jibing, or Peahi (aka "Jaws"), where surfers seasonally get to glide on 30- to 60-foot waves.

Treat the ocean with respect, and for your safety, choose activities that suit your skill level and level of fitness. If in doubt, skip the rental and pay for a lesson to have proper instructions in navigating swells and wind and someone with you in case you get in a bind. The ocean might be beautiful, but it can be unpredictable.

Surfing is enjoyed all year, and avid surfers live for the winter swells when the north and west coasts get really "lit up." Whale season on Maui is nothing short of majestic at its peak, late January–mid-March. You can spot them from the shore or get up close with a motorized raft or catamaran.

We know how tempting it is to spend your entire vacation on the beach (many days we're tempted as well), but if you do, you'll miss out on the "other side of Maui": the eerie, moonlike surface of Haleakala Crater, the lush rain forests of East Maui, and the geological wonder that is Iao Valley State Monument, to name just a few. Even playing a round of golf on one of the world-class courses provides breathtaking vistas, reminding you just why you chose to come to Maui in the first place.

Maui's exceptional climate affords year-round opportunities for outdoor adventures, whether it's exploring cascading waterfalls on a day hike, riding horseback through verdant valleys, soaring across vast gulches on a zip line, or taking an exhilarating bicycle ride down Haleakala. When you take the time to get off the beaten path, you'll discover why Maui *no ka oi* (is the best). But make sure not to overbook yourself—one or two activities per day is plenty. You're on vacation, remember.

Adventure Sports

Rappel Maui
LOCAL SPORTS | If the idea of walking backward down waterfalls appeals to you, this company stands ready, willing, and able to accommodate. Friendly, knowledgeable guides encourage and assist you literally every step of the way. You must be at least ten years old to participate, have a waist size between 22 and 48 inches, and weigh between 70 and 249 pounds. Rappelling is a moderately strenuous activity, so be prepared for a workout that includes hiking and swimming in addition to rappelling. The tour price includes all gear, a snack, bottled water, and mosquito repellent. You'll need a rental car to make the 26.5-mile

(one-hour) drive from the Kahalui airport to the Garden of Eden Arboretum along the road to Hana. Arrive early and get ready to explore your inner canyoneer! ✉ *10600 Hana Hwy., Haiku-Pauwela* ☎ *808/270–1500* ⊕ *rappelmaui.com* ✍ *$229 per person.*

Air Tours

Helicopter flight-seeing excursions can take you over the West Maui Mountains, Haleakala Crater, or the Island of Molokai. Flying is a beautiful, thrilling way to see the Island and the *only* way to see some of its most scenic areas and waterfalls. Tour prices usually include a digital video of your trip so you can relive the experience at home. Fees run about $250 for a half-hour flight and more than $350 for a 75-minute tour with an ocean or cliffside landing. Discounts may be available online or if you're willing to take a chance by calling at the last minute.

Tour operators come under sharp scrutiny for passenger safety and equipment maintenance. Don't be shy; ask about a company's safety record, flight paths, age of equipment, and level of operator experience. Generally, though, if it's still in business, it's doing something right.

Blue Hawaiian Helicopters
AIR EXCURSIONS | Since 1985, this company has provided aerial adventures in Hawaii and has been integral in some of Hollywood's filming on Maui. Complete Island tours start at 65 minutes and include views of lush valleys, waterfalls, rain forests, and Haleakala crater. A bonus option is to land at a remote location along the Haleakala slopes. Its A-Star and Eco-Star helicopters are air-conditioned and have Bose noise-blocking headsets for all passengers. Charter flights are also available. ✉ *1 Lelepio Pl., Hangar 105, Kahului* ☎ *808/871–8844 local, 800/745–2583 toll*

free ⊕ bluehawaiian.com ✉ Tours start at $369 per person.

Sunshine Helicopters

AIR EXCURSIONS | The 45-minute Hana-Haleakala tour soars past Haleakala National Park, revealing its many faces, including the arid moonlike crater and lush eastern edge dripping with waterfalls and rain forests. First-class seating is available for an additional fee. Charter flights can be arranged. A pilot-narrated digital record of your actual flight is available for purchase. ⊠ *Kahului Airport Rd., Hangar 107, Kahului* ☎ *808/270–3999, 866/501–7738 ⊕ sunshinehelicopters. com* ✉ *Tours start at $254.*

Biking

Long distances and mountainous terrain keep biking from being a practical mode of travel on Maui. Still, painted bike lanes enable cyclists to travel from Makena to Kapalua, and you'll see hardy souls battling the trade winds under the hot Maui sun.

Several companies offer guided bike tours down Haleakala. This activity is a great way to enjoy an easy, gravity-induced bike ride but isn't for those not confident on a bike. The ride is inherently dangerous due to the slope, sharp turns, and the fact that you're riding down an actual road with cars on it. That said, the guided bike companies take every safety precaution. A few companies offer unguided (or, as they like to say, "self-guided") tours where they provide you with the bike and transportation to the mountain, and then you're free to descend at your own pace. Most companies offer discounts for Internet bookings.

Haleakala National Park no longer allows commercial downhill bicycle rides within the park's boundaries. As a result, tour amenities and routes differ by company. Ask about sunrise viewing from the Haleakala summit (be prepared to leave *very* early in the morning) if this is an essential feature for you. Some lower-price tours begin at the 6,500-foot elevation just outside the national park boundaries, where you will be unable to view the sunrise over the crater. Weather conditions on Haleakala vary greatly, so a visible sunrise can never be guaranteed. Sunrise is downright cold at the summit, so be sure to dress in layers and wear closed-toe shoes.

Each company has age and weight restrictions, and pregnant women are discouraged from participating, although they are generally welcome in the escort van. Reconsider this activity if you have difficulty with high altitudes, have recently been scuba diving, or take medications that may cause drowsiness.

BEST SPOTS

Thompson Road in Keokea and Polipoli Spring State Recreation Area in Kula are popular areas for cycling in Maui, and Makawao Forest Reserve is attracting riders of all ages and ability levels with its well-maintained, clearly marked trails.

Makawao Forest Reserve

BIKING | Mountain bikers of all ages and ability levels will find something to please at this recreation area that features seven trails and three skill areas. Trails are well marked, and there are maps posted at each intersection. ⊠ *Kahakapao Rd., Makawao* ✛ *To get here from Piiholo Rd., turn left on Waiahiwi Rd. and then right on Kahakapao Rd.*

Polipoli Spring State Recreation Area

BIKING | Mountain bikers favor the remote Polipoli Spring State Recreation Area for its bumpy trail through an unlikely forest of conifers. Polipoli Spring is often closed following heavy storms due to fallen trees and other damage. Check the Hawaii State Parks website prior to making the drive up there. ⊠ *End of Waipoli Rd., off Rte. 377, Kula ⊕ hawaiistateparks.org.*

Thompson Road

BIKING | Street bikers will want to head out to scenic Thompson Road. It's quiet, gently curvy, and flanked by gorgeous views on both sides. Because it's at a higher elevation, the air temperature is cooler and the wind lighter. The coast back down toward Kahului on the Kula Highway is worth the ride up. ⊠ *Kula Hwy., off Rte. 37, Keokea.*

EQUIPMENT AND TOURS

★ Cruiser Phil's Volcano Riders

BIKING | In the downhill bicycle industry since 1983, "Cruiser" Phil Feliciano offers both group and private tours that include hotel transfers, coffee and snacks, and a guided 23-mile ride down the mountain. Participants should be older than 12, at least five feet tall, weigh less than 280 pounds, and have ridden a bike in the past year. Feliciano also offers structured independent bike tours, van-only tours, and packages that include a zip-lining experience. Discounts are available for online bookings. ⊠ *810 Haiku Rd. #120, Haiku-Pauwela* ☎ *808/575–9575* ⊕ *cruiserphils.com* ✉ *Tours start at $130 per person.*

Go Cycling Maui

BIKING | Serious cyclists can join an exhilarating group ride with Donnie Arnoult, a fixture on the Maui cycling scene since 1999. Routes include Haiku to Keanae, Kula to Kahikinui, and the ultimate Maui cycling challenge: Paia to the top of the Haleakala crater. You bring your own cycling shoes, pedals, and clothes, and Donnie provides the bicycle, helmet, gloves, water bottle, snacks, and energy drinks. His shop is also a full-service cycling store offering sales, rentals, and repairs. ⊠ *99 Hana Hwy., Unit A, Paia* ☎ *808/579–9009* ⊕ *gocyclingmaui.com* ✉ *One-day rides $199 per person ($245 to the crater).*

Island Biker

BIKING | Maui's premier bike shop for rentals, sales, and service offers standard front-shock bikes, road bikes, and full-suspension mountain bikes. Rental prices include a helmet, pump, water bottle, cages, tire-repair kit, and spare tube. Car racks are included with weekly rentals. The staff can suggest routes appropriate for mountain or road biking. ⊠ *415 Dairy Rd. Suite C, Kahului* ☎ *808/877–7744* ✉ *Daily rentals start at $75. Weekly rates start at $250.*

Krank Cycles

BIKING | Krank Cycles is located in Kahului and Upcountry Maui, close to the Makawao Forest Reserve. They offer full-day and weekly rentals of high-end road and mountain bikes. Owner Moose will provide you with maps and trail reports, in addition to your rental bike and gear. ⊠ *1120 Makawao Ave., Makawao* ☎ *808/572–2299* ⊕ *krankmaui.com* ✉ *Daily rental $59 and up.*

Maui Mountain Cruisers

BIKING | This partially guided bike tour begins at the company's Paia shop, where you'll be outfitted before being shuttled 6,500 feet to the Haleakala National Park entrance. Once there, you're free to "cruise" the approximately 26 miles downhill to your starting point, stopping at the many shops, eateries, and historic sites along the way. ⊠ *381 Baldwin Ave. #C, Paia* ☎ *808/871–6014* ⊕ *mauimountaincruisers.com* ✉ *$85.*

West Maui Cycles

BIKING | Serving the island's west side, West Maui Cycles offers a range of bikes, including cruisers, hybrids, and performance road bikes. They offer discounted rates for longer-term rentals. Sales and service are also available. ⊠ *1087 Limahana Pl., No. 6, Lahaina* ☎ *808/661–9005* ⊕ *westmauicycles.com* ✉ *Cruisers $20 per day, hybrids $40 per day, and performance road bikes $60–$100 per day.*

How to Catch a Wave

The technique for catching waves is the same with or without a board. Swim out to where the swell is just beginning to break, and position yourself toward shore. When the next wave comes, lie on your bodyboard (if you have one), kick like crazy, and catch it. You'll feel the push of the wave as you glide in front of the gurgling foamy surf. When bodysurfing, put your arms over your head, bring your index fingers together (so you look like the letter "A"), and stiffen your body like a board to achieve the same effect.

If you don't like to swim too far out, stick with bodyboarding and bodysurfing close to shore. Shore breaks (if they aren't too steep) can be exhilarating to ride. You'll know it's too steep if you hear the sound of slapping when the waves hit the sand. You're looking for waves that curl over and break farther out, then roll, not slap onto the sand. Always watch first to make sure the conditions aren't too strong.

Bodyboarding and Bodysurfing

Bodysurfing and "sponging" (as bodyboarding is called by the regulars; "boogie boarding" is another variation) are great ways to catch some waves without having to master surfing—and there's no balance or coordination required. A bodyboard (or "sponge") is softer than a hard fiberglass surfboard, which means you can ride safely in the rough-and-tumble surf zone. If you get tossed around—which is half the fun—you don't have a heavy surfboard nearby to bang your head on but you do have something to hang onto. Serious spongers invest in a single short-clipped fin to help propel them into the wave.

BEST SPOTS

In West Maui, **D. T. Fleming Beach** offers great surf almost daily along with some nice amenities: ample parking, restrooms, a shower, grills, picnic tables, and a daily lifeguard. Caution is advised, especially during winter months, when the current and undertow can get rough.

Between Kihei and Wailea on the South Shore, **Kamaole III** is a good spot for bodysurfing and bodyboarding. It has a sandy floor, with one- to three-foot waves breaking not too far out. It's often crowded late in the day, especially on weekends when local kids are out of school. Don't let that chase you away; the waves are wide enough for everyone.

If you don't mind public nudity (officially illegal but practiced nonetheless), Puu Olai **(aka Little Beach)** on the South Shore is the best break on the island for bodyboarding and bodysurfing. The shape of the sandy shoreline creates waves that break a long way out and tumble into shore. Because it's sandy, you only risk stubbing a toe on the few submerged rocks. Don't try bodyboarding at neighboring Oneloa **(aka Big Beach)**—waves will slap you onto the steep shore. To get to Little Beach, take the first entrance to Makena State Beach Park; climb the rock wall at the north end of the beach.

On the North Shore, **Paia Bay** has waves suitable for spongers and bodysurfers. The beach is just before Paia town, beyond the large community building and grass field.

EQUIPMENT

Most condos and hotels have bodyboards available to guests—some in better condition than others (beat-up boards work just as well for beginners). You can also pick up a bodyboard from any discount shop, such as Target or Longs Drugs (now owned by CVS), for upwards of $30.

Auntie Snorkel

WATER SPORTS | You can rent decent bodyboards and all types of affordable watersport equipment at Auntie Snorkel. Check online for specials and discounts. ✉ 2439 S. Kihei Rd., Kihei ☎ 808/298–3021 ⊕ auntiesnorkel.com ⊠ Bodyboard rentals $6.95 a day or $20 a week.

West Maui Sports and Fishing Supply

WATER SPORTS | This old country store has been around since 1987 and has some of the best prices on the west side for surfboards and bodyboards. Snorkel and fishing gear, beach chairs, and umbrellas are also available. ✉ 843 Wainee St., Lahaina ☎ 808/661–6252 ⊕ westmauisports.com ⊠ Surfboards $70 per week. Bodyboards $3 per day, $15 per week.

Deep-Sea Fishing

If fishing is your sport, Maui is your island. In these waters, you'll find *ahi* (yellowfin tuna), *aku* (skipjack tuna), barracuda, bonefish, *kawakawa* (bonito), *mahimahi* (dolphinfish), Pacific blue marlin, *ono* (wahoo), and *ulua* (giant trevally). You can fish year-round, and you don't need a license.

Plenty of fishing boats run out of Lahaina and Maalaea harbors. If you charter a private boat, expect to spend in the neighborhood of $700 to $1,000 for an exciting half day in the swivel seat. You can share a boat for much less if you don't mind close quarters with a stranger. Before you sign up, you should know that some boats keep the catch. Most will, however, fillet a nice piece for you to take

home. And if you catch a real beauty, you might even be able to have it professionally mounted.

■**TIP**➔ **Because boats fill up fast during busy seasons, make reservations before coming to Maui.**

You're expected to bring your lunch and beverages in unbreakable containers. (Shop the night before; it's hard to find snacks at 5 am.) Boats supply coolers, ice, and bait. A 7.5% tax is added to the cost of a trip, and a 15%–20% tip for the crew is suggested.

BOATS AND CHARTERS

Die Hard Sportfishing

FISHING | Captain Fuzzy Alboro runs a highly recommended operation on the 33-foot *Die Hard.* Check-in times vary between 10 pm and 3 am, depending on the moon's location, and trips range from four to eight hours. He takes a minimum of four and a maximum of six people. ✉ Lahaina Harbor, 654 Wharf St., Slip 9, Lahaina ☎ 808/344–5051 ⊕ diehardsportfishing.com ⊠ $300 for shared boat or $1,520 for private charter.

Finest Kind Sportfishing

FISHING | A record 1,118-pound pacific blue marlin was reeled in by the crew aboard *Finest Kind,* a lovely 37-foot Merritt kept so clean you'd never guess the action it's seen. Captain David Hudson has been around these waters for about 40 years, long enough to befriend other expert fishers. This three-generation family-run company operates three boats and specializes in skilled trolling. No bananas on board, please; the captain thinks they're bad luck for fishing. ✉ Lahaina Harbor, 675 Wharf St., Slip 7, Lahaina ☎ 808/661–0338 ⊕ finestkindsportfishingmaui.com ⊠ Shared charters $300 for four hours, $475 for full day. Full-day private charter $2,300.

Hinatea Sportfishing

FISHING | This family-run company has built an excellent reputation. The active crew aboard *Hinatea,* the 41-foot

Hatteras Convertible, has one motto: "No boat rides here—we go to catch fish!" ✉ *Lahaina Harbor, 675 Wharf St., Slip 27, Lahaina* ☎ *808/667–7548* ⊕ *hi-natea-sportfishing.com* ✉ *Shared boat charters $275–$350. Private charters $1,000–$1,600.*

Jayhawk Charters

FISHING | This ultraluxe, 48-foot *Cabo* is available for private charters and takes a maximum of six passengers. It's equipped with air-conditioning, two bathrooms, a salon, and two comfy staterooms with a flat-screen TV, a Bose stereo system, and leather couches. For serious anglers, the boat also has Shimano rods and reels, a black-box sonar, and the latest in fish finders, GPS, and chart plotters. ✉ *Lahaina Harbor, Slip 63, Lahaina* ☎ *866/326–0636* ⊕ *jayhawkmaui. squarespace.com* ✉ *$916 per hour (full-day runs last up to eight hours).*

Strike Zone

FISHING | This charter company is one of the few to offer bottom-fishing trips (for smaller fish like snapper) and pelagic trips (for the big ones—*ono* (wahoo), *ahi* (yellowfin tuna), *mahimahi* (dolphinfish), and marlin. *Strike Zone* is a 43-foot Delta that offers plenty of room for 28 people. Soft drinks and lunch or snacks included. The entire boat shares the catch. ✉ *Maalaea Harbor, 101 Maalaea Boat Harbor Rd., Slip 40, Maalaea* ☎ *808/879–4485* ⊕ *strikezonemaui.com* ✉ *6-hour trip $188 per person for a pole; spectators $94. 4-hour charters offered on Sun., Tues., and Thurs. at $154.*

Golf

Maui's natural beauty and surroundings offer some of the most jaw-dropping vistas imaginable on a golf course; add a variety of challenging, well-designed courses, and it's easy to explain the Island's popularity with golfers. Holes run across small bays, past craggy lava outcrops, and up into cool forested mountains. Most courses have mesmerizing ocean views, some close enough to feel the salt in the air. Although many golf courses are affiliated with resorts (and therefore a little pricier), the general-public courses are no less impressive. Playing on Lanai is another option.

Greens Fees: Golf can be costly on Maui. Greens fees listed here are the highest course rates per round on weekdays and weekends for U.S. residents. (Some courses charge non-U.S. residents higher prices.) Rental clubs may or may not be included with the greens fee. Discounts are often available for resort guests, for twilight tee times, and for those who book online.

■ **TIP**→ Resort courses, in particular, offer more than the usual three sets of tees, so bite off as much or as little challenge as you like. Tee it up from the tips and you can end up playing a few 600-yard par 5s and see a few 250-yard forced carries.

DISCOUNTS AND DEALS
Maui Golf Shop

GOLF | This operation has the biggest rental fleet of over 150 club sets and offers discounted tee times. ✉ *1215 S. Kihei Rd., Kihei* ☎ *808/875–4653 local, 800/981–5512 toll free* ⊕ *golf-maui.com.*

MAUI GOLF TOURNAMENTS

Maui has a number of golf tournaments, many of which are fundraisers for local charities, and one kicks off the PGA Tour every year.

Ka Lima O Maui 100 Holes of Golf

SPECTATOR SPORTS | Every May, self-proclaimed "lunatic" golfers play from sunrise to sunset in Wailea's annual Memorial Day weekend fundraiser for Ka Lima O Maui, a local charity that provides job training and employment for disabled adults. ✉ *127 Mahalani St., Wailuku* ☎ *808/875–7450* ⊕ *kalimaomaui.org.*

Tips for Golfing on Maui

Golf is golf, and Hawaii is part of the United States, but Island golf has its quirks. Here are a few tips to make your golf experience in the Islands more pleasant.

■ Sunscreen: Buy it, apply it (we're talking a minimum of 30 SPF). The subtropical rays of the sun are intense, even in December. Good advice is to apply sunscreen, at a minimum, on the 1st and 10th tees.

■ Stay hydrated. Spending four-plus hours in the sun and heat means you'll sweat away many fluids and energy.

■ All resort courses and many daily-fee courses provide rental clubs. In many cases, they're the latest lines from top manufacturers. Valid both for men and women and for left-handers, which means you don't have to schlep clubs across the Pacific.

■ Pro shops at most courses are well stocked with balls, tees, and other accoutrements, so it doesn't weigh a ton even if you bring your bag.

■ Come spikeless—few Hawaii courses still permit metal spikes. Also, most of the resort courses require a collared shirt.

■ Maui is notorious for its trade winds. Consider playing early or at twilight if you want to avoid the breezes, and remember that although they will frustrate you at times and make club selection difficult, you may well see some of your longest drives ever.

■ In theory, you can play golf in Hawaii 365 days a year, but there's a reason the Hawaiian Islands are so green: an umbrella and light jacket can come in handy.

■ Unless you play a muni or specific daily-fee courses, plan on taking a cart. Riding carts are mandatory at most courses and are included in the greens fee.

Sentry Tournament of Champions

SPECTATOR SPORTS | Held in January on Kapalua's Plantation Course, this tournament is an attention-getter—the first official PGA tour event. ⊠ *2000 Plantation Club Dr., Lahaina* ☎ *808/669–8044* ⊕ *golfatkapalua.com.*

WEST MAUI

Kaanapali Golf Courses

GOLF | In 1962, the Royal Kaanapali (North) Course opened and was one of three in Hawaii designed by Robert Trent Jones Sr., the godfather of modern golf architecture. The greens average a whopping 10,000 square feet, necessary because of the often-severe undulation. The par-4 18th hole course is challenging (the prevailing trade breezes, with out-of-bounds on the left and a lake on the right). Designed by Arthur Jack Snyder, the Kaanapali Kai (South) Course (opened in 1976) shares similar seaside-into-the-hills terrain. Still, it is rated a couple of strokes easier, mainly because putts are less treacherous. ⊠ *2290 Kaanapali Pkwy., Lahaina* ☎ *808/661–3691, 866/454–4653* ⊕ *kaanapaligolfcourses.com* 🖼 *Royal Kaanapali (North) Course $255, Kaanapali Kai (South) Course $205* 🎋 *Royal Kaanapali (North) Course: 18 holes, 6700 yards, par 71; Kaanapali Kai (South) Course: 18 holes, 6400 yards, par 70.*

★ Kapalua Golf

GOLF | Perhaps Hawaii's best-known golf resort and the crown jewel of golf on Maui, Kapalua hosts the PGA Tour's first event each January: the Sentry Tournament of Champions at the Plantation Course. On this famed course, Ben Crenshaw and Bill Coore (1991) tried to incorporate traditional shot values in a nontraditional site, taking into account slope, gravity, and the prevailing trade winds. The par-5 18th hole, for instance, plays 663 yards from the back tees (600 yards from the resort tees). The hole drops 170 feet in elevation, narrowing as it goes to a partially guarded green, and plays downwind and down-grain. Despite the longer-than-usual distance, the slope is great enough and the wind at your back usually brisk enough to reach the green with two well-struck shots—a truly unbelievable finish to a course that will challenge, frustrate, and reward the patient golfer.

The Bay Course (Arnold Palmer and Francis Duane, 1975) is the more traditional of Kapalua's courses, with gentle rolling fairways and generous greens. The most memorable hole is the par-3 5th hole, with a tee shot that must carry over a turquoise inlet of Oneloa Bay. Each of the courses has a separate clubhouse. ⊠ *2000 Plantation Club Dr., Kapalua* ☎ *808/669–8044, 877/527–2582* ⊕ *golfatkapalua.com* ✆ *Plantation Course $329, Bay Course $229* ⚐ *Plantation Course: 18 holes, 7411 yards, par 73. Bay Course: 18 holes, 6600 yards, par 72.*

Kapalua Golf Academy

GOLF | It is a state-of-the-art golf school and training facility designed by three-time US Open Champion Hale Irwin. With 23 acres of practice turf, an 18-hole putting course, and a 3-hole walking course, the Kapalua Golf Academy offers individual lessons, corporate clinics, golf schools, daily clinics, and custom off-site instruction by its renowned staff of PGA professionals. ⊠ *1000 Office Rd., Kapalua* ☎ *808/665–5455, 877/527–2582* ⊕ *golfatkapalua.com* ✆ *Private instruction starts at $185 for a 50-minute lesson.*

THE SOUTH SHORE

Maui Nui Golf Club

GOLF | Maui Nui Golf Club offers challenging but fair greens. Fairways tend to be narrow, especially in landing areas, and can be arduous when the trade winds come up in the afternoon. Friendly staff make the course suitable for beginners. ⊠ *1345 Piilani Hwy., Kihei* ☎ *808/874–0777* ⊕ *mauinuigolfclub.com* ✆ *$79 and up* ⚐ *18 holes, 6404 yards, par 71.*

Wailea Blue Course

GOLF | Wailea's original course, the Blue Course (1971), nicknamed "The Grand Lady of Wailea," is operated from a separate clubhouse from the Gold and Emerald courses, its newer siblings. Here, judging elevation change is key. Fairways and greens tend to be wider and more forgiving than on the newer courses, and they run through colorful flora that includes hibiscus, wiliwili, bougainvillea, and plumeria. ⊠ *100 Wailea Ike Dr., Wailea* ☎ *808/875–7450, 888/328–6284* ⊕ *waileagolf.com* ✆ *$190* ⚐ *18 holes, 6765 yards, par 71.*

★ Wailea Golf Club

GOLF | Wailea is the only Hawaii resort to offer three courses: Gold, Emerald, and Blue—the latter at a different location with another pro shop. Designed by Robert Trent Jones Jr. (Gold and Emerald) and Arthur Jack Snyder (Blue), these courses share similar terrain, carved into the leeward slopes of Haleakala. Although the ocean does not come into play, its beauty is visible on almost every hole.

■TIP→ **Remember, putts break dramatically toward the ocean.**

Jones refers to the Gold Course at Wailea (1994) as the "masculine" course. It's all trees and lava, and regarded as the hardest of the three courses. The trick here is to note even subtle changes in elevation. The par-3 8th, for example, plays from an elevated tee across a lava ravine to a large, well-bunkered green framed

Places to Relax After a Round

Among golf's great traditions is the so-called 19th hole. No matter how the first 18 go, the 19th is sure to offer comfort and cheer, not to mention a chilled beverage. Here's a look at some of the best.

Kapalua boasts three 19th holes with excellent fare and views: the **Plantation House** has a commanding view of the Plantation Course's 18th hole, the Pailolo Channel, and the Island of Molokai beyond; the **Pineapple Grill** overlooks the Bay Course's 18th, and **Merriman's Kapalua** sits beside the ocean at Kapalua Bay.

At Wailea's Gold and Emerald courses, **Gannon's** overlooks the sea in a lovely garden setting and serves excellent food. The restaurant is owned and managed by famed chef Beverly Gannon of Haliimaile General Store with its elegant Red Bar.

The **Kahili Restaurant**, a plantation-style clubhouse at the King Kamehameha Golf Club's Kahili Course, offers commanding views of the ocean on both sides of the Island and 10,000-foot Haleakala.

Café O'Lei at the Dunes at Maui Lani offers indoor and outdoor seating overlooking the golf course, as well as a stunning view of the West Maui Mountains. Kono's on the Green at Maui Nui Golf Club has a welcoming lanai for sunset watching or just generally kicking back.

by palm trees, the blue sea, and tiny Molokini. The course demands strategy and careful club selection. The Emerald Course (1994) is the "feminine" layout with lots of flowers and bunkering away from greens. Although this may seem to render the bunker benign, the opposite is true. A bunker well in front of a green disguises the distance to the hole. Likewise, the Emerald's extensive flower beds are dangerous distractions because of their beauty. The Gold and Emerald courses share a clubhouse, practice facility, and 19th hole. ⊠ *100 Wailea Golf Club Dr., Wailea* ☎ *808/875–7450, 888/328–6284* ⊕ *waileagolf.com* 🍽 *Gold Course $279, Emerald Course $279* ⅄ *Gold Course: 18 holes, 7078 yards, par 72; Emerald Course: 18 holes, 6825 yards, par 72.*

CENTRAL MAUI

★ The Dunes at Maui Lani

GOLF | Robin Nelson is at his minimalist best here, creating British-style links in the middle of the Pacific. Holes run through ancient, lightly wooded sand dunes, 5 miles inland from Kahului Harbor. Thanks to the natural humps and slopes of the dunes, Nelson had to move very little dirt and created a natural beauty. During the design phase, he visited Ireland, and not so coincidentally the par-3 3rd looks a lot like the Dell at Lahinch: a white dune on the right sloping down into a deep bunker and partially obscuring the right side of the green—just one of several blind to semi-blind shots here. ⊠ *1333 Maui Lani Pkwy., Kahului* ☎ *808/873–0422* ⊕ *dunesatmauilani.com* 🍽 *$99 (prices drop later in the day)* ⅄ *18 holes, 6841 yards, par 72.*

Waiehu Golf Course

GOLF | Maui's lone municipal course and undoubtedly the best bargain on the Island, Waiehu is really two courses in one. The front nine, dating to 1930, feature authentic seaside links that run along Waihee Reef. The back nine, built on a series of sand dunes that look up toward the lush valleys of the West Maui Mountains, were designed by Arthur Jack Snyder and opened in 1963. ⊠ *200 Halewaiu Rd., Wailuku* ☎ *808/270–7400*

⊕ waiehugolf.com ✉ Weekdays $57, weekends $67 ⛳ 18 holes, 6330 yards, par 72.

UPCOUNTRY
Pukalani Country Club
GOLF | At 1,110 feet above sea level, Pukalani (Bob Baldock, 1980) provides one of the finest vistas in all Hawaii. Holes run up, down, and across the slopes of Haleakala. The trade winds tend to come up in the late morning and afternoon. Winds combined with frequent elevation change, makes club selection a test. The fairways tend to be wide, but greens are undulating and quick. ✉ 360 Pukalani St., Pukalani ☎ 808/572–1314 ⊕ pukalanigolf.com ✉ $89; Twilight rate $69 from 11 am–1 pm ⛳ 18 holes, 6962 yards, par 72.

Hang Gliding and Paragliding

If you've always wanted to know what it feels like to fly, hang gliding or paragliding might be your perfect Maui adventure. You'll get open-air, bird's-eye views of the Valley Isle that you'll likely never forget. And you don't need to be a daredevil to participate.

EQUIPMENT AND LESSONS
Hang Gliding Maui
HANG GLIDING & PARAGLIDING | Armin Engert will take you on an instructional powered hang-gliding trip out of Hana Airport in East Maui. With more than 13,000 hours in the air and a perfect safety record, Armin flies you over Maui's most beautiful coast. Snapshots of your flight from a wing-mounted camera cost an additional $50, and a 34-minute DVD of the flight from a wing-mounted camera is available for $100. Reservations are required. ✉ Hana Airport, Alalele Pl., off Hana Hwy., Hana ☎ 808/264–3287 ⊕ hanggldingmaui.com ✉ 30-minute

flight lesson $240, 45-minute lesson $320, and 60-minute lesson $400.

Paraglide Maui
HANG GLIDING & PARAGLIDING | The only paragliding outfit on Maui to offer solo, tandem, and instruction is at Polipoli Spring State Recreation Area. The leeward slope of Haleakala lends itself to paragliding with breathtaking scenery and air currents that increase during the day. Polipoli creates tremendous thermals that allow you to descend 3,000 feet peacefully to land. Solo paragliding certification is also available. ✉ 1100 Waipoli Rd., Kula ☎ 808/874–5433 ⊕ paraglidemaui.com ✉ Tandem instruction prices $175 to $295.

Hiking

Hikes on Maui include treks along the coastal seashore, verdant rain forest, and alpine desert. Orchids, hibiscus, ginger, heliconia, and anthuriums grow wild on many trails, and exotic fruits like mountain apple, lilikoi (passion fruit), and strawberry guava provide refreshing snacks for hikers. During your hike, don't hike alone, wear bright clothing, stay on the trail, and be aware that you may encounter hunters who are hunting off the trail.

■ TIP→ Hawaii possesses some of the world's rarest plants, insects, and birds. Pocket field guides are available at most grocery or drug stores and can really illuminate your walk.

BEST SPOTS
HALEAKALA NATIONAL PARK
★ Haleakala Crater
NATURE SIGHT | The park's main attraction is the eroded depression found at the Summit District known as Haleakala Crater. And, undoubtedly, the island's best hiking is found here. If you're in good shape, do a day hike descending from the summit along Keoneheehee Trail (Sliding Sands Trail) to the crater

floor. You might also consider spending several days here amid the cinder cones, lava flows, and all that loud silence. Entering the crater is like landing on a different planet. In the early 1960s, NASA brought moon-suited astronauts here to practice what it would be like to "walk on the moon." Tent camping and cabins are available with permits. On the 30 miles of trails, you can traverse black sand and wild lava formations, follow the blooming *ahinahina* (silverswords) path, and take in tremendous views of the big sky and burned-red cliffs.

The best time to go into the crater is summer when the conditions are generally more predictable. Be sure to bring layered clothing—and plenty of warm clothes if you're staying overnight. It may be scorching hot during the day, but it gets mighty chilly after dark. Bring drinking water, as potable water is available only at the two visitor centers. Overnight visitors must get a permit at park headquarters before entering the crater. ⊠ *Haleakala Crater Rd., Haleakala National Park* ☎ *808/572–4400* ⊕ *www. nps.gov/hale* ☎ *$30 entrance fee per vehicle (good for 3 days).*

IAO VALLEY STATE MONUMENT

In Hawaiian, Iao means "supreme cloud." When you enter this mystical valley in the middle of an unexpected rain forest near Wailuku in West Maui, you'll know why. At 750 feet above sea level, the 10-mile valley clings to the clouds as if it's trying to cover its naked beauty. One of Maui's great wonders, the valley is the site of a famous battle to unite the Hawaiian Islands. Out of the clouds, the Iao Needle, a tall chunk of volcanic rock, stands as a monument to the long-ago lookout for Maui warriors. Today, the valley is a peaceful land of lush tropical plants, clear pools and a running stream, and easy enjoyable strolls.

To get to Iao Valley State Monument, head to the western end of Route 32. The road dead-ends into the parking lot

($25 per car). The park is open daily 7 am–6 pm with an entrance fee ($5 per person). Facilities are available, but there is no drinking water.

★ Iao Needle Lookout Trail & Ethnobotanical Loop

HIKING & WALKING | Anyone can do this short walk from the parking lot at Iao Valley State Monument. On your choice of two paved walkways, you can cross the Iao Stream and explore the junglelike area. Ascend the stairs up to the Iao Needle for spectacular views of Central Maui. Be sure to stop at the lovely Kepaniwai Heritage Gardens, which commemorate the cultural contributions of various immigrant groups. Open daily from 7 am–6 pm. *Easy.* ⊠ *Trailhead: Iao Valley State Monument parking lot, Rte. 32, Wailuku* ⊕ *dlnr.hawaii.gov/dsp/parks/maui/iao-valley-state-monument* ☎ *$5 per person; $25 parking per car.*

OHEO GULCH

A branch of Haleakala National Park, Oheo Gulch is famous for its pools (Seven Sacred Pools). There are more than seven pools when the water levels are up. A former owner of the Travaasa Hotel in Hana started calling the area Seven Sacred Pools to attract the masses to sleepy old Hana. His plan worked, and the name stuck, much to the chagrin of many locals.

The best time to visit the pools is in the morning before the crowds and tour buses arrive. Start your day with a vigorous hike. Oheo has some fantastic trails to choose from, including our favorite, the Pipiwai Trail. At the end of your walk, nothing could be better than going to the pools, lounging on the rocks, and cooling off in the freshwater reserves. Keep in mind that the park periodically closes the pools when the potential for flash flooding exists.

You can find Oheo Gulch on Route 31, 10 miles past Hana town. To visit, you must pay the $30-per-car National Park fee,

Tips for Day Hikes

Hiking is a perfect way to see Maui. Just wear sturdy shoes to spare your ankles from a crash course in loose lava rock. The weather is guaranteed to be extreme at upper elevations—alternately chilly or blazing—so layers are good.

When hiking near streams or waterfalls, be cautious: flash floods can occur at any time. Don't drink stream water or swim in streams if you have open cuts; bacteria and parasites are not the souvenirs you want to take home with you.

Here's a checklist for what to take for a great hike:

■ Water (at least two quarts per person; drink even if you're not thirsty)

■ Food—fruit, trail mix, and lunch

■ Rain gear—especially if going into the crater

■ Sturdy hiking shoes

■ Layered clothing

■ Wide-brimmed hat and sunglasses

■ Sunscreen (SPF 30 or higher recommended)

■ Mosquito repellent (a must around waterfalls and pools)

---

which is valid for three days and can be used at Haleakala's summit (keep your receipt). For information about scheduled orientations and cultural demonstrations, be sure to visit Haleakala National Park's Kipahulu Visitor Center, 10 miles past Hana. Note that there is no drinking water here—plan accordingly.

Kahakai Trail

TRAIL | This quarter-mile hike (more like a walk) stretches between Kuloa Point and the Kipahulu campground. It provides rugged shoreline views, and there are places where you can stop to gaze at the surging waves below. *Easy.* ✉ *Hana* ✥ *Trailhead: Kuloa Point* ⊕ *nps.gov/hale* ✉ *$30 entrance fee per vehicle (good for 3 days).*

Kuloa Point Trail

TRAIL | A half-mile walk, this trail takes you from the Kipahulu Visitor Center down to the pools of Oheo at Kuloa Point, where the freshwater pools and ocean meet. On the trail, you pass native trees and pre-contact Hawaiian sites. *Easy.* ■TIP➜ **Tempting as it is, swimming in the ocean is strongly discouraged. While** it may seem calm near sea level, unpredictable conditions at higher elevations cause flash flooding and other dangers. ✉ *Hana Hwy., Hana* ✥ *Trailhead: Kipahulu Visitor Center* ⊕ *nps.gov/hale* ✉ *$30 entrance fee per vehicle (good for 3 days).*

★ Pipiwai Trail

TRAIL | This popular 2-mile trek upstream reveals two magnificent waterfalls: Makahiku Falls at about half a mile in, and the grand finale 400-foot Waimoku Falls, pounding down in all its power and glory. Following signs from the parking lot, head across the road and uphill into the forest. The trail borders a stunning gorge and passes onto a boardwalk through an impenetrable forest of giant bamboo. This stomp through muddy and rocky terrain takes around three hours to enjoy fully. Although this trail is never truly crowded, it's best done early in the morning before the tours arrive. Be sure to bring mosquito repellent. *Moderate.* ✉ *Hana Hwy., Hana* ✥ *Trailhead: Near mile marker 42* ⊕ *nps.gov/hale* ✉ *$30 entrance fee per vehicle (good for 3 days).*

POLIPOLI SPRING STATE RECREATION AREA

A hiking area with great trails for all levels—and something unexpected on a tropical island—is the Kula Forest Reserve at Polipoli Spring State Recreation Area in Upcountry Maui. During the Great Depression, the government began a program to reforest the mountain, and soon cedar, pine, cypress, and even redwood took hold. At an elevation of 6,200 feet, the area feels more like Vermont than Hawaii. It's cold and foggy and often wet, but there's something about the enormity of the trees, quiet mist, and mysterious caves that make you feel you've discovered an unspoken secret. Hikers should wear brightly colored clothing, as hunters may be in the area.

To reach the forest, take Route 37 out to the far end of Kula, then turn left at Route 377. After about a half-mile, turn right at Waipoli Road. You'll encounter switchbacks; after that, the road is bad but passable. Although standard cars have been known to make it, four-wheel-drive vehicles are strongly recommended. Use your best judgment.

. ■ TIP→ **Polipoli Spring is often closed following heavy storms due to fallen trees and other damage. Check the Hawaii State Parks website before making the drive up there.**

Boundary Trail

HIKING & WALKING | This 4-mile trail begins just past the Kula Forest Reserve boundary cattle guard on Polipoli Road and descends into the lower boundary southward, all the way to the ranger's cabin at the junction of the Redwood and Plum trails. Combine them, and you've got a hearty 5-mile day hike. The trail crosses many scenic gulches, with an overhead of tall eucalyptus, pine, cedar, and plum trees. Peep through the trees for wide views of Kula and Central Maui. *Moderate.* ✉ *Trailhead: Polipoli Campground, Polipoli Rd., Kula* ⊕ *dlnr.hawaii. gov/recreation/nah/maui.*

Kalaupapa Trail

You can take an overnight trip to the Island of Molokai for a day of hiking down to Kalaupapa Peninsula and back, by means of a 3-mile, 26-switchback trail. The trail is nearly vertical, traversing the face of some of the highest sea cliffs in the world. See Kalaupapa Peninsula in Chapter 11, Molokai, for more information.

Redwood Trail

HIKING & WALKING | This colorful 1.7-mile hike winds through redwoods and conifers past the short Tie Trail down to the old ranger's cabin. Although the views are limited, groves of trees and flowering bushes abound. The end of the trail is an old cabin site and the three-way junction with the Plum Trail and the Boundary Trail. *Moderate.* ✉ *Trailhead: Near Polipoli Campground, Polipoli Rd., Kula* ⊕ *dlnr. hawaii.gov/dsp/hiking/maui/redwood-trail.*

Upper Waiakoa Trail

HIKING & WALKING | Start this scenic albeit rugged trail at the Polipoli Access Road (look for trailhead signs) and proceed up Haleakala through mixed pine and past caves and thick shrubs. The path crosses the land of Kaonoulu to the land of Waiakoa, where it reaches its highest point (7,800 feet). Here you'll find yourself in barren raw terrain with fantastic views. At this point, you can either turn around or continue on to the 3-mile Waiakoa Loop for a 14-mile journey. Other than a cave shelter, there's no water or other facilities on these trails, so come prepared. *Difficult.* ✉ *Trailhead: Polipoli Access Rd., Kula* ⊕ *dlnr.hawaii.gov/ recreation/nah/maui.*

THE SOUTH SHORE AND WEST MAUI

In addition to the trails listed below, the Kapalua Resort offers free access to 100 miles of self-guided hikes. Trail information and maps are available at the Kapalua Adventure Center.

Hoapili Trail (King's Trail)

HIKING & WALKING | This 5½-mile coastal trail beyond the Ahihi-Kinau Natural Area Reserve offers a challenging hike through eye-popping scenery. Named after a king, it follows the shoreline, threading through the remains of ancient villages. King Hoapili created an islandwide road, and this broad path of stacked lava rocks is a marvel to look at and walk on. (It's not the easiest surface for the ankles and feet, so wear sturdy shoes.) The trail takes you through brutal territory with little shade and no facilities, and extra water is a must. To get here, follow Makena Road to La Perouse Bay. The trail can be a challenge to find—walk south along the ocean through the *kiawe* (mesquite, or algaroba) trees, where you'll encounter numerous wild goats (don't worry—they're gentle), and past a scenic little bay. The trail begins just around the corner to the left. *Difficult.* ⊠ *Trailhead: La Perouse Bay, Makena Rd., Makena.*

Kapalua Resort

HIKING & WALKING | The resort offers free access to miles of hiking trails as a self-guided experience. Trail information and maps are available at the Kapalua Village Center. The Village Walking Trails offer a network of exercise opportunities on former golf cart paths, including the 3.6-mile Lake Loop, which features sweeping views and a secluded lake populated with quacking ducks. The Coastal Trail provides views of the ocean and wildlife as it crosses the golden sand dunes of Oneloa Bay and past Ironwood Beach and the Ritz-Carlton, Kapalua, to its terminus at D. T. Fleming Beach Park. Sightings of green sea turtles, dolphins, and humpback whales (in season) are likely, along with wedge-tailed sheerwater seabirds called *uau kani.* Guided 1½-mile hikes on the coastal trail that include tide pool exploration are available for $100 through the Jean-Michel Cousteau Ambassadors of the Environment program at the Ritz-Carlton, Kapalua. ⊠ *2000 Village Rd., corner of Office Rd., Kapalua* ☎ *808/665–4386 Kapalua Village Center concierge, 808/665–7292 Jean-Michel Cousteau Ambassadors of the Environment* ⊕ *kapalua.com.*

Makaluapuna Point (Dragon's Teeth)

HIKING & WALKING | The forceful winds that sweep over the point caused lava formations to harden upward into jagged points resembling giant teeth, hence this attraction's nickname of Dragon's Teeth. To get there, park in the small paved lot to the right at the end of Office Road, and follow the path at the edge of the Bay Golf Course (watch for errant golf balls, and be respectful of the golfers). Along the way, there's a labyrinth where you can experience a meditative walk. ■TIP→ **Wear sturdy shoes and bring water, as there are no facilities here.** ⊠ *Office Rd., Kapalua.*

Waihee Ridge

HIKING & WALKING | This 4¾-mile hike in West Maui offers a generous reward at the top: breathtaking panoramic views of the windward coast and the ridges that rise inland, as well as Mt. Lanilili, Puu Kukui, Eke Crater, and the remote village of Kahakuloa. In rainy conditions the trail can quickly turn into a muddy slippery affair. To get here from Highway 340, turn left across the highway from Mendes Ranch and drive three-quarters of a mile up a partially paved road to the signed trailhead. *Moderate.* ⊠ *Trailhead: Opposite Mendes Ranch, Hwy. 340, Wailuku.*

GOING WITH A GUIDE

Guided hikes can help you see more than you might on your own. If the company is driving you to the site, be sure to ask about drive times; they can be fairly lengthy for some hikes.

★ Friends of Haleakala National Park

HIKING & WALKING | This nonprofit offers overnight trips into the volcanic crater. The purpose of your trip, the service work itself, isn't too much—mostly native planting, removing invasive plants, and light cabin maintenance. But participants are asked to check the website to learn more about the trip and certify readiness for service work. A knowledgeable guide accompanies each trip, taking you to places you'd otherwise miss and teaching you about the native flora and fauna. ✉ *Makawao* ☎ *808/876–1673* ⊕ *fhnp.org.*

★ Hike Maui

HIKING & WALKING | Started in 1983, the area's oldest hiking company remains extremely well regarded for its hikes led by enthusiastic, highly trained guides who weave botany, geology, ethnobotany, culture, and history into the outdoor experience. The seven-hour Haleakala tour includes two hikes, each revealing vastly different environments that make up this national park. The 11-hour Hana excursion takes you to the park's remote eastern edge, where you'll explore a bamboo forest that leads to a stunning 400-foot waterfall, among other stops. Hike Maui supplies day packs, rain gear, mosquito repellent, first-aid supplies, bottled water, snacks, lunch, and transportation to and from the site. ✉ *Kahului* ☎ *808/784–7982* ⊕ *hikemaui.com* 🎫 *Tours start at $109.*

Kipahulu Ohana

HIKING & WALKING | Native Hawaiian guides from this nonprofit organization lead cultural interpretive hikes and taro patch tours at Kipahulu near Hana through a cooperative agreement with Haleakala National Park. The two-hour walk takes you to scenic overlooks and past remnants from the sugarcane industry, culminating at an ancient taro farm that was restored to active production. A three-hour hike includes a side trip to 400-foot Waimoku Falls. You can park at Kipahulu Visitor Center ($30 per car) and meet your guide at the Hale Kuai, the traditional thatched house near the center. ✉ *Hana* ☎ *808/248–8558* ⊕ *kipahulu.org* 🎫 *Two-hour hike $49, three-hour $79.*

Sierra Club

HIKING & WALKING | One great avenue into the island's untrammeled wilderness is Maui's chapter of the Sierra Club. Join one of the club's hikes into pristine forests, along ancient coastal paths, to historic sites, and to Haleakala Crater. Some outings require volunteer service, but most are just for fun. Bring your own food and water, rain gear, sunscreen, sturdy shoes, and a suggested donation of $5 for hikers over age 14 ($3 for Sierra Club members). This is a true bargain. ✉ *Paia* ☎ *808/867–6001* ⊕ *mauisierraclub.org.*

Horseback Riding

Mendes Ranch

HORSEBACK RIDING | Family-owned and -run, Mendes Ranch operates out of the beautiful ranch land of Kahakuloa on the windward slopes of the West Maui Mountains. Morning and afternoon trail rides lasting 1½ hours are available. Paniolos take you cantering up rolling pastures into the lush rain forest, and then you'll descend all the way down to the ocean for a photo op with a dramatic backdrop. Don't expect a Hawaiian cultural experience here—it's all about the horses and the ride. Mendes also offers a horseback riding and helicopter tour in partnership with Sunshine Helicopters. ✉ *3530 Kahekili Hwy., Wailuku* ☎ *800/871–5222* ⊕ *mendesranch.com* 🎫 *Rides start at $135.*

Kayaking

Kayaking is a fantastic and eco-friendly way to experience Maui's coast up close. Floating aboard a "plastic Popsicle stick" is easier than you might think, and it allows you to cruise out to vibrant, living coral reefs and waters where dolphins and even whales roam. Kayaking can be a leisurely paddle or a challenge of heroic proportions, depending on your ability, the location, and the weather.

■TIP→ **Although you can rent kayaks independently, we recommend hiring a guide.**

A calm surface can hide powerful ocean currents. Most guides are naturalists who will steer you away from surging surf, lead you to pristine reefs, and point out camouflaged fish, like the stalking hawkfish. Not having to schlep your gear on top of your rental car is a bonus. A half-day tour runs around $75.

If you decide to strike out on your own, tour companies will rent kayaks for the day with paddles, life vests, and roof racks, and many will meet you near your chosen location. Ask for a map of good entries and plan to avoid paddling back to shore against the wind (schedule extra time for the return trip regardless). Read weather conditions, bring binoculars, and take a careful look from the bay before heading in. Get there early before the trade wind kicks in, and stick close to shore. When you're ready to snorkel, secure your belongings in a dry pack on board and drag your kayak by its bowline behind you. (This isn't as hard as it sounds.)

BEST SPOTS

Makena Landing is an excellent starting point for a South Shore adventure. Enter from the paved parking lot or the small sandy beach a little south. The shoreline is lined with million-dollar mansions. The bay itself is virtually empty, but the right edge is flanked with brilliant coral heads and juvenile turtles. If you round the point on the right, you come across Five Caves, a system of enticing underwater arches. In the morning you may see dolphins, and the arches are havens for lobsters, eels, and spectacularly hued butterfly fish.

In West Maui, past the steep cliffs on the Honoapiilani Highway, there's a long stretch of inviting coastline that includes **Ukumehame Beach.** This is a good spot for beginners; entry is easy, and there's much to see in every direction. Pay attention if trade winds pick up from the late morning onward; paddling against them can be challenging. If you want to snorkel, the best visibility is farther out at Olowalu Beach. Watch for sharp *kiawe* (mesquite) thorns buried in the sand on the way into the water. Water shoes are recommended.

EQUIPMENT, LESSONS, AND TOURS

Kelii's Kayak Tours

KAYAKING | One of the highest-rated kayak outfitters on the Island, Kelii's offers kayaking trips and combo adventures where you can also surf, snorkel, or hike to a waterfall. Leading groups of up to eight people, the guides show what makes each reef unique. Most popular is the kayak and snorkel combo to Turtle Town—explore colorful reefs, endangered green sea turtles, and you might see a dolphin or two. Trips are available on the Island's north, south, and west shores. ⊠ *1993 S. Kihei Rd., Suite 12, Kihei* ☎ *808/874-7652* ⊕ *keliiskayak.com* ⊠ *$84 and up.*

★ South Pacific Kayaks

KAYAKING | These guys pioneered recreational kayaking on Maui, so they know their stuff. Guides are friendly, informative, and eager to help you get the most out of your experience; we're talking genuine, fun-loving, kayak geeks who will maneuver away from crowds when exploring prime snorkel spots. South Pacific stands out as adventurous and environmentally responsible, plus their gear and equipment are well maintained. They offer a variety of trips leaving from both West Maui and South Shore locations. ⊠ *95 Halekuai St., Kihei* ☎ *808/875-4848* ⊕ *southpacifickayaks. com* ⊠ *From $85.*

Kiteboarding

Kiteboarders soar above the Pacific, catapulting up to 40 feet above the breaking surf. Silken kites hold these athletes aloft for precious seconds—long enough for the execution of mind-boggling tricks—then deposit them back in the sea. This sport is not for the weak-kneed. No matter what people might tell you, it's harder to learn than windsurfing. The unskilled (or unlucky) can be caught in an upwind and carried far out in the ocean, or worse—dropped smack on the shore. Because of insurance (or the lack thereof), companies are not allowed to rent equipment. Beginners must take lessons and then purchase their own gear. Devotees swear that after your first few lessons, committing to buying your kite is easy.

BEST SPOTS

The steady tracks on **Kanaha Beach** make this North Shore spot primo for learning. Specific areas are set aside for different water activities, so launch and land only in kiteboarding zones, and kindly give way to swimmers, divers, anglers, and paddlers.

LESSONS

Aqua Sports Maui

WATER SPORTS | A local favorite of kiteboarding schools, Aqua Sports is conveniently located near Kite Beach, at the west end of Kanaha Beach, and offers basic to advanced kiteboarding lessons taught by certified instructors. Students enjoy a 10% discount at several Maui kite and surf shops. ⊠ *111 Hana Hwy., Suite 110, near Kite Beach, Kahului* ☎ *808/242–8015* ⊕ *mauikiteboardinglessons.com* ⬚ *Rates start at $300 for a three-hour beginners course.*

★ Hawaiian Sailboarding Techniques

WATER SPORTS | Experienced instructors will have you safely ripping in no time at lower Kanaha Beach Park. Instead of observing from the shore, instructors follow after students on a chase boat to give immediate feedback. The company is part of Hi-Tech Surf Sports, in the Triangle Square shopping center. ⊠ *Triangle Square, 425 Koloa St., Kahului* ☎ *808/871–5423* ⊕ *hstwindsurfing.com* ⬚ *$300 and up.*

Kiteboarding School of Maui

WATER SPORTS | One of the first kiteboarding schools in the United States, KSM offers one-on-one "flight lessons." Pro kiteboarders will induct you at Kite Beach, at the west end of Kanaha Beach, providing private instruction with quality equipment. ⊠ *111 Hana Hwy., Suite 110, Kahului* ☎ *808/873–0015* ⊕ *ksmaui.com* ⬚ *Rates start at $99 for a 90-minute lesson.*

Parasailing

Parasailing is an easy, exhilarating way to earn your wings: strap on a harness attached to a parachute, and a power-boat pulls you up and over the Pacific ocean from a launching dock or a boat's platform.

■TIP→ **Parasailing is limited to West Maui, and "thrill craft"—including parasails—are prohibited in Maui waters during hump-back-whale calving season, December 15–May 15.**

LESSONS AND TOURS

UFO Parasail

HANG GLIDING & PARAGLIDING | This cheekily named company offers single, tandem, and triple rides. Depending on the number of passengers, rides last 8–12 minutes. It's more fun to take the "dip" (when the boat slows down to let the parachute descend slowly in the water). You'll get a little wet, though you'll probably catch more water while on the boat watching the others take flight. Observers are welcome aboard for $79. Trips leave from Kaanapali Beach, which fronts Whalers Village shopping center. ■ TIP➜ **No parasailing during whale season.** ✉ 2435 Kaanapali Parkway, Kaanapali ☎ 808/427–2250 ⊕ ufoparasail. net ✆ Starting at $136.

West Maui Parasail

HANG GLIDING & PARAGLIDING | Soar at 800 feet above the ocean for a bird's-eye view of Lahaina, or be daring at 1,200 feet for smoother rides and even better views. The captain will be glad to let you experience a "toe-dip" or "freefall" if you request it. Hour-long trips from Lahaina Harbor and Kaanapali Beach include 8- to 10-minute flights. ■ TIP➜ **No parasailing during whale season.** ✉ Lahaina Harbor, 675 Wharf St., Slip 15, Lahaina ☎ 808/661–4060 ⊕ westmauiparasail. com ✆ Starting at $125.

Rafting

The high-speed, inflatable rafts you find on Maui are nothing like the raft that Huck Finn used to drift down the Mississippi. While passengers grip straps, these rafts fly, skimming and bouncing across the sea. Because they're so maneuverable, they go where the big boats can't—secret coves, sea caves, and remote beaches.

■ TIP➜ **Although safe, these trips are not for the faint of heart. If you have back or neck problems or are pregnant, you should reconsider this activity.**

TOURS

Blue Water Rafting

BOATING | One of the few ways to get to the stunning Kanaio Coast (the roadless southern coastline beyond Ahihi-Kinau), this rafting tour begins conveniently at the Kihei Boat Ramp on the South Shore. Dolphins, turtles, and other marine life are the highlight of this adventure, along with majestic sea caves, lava arches, and views of Haleakala. The Molokini stop is usually timed between the bigger catamarans, so you can enjoy

the crater without the usual massive crowd. If conditions permit, you'll be able to snorkel the back wall, which has much more marine life than the inside. ✉ Kihei Boat Ramp, S. Kihei Rd., Kihei ☎ 808/879–7238 ⊕ bluewaterrafting.com ✆ From $60.

Ocean Riders

BOATING | Start the day with a spectacular view of the sun rising above the West Maui Mountains, then cross the Auau Channel to Lanai's Kaiolohia (commonly referred to as Shipwreck Beach). After a short swim at a secluded beach, this tour circles Lanai, allowing you to view the Island's 70 miles of remote coast. The "back side" of Lanai is one of Hawaii's unsung marvels, and you can expect to stop at three protected coves for snorkeling. You might chance upon *honu* (sea turtles), monk seals, and a friendly reef shark, as well as rare varieties of angelfish and butterflyfish. Guides are knowledgeable and slow down long enough for you to marvel at sacred burial caves and interesting rock formations. Sit toward the backbench if you are sensitive to motion sickness. Tours include snorkel gear, a fruit breakfast, and a satisfying deli lunch. ✉ Mala Wharf, Front St., Lahaina ☎ 808/661–3586 ⊕ mauioceanriders. com ✆ From $186.

★ Redline Rafting

WATER SPORTS | This company's raft tours begin with a trip to Molokini Crater for some snorkeling. If weather permits, the raft explores the crater's back wall, too. There's a quick stop at La Perouse Bay to spot dolphins, and then it's off to Makena for more underwater fun and a deli lunch. The rafts provide great seating, comfort, and shade. ✉ Kihei Boat Ramp, 2800 S. Kihei Rd., Kihei ☎ 808/201–7450 ⊕ redlinerafting.com ✆ Whale-watching excursions start at $85, snorkel trips at $139.

Sailing

With the islands of Molokai, Lanai, Kahoolawe, and Molokini a stone's throw away, Maui's waters offer visually arresting backdrops for sailing adventures. Sailing conditions can be fickle, so some operations throw in snorkeling or whale-watching, and others offer sunset cruises. Winds are consistent in summer but variable in winter, and afternoons are generally windier throughout the year.

■ TIP➔ **You won't be sheltered from the elements on the trim racing boats, so be sure to bring a hat that won't blow away, a light jacket, sunglasses, and sunscreen.**

BOATS AND CHARTERS

Kai Kanani

SAILING | As the only sailing vessel that leaves from Wailea (the others on the South Shore depart from Maalaea), the Kai Kanani stays moored off of Maluaka Beach in Makena-Wailea. It's also the only boat that beach-loads, rather than loading from a dock, which means you may get a bit wet when boarding—but that's all part of the fun. Cruises include the earliest Molokini snorkel on the Island and run throughout the day, ending with their sunset adventure cruise. Food and beverages come included in the ticket price. ✉ 34 Wailea Gateway Pl., Wailea ☎ 808/879–7218 ⊕ kaikanani.com ⎙ Tours from $175.

Paragon Sailing Charters

SAILING | If you want to snorkel and sail, this is your boat. Many snorkel cruises claim to sail, but motor most of the way—Paragon is an exception. Both Paragon vessels (one catamaran in Lahaina, the other in Maalaea) are shipshape, and crews are accommodating and friendly. Its mooring in Molokini Crater is particularly good, and tours will often stay after the masses have left. The Lanai trip includes a picnic lunch at Manele Bay, snorkeling, and a quick afternoon blue-water swim. Extras on

the trips to Lanai include mai tais, sodas, dessert, and champagne. Hot and cold appetizers come with the sunset sail, which departs daily from Lahaina Harbor. ✉ Maalaea Harbor, Maalaea ☎ 808/244–2087 ⊕ www.sailmaui.com ⎙ Sunset sail starts at $85, snorkel at $160.

Scotch Mist Charters

SAILING | Follow the wind aboard this 50-foot Santa Cruz sailing yacht. The four-hour snorkeling excursion and two-hour whale-watching and sunset sail trips carry no more than 22 passengers. The two-hour sunset sails include soft drinks, wine, beer, champagne, and chocolate. ✉ Lahaina Harbor, Slip 2, Lahaina ☎ 808/661–0386 ⊕ scotchmistsailingcharters.com ⎙ Starts at $74.

★ Trilogy Excursions

SAILING | With more than four decades of experience and some good karma from their reef-cleaning campaigns, Trilogy has an excellent reputation in the community. It's one of only two companies that sail to Molokini Crater rather than motor. Their two-hour sunset sail includes appetizers, beer, wine, champagne, margaritas, and mai tais. Tours depart from Lahaina Harbor, Maalaea Harbor, and, in West Maui, in front of the Kaanapali Beach Hotel. ✉ Lahaina Harbor, 675 Wharf St., Lahaina ☎ 808/874–5649, 888/225–6284 ⊕ sailtrilogy.com ⎙ Starts at $99.

PRIVATE CHARTERS

Hiring a private charter for a sail will cost you more, but it's one way to avoid crowds. Although almost all sailing vessels offer private charters, a few cater to them specifically.

Cinderella Sailing Charters

BOATING | This swift and elegant 51-foot Peterson costs $350 per hour for a charter of up to six people, including beverages and light appetizers (two-hour minimum). Cinderella's ultimate five-hour snorkel and sail package with soft drinks and lunch is $1,900. Sunset sails are $750 for two hours. BYOB.

■**TIP→ Discounts are available for multiple trips booked.** ✉ *Maalaea Harbor, Slip 41* ☏ *808/344–3906* ⊕ *cinderellasailing.com.*

Island Star

BOATING | This 57-foot Columbia offers customized trips out of Maalaea. *Island Star* is equipped with a galley for onboard food preparation and a master stateroom with a king-size bed. ✉ *Maalaea Harbor, Slip 42, Maalaea* ☏ *808/669–7827* ⊕ *islandstarmaui.com* ✑ *$700 per hour, minimum two hours.*

Shangri-La

BOATING | A 65-foot catamaran, *Shangri-La* is the largest and most luxurious boat catering to private charters. This gorgeous yacht can accommodate up to 49 guests. A private chef and premium alcohol are available for additional fees. ✉ *Kaanapali Beach, Lahaina* ☏ *808/665–0077* ⊕ *sailingmaui.com* ✑ *Starts at $1,700 for a private charter (two-hour minimum).*

Scuba Diving

Maui has been rated one of the top 10 dive spots in the United States. It's common to see huge sea turtles, eagle rays, and small reef sharks, not to mention many varieties of angelfish, parrotfish, eels, and octopuses. Most of the species are unique to this area, unlike other popular dive destinations. In addition, the terrain itself is different from other dive spots. Here you can find ancient and intricate lava flows full of nooks where marine life hide and breed. Although the water tends to be a bit rougher—not to mention colder—divers are given an incredible thrill during the humpback-whale season, when you can hear whales singing underwater. Be sure to check conditions before you head out.

Some of the finest diving spots in all of Hawaii lie along the Valley Isle's western and southwestern shores. Dives are best in the morning when visibility can hold a steady 100 feet. If you're a certified diver, you can rent gear at any Maui dive shop simply by showing your PADI or NAUI card. Unless you're familiar with the area, however, it's probably best to hook up with a dive shop for an underwater tour. Shops also offer introductory dives for those who aren't certified.

■**TIP→ Before signing on with any outfitter, it's a good idea to ask a few pointed questions about your guide's experience, the weather outlook, and the condition of the equipment.**

BEST SPOTS

Honolua Bay, a marine preserve in West Maui, is alive with many varieties of coral and tame tropical fish, including large *ulua* (giant trevally), *kahala* jack fish family), barracuda, and manta rays. With depths of 20–50 feet, this is a popular summer dive spot, good for all levels.

■**TIP→ High surf often prohibits winter dives.**

On the South Shore, one of the most popular dive spots is **Makena Landing** (also called Nahuna Point, Five Graves, or Five Caves). You can revel in underwater delights—caves, ledges, coral heads, and an outer reef home to a large green–sea turtle colony called Turtle Town.

■**TIP→ Entry is rocky lava, so be careful where you step. This area is for more experienced divers.**

Three miles offshore from Wailea on the South Shore, **Molokini Crater** is world-renowned for its deep, crystal clear, fish-filled waters. A crescent-shape islet formed by the eroding top of a volcano, the crater is a marine preserve ranging 10–80 feet deep. The numerous tame fish and brilliant coral within the crater make it a popular introductory dive site. On calm days, the back side of Molokini Crater (called Back Wall) can be a dramatic sight for advanced divers, with visibility of up to 150 feet. The enormous drop-off into the Alalakeiki Channel offers awesome seascapes, black coral, and chance sightings of larger fish and sharks.

Some of the southern coast's best diving is at **Ahihi Bay,** part of the Ahihi-Kinau Natural Area Reserve. The area frequently closes due to shark sightings; call ahead before visiting. The area is best known for its "Fishbowl," a small cove right beside the road, next to a hexagonal house. Here you can find excellent underwater scenery, with many types of fish and coral.

■ TIP → **Be careful of the rocky-bottom entry (wear reef shoes if you have them).**

The Fishbowl can get crowded, especially in high season. If you want to steer clear of the crowds, look for a second entry ½ mile farther down the road—a gravel parking lot at the surf spot called Dumps. Entry into the bay here is trickier, as the coastline is all lava.

Formed from the last lava flow two centuries ago, **La Perouse Bay** brings you the best variety of fish—more than any other site. The lava rock provides a protective habitat, and all four types of Hawaii's angelfish can be found here. To dive into the spot called Pinnacles, enter anywhere along the shore, just past the private entrance to the beach. Wear your reef shoes, as entry is sharp. To the right, you'll be in the Ahihi-Kinau Natural Area Reserve; to the left, you're outside. Look for the white sandy bottom with massive coral heads. Pinnacles is for experienced divers only.

EQUIPMENT, LESSONS, AND TOURS

Extended Horizons

DIVING & SNORKELING | This eco-friendly dive boat stands apart by being the only commercial vessel on Maui to run on 100% locally made biodiesel. Its popular Lanai charter has divers swimming through dramatic archways and lava structures, while other trips venture along West Maui. Shore and night dives

are also available. Tours are run by enthusiastic and professional guides who are keen at not only identifying underwater creatures but also interpreting their behavior. ✉ *Mala Boat Ramp, Lahaina* ☎ *808/667–0611* ⊕ *extendedhorizons. com* 🚢 *From $179.*

Lahaina Divers

SCUBA DIVING | With over 40 years of diving experience, this West Maui shop offers tours of Maui, Molokini, Molokai, and Lanai. Big charter boats (which can be crowded, with up to 25 divers per boat) leave daily for Molokini Crater, Back Wall, Lanai, Turtle Reef, and other destinations. Breakfast pastries and deli lunch are included. For uncertified divers, there's a daily "Discover Scuba" lesson off one of the Turtle Reef sites or the Mala ramp wreckage, depending on conditions. ✉ *143 Dickenson St., Lahaina* ☎ *808/667–7496* ⊕ *lahainadivers.com* 🚢 *From $229.*

Maui Dive Shop

SCUBA DIVING | Maui Dive Shop offers scuba charters, diving instruction, and equipment rental at its Kihei location. Excursions go to Molokini, Shipwreck Beach, and Cathedrals on Lanai. Intro dives are done offshore. Night dives, scooter dives, and customized trips are available, as are full SSI and PADI certificate programs. ✉ *1455 S. Kihei Rd., Kihei* ☎ *808/875–0333 local, 800/542–3483 toll free* ⊕ *mauidiveshop.com* 🚢 *From $189.*

★ Mike Severns Diving

SCUBA DIVING | This popular and reliable company has been around for more than four decades and takes groups of up to seven certified divers, with two dive masters, to both popular and off-the-beaten-path dive sites. Marine biologists or naturalists offer informative briefings, and boat trips leave from Kihei Boat Ramp and go wherever conditions are best: the Molokini Marine Life Conservation District, Molokini Crater's Back Wall, Makena, or beyond La Perouse Bay. ✉ *Kihei Boat Ramp, 2988 S. Kihei Rd.,*

Kihei ☎ *808/879–6596* ⊕ *mikesevernsdiving.com* ✉ *Dives from $224 (BYO gear) or $269 (gear included).*

Prodiver Maui

DIVING & SNORKELING | Known for its professional crew, top-notch gear, and action-packed dive sites, this company leads trips to Molokini's back wall and other South Maui spots. Shore dives are an option, and Discover Scuba introductory lessons begin in the pool, allowing novices to learn in a controlled environment. The three-tank dive is designed for maximum time underwater and is for experts. ✉ *22 Alahele Place, #4, Kihei* ☎ *808/875–4004* ⊕ *prodivermaui.com* ✉ *Dives start at $149; rental gear packages from $45.*

Shaka Divers

SCUBA DIVING | Since 1983, owner Doug Corbin has led personalized dives, including great four-hour intro dives, refresher courses, scuba certifications, and south shore dives to Ulua, Nahuna Point or Turtle Town (also called Five Caves or Five Graves), and Bubble Cave. Typical dives last about an hour. Dives can be booked on short notice, with afternoon tours available (hard to find on Maui). Shaka also offers night dives and torpedo-scooter dives. The twilight two-tank dive is nice for day divers who want to ease into night diving. ✉ *24 Hakoi Pl., Kihei* ☎ *808/250–1234* ⊕ *www.shakadivers.com* ✉ *From $59.*

Tiny Bubbles Scuba

DIVING & SNORKELING | Owner and dive master Tim Rollo has led customized, private shore dives along West Maui since 1995. He'll take only four to six divers at a time, and can cater to the most novice diver. Intro dives include gear and air. Night dives, scooter dives, and scuba certifications are also offered. ✉ *104 Kaanapali Shores, Lahaina* ☎ *808/870–0878, 808/870–2738 reservations* ⊕ *tinybubblesscuba.com* ✉ *Dives from $89.*

Snorkeling

There are two ways to approach snorkeling—by land or by sea. At around 7 am daily, a parade of boats heads out to Lanai or to Molokini Crater, that ancient cone of volcanic cinder off the coast of Wailea. Boat trips offer some advantages—deeper water, seasonal whale-watching, crew assistance, lunch, and gear. But much of Maui's best snorkeling is found just steps from the road. Nearly the entire leeward coastline from Kapalua south to Ahihi-Kinau offers opportunities to ogle fish and turtles. If you're patient and sharp-eyed, you may glimpse eels, octopuses, lobsters, eagle rays, and even a rare shark or monk seal.

■ TIP➔ **Visibility is best in the morning, before the trade winds pick up.**

BEST SPOTS

Snorkel sites are listed from north to south, starting at the northwest corner of the Island. The **Honolua Bay Marine Life Conservation District** *has a superb reef for snorkeling just north of Kapalua.*

■ TIP➔ **Bring a fish key with you, as you're sure to see many species of triggerfish, filefish, and wrasses.**

The coral formations on the right side of the bay are particularly dramatic, with pink, aqua, and orange varieties. On a lucky day, you might even be snorkeling with a pod of dolphins nearby. Take care entering the water; there's no beach, and the rocks and concrete ramp can be slippery. The northeast corner of this windward bay periodically gets hammered by big waves in winter. Avoid the bay then, as well as after heavy rains.

Minutes south of Honolua Bay, dependable **Kapalua Bay** beckons. As beautiful above the water as it is below, Kapalua is exceptionally calm, even when other spots get testy. Needle and butterfly fish dart just past the sandy beach, which is why it's sometimes crowded.

Snorkelers can see adorable green sea turtles around Maui.

■TIP→ The sand can be particularly hot here—watch your toes!

Puu Kekaa (nicknamed Black Rock), in front of the Sheraton Maui Resort & Spa at the northernmost tip of **Kaanapali Beach,** is great for snorkelers of any skill level. The entry couldn't be easier—dump your towel on the sand and in you go. Beginners can stick close to shore and still see lots of action. Advanced snorkelers can swim to the tip of Puu Kekaa to see larger fish and eagle rays. One of the underwater residents here is a turtle whose hefty size earned him the name Volkswagen. He sits very still, so you have to look closely. Equipment can be rented on-site. Parking, which is in a small lot adjoining the hotel, is the only hassle.

Along Honoapiilani Highway, there are several favorite snorkel sites, including the area just out from the cemetery at **Hanakaoo Beach Park.** At depths of 5 and 10 feet, you can see a variety of corals, especially as you head south toward Wahikuli Wayside Park.

South of Olowalu General Store, the shallow coral reef at **Olowalu** is good for a quick underwater tour, but if you're willing to venture out about 50 yards, you'll have easy access to an expansive coral reef with abundant turtles and fish—no boat required. Swim offshore toward the pole sticking out of the reef. Except for during a south swell, this area is calm, and good for families with small children. Boats sometimes stop here (they refer to this site as Coral Gardens) when conditions in Honolua Bay are not ideal. During low tide, be extra cautious when hovering above the razor-sharp coral.

Excellent snorkeling is found down the coastline between Kihei and Makena on the South Shore.

■TIP→ The best spots are along the rocky fringes of Wailea's beaches—Mokapu, Ulua, Wailea, and Polo—off Wailea Alanui Drive.

Find one of the public parking lots sandwiched between Wailea's luxury resorts (look for a blue sign reading "Shoreline

Access" with an arrow pointing to the lot). Enjoy the sandy and calm waters with relatively good visibility and a variety of fish. Of the four beaches, Ulua has the best reef. You may listen to snapping shrimp and parrotfish nibbling on coral.

In South Maui, the end of the paved section of Makena Road is where you'll find the **Ahihi-Kinau Natural Area Reserve.** Despite its lava-scorched landscape, the area is very popular, especially with sharks, causing the area to be closed quite frequently. Call ahead to make sure it's open. It's difficult terrain and the area sometimes gets crowded, but it's worth visiting to experience some of the reserve's outstanding treasures, such as the sheltered cove known as the Fish Bowl.

■ TIP→ **Be sure to bring water: this is a hot and unforgiving wilderness.**

Between Maui and neighboring Kahoolawe you'll find the world-famous **Molokini Crater.** Its crescent-shape rim acts as a protective cove from the wind and provides a sanctuary for birds and colorful marine life. Most snorkeling tour operators offer a Molokini trip, and it's not unusual for your charter to share this dormant volcano with five or six other boats. The journey to this sunken crater takes more than 90 minutes from Lahaina, an hour from Maalaea, and less than half an hour from the South Shore.

EQUIPMENT
Most hotels and vacation rentals offer complimentary use of snorkel gear. Beachside stands fronting the major resort areas rent equipment by the hour or day. If you're squeamish about using someone else's gear (or need a prescription lens), pick up your own at any discount shop. Costco and Longs Drugs have better prices than ABC Stores; dive shops have superior equipment.

■ TIP→ **Don't shy away from asking for instructions; a snug fit makes all the difference in the world. A mask fits if it sticks to**

your face when you inhale deeply through your nose. Fins should cover your entire foot (unlike diving fins, which strap around your heel).

Maui Dive Shop
SNORKELING | You can rent pro gear (including optical masks, bodyboards, and wet suits) at their Kihei location. Daily and weekly rates are available. Pump these guys for weather info before heading out; they'll know better than last night's news forecaster, and they'll give you the real deal on conditions. ⊠ *1455 S. Kihei Rd., Kihei* ☎ *808/875–0333* ⊕ *mauidiveshop.com.*

Snorkel Bob's
SNORKELING | Here you can rent fins, masks, and snorkels, and Snorkel Bob's will throw in a carrying bag, map, and snorkel tips. Avoid the circle masks and go for the split-level or premium snorkel package; it's worth the extra money. There are seven Snorkel Bob's locations on Maui, including Kihei, Wailea, Lahaina, Kahana, and Napili. ⊠ *5425 C Lower Honoapiilani Hwy., Napili* ☎ *808/669–9603* ⊕ *snorkelbob.com* ✉ *Weekly rentals from $10–$72.*

TOURS
The same boats that offer whale-watching, sailing, and diving also offer snorkeling excursions. Trips usually include visits to two locales, lunch, gear, instruction, and possible whale or dolphin sightings. Some captains troll for fish along the way.

The most popular snorkel cruise destination is Molokini Crater, a crescent about 3 miles offshore from Wailea. You can spend half a day floating above the fish-filled crater for about $80. Some say it's not as good as it's made out to be and that it's too crowded, but others consider it one of the best spots in Hawaii. Visibility is generally outstanding, and fish are incredibly tame. Your second stop will

Continued on page 222

SNORKELING IN HAWAII

Molokini Crater

The waters surrounding the Hawaiian Islands are filled with life—from giant manta rays cruising off the Big Island's Kona Coast to humpback whales giving birth in the waters around Maui. Dip your head beneath the surface to experience a spectacularly colorful world: pairs of milletseed butterflyfish dart back and forth, redlipped parrotfish snack on coral algae, and spotted eagle rays flap past like silent spaceships. Sea turtles bask at the surface while tiny wrasses give them the equivalent of a shave and a haircut. The water quality is typically outstanding; many sites afford 30-foot-plus visibility. On snorkel cruises, you can often stare from the boat rail right down to the bottom.

Certainly few destinations are as accommodating to every level of snorkeler as Hawaii. Beginners can tromp in from sandy beaches while more advanced divers descend to shipwrecks, reefs, craters, and sea arches just offshore. Because of Hawaii's extreme isolation, the island chain has fewer fish species than Fiji or the Caribbean—but many of the fish that live here exist nowhere else. The Hawaiian waters are home to the highest percentage of endemic fish in the world.

The key to enjoying the underwater world is slowing down. Look carefully. Listen. You might hear the strange crackling sound of shrimp tunneling through coral, or you may hear whales singing to one another during winter. A shy octopus may drift along the ocean's floor beneath you. If you're hooked, pick up a waterproof fishkey from Long's Drugs. You can brag later that you've looked the Hawaiian turkeyfish in the eye.

Picasso Triggerfish

Milletseed Butterflyfish*

Yellow Tang

Moorish Idol

Hawaiian Whitespotted Toby*

Saddleback Wrasse*

Redlip Parrotfish

Hawaiian Turkeyfish*

Zebra Moray Eel

Stocky Hawkfish

Green Sea Turtle (Honu)

Spotted Eagle Ray

*endemic to Hawaii

POLYNESIA'S FIRST CELESTIAL NAVIGATORS: HONU

Honu is the Hawaiian name for two native sea turtles, the hawksbill and the green sea turtle. Little is known about these dinosaur-age marine reptiles, though snorkelers regularly see them foraging for *limu* (seaweed) and the occasional jellyfish in Hawaiian waters. Most female honu nest in the uninhabited Northwestern Hawaiian Islands, but a few sociable ladies nest on Maui and Big Island beaches. Scientists suspect that they navigate the seas via magnetism—sensing the earth's poles. Amazingly, they will journey up to 800 miles to nest—it's believed that they return to their own birth sites. After about 60 days of incubation, nestlings emerge from the sand at night and find their way back to the sea by the light of the stars.

SNORKELING

Many of Hawaii's reefs are accessible from the shore.

The basics: Sure, you can take a deep breath, hold your nose, squint your eyes, and stick your face in the water in an attempt to view submerged habitats . . . but why not protect your eyes, retain your ability to breathe, and keep your hands free to paddle about when exploring underwater? That's what snorkeling is all about.

Equipment needed: A mask, snorkel (the tube attached to the mask), and fins. In deeper waters (any depth over your head), life jackets are advised.

Steps to success: If you've never snorkeled before, it's natural to feel a bit awkward at first, so don't sweat it. Breathing through a mask and tube, and wearing a pair of fins take getting used to. Like any activity, you build confidence and comfort through practice.

If you're new to snorkeling, begin by submerging your face in shallow water or a swimming pool and breathing calmly through the snorkel while gazing through the mask.

Next you need to learn how to clear water out of your mask and snorkel, an essential skill since splashes can send water into tube openings and masks can leak. Some snorkels have built-in drainage valves, but if a tube clogs, you can force water up and out by exhaling through your mouth. Clearing a mask is similar: lift your head from water while pulling forward on mask to drain. Some masks have built-in purge valves, but those without can be cleared underwater by pressing the top to the forehead and blowing out your nose (charming, isn't it?), allowing air to bubble into the mask, pushing water out the bottom. If it sounds hard, it really isn't. Just try it a few times and you'll soon feel like a pro.

Never touch or stand on coral.

Now your goal is to get friendly with fins—you want them to be snug but not too tight—and learn how to propel yourself with them. Fins won't help you float, but they will give you a leg up, so to speak, on smoothly moving through the water or treading water (even when upright) with less effort.

Flutter stroking is the most efficient underwater kick, and the farther your foot bends forward the more leg power you'll be able to transfer to the water and the farther you'll travel with each stroke. Flutter kicking movements involve alternately separating the legs and then drawing them back together. When your legs separate, the leg surface encounters drag from the water, slowing you down. When your legs are drawn back together, they produce a force pushing you forward. If your kick creates more forward force than it causes drag, you'll move ahead.

Submerge your fins to avoid fatigue rather than having them flailing above the water when you kick, and keep your arms at your side to reduce drag. You are in the water—stretched out, face down, and snorkeling happily away—but that doesn't mean you can't hold your breath and go deeper in the water for a closer look at some fish or whatever catches your attention. Just remember that when you do this, your snorkel will be submerged, too, so you won't be breathing (you'll be holding your breath). You can dive head-first, but going feet-first is easier and less scary for most folks, taking less momentum. Before full immersion, take several long, deep breaths to clear carbon dioxide from your lungs.

If your legs tire, flip onto your back and tread water with inverted fin motions while resting. If your mask fogs, wash condensation from the lens and clear water from your mask.

TIPS FOR SAFE SNORKELING

- Snorkel with a buddy and stay together.
- Plan your entry and exit points prior to getting in the water.
- Swim into the current on entering and then ride the current back to your exit point.
- Carry your flippers into the water and then put them on, as it's difficult to walk in them, and rocks may be slippery.
- Make sure your mask fits properly and is not too loose.
- Pop your head above the water periodically to ensure you aren't drifting too far out, or too close to rocks.
- Think of the water as someone else's home—don't take anything that doesn't belong to you, or leave any trash behind.
- Don't touch any sea creatures; they may sting.
- Wear a T-shirt over your swimsuit to help protect you from being fried by the sun.
- When in doubt, don't go without a snorkeling professional; try a guided tour.
- Don't go in if the ocean seems rough.

Green sea turtle (Honu)

Tips on Safe Snorkeling

■ Snorkel with a buddy and stay together.

■ Choose a location where lifeguards are present.

■ Ask the lifeguard about conditions before getting in the water.

■ Plan your entry and exit points prior to getting in the water.

■ Swim into the current on entering and then ride the current back to your exit point.

■ Pop your head above the water periodically to ensure you aren't drifting too far out or near rocks.

■ Think of the ocean as someone else's home—don't take anything that doesn't belong to you or leave any trash behind.

■ Don't touch any ocean creatures; they may reveal hidden stingers.

■ Do not bump against or step on coral. Touching it can kill the delicate creatures that reside within the hard shell. Coral reefs grow only an inch or two a year.

■ Wear a rash guard; it will keep you from being fried by the sun.

■ Apply mineral sunscreen at least 30 minutes before you embark on your trip, so less of it enters the water.

■ When in doubt, don't go without a snorkeling professional; try a tour.

---

be somewhere along the leeward coast, either Turtle Town near Makena or Coral Gardens toward Lahaina.

■ TIP→ **On windy mornings, there's a good chance the waters will be too rough to moor in Molokini Crater, and you'll end up snorkeling somewhere off the shore, where you could have driven for free.**

If you've tried snorkeling and are tentatively thinking about scuba, you may want to try "snuba," a cross between the two. With snuba, you dive 20 feet below the surface; only you're attached to an air hose from the boat. Many boats now offer snuba (for an extra fee of $45–$65) and snorkeling.

Snorkel cruises vary—some serve mai tais and steaks, whereas others offer beer and cold cuts. You might prefer a large ferryboat to a smaller sailboat, or vice versa. Be sure you know where to go to board your vessel; getting lost in the harbor at 6 am is a lousy start to your day.

■ TIP→ **Bring sunscreen, an underwater camera (they're double the price onboard), a towel, and a cover-up for the windy return trip.**

Even tropical waters get chilly after hours of swimming, so consider wearing a rash guard or renting wetsuits for a fee.

Alii Nui Maui

SNORKELING | On this 65-foot luxury catamaran, you can come as you are (with a bathing suit, of course); towels, sunblock, and all your gear are provided. Because the owners also operate Maui Dive Shop, snorkel and dive equipment are top-of-the-line. Wet-suit tops are available to use for sun protection or to keep extra warm in the water. The boat, which holds a maximum of 60 people, is nicely appointed. A morning snorkel sail (there's a diving option, too) heads to Turtle Town or Molokini Crater and includes a continental breakfast, lunch, and post-snorkel alcoholic drinks. The three-, five-, or six-hour snorkel trip offers transportation from your hotel. Videography and huka (similar to snuba) are available for a fee. ✉ *Maalaea Harbor, Slip 56, Maalaea* ☎ *800/542–3483, 808/875–0333* ⊕ *aliinuimaui.com* ✉ *From $109.*

Gemini Sailing Charters

SNORKELING | One of the main draws of this snorkel sail excursion is its affordable rates. The vacation-friendly 11 am departure is another plus. Honolua Bay is the primary destination, but Mala Wharf in Lahaina and Olowalu are possible options in case of choppy waters. The hot buffet lunch includes a selection of chicken, fish, and veggie options, plus fresh-baked cookies. You can find the company on Kaanapali Beach, fronting the Westin Maui Resort. ✉ *Westin Maui Resort & Spa, 2365 Kaanapali Pkwy., Kaanapali* ☎ *800/820–7245, 808/669–1700* ⊕ *geminisailing.com* ✉ *From $127.*

Hawaiian Sailing Canoe Adventure

SNORKELING | Few things could qualify as a more authentic Hawaiian experience than paddling in a *waapea* (sailing canoe) with this family-run outfit. Get a deep sense of history and mythology as you listen to your guide pray, chant, and bestow a wealth of knowledge about ancient Hawaii during this intimate excursion. The canoe makes a snorkel stop at a nearby reef. Refreshments and snorkel equipment are included. Trips begin at Polo Beach in front of the Fairmont Kea Lani. ✉ *Polo Beach, Wailea* ☎ *808/281–9301* ⊕ *mauisailingcanoe.com* ✉ *From $179.*

Maui Classic Charters

SNORKELING | **FAMILY** | Hop aboard the *Four Winds II*, a 55-foot, glass-bottom catamaran (great fun for kids), for one of the most dependable snorkel trips around. You'll spend more time than other charter boats at Molokini Crater and enjoy turtle-watching on the way home. The trip includes optional snuba ($62 extra), continental breakfast, barbecue lunch, beer, wine, and soda. With its reasonable price, the trip can be popular and crowded. The crew works hard to keep everyone happy, but if the trip is fully booked, you will be cruising with more than 100 new friends. For a more intimate experience, opt for the *Maui Magic*, Maalaea's fastest PowerCat, which holds fewer people than some of the larger vessels. ✉ *Maalaea Harbor, Slips 55 and 80, Maalaea* ☎ *808/879–8188, 800/736–5740* ⊕ *mauiclassiccharters.com* ✉ *From $65.*

Teralani Sailing Charters

SNORKELING | Choose between a standard or premier snorkel trip with a deli lunch or a top-of-the-line excursion that's an hour longer and includes two snorkel sites and a barbecue-style lunch. The company's cats could hold well over 100 people, but 49 is the maximum per trip. The boats are kept in pristine condition. Freshwater showers are available, as is an open bar after the second snorkel stop. A friendly crew provides all your gear, a flotation device, and a quick course in snorkeling. During whale season, only the premier trip is available. Boarding is right off Kaanapali Beach, fronting the Westin Maui Hotel. ✉ *Kaanapali Beach, Kaanapali* ☎ *808/661–7245* ⊕ *teralani.net* ✉ *From $139.*

★ Trilogy Excursions

SNORKELING | Many people consider a trip with Trilogy Excursions to be a highlight of their vacation. Maui's longest-running operation has comprehensive offerings, with six beautiful 54- to 65-foot sailing vessels at three departure sites. All excursions are staffed by energetic crews who will keep you well-fed and entertained with local stories and corny jokes. A full-day catamaran cruise to Lanai includes a continental breakfast and barbecue lunch, a guided tour of the island, a "Snorkeling 101" class, and time to snorkel in the waters of Lanai's Hulopoe Marine Preserve (Trilogy Excursions has exclusive commercial access). The company also offers Molokini Crater and Olowalu snorkel cruises that are top-notch. Tours depart from Lahaina

Harbor, Maalaea Harbor, and, in West Maui, in front of the Kaanapali Beach Hotel. ⊠ *Lahaina Harbor, 675 Wharf St., Lahaina* ☎ *808/874–5649, 888/225–6284* ⊕ *sailtrilogy.com* ⊠ *From $135.*

Stand-Up Paddling

Also called stand-up paddle surfing or paddleboarding, stand-up paddling is the "comeback kid" of surf sports; you stand on a longboard and paddle out with a canoe oar. While stand-up paddling requires even more balance and coordination than regular surfing, it is still accessible to every skill level. Most surf schools now offer stand-up paddle lessons. Advanced paddlers can amp up the adrenaline with a downwind coastal run that spans almost 10 miles from North Shore's Maliko Gulch to Kahului Harbor, sometimes reaching speeds up to 30 mph.

The fun thing about stand-up paddling is that you can enjoy it whether the surf is good or the water is flat. However, as with all water sports, being attentive and reading the environment is essential. Look at the sky and assess the wind by how fast the clouds move. Note where the whitecaps are going, and always point the nose of your board perpendicular to the wave.

■TIP➔ **Because of the size and speed of a longboard, stand-up paddling can be dangerous, so lessons are highly recommended, especially if you intend to surf.**

LESSONS

Stand-Up Paddle Surf School

WATER SPORTS | Maui's first school devoted solely to stand-up paddling was founded by the legendary Maria Souza, the first woman to surf the treacherous waves of Peahi (nicknamed "Jaws") on Maui's North Shore. Although most surf schools offer stand-up paddling, Maria's classes are in a league of their own. They include a proper warm-up with a hula-hoop and balance ball and a cool-down with yoga. Locations vary depending on conditions. ⊠ *185 Paka Pl., Kihei* ☎ *808/579–9231* ⊠ *Lessons from $199* ☞ *standuppaddlesurfschool.com.*

Surfing

Maui's coastline has surf for every skill level, beginners included. Waves on leeward-facing shores (West and South Maui) tend to break in gentle sets all summer long. Surf instructors in Kihei and Lahaina can rent you boards, give you onshore instruction, and then lead you out through the channel, where it's safe to enter the surf. They'll shout encouragement while you paddle like mad for the thrill of standing on the water—most will give you a helpful shove. These areas are great for beginners; the only danger is whacking a stranger with your board or stubbing your toe against the reef.

The North Shore is another story. Winter waves pound the windward coast, attracting water champions from every corner of the world. Jet Skis tow in adrenaline addicts to "Jaws," the legendary deep-sea break. Waves here periodically tower upward of 40 feet. The only spot for viewing this phenomenon (which happens just a few times a year) is on private property so, if you hear the surfers next to you crowing about "Jaws going off," cozy up and get them to take you with them.

Whatever your skill, there's a board, a break, and even a surf guru to accommodate you. A two-hour lesson is a good intro to surf culture.

You can get the wave report each day by checking page 2 of the *Maui News*, logging on to the Glenn James weather site (⊕ *hawaiiweathertoday.com*), or by calling ☎ *808/871–5054* (for the weather forecast) or ☎ *808/877–3611* (for the surf report).

BEST SPOTS

On the South Shore, beginners can hang ten at Kihei's **Cove Park,** a sometimes crowded but reliable one- to two-foot break. Boards can easily be rented across the street or neighboring Kalama Park's parking lot. Balancing the nine-plus-foot board on your head while crossing busy South Kihei Road is the only bummer.

For advanced wave riders, **Hookipa Beach Park** on the North Shore boasts several well-loved breaks, including "Pavilions," "Lanes," "the Point," and "Middles." Surfers have priority until 11 am when windsurfers move in on the action.

■ TIP→ **Competition is stiff here. If you don't know what you're doing, consider watching.**

Long- or shortboarders in West Maui can paddle out at **Launiupoko Beach Park.** The east end of the park has an easy break, suitable for beginners.

Also called Thousand Peaks, **Ukumehame** is one of the better beginner spots in West Maui. You'll soon see how the spot got its name—the waves here break again and again in wide and consistent rows, giving lots of room for beginning and intermediate surfers.

Good surf spots in West Maui include "Grandma's" at **Papalaua Park,** just after the *pali* (cliff), where waves are so easy a grandma could ride them. **Puamana Beach Park** for a mellow longboard day and **Lahaina Harbor** offers an excellent inside wave for beginners (called Breakwall) and the more advanced outside (a great lift if there's a big south swell).

EQUIPMENT AND LESSONS

Maui is the perfect place to learn to surf, with plenty of fantastic surf schools offering lessons that guarantee you'll catch a wave on your first day. Surf camps are becoming increasingly popular. One- or two-week camps offer a terrific way to build muscle and self-esteem simultaneously.

Watching Surfers

Even if you aren't a surfer, watching is just as fun (well, almost). Near-perfect waves can be seen at Honolua Bay, on the northern tip of West Maui. To get here, continue 2 miles north of D. T. Fleming Park on Highway 30 and take a left onto the dirt road next to a pineapple field; a path leads down the cliff to the beach. In addition, Hookipa Beach Park, just outside of Paia, gives you the perfect overlook to see pro surfers, windsurfers, and kiters.

Big Kahuna Adventures

SURFING | Rent soft-top longboards here for $35 for two hours. Weekly rates are $160. Call ahead to make an appointment. This company also offers surf lessons and rents kayaks, stand-up paddleboards, plus snorkel and beach gear. Look for the Big Kahuna truck at Kalama Park; lessons take place at Cove Park. ✉ *Kalama Park, 1900 S Kihei Rd., Kihei* ☎ *808/875–6395* ⊕ *bigkahunaadventures. com* ☑ *Lessons start at $95.*

Goofy Foot

SURFING | Surfing "goofy foot" means putting your right foot forward. They might be goofy, but we like the right-footed gurus here. This shop is just plain cool and only steps away from "Breakwall," a great beginner's spot in Lahaina. A two-hour class with five or fewer students is $85, and you're guaranteed to be standing by the end or it's free. ✉ *505 Front St., Suite 123, Lahaina* ☎ *808/244–9283* ⊕ *goofyfootsurfschool. com* ☑ *Group classes start at $85; private two-hour lessons $170.*

★ Hi-Tech Surf Sports

SURFING | Hi-Tech has some of the best boards, advice, and attitude around. It rents even its best surfboards—choose from longboards, shortboards, and hybrids—starting at $25 per day. There's another shop in Paia and a third location in Kihei across from Cove Park, a popular surf spot for beginners. ✉ *425 Koloa St., Kahului* ☎ *808/877–2111* ⊕ *surfmaui.com.*

★ Maui Surf Clinics

SURFING | **FAMILY** | Instructors here will get even the shakiest novice riding with the school's beginner program. They offer two-hour group lessons (up to five students) and private lessons with the patient and meticulous instructors. The company provides boards, rash guards, and water shoes, all in impeccable condition—and it's tops in the customer-service department. ✉ *505 Front St., S uite 201, Lahaina* ☎ *808/244–7873* ⊕ *mauisurfclinics.com* ✎ *Group lessons $85; private lessons $180.*

Maui Surfer Girls

SURFING | Maui Surfer Girls started in 2001 with surf camps for teen girls, but quickly branched out to offer surfing lessons year-round. Located away from the crowds, Maui Surfer Girls specializes in private lessons and small groups, and their ratio of four students per instructor is the smallest in the industry. ✉ *Ukumehame Beach Park, Lahaina* ☎ *808/670–3886* ⊕ *mauisurfergirls.com* ✎ *Group lesson $99, Semi-Private $145, Private $209.*

Outrageous Surf School

SURFING | If you're not too keen on onshore lessons, Outrageous Surf School might be your best bet. After a quick demo in the shop, head down to the Lahaina Breakwall to hit the waves. ✉ *640 Front St., Lahaina* ☎ *808/669–1400* ⊕ *youcansurf.com* ✎ *Group lessons $55 per person; semiprivate for two $150 each per person* ☉ *Sun.* .

Surf Report ☼

Before heading out for any water activity, be sure to get a weather and wave report, and make sure the surf report you get is the *full face value* of the wave. "Hawaiian-style" cuts the wave size in half. For instance, a Hawaiian might say a wave is 5 feet high, which means 10 feet if you're from New Jersey or Florida. For years, scientists and surfers were using different measurements, as Hawaii locals measured waves from median sea level to the crest. These days, most surf reports are careful to distinguish between the two.

Royal Hawaiian Surf Academy

SURFING | Owner Kimo Kinimaka grew up rippin' it with his uncle, legendary surfer Titus Kinimaka, so it's no wonder his passion translates to a fun memorable time at the novice-friendly Lahaina Breakwall. Group lessons are offered, as are privates where you can have your instructor's full attention. Rash guards and shoes are provided. ✉ *505 Front St., Suites 127 and 128, Lahaina* ☎ *808/276–7873* ⊕ *royalhawaiiansurfacademy.com* ✎ *Group lessons $75; Private lessons $175.*

Second Wind

SURFING | Surfboard rentals at this centrally located shop are a deal—good boards go for $30 per day or $210 for 10 days. The shop also rents and sells its own Elua Makani boards (which means "second wind" in Hawaiian). Surfing, kiteboarding, windsurfing, and stand-up paddling lessons are available for beginners and advanced students. ✉ *111 Hana Hwy., Kahului* ☎ *808/877–7467* ⊕ *secondwindmaui.com* ✎ *Semi-private lessons $100; Private $150.*

Tennis

Most courts charge by the hour but will let players continue after their initial hour for free, provided no one is waiting. Many hotels and condos charge a fee for non-guests.

BEST SPOTS

Kapalua Tennis Garden

TENNIS | This complex has 10 courts (4 lighted for night play) and a pro shop. The membership fee is $50 per person per week. Daily clinics for kids and adults are $50 per person with drop-in doubles play offered for $20 per person. ⊠ *100 Kapalua Dr., Kapalua* ☎ *808/662–7730* ⊕ *golfatkapalua.com.*

Lahaina Civic Center

TENNIS | The best free courts are the nine at the Lahaina Civic Center, near Wahikuli Wayside Park. They all have overhead lighting for night play and are available on a first-come, first-served basis. ⊠ *1840 Honoapiilani Hwy., Lahaina* ☎ *808/661–4685* ⊕ *mauicounty.gov/facilities/Facility/Details/209* ✉ *Free.*

Wailea Tennis Club

TENNIS | Featuring 11 Sportsmaster courts, this club also offers lessons, rentals, and ball machines. Daily clinics help you improve your ground strokes, serve, volley, or doubles strategy. The daily court fee, which guarantees 90 minutes of play for singles or doubles, is $27 per player. Lessons are also available for an additional fee. ⊠ *131 Wailea Ike Pl., Wailea* ☎ *808/879–1958* ⊕ *waileatennis.com* ✉ *$27 daily per person; Clinics $42.*

TOURNAMENTS

Kapalua Open Tennis Tournament

SPECTATOR SPORTS | Over Labor Day weekend, the Kapalua Open Tennis Tournament beckons Hawaii's hitters to Kapalua's Tennis Garden. ⊠ *100 Kapalua Dr., Kapalua* ☎ *808/662–7730* ⊕ *kapaluatennis.com* ✉ *$22 per player.*

Educational Excursions

Jean-Michel Cousteau's **Ambassadors of the Environment**, housed at the Ritz-Carlton, Kapalua, presents more of an educational excursion than a regular tour. An extensive youth program includes whale-watching, tide pool exploration, tracking green sea turtles, and more, with all sessions led by naturalists who link Hawaiian culture with conservation. For information, call ☎ *808/665-7292.*

Whale-Watching

From December into May, whale-watching becomes one of the most popular activities on Maui. During the season, *all* outfitters offer whale-watching in addition to their regular activities, and most do an excellent job. Boats leave the wharves at Lahaina and Maalaea in search of humpbacks, allowing you to enjoy the awe-inspiring size of these creatures in closer proximity. From November through May, the Pacific Whale Foundation sponsors the Maui Whale Festival, a variety of whale-related events for locals and visitors; check the calendar at ⊕ *mauiwhalefestival.org.*

As it's almost impossible *not* to see whales in winter on Maui, you'll want to prioritize: is an adventure or comfort your aim? If close encounters with the giants of the deep are your desire, pick a smaller boat that promises sightings. Those who think "green" usually prefer the smaller, quieter vessels that produce the least amount of negative impact on the whales' natural environment. If you want to sip mai tais as whales cruise by, stick with a sunset cruise ($50 and up)

Humpback whale calves are plentiful in winter; this one is breaching off West Maui.

on a boat with an open bar and *pupus* (appetizers).

■ **TIP➜ Afternoon trips are generally rougher because the wind picks up, but some say this is when the most surface action occurs.**

Every captain aims to please during whale season, getting as close as legally possible (100 yards). Crew members know when a whale is about to dive (after several waves of its heart-shaped tail) but can rarely predict breaches (when the whale hurls itself up and almost entirely out of the water). Prime viewing space (on the upper and lower decks, around the railings) is limited, so boats can feel crowded even when half full. Opt for a smaller boat with fewer bookings if you don't want to squeeze in beside strangers. Don't forget to bring sunscreen, sunglasses, a light long-sleeve cover-up, and a hat you can secure. Winter weather is less predictable and, at times, can be extreme, especially as the wind picks up. Arrive early to find parking.

BEST SPOTS

The northern end of **Keawakapu Beach** on the South Shore seems to be a whale magnet. Situate yourself on the sand or at the nearby restaurant and watch mamas and calves at play. From mid-December to mid-April, the Pacific Whale Foundation has naturalists at Ulua Beach and the scenic viewpoint at **Papawai Point Lookout.** You can spot whales along the *pali* of West Maui's Honoapiilani Highway all day long. Make sure to park safely before trying to take that perfect photo.

BOATS AND CHARTERS
Gemini Sailing Charters

WILDLIFE-WATCHING | Morning and afternoon whale-watching trips off the Kaanapali coast are available on this well-maintained catamaran staffed by an experienced and fun crew. You can find Gemini on Kaanapali Beach in front of the Westin Maui. ⊠ *Westin Maui Resort & Spa, 2365 Kaanapali Pkwy., Lahaina* ☎ *800/820–7245, 808/669–1700* ⊕ *geminisailing.com* ✉ *From $70.*

The Humpbacks' Winter Home

The humpback whales' attraction to Maui is legendary, and seeing them from December to May is a highlight for many visitors. More than half the Pacific's humpback population winters in Hawaii, especially in the waters around the Valley Isle, where mothers can be seen just a few hundred feet offshore, training their young calves in the fine points of whale etiquette. From shore, it's easy to catch sight of whales spouting or even breaching—when they leap almost entirely out of the sea, slapping back onto the water with a huge splash.

There were thousands of giant mammals, but a history of overhunting and marine pollution reduced the world population to about 1,500. In 1966, humpbacks were put on the endangered-species list. Hunting or harassing whales is illegal in the waters of most nations, and in the United States, boats and airplanes are prohibited from getting too close. However, the jury is still out on the effects of military sonar testing on marine mammals.

Marine biologists believe the humpbacks (much like humans) keep returning to Hawaii because of its warmth. Having fattened themselves in subarctic waters all summer, the whales migrate south in the winter to breed, and a rebounding population of thousands cruises Maui waters. Winter is calving time, and the young whales probably couldn't survive in the frigid Alaskan waters. No one has ever seen a whale give birth here, but experts know that calving is their main winter activity because the 1- and 2-ton youngsters suddenly appear while the whales are in residence.

Each season, the first sighting of a humpback whale spouts is exciting for locals on Maui. A collective sigh of relief can be heard: "Ah, they've returned." Flukes and flippers can rise above the ocean's surface at a not-so-far distance. It's hard not to anthropomorphize the tail waving; it looks like a friendly gesture. Each fluke is uniquely patterned, like a human's fingerprint, and is used to identify the giants as they travel halfway around the globe and back.

Maui Adventure Cruises

WILDLIFE-WATCHING | Whale-watching from this company's raft puts you right above the water surface and on the same level as the whales. You'll forgo the cocktail in your hand, but you won't have to deal with crowds, even if the vessel is at max capacity with 36 people. The whales can get up close if they like, and when they do, it's spectacular. These rafts can move faster than a catamaran, so you don't spend much time motoring between whales or pods. Refreshments are included; no children under five. ⊠ *Lahaina Harbor, Slip 11, Lahaina*

☎ *808/661–5550* ⊕ *mauiadventurecruises.com* ⊠ *Adults $64; Children 5–12 years old $49.*

★ Pacific Whale Foundation

WILDLIFE-WATCHING | **FAMILY** | This nonprofit organization pioneered whale-watching back in 1979. The crew includes a certified marine naturalist who offers insights into whale behavior and suggests ways for you to help save marine life worldwide. One of the best things about these trips is the underwater hydrophone that allows you to hear the whales sing. Trips meet at the organization's store, which sells whale-theme and local souvenirs.

You'll share the boat with a large group of people in stadium-style seating. If you prefer a smaller crowd, book their small-group experience instead. ✉ *612 Front St., Lahaina* ☎ *808/650–7056* ⊕ *pacificwhale.org* ⊠ *From $70.*

Windsurfing

Windsurfing, invented in the 1950s, found its true home at Hookipa on Maui's North Shore in 1980. Seemingly overnight, windsurfing pros from around the world flooded the area. Equipment evolved, amazing film footage was captured, and a new sport was born.

If you're new to the action, you can get lessons from the experts islandwide. For a beginner, the best thing about wind-surfing is that (unlike surfing) you don't have to paddle. Instead, you have to hold on tight to a flapping sail as it whisks you into the wind. Needless to say, you're going to need a little coordination and balance to pull this off. Instructors start you out on a beach at Kanaha. Lessons range from two-hour introductory classes to five-day advanced "flight school."

BEST SPOTS
After **Hookipa Bay** was discovered by windsurfers four decades ago, this windy North Shore beach 10 miles east of Kahului gained an international reputation. The spot is blessed with optimal wave-sailing wind and sea conditions and offers the ultimate aerial experience.

In the summer, the windsurfing crowd heads to **Kalepolepo Beach** on the South Shore. Trade winds build in strength, and by afternoon a swarm of dragonfly sails can be seen skimming the whitecaps, with Mauna Kahalawai (the West Maui Mountains) as a backdrop.

An excellent site for speed, **Kanaha Beach Park** is dedicated to beginners in the morning hours before the waves and

Ocean-Sports Tournaments 👁

The Jaws Big Wave Challenge is not for the faint of heart—and that includes spectators. Big-wave surfers test their skills at this surf break nicknamed "Jaws," (aka Peahi) known for producing waves up to 60 feet. The holding period for this contest is October–March, and only happens when the waves have reached monster heights. In November, top windsurfers compete in the **Maui Aloha Classic** at Hookipa. Cheer on the world's best women pro surfers during the Hawaii Pro at Honolua Bay, held in November and December.

wind get roaring. After 11 am, the professionals choose the size and shape best suited for the day's demands. This beach tends to have smaller waves and forceful winds—sometimes sending sailors flying at 40 knots. If you aren't ready to go pro, this is a great place for a picnic while you watch from the beach. To get here, use any of the three entrances on Amala Place, which runs along the shore just north of Kahului Airport.

EQUIPMENT AND LESSONS
Action Sports Maui

WINDSURFING | The quirky, friendly professionals will meet you at Kanaha Beach Park on the North Shore, outfit you with your sail and board, and guide you through your first "jibe," or turn. They promise that your learning time for windsurfing will be cut in half. Lessons begin at 9 am every day except Sunday. ✉ *96 Amala Pl., Kahului* ☎ *808/283–7913* ⊕ *actionsportsmaui.com* ⊠ *Lessons from $250.*

Did You Know?

Champion windsurfers come from around the world for the action at Hookipa Beach on the North Shore, where the sport developed. If you can't join in, relax, picnic, and watch the fun.

★ Hawaiian Sailboarding Techniques

WINDSURFING | Considered one of Maui's finest windsurfing schools, Hawaiian Sailboarding Techniques brings you quality instruction by skilled sailors. Founded by Alan Cadiz, an accomplished World Cup Pro, the school sets high standards for a safe, quality windsurfing experience. The company is inside Hi-Tech Surf Sports, which offers excellent equipment rentals. ⊠ *Hi-Tech Surf Sports, 425 Koloa St., Kahului* ☎ *808/871–5423* ⊕ *hstwindsurfing.com* ✉ *Lessons start at $189.*

Second Wind

WINDSURFING | Located in Kahului, this company rents boards for whatever kind of water sport you're into—windsurfing, kiteboarding, stand-up paddling, or surfing—plus lessons are offered in each discipline. Need ocean-inspired threads for when you're on dry land? They've got that, too. ⊠ *111 Hana Hwy., Kahului* ☎ *808/877–7467* ⊕ *secondwindmaui.com* ✉ *Lessons from $125.*

Zip Line Tours

Zip-lining on one of Maui's several courses lets you satisfy your inner Tarzan by soaring high above deep gulches and canyons—for a price that can seem steep. A harness keeps you fully supported on each ride. Each course has age minimums and weight restrictions, but generally, you must be at least 10 years old and weigh a minimum of 60–80 pounds and a maximum of 230–250 pounds. You should wear closed-toe athletic-type shoes and expect to get dirty.

■**TIP→ Reconsider this activity if you are pregnant, uncomfortable with heights, or have serious back or joint problems.**

★ Flyin' Hawaiian Zipline

ZIP-LINING | These guys have the longest line in the state (a staggering 3,600 feet) and a unique course layout. You build confidence on the first line, then board a four-wheel-drive vehicle that takes you 1,500 feet above the town of Waikapu to seven more lines that carry you over 11 ridges and nine valleys. The total distance covered is more than 2½ miles, and the views are astonishing. You must be able to hike over steep, sometimes slippery terrain while carrying a 10-pound metal trolley. Must be at least 10 years old or older and between 75–230 lbs. ⊠ *Maui Tropical Plantation, 1670 Honoapiiani Hwy., Wailuku* ☎ *808/463–5786* ⊕ *flyinhawaiianzipline.com* ✉ *$219.*

Kapalua Ziplines

ZIP-LINING | Begin with a 20-minute ride in a four-wheel-drive van through pineapple fields to the Mountain Outpost, a 3,000 square-foot observation deck boasting panoramic ocean and mountain views. If you're on the seven-line zip, you'll climb even higher above the Pacific Ocean in a Polaris Ranger to experience 2 miles of parallel zipping plus snacks. The shorter five-line zip and full moon zip are great if you're short on time. Must be 10 years old or older and between 60–250 lbs. ⊠ *500 Office Rd., Kapalua* ☎ *808/756–9147* ⊕ *kapaluaziplines.com* ✉ *Starting at $160.*

Skyline Eco Adventures

ZIP-LINING | The first company to open a zip line course in the United States, Skyline has expanded to offer Haleakala Sunrise tours followed by breakfast at picturesque Kula Lodge. The Haleakala Sunrise & Zip Tour adds on a zip-lining adventure that leads you across an Indiana Jones-style swinging bridge. You'll reach speeds over 45 mph on Hawaii's only pendulum line over the natural wonders of Maui. ⊠ *18303 Haleakala Hwy., Kula* ☎ *808/878–8400* ⊕ *skylinehawaii.com* ✉ *Starting at $129.*

Chapter 11

MOLOKAI

Updated by
Laurie Lyons-Makaimoku

◉ Sights	🍴 Restaurants	🛏 Hotels	🛍 Shopping	🍸 Nightlife
★★★★★	★★★★☆	★★★☆☆	★★★★☆	★☆☆☆☆

WELCOME TO MOLOKAI

TOP REASONS TO GO

★ **Kalaupapa Peninsula:** Hike or take a mule ride down the world's tallest sea cliffs, or take a plane to a fascinating historic community that still houses a few former Hansen's disease patients and learn more about the people who have been hidden away from the world.

★ **A waterfall hike in Halawa:** A fascinating guided (intermediate) hike through private property takes you past ancient ruins, restored taro patches, and a sparkling cascade.

★ **Deep-sea fishing:** Sport fish are plentiful in these waters, as are gorgeous views of several islands. Fishing is one of the Island's great adventures.

★ **Closeness to nature:** Deep valleys, sheer cliffs, endless rainbows, and the untamed ocean are the main attractions on Molokai.

★ **Papohaku Beach:** This 3-mile stretch of golden sand is one of the most sensational beaches in all of Hawaii. Sunsets and barbecues are perfect here.

Molokai is about 10 miles wide on average and four times that long. It comprises east, west, and central regions, plus the Kalaupapa Peninsula and the Kalaupapa National Historic Park. The north shore thrusts up from the sea to form the tallest sea cliffs on Earth, while the south shore slides almost flat into the water, then fans out to form the largest shallow-water reef system in the United States. Kaunakakai, the island's main town, has most of the stores and restaurants. Surprisingly, the highest point on Molokai rises to only 4,970 feet.

1 West Molokai. The most arid part of the island, known as the west end, has two inhabited areas: the coastal stretch includes a few condos and luxury homes, along with the largest beaches on the island; nearby is the fading hilltop hamlet of Maunaloa, a former plantation town, whose backdrop is the dormant volcano that shares its name. Papohaku Beach, one of the remote beaches found here, is the Hawaiian Islands' second-longest white-sand beach.

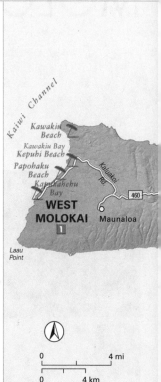

2 Central Molokai. The island's only true town, Kaunakakai, with its mile-long wharf, is here. Nearly all the island's eateries and stores are in or close to Kaunakakai. Highway 470 crosses the center of the island, rising to the top of the sea cliffs and the Kalaupapa overlook. At the base of the cliffs is Kalaupapa National Historical Park, a top attraction.

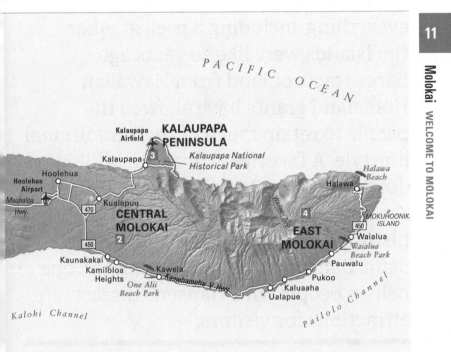

PACIFIC OCEAN

KALAUPAPA PENINSULA

Kalaupapa Airfield

Kalaupapa ③

Kalaupapa National Historical Park

Hoolehua

Hoolehua Airport

Maunaloa Hwy.

Kualapuu

470

CENTRAL MOLOKAI

②

450

Kaunakakai

Kamiloloa Heights

Kawela

One Alii Beach Park

Kamehameha V Hwy.

④

EAST MOLOKAI

Wailau Trail

Halawa

Halawa Beach

MOKUHOONIKI ISLAND

450

Waialua

Waialua Beach Park

Pauwalu

Pukoo

Kaluaaha

Ualapue

Kalohi Channel

Pailolo Channel

③ Kalaupapa Peninsula.
One of the most remote areas in the entire Hawaiian Islands is currently accessible only by air. It is typically accessible by foot or on a mule, but as of late 2019 the path is closed indefinitely due to a landslide. It's a place of stunning beauty with a tragic history.

④ East Molokai.
The scenic drive on Route 450 around this undeveloped area, also called the east end, passes through the green pastures of Puu O Hoku Ranch and climaxes with a descent into Halawa Valley. As you continue east, the road becomes increasingly narrow and the island ever more lush.

With sandy beaches to the west, sheer sea cliffs to the north, and a rainy, lush eastern coast, Molokai offers a bit of everything, including a peek at what the Islands were like 50 years ago. Large tracts of land from Hawaiian Homeland grants have allowed the people to retain much of their traditional lifestyle. A favorite expression is "Slow down, you're on Molokai." Exploring the great outdoors and visiting the historic Kalaupapa Peninsula, where Saint Damien and Saint Marianne Cope helped people with Hansen's disease, are attractions for visitors.

Molokai is generally thought of as the last bit of "real" Hawaii. Tourism has been held at bay by the Island's unique history and the pride of its predominantly Native Hawaiian population. Only 38 miles long and 10 miles wide at its widest point, Molokai is the fifth-largest island in the Hawaiian archipelago. Eight thousand residents call Molokai home, nearly 60% of whom are Hawaiian.

Molokai is a great place to be outdoors. There are no tall buildings, no traffic lights, no streetlights, no stores bearing the names of national chains, and nothing at all like a resort. You will, however, find 15 parks and more than 100 miles of shoreline to play on. At night the whole Island grows dark, creating a velvety blackness and a wonderful rare silence.

The first thing to do on Molokai is to drive everywhere. It's a feat you can accomplish comfortably in two days. Depending on where you stay, spend a day exploring the west end and another exploring the east end. Basically, you have one 40-mile west–east highway (two lanes, no stoplights) with three side trips: the nearly deserted little west-end town of Maunaloa; the Highway 470 drive (just a few miles) to the top of the north shore and the overlook of Kalaupapa Peninsula; and the short stretch of shops in Kaunakakai town. After you learn the general lay of the land, you can return to the places that interest you most. Directions on the

Island—as throughout Hawaii—are often given as *mauka* (toward the mountains) and *makai* (toward the ocean).

■ TIP→ **Most Molokai establishments cater to the needs of locals, not tourists, so you may need to prepare a bit more than if you were going to a more popular destination. Pick up a disposable cooler in Kaunakakai town, and then buy supplies in local markets. Don't forget to carry some water, and bring sunscreen and mosquito repellent to the Island with you.**

GEOGRAPHY

Molokai was created when two large volcanoes—Kamakou in the east and Maunaloa in the west—broke the surface of the Pacific Ocean to create an island. Afterward, a third section of the Island emerged when a much smaller caldera, Kauhako, popped up to form the Kalaupapa Peninsula. But it wasn't until an enormous landslide sent much of Kauhako Mountain into the sea that the island was blessed with the sheer sea cliffs—the world's tallest—that make Molokai's north shore so spectacularly beautiful.

HISTORY

Molokai is named in chants as the child of the moon goddess Hina. For centuries the Island was occupied by native people, who took advantage of the reef fishing and ideal conditions for growing taro.

When leprosy broke out in the Hawaiian Islands in the 1840s, the Kalaupapa Peninsula, surrounded on three sides by the Pacific and accessible only by a steep trail, was selected as the place to exile people suffering from the disease. The first patients were thrown into the sea to swim ashore as best they could, and left with no facilities, shelter, or supplies. In 1873, a missionary named Father Damien arrived and began to serve the peninsula's suffering inhabitants. He died in 1889 from leprosy and was canonized as a saint by the Catholic Church in 2009. In 1888, a nun named Mother Marianne

Cope moved to Kalaupapa to care for the dying Father Damien and continue his vital work. Mother Marianne stayed at Kalaupapa until her death in 1918; she was canonized in 2012.

Although leprosy, known now as Hansen's disease, is no longer contagious and can be remitted, the buildings and infrastructure created by those who were exiled here still exist, and some longtime residents have chosen to stay in their homes. Today the area is Kalaupapa National Historical Park. Visitors are typically welcome with a tour group, but the Kalaupapa Trail and Kalaupapa Trail are currently closed to protect the residents from the pandemic.

THE BIRTHPLACE OF HULA

Tradition has it that, centuries ago, Lailai came to Molokai and lived on Puu Nana at Kaana. She brought the art of hula and taught it to the people, who kept it secret for her descendants, making sure the sacred dances were performed only at Kaana. Five generations later, Laka was born into the family and learned hula from an older sister. She chose to share the art and traveled throughout the Islands teaching the dance, although she did so without her family's consent. The yearly Ka Hula Piko Festival, held on Molokai in May, celebrates the birth of hula at Kaana.

Planning

When to Go

If you're keen to explore Molokai's beaches, coral beds, or fishponds, summer is your best bet for nonstop calm seas and sunny skies. The weather mimics that of the other Islands: low to mid-80s year-round, slightly rainier in winter. As you travel up the mountainside, the weather changes with bursts of downpours. The strongest storms occur in winter when winds and rain shift to come in from the south.

For a taste of Hawaiian culture, plan your visit around a festival. In January, Islanders and visitors compete in ancient Hawaiian games at the Ka Molokai Makahiki Festival. The Molokai Ka Hula Piko, an annual daylong event in May, draws premier hula troupes, musicians, and storytellers. Long-distance canoe races from Molokai to Oahu are in late September and early October. Although never crowded, the Island is busier during these events—book accommodations and transportation six months in advance.

Note: Some events have been modified due to the COVID-19 pandemic and are slow to return.

Getting Here and Around

AIR

If you're flying in from the mainland United States, you must first make a stop in Honolulu, Oahu or Kahului, Maui. From either of those, Molokai is just a short hop away. Molokai's transportation hub is Molokai Airport (MKK), a tiny airstrip 8 miles west of Kaunakakai and about 18 miles east of Maunaloa. An even smaller airstrip serves the little community of Kalaupapa on the north shore.

From Molokai Airport (sometimes called Hoolehua Airport), it takes about 10 minutes to reach Kaunakakai and 25 minutes to reach the west end of the Island by car. There's no public bus. A taxi will cost about $27 from the airport to Kaunakakai with Hele Mai Taxi. Keep in mind, however, that it's difficult to visit the Island without a rental car.

AIRPORT CONTACTS Molokai Airport (MKK). ⊠ *3980 Airport Loop, Hoolehua* ☎ *808/567–9660* ⊕ *airports.hawaii.gov/ mkk.*

TAXI CONTACTS Hele Mai Taxi. ⊠ *Kaunakakai* ☎ *808/336–0967* ⊕ *molokaitaxi. com.*

CAR

If you want to explore Molokai from one end to the other, you must rent a car. With just a few main roads to choose from, it's a snap to drive around here. The gas stations are in Kaunakakai. Ask your rental agent for a free *Molokai Drive Guide.*

Alamo maintains a counter at Molokai Airport. Make arrangements in advance, because the number of rental cars on Molokai is limited. Be sure to check that the vehicle's four-wheel drive is working before you depart from the agency. Off-road driving is not allowed; beware of fees for returning the car dirty. If Alamo is fully booked, check out Molokai Car Rental.

CONTACTS Alamo Rent a Car. ⊠ *3980 Airport Loop, Building 2, Hoolehua* ☎ *808/567–6381* ⊕ *www.alamo.com.* **Mobettah Car Rentals.** ⊠ *3980 Airport Loop, Hoolehua* ☎ *808/308–9566* ⊕ *www.mobettahcarrentals.com.*

Beaches

Molokai's unique geography gives the Island plenty of drama and spectacle along the shorelines but not so many places for seaside basking and bathing. The long north shore consists mostly of towering cliffs that plunge directly into the sea and is inaccessible except by boat, and even then only in summer. Much of the south shore is enclosed by a huge reef, which stands as far as a mile offshore and blunts the action of the waves. Within this reef you can find a thin strip of sand, but the water here is flat, shallow, and at times clouded with silt. This reef area is best suited to wading, pole fishing, kayaking, and paddleboarding.

The big, fat, sandy beaches lie along the west end. The largest of these—the second largest in the Islands—is Papohaku Beach, which fronts a grassy park shaded by a grove of *kiawe* (mesquite) trees. These stretches of west-end sand are generally unpopulated. At the east end, where the road hugs the sinuous shoreline, you encounter a number of pocket-size beaches in rocky coves, good for snorkeling. Don't venture too far out, however, or you can find yourself caught in dangerous currents. The Island's east-end road ends at Halawa Valley with its unique double bay, which is not recommended for swimming.

■ TIP→ **To rent kayaks, SUPs, and snorkel gear, check out Molokai Outdoors at** ⊕ *molokai-outdoors.com.*

Hotels

Molokai appeals most to travelers who appreciate genuine Hawaiian ambience rather than swanky digs. Most hotel and condominium properties range from adequate to funky, but the prices are significantly lower than hotels on the other Islands. Visitors who want to lollygag on the beach should choose one of the condos or home rentals in West Molokai. Travelers who want to immerse themselves in the spirit of the Island should seek out a condo or cottage, the closer to East Molokai the better. Hotel Molokai in Kaunakakai is the closest thing you'll find to a resort.

■ TIP→ **Maui County has regulations concerning vacation rentals; to avoid disappointment, always contact the property manager or the owner and ask if the accommodations have the proper permits and are in compliance with local ordinances.**

The coastline along Molokai's west end has ocean-view condominium units and luxury homes available as vacation rentals. Central Molokai offers seaside condominiums. The only lodgings on the east end are some guest cottages in magical settings and the cottages and ranch lodge at Puu O Hoku. Note that room rates do not include the 13.42% sales tax.

Hotel reviews have been shortened. For full information, visit Fodors.com. Hotel prices are the lowest cost of a standard double room in high season. Condo price categories reflect studio and one-bedroom rates.

WHAT IT COSTS in U.S. Dollars			
$	$$	$$$	$$$$
HOTELS			
under $181	$181–$260	$261–$340	over $340

Molokai Vacation Rentals

HOTEL | FAMILY | Vacasa Vacation Rentals handles condo rentals across the Island. There is a two-night minimum on all properties. Contactless check-in is available at most properties. ✉ *130 Kamehameha V Hwy., Kaunakakai* ☎ *808/460–4421* ⊕ *www.molokaivacationrental.com.*

Restaurants

Dining on Molokai, for the most part, is simply a matter of eating—there are no fancy restaurants, just pleasant low-key places to dine. Paddlers Restaurant and Bar and Hiro's Ohana Grill currently have the best dinner and ambience offerings. Other options include burgers, plate lunches, pizza, coffee shop-style sandwiches, and make-it-yourself fixings.

During a week's stay, you might easily hit all the dining spots worth a visit and then return to your favorites for a second round. The dining scene is fun because it's a microcosm of Hawaii's diverse cultures. You can find locally grown vegetarian foods, spicy Filipino cuisine, or Hawaiian fish with a Japanese influence—such as tuna, mullet, and moonfish that's grilled, sautéed, or mixed with seaweed to make poke (salted and seasoned raw fish).

Most eating establishments are on Ala Malama Street in Kaunakakai. If you're heading to West Molokai for the day, be sure to stock up on provisions, as there is no place to eat there. If you are on the east end, stop by **Manae Goods & Grindz** (☎ 808/558–8186) near mile marker 16 for good local seafood plates, burgers, and ice cream.

Restaurant reviews have been shortened. For full information, visit Fodors.com. Restaurant prices are the average cost of a main course at dinner or, if dinner is not served, at lunch.

WHAT IT COSTS in U.S. Dollars

$	$$	$$$	$$$$
RESTAURANTS			
under $18	$18–$26	$27–$35	over $35

Nightlife

Local nightlife consists mainly of gathering with friends and family, sipping a few cold ones, strumming ukuleles and guitars, singing old songs, and talking story. Still, there are a few ways to kick up your heels. Pick up a copy of the weekly *Molokai Dispatch* and see if there's a concert, church supper, or dance. Paddlers Restaurant is a great option for live music and a full bar most nights of the week.

Shopping

Molokai has one main commercial area: Ala Malama Street in Kaunakakai. There are no department stores or shopping malls, and the clothing is typical island wear. A small number of family-run businesses defines the main drag of Maunaloa, a rural former plantation town, and there are a couple of general stores and other random stores throughout the Island. Most stores in Kaunakakai are open Monday–Saturday 10 am–6 pm, but posted hours are sometimes just a suggestion. If you find that a store isn't open at the posted time, grab a coffee, shop at a couple of other spots, then circle back around. Almost everything shuts down on Sundays, so be sure to plan ahead.

Visitor Information

CONTACTS Destination Molokai Visitors Bureau. ✉ 3980 Airport Loop, Hoolehua ☎ 808/553–5221 ⊕ gohawaii.com/molokai.

West Molokai

Papohaku Beach is 17 miles west of the airport; Maunaloa is 10 miles west of the airport.

The remote beaches and rolling pastures on Molokai's west end are presided over by Maunaloa, a dormant volcano, and a sleepy little former plantation town of the same name. Papohaku Beach, the Hawaiian Islands' second-longest white-sand beach, is one of the area's biggest draws.

GETTING HERE AND AROUND

The sometimes winding paved road through West Molokai begins at Highway 460 and ends at Kapukahehu Bay. The drive from Kaunakakai to Maunaloa is about 30 minutes.

◉ Sights

Kaluakoi

TOWN | Although the mid-1970s Kaluakoi Hotel and Golf Club is closed and forlorn, some nice condos and a gift shop are operating nearby. Kepuhi Beach, the white-sand beach along the coast, is worth a visit. ✉ *Kaluakoi Rd., Maunaloa.*

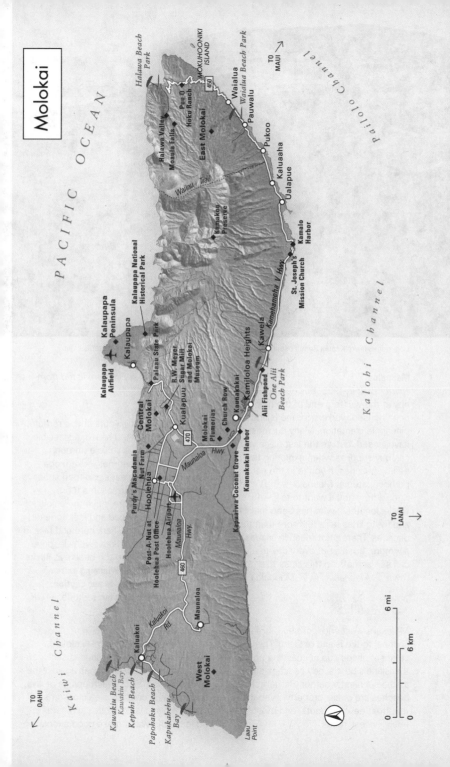

Molokai

PACIFIC OCEAN

Halawa Beach Park

MOKUHOONIKI ISLAND

Halawa Valley
Moaula Falls

Puu O Hoku Ranch

Waialua
Waialua Beach Park

TO MAUI

Pauwalu

Pukoo

Kaluaaha

East Molokai

Ualapue

Wailau Trail

Kamakou Preserve

Kalaupapa Peninsula

Kalaupapa

Kamalo Harbor

Kalaupapa National Historical Park

St. Joseph's Mission Church

Kalaupapa Airfield

Palaau State Park

R.W. Meyer Sugar Mill and Molokai Museum

Kualapuu

Kawela

Kamehameha V Hwy.

Central Molokai

Kamiloloa Heights

Molokai Plumerias

Church Row

Kaunakakai

Ailii Fishpond
One Alii Beach Park

470

Kaunakakai Harbor

Kapuaiwa Coconut Grove

Maunaloa Hwy.

Purdy's Macadamia Nut Farm

Hoolehua

Post-A-Nut at Hoolehua Post Office

Hoolehua Airport

Maunaloa Hwy.

TO LANAI

460

Kaluakoi

Kaluakoi Rd

Maunaloa

Kawakiu Beach
Kawakiu Bay

Kepuhi Beach

Papohaku Beach

West Molokai

Kapukahehu Bay

Laau Point

Kaiwi Channel

TO OAHU

Paailolo Channel

Kalohi Channel

6 mi

6 km

0

Lava ridges make Kepuhi Beach beautiful, but swimming here is difficult unless the water is calm.

Maunaloa

TOWN | Built in 1923, this quiet community at the western end of the highway once housed workers for the Island's pineapple plantation. Many businesses have closed, but it's the last place you can buy supplies when exploring the nearby beaches. If you're in the neighborhood, stop at Maunaloa's Big Wind Kite Factory. You'll want to talk with Uncle Jonathan, who has been making and flying kites here for more than three decades. There's not much in Maunaloa anymore, but it's not every day that you can see something this close to a ghost town. ⊠ *Maunaloa Hwy., Maunaloa.*

😊 Beaches

Molokai's west end looks across a wide channel to the island of Oahu. This crescent-shape cup of coastline holds the island's best sandy beaches as well as the sunniest weather. Remember: all beaches are public property, even those that front developments, and most have public access roads.

Beaches in this section are listed from north to south.

Kawakiu Beach

BEACH | Seclusion is yours at this remote, beautiful, white-sand beach, accessible by four-wheel-drive vehicle (through a gate that is sometimes locked) or a 45-minute walk (wear close-toed shoes as you may find yourself in a thorny situation). To get here, drive to Paniolo Hale off Kaluakoi Road and look for a dirt road off to the right. Park here and hike in or, with a four-wheel-drive vehicle, drive along the dirt road to the beach. ⚠ **Rocks and undertow make swimming extremely dangerous at times, so use caution. Amenities:** none. **Best for:** solitude. ⊠ *Off Kaluakoi Rd., Maunaloa.*

Kepuhi Beach

BEACH | The Kaluakoi Hotel is closed, but its half mile of ivory sand is still accessible. The beach shines against the turquoise sea, black outcroppings of lava, and magenta bougainvillea blossoms. When the sea is perfectly calm, lava ridges in the water make good snorkeling spots. With any surf at all, however, the water around these rocky places churns and foams, wiping out visibility and making it difficult to avoid being slammed into the jagged rocks. Stick to the northern part of the beach to avoid as many of the rocks as possible. If the surf is too big for snorkeling, there's a nice bench up the path that lets you relax and take it all in. **Amenities:** none. **Best for:** snorkeling; walking. ⊠ *Kaluakoi Rd., Maunaloa.*

★ Papohaku Beach

BEACH | One of the most sensational beaches in Hawaii, Papohaku is a three-mile-long strip of white sand, the longest of its kind on the Island. There's so much sand here that Honolulu once purchased bargeloads of the stuff to replenish Waikiki Beach. A shady beach park just inland is the site of the Ka Hula Piko Festival, held each year in May. The park is also a great sunset-facing spot for a rustic afternoon barbecue. A park ranger patrols the area periodically. ⚠ **Swimming is not recommended, except on exceptionally calm summer days, as there's a dangerous undertow. Amenities:** showers; toilets. **Best for:** sunset; walking. ⊠ *Kaluakoi Rd., Maunaloa* ✢ *2 miles south of the former Kaluakoi Hotel.*

🛏 Hotels

If you want to stay in West Molokai so you'll have access to unspoiled beaches, you can choose from condos or vacation homes. Note that units fronting the abandoned Kaluakoi golf course present a bit of a dismal view.

Ke Nani Kai

$ | **APARTMENT** | These pleasant, spacious one- and two-bedroom condos near the beach—each with a washer, dryer, and a fully equipped kitchen—have ocean views and nicely maintained tropical landscaping. **Pros:** on island's secluded west end; uncrowded pool; beach across the road. **Cons:** far from commercial center; some units overlook abandoned golf

Beach Safety 🏄

Unlike protected shorelines like Kaanapali on Maui, the coasts of Molokai are exposed to rough sea channels and dangerous rip currents. The ocean tends to be calmer in the morning and in summer. No matter what the time, however, always study the sea before entering. Unless the water is placid and the wave action minimal, it's best to stay on shore, even though locals may be in the water. Don't underestimate the power of the ocean. Protect yourself with sunblock; cool breezes make it easy to underestimate the power of the sun as well.

course; amenities vary from unit to unit. $ *Rooms from: $162* ⊠ *50 Kepuhi Pl., Maunaloa* ☎ *808/460–4421* ⊕ *molokai-vacation-rental.net* ➘ *120 units* ⧇ *No Meals.*

★ Paniolo Hale

$ | **APARTMENT** | Perched high on a ridge overlooking a favorite local surfing spot, this is Molokai's best condominium property and boasts mature tropical landscaping and a private serene setting. **Pros:** close to beach; quiet surroundings; perfect if you are an expert surfer. **Cons:** far from shopping; golf course units front abandoned course; amenities vary. $ *Rooms from: $167* ⊠ *100 Lio Pl., Maunaloa* ☎ *808/460-4221* ⊕ *molokai-vacation-rental.net* ➘ *77 units* ⧇ *No Meals.*

🛍 Shopping

ARTS AND CRAFTS
★ Big Wind Kite Factory

CRAFTS | The factory has custom-made kites you can fly or display. Designs range from Hawaiian flags to Hawaiian animals like *pueo* (owls) with a little bit of mermaid fun in between. Also in stock are paper kites, mini kites, and wind socks. The adjacent gallery carries an eclectic collection of merchandise, including locally made crafts, Hawaiian books and CDs, jewelry, and other souvenirs. ⊠ *120 Maunaloa Hwy., Maunaloa* 🕾 *808/552–2364* ⊕ *bigwindkites.com.*

FOOD

Maunaloa General Store

FOOD | Stocking meat, produce, beverages, and dry goods, this shop is a convenient stop if you're planning a picnic at one of the west-end beaches. Stop for other treats as well—they've got ice cream, beer, and plenty of tasty snacks. ⊠ *200 Maunaloa Hwy., Maunaloa* 🕾 *808/552–2346.*

Kalaupapa Peninsula

One of the more remote areas in the Hawaiian Islands is a place of stunning natural beauty coupled with a tragic past. It's here that residents of Hawaii who displayed symptoms of Hansen's disease were permanently exiled beginning in 1866. Today, the peninsula is still isolated. But a day spent here is, without a doubt, a profound, once-in-a-lifetime experience.

GETTING HERE AND AROUND

Unless you fly (through Makani Kai Air on-island or Mokulele Airlines off-island), the only way into Kalaupapa National Historical Park is to travel down a dizzying switchback trail, either on foot or by mule. Going down on foot takes at least an hour, but you must allow 90 minutes for the return; going down by mule is even slower, taking two hours down, and the same to travel back up. The switchbacks are numbered—26 in all—and descend 1,700 feet to sea level in just under 3 miles. The steep trail is more of a staircase, and most of the trail is shaded. However, the footing is uneven, and there is little to keep you from pitching over the side. If you don't mind heights, you can stare straight down to the ocean

Closures at Kaluapapa 👁

While the Kalaupapa Peninsula is most definitely a highlight of visiting Molokai, the park is currently closed to the general public and commercial tours in order to protect residents from exposure to COVID-19. Access to the park has always been somewhat difficult, and it has been closed in the past, but we are confident it will reopen soon. Be sure to check with the National Park Service (⊕ *nps.gov/kala*) for updates and closure information before planning your trip.

for most of the way. It's strenuous regardless of which method you choose.

The Kalaupapa Trail and Peninsula are all part of Kalaupapa National Historical Park (🕾 *808/567–6802*), which is open every day but Sunday for tours only. Keep in mind there are no public facilities (except an occasional restroom) anywhere in the park. Pack your own food and water, as well as light rain gear, sunscreen, and bug repellent. ■ TIP→ **To learn more about this unique place be sure to visit the Molokai Museum and view the community from the Kaulapapa Overlook.**

TOURS

★ **Kalaupapa Guided Mule Tour**

SCENIC DRIVE | Mount a friendly, well-trained mule and wind along a thrilling 3-mile, 26-switchback trail to reach the town of Kalaupapa, which was once home to patients with leprosy who were exiled to this remote spot. The path was built in 1886 as a supply route for the settlement below. Once in Kalaupapa, you take a guided tour of the town and enjoy a light picnic lunch. The trail traverses some of the highest sea cliffs in the world, and views are spectacular.

Only those in good shape should attempt the ride, as two hours each way on a mule can take its toll. You must be at least 16 years old and weigh no more than 250 pounds; pregnant women are not allowed. The entire event takes seven hours. The same outfit can arrange for you to hike down or fly in. No one is allowed in the park or on the trail without booking a tour. ⚠ **Currently closed in order to protect residents from exposure to COVID-19. Call** ☎ *808/567-6088* **for updates.** ✉ *100 Kalae Hwy., Kualapuu* ☎ *808/567-6088, 800/567-7550* ⊕ *www.muleride.com* 🖃 *$209.*

Mokulele Airlines

AIR EXCURSIONS | To fly into Kalaupapa from another island your only option is Mokulele Airlines (they'll make a layover at the Molokai Airport). As with other ways of traveling into the area, you'll need to arrange a tour so that they can secure permits for you—all visitors must have a sponsor and may not roam around Kalaupapa freely; your tour company serves as your sponsor. Mokulele will require sponsor information before booking. Mokulele Airlines is now part of Southern Airways. ✉ *Kalaupapa* ☎ *866/260–7070 Reservations only.*

⊙ Sights

Kalaupapa National Historical Park

NATIONAL PARK | For 100 years, this remote strip of land was "the loneliest place on Earth," a beautiful yet feared place of exile for those suffering from leprosy (now known as Hansen's disease). Today, visitors to Molokai's Kalaupapa Peninsula, open every day but Sunday, can admire the tall sea cliffs, rain-chiseled valleys, and tiny islets along the coast. The park tells a poignant human story, as the Kalaupapa Peninsula was once a community of about 1,000 people who were banished from their homes in Hawaii. It also recounts the wonderful work of Father Damien, a Belgian missionary who arrived in 1873

Hawaii's First Saint ⊙

A long-revered figure on Molokai and in Hawaii, Father Damien, who cared for the desperate patients at Kalaupapa, was elevated to sainthood in 2009. Visitors who cannot visit Kalaupapa can find information on Saint Damien at St. Damien Church in Kaunakakai and may worship at Our Lady of Seven Sorrows (just west of Kaunakakai), St. Damien Church, or at St. Vincent Ferrer in Maunaloa.

to work with the patients. He died in 1889 from leprosy and was canonized as a saint by the Catholic Church in 2009. Mother Marianne Cope, who continued St. Damien's work after his death, was canonized in 2012.

Today there are about eight patients still living in Kalaupapa—now by choice, as the disease is treatable. Out of respect to these people, visitors must be at least 16 years old, cannot stay overnight, and must be on a guided tour or invited by a resident. Photographing patients without their permission is forbidden. There are no public facilities (except an occasional restroom) anywhere in the park. Pack your own food and water, as well as light rain gear, sunscreen, and bug repellent. ✉ *Hwy. 470, Kualapuu* ☎ *808/567–6802* ⊕ *www.nps.gov/kala.*

Central Molokai

Kaunakakai is 8 miles southeast of the airport.

Most residents live centrally, near the Island's one and only true town, Kaunakakai. It's just about the only place on the Island to get food and supplies—it

Kapuaiwa Coconut Grove in Central Molokai is a survivor of royal plantings from the 19th century.

is Molokai. Go into the shops along and around Ala Malama Street to shop and talk with the locals. Take your time, and you'll really enjoy being a visitor. On the north side is Coffees of Hawaii, a 500-acre coffee plantation, and the Kalaupapa National Historical Park, one of the Island's most notable sights.

GETTING HERE AND AROUND

Central Molokai is the hub of the Island's road system, and Kaunakakai is the commercial center. Enjoy the slow pace, and watch for kids, dogs, and people crossing the street downtown.

◉ Sights

Church Row

CHURCH | Standing together along the highway are seven houses of worship with primarily native-Hawaiian congregations. Notice the unadorned, boxlike architecture so similar to missionary homes. ⊠ *Rte. 460, Kaunakakai* ✦ *5½ miles south of airport.*

Kapuaiwa Coconut Grove

HISTORIC SIGHT | From far away this spot looks like a sea of coconut trees. Closer up you can see that the tall stately palms are planted in long rows leading down to the sea. This is a remnant of one of the last surviving royal groves planted for Prince Lot, who ruled Hawaii as King Kamehameha V from 1863 until his death in 1872. The grove is planted on private property—visitors should observe from outside of the perimeter fence. ⊠ *30 Mauna Loa Hwy., Kaunakakai.*

Kaunakakai

TOWN | Central Molokai's main town looks like a classic 1940s movie set. Along the short main drag is a cultural grab bag of restaurants and shops, and many people are friendly and willing to supply directions or just "talk story." Preferred dress is shorts and a tank top, and no one wears anything fancier than a cotton skirt or aloha shirt. ⊠ *Rte. 460, 3 blocks north of Kaunakakai Wharf, Kaunakakai.*

The Truth About Hansen's Disease ⊙

- A cure for leprosy has been available since 1941. Multi-drug therapy, a rapid cure, has been available since 1981.

- With treatment, none of the disabilities traditionally associated with leprosy need occur.

- Most people have a natural immunity to leprosy. Only 5% of the world's population is even susceptible to the disease.

- There are still more than 200,000 new cases of leprosy each year; the majority are in India.

- All new cases of leprosy are treated on an outpatient basis.

- The term "leper" is offensive and should not be used. It is appropriate to say "a person is affected by leprosy" or "by Hansen's disease."

Kaunakakai Harbor

MARINA/PIER | Once bustling with barges exporting pineapples, these docks now host visiting boats and the regular barge from Oahu. The wharf, the longest in the state, is also the starting point for fishing, sailing, snorkeling, whale-watching, and scuba-diving excursions. It's a nice place at sunset to watch fish rippling the water. To get here, take Kaunakakai Place, which dead-ends at the wharf. ⊠ *Rte. 450, at Ala Malama St., Kaunakakai* ⊕ *kaunakakaiharbor.com.*

Molokai Plumerias

GARDEN | The sweet smell of plumeria surrounds you at this 10-acre orchard containing thousands of these fragrant trees. Purchase a lei to go, or for $25 owner Dick Wheeler will give you a basket, set you free to pick your own blossoms, then teach you how to string your own lei. Whether purchasing a lei or making your own, it's best to call first for an appointment or to order your lei in advance. ⊠ *1342 Maunaloa Hwy., Kaunakakai* ☎ *808/553–3391* ⊕ *molokaiplumerias.com.*

★ Palaau State Park

FOREST | **FAMILY** | One of the Island's few formal recreation areas, this 233-acre retreat sits at a 1,000-foot elevation. A short path through an ironwood forest leads to Kalaupapa Lookout, a magnificent overlook with views of the town of Kalaupapa and the 1,664-foot-high sea cliffs protecting it. Informative plaques have facts about leprosy, Saint Damien, and the colony. The park is also the site of Kaule O Nanahoa (Phallus of Nanahoa), where women in old Hawaii would come to the rock to enhance their fertility; it is said some still do. Because the rock is a sacred site, be respectful and don't deface the boulders. The park is well maintained, with trails, camping facilities, restrooms, and picnic tables. ⊠ *Rte. 470, Kualapuu* ✛ *Take Hwy. 460 west from Kaunakakai and then head mauka (toward the mountains) on Hwy. 470, which ends at the park* ☎ *808/567–6923* ⊕ *dlnr. hawaii.gov/dsp/parks/molokai/palaau-state-park* ☜ *Free.*

Post-A-Nut at Hoolehua Post Office

GOVERNMENT BUILDING | At this small, rural post office you can mail a coconut anywhere in the world. Postmaster Gary Lam provides the coconuts and colored markers. You decorate and address your coconut, and Gary affixes eye-catching stamps on it from his extensive collection. Costs vary according to destination, but for domestic addresses they start around $10. ⊠ *69-2 Puupeelua Ave.,*

Kaule O Nanahoa at Palaau State Park

Hoolehua ☎ 808/553–5112 ⊕ postanut. com ☉ Closed weekends.

Purdy's Macadamia Nut Farm

FARM/RANCH | Molokai's only working macadamia nut farm is open for educational tours hosted by the knowledgeable and entertaining owners. A family business in Hoolehua, the farm takes up 1½ acres with a flourishing grove of 50 original trees that are more than 90 years old, as well as several hundred younger trees. The nuts taste delicious right out of the shell, home roasted, or dipped in macadamia-blossom honey. Look for Purdy's sign behind Molokai High School. *⊠ Lihi Pali Ave., Hoolehua ☎ 808/567–6601 ⊕ molokai-aloha.com/ macnuts ☜ Free ☉ Sun. and holidays by appointment only.*

★ R. W. Meyer Sugar Mill and Molokai Museum

HISTORY MUSEUM | Built in 1877, the fully restored, three-room sugar mill has been reconstructed as a testament to Molokai's agricultural history. It is located next to the Molokai Museum and is usually included in the museum tour. Several interesting machines from the past are on display, including a mule-driven cane crusher and a steam engine. The museum contains changing exhibits on the Island's early history and has a gift shop. Currently (and for the foreseeable future) the museum is home to an incredible photography exhibit that showcases the people of and life in Kalaupapa; attending the exhibit and speaking with docents is a great way to learn more about the community if you aren't able to visit. Be sure to step into the gift shop for some unique, locally made items. *⊠ Rte. 470, Kualapuu ✛ 2 miles southwest of Palaau State Park ☎ 808/567–6436 ☜ $5 (cash only) ☉ Closed Sun.*

🏖 Beaches

The south shore is mostly a huge, reef-walled expanse of flat saltwater edged with a thin strip of gritty sand and stones, mangrove swamps, and the amazing system of fishponds constructed by the chiefs of ancient Molokai. From this shore you can look out across glassy water to see people standing on top of the sea—actually, way out on top of the reef—casting fishing lines into the distant waves. This is not a great area for swimming beaches, but it is a good place to snorkel or wade in the shallows.

One Alii Beach Park

BEACH | Clear, close views of Maui and Lanai across the Pailolo Channel dominate One Alii Beach Park (*One* is pronounced "o-nay," not "won"), the only well-maintained beach park on the Island's south-central shore. Molokai folks gather here for family reunions and community celebrations; the park's tightly trimmed expanse of lawn could almost accommodate the entire Island's population. Swimming within the reef is perfectly safe, but don't expect to catch any waves. Nearby is the restored One Alii fishpond (it is appropriate only for Native Hawaiians to fish here). **Amenities:** playground; showers; toilets. **Best for:** parties; swimming. ⊠ *Rte. 450, Kaunakakai* ✛ *east of Hotel Molokai.*

🍴 Restaurants

★ Hiro's Ohana Grill

$$$ | **MODERN HAWAIIAN** | Located in Hotel Molokai, the Island's only oceanfront restaurant is also its fanciest and best place to grab a drink or watch the game on TV. Enjoy pasta, steak, shrimp, or fish while watching the sunset and listening to live music, and don't be surprised if the couple you saw hiking is seated at the table right next to you. **Known for:** live music and hula; whale-watching from your table in winter; shrimp pesto over linguini. ⑤ *Average main: $31* ⊠ *Hotel Molokai, 1300 Kamehameha V Hwy., Kaunakakai* ☎ *808/660–3400* ⊕ *hirosohanagrill.com* ☞ *Breakfast available on Sundays.*

Kamoi Snack-n-Go

$ | **AMERICAN** | **FAMILY** | The old school interior at this "Molokai rest stop" feels

Molokai Vibes 👁

Molokai is one of the last places in Hawaii where most of the residents are living an authentic rural lifestyle and wish to retain it. Many oppose developing the Island for visitors or outsiders, so you won't find much to cater to your needs; but if you take time and talk to the locals, you will find them hospitable and friendly. Some may even invite you home with them. It's a safe place, but don't interrupt private parties on the beach or trespass on private property. Consider yourself a guest in someone's house, rather than a customer.

a bit like a time warp, making it the perfect place to try one (or two) of the 30 or more flavors of Dave's Hawaiian Ice Cream; it's the only place that serves it on the Island. Sit in the refreshing breeze on one of the benches outside to enjoy your cone and pick up snacks, crack seed, water, and cold drinks. **Known for:** Icees; grab-n-go snacks and drinks; unique, tropical flavors of Dave's Hawaiian Ice Cream. ⑤ *Average main: $6* ⊠ *28 Kamoi St., Kaunakakai* ☎ *808/553–3742* ⊕ *facebook.com/kamoisnack.*

★ Kanemitsu's Bakery and Coffee Shop

$ | **CAFÉ** | Stop at this James Beard–nominated Molokai institution for morning coffee, a *loco moco* (white rice, burger patty, fried egg, and brown sauce), and some Molokai bread—a sweet, pan-style white loaf that makes excellent cinnamon toast. Prices are nice and portions are large; breakfast can easily carry you through lunch. **Known for:** taro pancakes; poi donuts; fast and friendly service. ⑤ *Average main: $9* ⊠ *79 Ala Malama St., Kaunakakai* ☎ *808/553–5855* ⊙ *Closed Tues.*

Kualapuu Cookhouse

$ | **AMERICAN** | Across the street from Kualapuu Market, this laid-back diner is a local favorite set in a classic, refurbished, green-and-white plantation house that's decorated with local photography and artwork and accented with a shady lanai. Typical fare at Kualapuu's only restaurant is a plate of chicken, pork, or hamburger steak served with rice, but there's also the more expensive spicy crusted *ahi* (yellowfin tuna) at dinner and daily specials. **Known for:** BYOB; Thursday night prime rib; chicken katsu. $ *Average main: $13 ⊠ 102 Farrington Ave., one block west of Rte. 470, Kualapuu* ☎ *808/567–9655* ▤ *No credit cards* ◷ *Closed for dinner Sun. and Mon.*

Manae Goods & Grindz

$ | **HAWAIIAN** | The best place to grab a snack or picnic supplies is this store, 16 miles east of Kaunakakai. It's the only place on the east end where you can find essentials such as ice and bread, and not-so-essentials such as seafood plate lunches, bentos, burgers, shakes, and refreshing smoothies. **Known for:** hurricane chips with seaweed and spicy mayo; *loco moco* (white rice and a burger patty topped with a fried egg and gravy) and plate lunches; famous macaroni salad. $ *Average main: $9 ⊠ 8615 Kamehameha V Hwy., Kaunakakai* ☎ *808/558–8498* ◷ *Lunch counter closed Wed.; no dinner.*

Molokai Burger

$ | **BURGER** | Clean and cheery, Molokai Burger offers both drive-through and eat-in options. Often compared to In-n-Out, this is the Island's version of fast food, and the tasty burger buns and super crispy fries (including enormous waffle fries as an option) help to elevate this past a typical experience. **Known for:** twofer Tuesdays; air-conditioning and Wi-Fi; affordable burgers. $ *Average main: $9 ⊠ 20 W. Kamehameha V Hwy., Kaunakakai* ☎ *808/553–3533* ⊕ *facebook. com/molokaiburgerHI* ◷ *Closed Sun.*

Molokai Pizza Cafe

$ | **AMERICAN** | **FAMILY** | This is a popular gathering spot for local families and a good place to pick up food for a picnic. Pizza, sandwiches, burgers, salads, pasta, and chicken are simply prepared and served without fuss. **Known for:** linguine alfredo; open Sundays; vegetarian options. $ *Average main: $15 ⊠ 15 Kaunakakai Pl., at Wharf Rd., Kaunakakai* ☎ *808/553–3288.*

★ Paddlers Restaurant and Bar

$$ | **AMERICAN** | New owners breathed new life—and a new menu—into this popular Molokai standout, and the result is a laid-back setting and a fusion of gourmet cuisine that stays true to the Island's roots, highlighted by excellent burgers, garlic shrimp, and nightly specials. The bar has the Island's only draft beer, there's live music and dancing most nights, and produce is locally sourced when available—especially with daily fish specials. **Known for:** tomato jam burger; live music at night; an umami explosion in the Paddler Fries. $ *Average main: $18 ⊠ 10 S. Mohala St., Kaunakakai* ☎ *808/553–3300* ⊕ *paddlersrestaurant. com* ◷ *Closed Sun.*

Sundown Deli

$ | **SANDWICHES** | A Molokai staple for more than 20 years, this small deli focuses on freshly made takeout food. Sandwiches come on a half dozen types of bread, and the homemade soups are outstanding. **Known for:** homemade soups; small but lovely breakfast menu; super friendly owner. $ *Average main: $9 ⊠ 145 Puali Pl., Kaunakakai* ☎ *808/553–3713* ⊕ *sundowndeli.com* ◷ *Closed weekends. No dinner.*

🛏 Hotels

Hotel Molokai is the closest thing to a resort that can be found on the Island, with a pool, on-site dining, activities desk, and more. In addition, there are two condo properties in this area, one close to shopping and dining in Kaunakakai, and the other on the way to the east end.

★ Hotel Molokai

$$ | HOTEL | FAMILY | At this local favorite, Polynesian-style bungalows are scattered around the nicely landscaped property, many overlooking the reef and distant Lanai. **Pros:** five minutes to town; some units have kitchenettes; authentic Hawaiian entertainment. **Cons:** lower-priced rooms are small and plain; walls can feel thin; Wi-Fi can be somewhat spotty. $ *Rooms from: $217* ✉ *1300 Kamehameha V Hwy., Kaunakakai* ☎ *808/660–3408, 877/553–5347 Reservations only* ⊕ *hotelmolokai.com* ⇨ *40 rooms* ⦿ *No Meals.*

Molokai Shores

$ | APARTMENT | Many of the units in this three-story condominium complex have a view of the ocean and Lanai in the distance, and there's a chance to see whales in season. **Pros:** convenient location; some units upgraded; near water. **Cons:** units close to highway can be noisy; beach is narrow and water is too shallow for swimming; Internet can be spotty in this area. $ *Rooms from: $175* ✉ *1000 Kamehameha V Hwy., Kaunakakai* ☎ *808/460-4421* ⊕ *molokai-vacation-rental.net* ⇨ *100 units* ⦿ *No Meals.*

Wavecrest

$ | APARTMENT | This 5-acre oceanfront condominium complex is convenient if you want to explore the east side of the Island—it's 13 miles east of Kaunakakai, with access to a beautiful reef, excellent snorkeling, and kayaking. **Pros:** friendly staff; good value; nicely maintained grounds. **Cons:** far from shopping; area sometimes gets windy; cell and Internet service can be spotty. $ *Rooms from: $150* ✉ *7148 Kamehameha V Hwy., near mile marker 13, Kaunakakai* ☎ *808/460–4421* ⊕ *molokai-vacation-rental.net* ⇨ *126 units* ⦿ *No Meals.*

🍸 Nightlife

Nightlife on Molokai may not be exactly what you think of for a typical night on the town, but that's what makes it special. It's easy to get to know locals and other travelers when you're singing karaoke, tasting Island-brewed beers, or enjoying the sounds of the ukulele at sunset.

Hiro's Ohana Grill

LIVE MUSIC | The bar at Hiro's Ohana Grill at Hotel Molokai is always a good place to enjoy a drink and beautiful views, with a rotating lineup of local musicians adding ambience to stunning sunset views. ✉ *1300 Kamehameha V Hwy., Kaunakakai* ☎ *808/660–3400* ⊕ *hirosohanagrill.com.*

★ Paddlers Restaurant and Bar

BARS | Paddlers Restaurant and Bar offers the most diverse nightlife on the Island, with music and dancing most nights of the week. Start off with happy hour from 2 to 5 pm Monday through Saturday, then stick around for the fun. If you're looking for a football game or UFC fight, this is the place for it. ✉ *10 Mohala St., Kaunakakai* ☎ *808/553–3300* ⊕ *paddlersrestaurant.com* ☾ *Closed Sun. and Mon.*

🛍 Shopping

GIFTS

Imports Gift Shop

MIXED CLOTHING | You'll find soaps and lotions, a small collection of 14-karat-gold chains, rings, earrings, and bracelets, and a jumble of Hawaiian quilts, pillows, souvenirs, books, and postcards at this local favorite. T-shirts, aloha wear, beach clothes, and muu muu are all available if you're clothes shopping. ✉ *82 Ala Malama St., Kaunakakai* ☎ *808/553–5734* ⊕ *molokaiimports.com.*

ARTS AND CRAFTS

Molokai Art from the Heart

CRAFTS | A small downtown shop, this arts and crafts co-op has locally made folk art like dolls, clay flowers, silk sarongs, and children's items. The shop also carries rotating original art by more than 100 Molokai artists and Giclée prints, jewelry, locally produced music, and Saint Damien keepsakes. ⊠ *64 Ala Malama St., Kaunakakai* ☎ *808/553–8018* ⊕ *molokaigallery.com* ⊗ *Closed Sun.*

CLOTHING AND SHOES
★ All Things Molokai
MIXED CLOTHING | This vibrant shop on the Ala Malama strip sells quirky souvenirs like funny T-shirts, jewelry, and local products. They have a café counter offering sandwiches, smoothies, and salads. The owners act as informal area guides, helping visitors find their way around and arrange services that they may need. ⊠ *61 Ala Malama Ave., Unit 3, Kaunakakai* ☎ *808/553–3299* ⊕ *allthingsmolokai.com* ⊗ *Closed Sun.*

★ Hawaii's Finest
MIXED CLOTHING | FAMILY | One of Hawaii's better-known clothing lines for contemporary aloha apparel, Hawaii's Finest sells just that, and at fair prices. This shop on the Ala Malama shopping strip fits in with the Hawaiian pride that permeates Molokai's culture. Their modern designs and bold colors adorn light cotton fabrics and accessories, and the apparel comes in a variety of sizes. This is your best option if you're looking for matching family wear. ⊠ *75B Ala Malama Ave., Kaunakakai* ☎ *808/553–5403* ⊕ *hifinest. com* ⊗ *Closed Sun.*

FOOD
Friendly Market Center
FOOD | The best-stocked supermarket on the Island has a slogan ("Your family store on Molokai") that is truly credible. Sun-and-surf essentials keep company with fresh produce, meat, groceries, and liquor. Locals say the food is fresher here than at the other major supermarket. ⊠ *90 Ala Malama St., Kaunakakai* ☎ *808/553–5595* ⊕ *friendlymkt.com* ⊗ *Closed Sun.*

Kualapuu Market
FOOD | This small market that's been open since 1938 has a little bit of everything and is a good stop for provisions, drinks, and other goodies before visiting the western or northern part of the Island. This multigenerational mom-and-pop store is run by the same family as Molokai Wines and Spirits. ⊠ *311 Farrington Hwy., Kualapuu* ☎ *808/567–6223* ⊕ *kualapuumarket.wixsite.com/kmltd* ⊗ *Closed Sun.*

★ Molokai Wines and Spirits
WINE/SPIRITS | Don't let the name fool you; along with a surprisingly good selection of fine wines and liquors, the store also carries cheeses and snacks for a nice wine and cheese at sunset experience. ⊠ *77 Ala Malama St., Kaunakakai* ☎ *808/553–5009* ⊕ *kualapuumarket. wixsite.com/kmltd* ⊗ *Closed Sun.*

SPORTING GOODS
★ Molokai Fish & Dive
SPORTING GOODS | This is the source for your sporting needs, from snorkels to free and friendly advice. Other island essentials like high-quality sunglasses and wide-brimmed hats are also for sale. This is also a good place to pick up original-design Molokai T-shirts, water sandals, books, and gifts. ⊠ *53 Ala Malama St., Kaunakakai* ☎ *808/553–5926* ⊕ *molokaifishanddive.com.*

East Molokai

Halawa Valley is 36 miles northeast of the airport.

On the beautifully undeveloped east end of Molokai you can find ancient fishponds, a magnificent coastline, splendid ocean views, and a fertile valley that's been inhabited for 14 centuries. The eastern uplands are flanked by Mt. Kamakou, the Island's highest point at 4,970 feet and home to the Nature Conservancy's Kamakou Preserve. Mist hangs over

Halawa Valley is an iconic site in East Molokai.

waterfall-filled valleys, and ancient lava cliffs jut out into the sea.

GETTING HERE AND AROUND
Driving the east end is a scenic adventure, but the road narrows and becomes curvy after the 20-mile marker. Take your time, especially in the seaside lane, and watch for oncoming traffic. Driving at night is not recommended.

⊙ Sights

★ Alii Fishpond
RUINS | With its narrow rock walls arching out from the shoreline, Alii is typical of the numerous fishponds that define southern Molokai. Many were built around the 13th century under the direction of powerful *alii* (chiefs), who were typically the only ones allowed to eat the harvest from the ponds. This early type of aquaculture, particular to Hawaii, exemplifies the ingenuity of Native Hawaiians. One or more openings were left in the wall, where gates called *makaha* were installed. These gates

allowed seawater and tiny fish to enter the enclosed pond but kept larger predators out. The tiny fish would then grow too big to get out. At one time there were 62 fishponds around Molokai's coast. Visits are available via guided tours with Ka Honua Momona International with a recommended donation of $25 per person. ✉ *Kamehameha V Hwy., Kaunakakai* ✛ *1/4 mile past Hotel Molokai* ⊕ *kahonuamomona.org* 🖃 *$25 per adult* ⌂ *Reserve online.*

★ Halawa Valley
RUINS | The Solatorio *ohana* (family) leads hikes through the valley, the oldest recorded habitation on Molokai. It is home to two sacrificial temples and many historic sites. Inhabitants grew taro and fished from 650 until the 1960s when an enormous flood wiped out the taro patches and forced old-timers to abandon their traditional lifestyle. Now, a new generation of Hawaiians has begun the challenging task of restoring the taro fields. Much of this work involves rerouting streams to flow through carefully

engineered level ponds called *loi*. Taro plants, with their big, dancing leaves, grow in the submerged mud of the *loi*, where the water is always cool and flowing. Hawaiians believe that the taro plant is their ancestor and revere it both as sustenance and as a spiritual necessity. The 3.4-mile round-trip valley hike, which goes to Moaula Falls, a 250-foot cascade, is rated intermediate to advanced and includes two moderate river crossings (so your feet will get wet). A $70 fee per adult supports restoration efforts. ⊠ *Eastern end of Rte. 450* ☎ *808/542–1855* ⊕ *halawavalleymolokai.com* 🖃 *$70.*

Kamalo Harbor

VIEWPOINT | A natural harbor used by small cargo ships during the 19th century and a favorite fishing spot for locals, Kamalo Harbor is a quick stop worth making to take in the quiet calm and hang out with shore birds; look for the "Drive Slow" signs just before the highway bends. This area is also the location of St. Joseph's Church, a tiny white church built by Saint Damien of the Kalaupapa colony in the 1880s. ⊠ *Rte. 450, Kaunakakai* ⊹ *11 miles east of Kaunakakai.*

Puu O Hoku Ranch

FARM/RANCH | A 14,000-acre private ranch in the highlands of East Molokai, Puu O Hoku was developed in the 1930s by wealthy industrialist Paul Fagan. Route 450 ambles right through this rural treasure with its pastures and grazing horses and cattle. As you drive slowly along, enjoy the splendid views of Maui and Lanai. The small Island off the coast is Mokuhooniki, a favorite spot among visiting humpback whales and nesting seabirds. The ranch is also a retreat center and organic farm, and it offers limited accommodations. ⊠ *Rte. 450, mile marker 25, Kaunakakai* ⊹ *25 miles east of Kaunakakai* ☎ *808/558–8109* ⊕ *puuohoku.com.*

St. Joseph's Mission Church

CHURCH | At this small, white church, a quick stop off the highway, you can learn more about Father Damien and his work. It's a state historic site and place of pilgrimage. The door is often open; if it is, slip inside, sign the guest book, and make a donation. The congregation keeps the church in beautiful condition. ⊠ *Kamehameha V Hwy., Kaunakakai* ☎ *808/558–0109* ⊕ *damienchurchmolokai. org.*

🌀 Beaches

The east end unfolds as a coastal drive with turnouts for tiny cove beaches—good places for snorkeling, shore fishing, or scuba exploring. Rocky little Mokuhooniki Island marks the eastern point of the Island and serves as a nursery for humpback whales in winter, nesting seabirds in spring, and hammerhead sharks in the fall. The road loops around the east end, then descends and ends at Halawa Valley.

Halawa Beach Park

BEACH | The vigorous water that gouged the steep, spectacular Halawa Valley also carved out two adjacent bays. Accumulations of coarse sand and river rock have created some protected pools that are good for wading or floating around. You might see surfers, but it's not wise to entrust your safety to the turbulent open ocean along this coast. Most people come here to hang out and absorb the beauty of Halawa Valley. The valley itself is private property, so do not wander without a guide. **Amenities:** toilets. **Best for:** solitude. ⊠ *End of Rte. 450, Kaunakakai.*

Waialua Beach Park

BEACH | Also known as Twenty Mile Beach, this arched stretch of sand leads to one of the most popular snorkeling spots on the Island. The water here, protected by the flanks of the little bay, is often so clear and shallow that even

St. Joseph's Church is one of Molokai's most historic sites.

from land you can watch fish swimming among the coral heads. Watch out for traffic when you enter the highway. ■ TIP→ **This is a pleasant place to stop on the drive around the east end. Amenities:** none. **Best for:** snorkeling; swimming. ✉ Rte. 450 near mile marker 20.

🛌 Hotels

Two unique lodging options await on the remote, far east end of the Island. Dunbar Beachfront Cottages, which lives up to its name as it's just steps from the sand, is great for families. Puu O Hoku Ranch, an active ranch and retreat facility, offers on-site ocean and waterfall views.

★ Dunbar Beachfront Cottages

$$ | HOUSE | FAMILY | Perfect for a comfortable base in the country, think of these two oceanfront, plantation-style cottages as your own private beach home on Molokai's east end; each has a full kitch-. en, washer and dryer, and ocean-facing lanai. **Pros:** complete privacy; well-stocked kitchens; convenient location

to east end beaches. **Cons:** very popular, so bookings can be hard to come by; additional cleaning fee; isolated and far from town. ⑤ Rooms from: $240 ✉ 9750 Kamehameha V Hwy., Kaunakakai ⊕ Just past mile marker 18 ☎ 808/336–0761 ⊕ www.molokaibeachfrontcottages.com ⇥ 2 cottages ❢◯❚ No Meals.

Puu O Hoku Ranch

$$$$ | B&B/INN | At the east end of Molokai, these ocean-view accommodations are on 14,000 isolated acres of pasture and forest—a remote and serene location for people who want to get away from it all or meet in a retreat atmosphere. **Pros:** on-site store with unique gifts and treats; authentic working ranch; great hiking. **Cons:** road to property is narrow and winding; very high cleaning fee; on remote east end of island. ⑤ Rooms from: $445 ✉ Rte. 450 near mile marker 25, Kaunakakai ☎ 808/558–8109 ⊕ puuo-hoku.com ⇥ 2-room cottage, 11-room lodge ❢◯❚ No Meals.

Activities

Molokai's shoreline topography limits opportunities for water sports. Sea cliffs dominate the north shore; the south shore is largely encased by a huge, taming reef.

⚠ **Open-sea access at west-end and east-end beaches should be used only by experienced ocean swimmers, and even then with caution as seas are rough, especially in winter.**

Generally speaking, there's no one around—certainly not lifeguards—if you are in need of assistance. For this reason alone, guided excursions are recommended. At the very least, be sure to ask for advice from outfitters or residents. Two kinds of water activities predominate: kayaking within the reef area and open-sea excursions on charter boats, most of which tie up at Kaunakakai Wharf.

Activity vendors in Kaunakakai are a good source of information on outdoor adventures on Molokai. For a mellow round of golf, head to the island's only golf course, Ironwood Hills, where you'll likely share the greens with local residents. Molokai's steep and uncultivated terrain offers excellent hikes and some stellar views. Although the island is largely wild, most land is privately owned, so get permission before hiking.

Biking

Cyclists who like to eat up the miles love Molokai, because its few roads are long, straight, and extremely rural. You can really go for it—there are no traffic lights and (most of the time) no traffic.

Molokai Bicycle

BIKING | You can rent a bike here for the day; prices depend on the model, with reductions for additional days or weeklong rentals. Bike trailers (for your drinks cooler, perhaps), including doubles for the kids, are also available. Hours are limited due to the owner's teaching schedule, but drop-offs and pickups are available for free at certain locations and for $25 at the airport. ⊠ *80 Mohala St., Kaunakakai* ☎ *808/553–5740* ⊕ *maui-molokaibicycle.com* 🚲 *Bikes from $25 per day, bike trailers from $15 per day.*

Deep-Sea Fishing

For Molokai people, as in days of yore, the ocean is more of a larder than a playground. It's common to see residents fishing along the shoreline or atop South Shore Reef, using poles or lines. Deep-sea fishing by charter boat is a great Molokai adventure. The sea channels here, though often rough and windy, provide gorgeous views of several islands. Big fish are plentiful in these waters, especially *mahimahi* (dolphinfish), marlin, and various kinds of tuna. Generally speaking, boat captains will customize the outing to your interests, share a lot of information about the island, and let you keep some or all of your catch.

EQUIPMENT
Molokai Fish & Dive

FISHING | If you'd like to try your hand at fishing, you can rent or buy equipment, book a trip, and ask for advice from the friendly staff here. They also host snorkel, scuba, and whale-watching tours. ⊠ *53 Ala Malama St., Kaunakakai* ☎ *808/553–5926* ⊕ *molokaifishanddive.com.*

BOATS AND CHARTERS
Alyce C.

FISHING | This 31-foot cruiser runs excellent sportfishing excursions in the capable hands of Captain Joe. Full-day, half-day, ¾-day, and full around-the-island trips are available upon the six-passenger boat; gear is provided. It's a rare day when you don't snag at least one memorable fish. Whale-watching trips are also available. ⊠ *Kaunakakai Wharf, Kaunakakai Pl., Kaunakakai* ☎ *808/558–8377* ⊕ *www.alycecsportfishing.com* 🚲 *From $450.*

Fun Hogs Sportfishing

FISHING | Trim and speedy, the 27-foot flybridge boat named *Ahi* offers four-hour, six-hour, and eight-hour sportfishing excursions, either near-shore or deep-sea. Skipper Mike Holmes also provides sunset cruises, scuba and snorkeling excursions, and whale-watching trips in winter. ☒ *Kaunakakai Wharf, Kaunakakai Pl., Kaunakakai* ☎ *808/336–0047* ⊕ *www. molokaifishing.com* ✉ *From $450.*

Molokai Action Adventures

FISHING | Walter Naki has traveled (and fished) all over the globe. He will create customized fishing expeditions and gladly share his wealth of experience. He will also take you to remote beaches for a day of swimming. If you want to explore the north side under the great sea cliffs, this is the way to go. His 21-foot Boston Whaler is usually seen in the east end at the mouth of Halawa Valley. ☒ *Kaunakakai* ☎ *808/558–8184* ✉ *From $300.*

Golf

Molokai is not a prime golf destination, but the sole nine-hole course makes for a pleasant afternoon.

Ironwood Hills Golf Course

GOLF | Like other nine-hole plantation-era courses, Ironwood Hills is in a prime spot, with basic fairways and not always manicured greens. It helps if you like to play laid-back golf with locals and can handle occasionally rugged conditions. On the plus side, most holes offer views of the ocean, as well as those of peaks of Oahu and Molokai's sea cliffs. Fairways are *kukuya* grass and run through pine, ironwood, and eucalyptus trees. Clubs are rented on the honor system; there's not always someone there to assist you and you should bring your own water. Access is via a bumpy, unpaved road. ☒ *Kalae Hwy., Kualapuu* ☎ *808/567–6000* ✉ *$20 for 9 holes* ⚐ *9 holes, 3088 yards, par 34.*

Hiking

Rural and rugged, Molokai is an excellent place for hiking. Roads and developments are few. The island is steep, so hikes often combine spectacular views with hearty physical exertion. Because the island is small, you can come away with the feeling of really knowing the place. And you won't see many other people around. Much of what may look like deserted land is private property, so be careful not to trespass—seek permission or use an authorized guide.

BEST SPOTS

Kalaupapa Trail

HIKING & WALKING | You can hike down to the Kalaupapa Peninsula and back via this 3-mile, 26-switchback route. The trail is often nearly vertical, traversing the face of the high sea cliffs. You can reach Kalaupapa Trail off Highway 470 near Kalaupapa Overlook. Only those in excellent shape should attempt it. You must have made prior arrangements with Kekaula (Mule Ride) Tours in order to access Kalaupapa via this trail. ☒ *Off Hwy. 470, Kualapuu* ☎ *808/567–6088 Kekaula Tours* ⊕ *nps.gov/kala.*

GOING WITH A GUIDE

★ Halawa Valley Falls Cultural Hike

HIKING & WALKING | This gorgeous, steep-walled valley was carved by two rivers and is rich in history. Site of the earliest Polynesian settlement on Molokai, Halawa is a sustained island culture with its ingeniously designed *loi,* or taro fields. Because of a tsunami in 1948 and changing cultural conditions in the 1960s, the valley was largely abandoned. The Solatorio *ohana* (family) is restoring the loi and taking visitors on guided hikes through the valley, which includes two of Molokai's *luakini heiau* (sacred temples), many historic sites, and the trail to Moaula Falls, a 250-foot cascade. Bring water, food, a *hookupu* (small gift or offering), insect repellent, and wear sturdy shoes that can get wet. The 3½-mile round-trip hike is rated intermediate to advanced and includes two moderate river crossings. ⊠ *14777 Kamehameha V Hwy., Kaunakakai* ✛ *Guide will meet you at the Halawa Beach Park pavilion* ☎ *808/542–1855* ⊕ *halawavalleymolokai. com* ⌦ *$70.*

Kayaking

Molokai's south shore is enclosed by the largest reef system in the United States—an area of shallow, protected sea that stretches over 30 miles. This reef gives inexperienced paddlers an unusually safe, calm environment for shoreline exploring.

⚠ **Outside the reef, Molokai waters are often rough, and strong winds can blow you out to sea. Kayakers out here should be strong, experienced, and cautious.**

BEST SPOTS
South Shore Reef
KAYAKING | This reef's area is superb for flat-water kayaking any day of the year. Get out in the morning before the wind picks up and paddle east, exploring the ancient Hawaiian fishponds. When you turn around, the wind will usually give you a push home. ■**TIP➜ For a kayak or paddleboard lessons, check out Molokai Outdoors at** ⊕ *molokai-outdoors.com.* ⊠ *Kaunakakai.*

EQUIPMENT, LESSONS, AND TOURS
★ Molokai Outdoors
KAYAKING | For guided kayak and paddleboard tours, this longtime Molokai activity company offers guided downwind runs along Molokai's southern coast, options for sunset and sunrise tours, as well as kayak and paddleboards for those looking to go solo. ⊠ *1529 Kamehameha V Hwy, Kaunakakai* ✛ *inside Hotel Molokai* ☎ *808/633–8700, 855/208–0811* ⊕ *molokai-outdoors.com* ⌦ *From $99 per person.*

Scuba Diving

Molokai Fish & Dive is the only PADI-certified dive company on Molokai and offers opportunities for beginner through advanced divers. Shoreline access for divers is extremely limited, even nonexistent in winter. Boat diving is the way to go. Without guidance, visiting divers can easily find themselves in risky situations with wicked currents. Proper guidance, however, opens an undersea world rarely seen.

Snorkeling

Snorkeling is particularly nice in Molokai with its beautiful fringed reef that hasn't been decimated by sunscreen and global warming. During the times when swimming is safe—mainly in summer—just about every beach on Molokai offers good snorkeling along the lava outcroppings in the Island's clean and pristine waters. Although rough in winter, Kepuhi Beach is a prime spot in summer. Certain spots inside the Souwth Shore Reef are also worth checking out.

BEST SPOTS
During the summer, **Kepuhi Beach** on Molokai's west end offers excellent snorkeling opportunities. The ½-mile-long stretch has plenty of rocky nooks that swirl with sea life. Take Kaluakoi Road all the way to the west end, park at the now-closed Kaluakoi Resort, and walk to the beach. Avoid Kepuhi Beach in winter, as the sea is rough here.

At **Waialua Beach Park,** on Molokai's east end, you'll find a thin curve of sand that rims a sheltered little bay loaded with coral heads and aquatic life. The water here is shallow—sometimes so shallow that you bump into the underwater landscape—and it's crystal clear. Pull off the road near mile marker 20.

Did You Know?

A hike through the Kamakou Preserve in East Molokai, on the slopes of the island's highest peak, reveals a lush rain forest with bogs and native wildlife. Sign up well in advance for a monthly guided hike with the Nature Conservancy, it's the only access available.

EQUIPMENT AND TOURS

All the charter boats carry snorkel gear and include dive stops.

Fun Hogs Sportfishing

SNORKELING | Mike Holmes, captain of the 27-foot *Ahi*, knows the island waters intimately, likes to have fun, and is willing to arrange any type of excursion—for example, one dedicated entirely to snorkeling. His two-hour snorkel whale-watch trips leave early in the morning and explore rarely seen fish and turtle sites outside the reef. ⊠ *Kaunakakai Wharf, Kaunakakai Pl., Kaunakakai* ☎ *808/336–0047* ⊕ *molokaifishing.com* 🍴 *From $75 per person.*

Spas

Molokai Acupuncture & Massage

SPAS | This relaxing retreat offers acupuncture, massage, herbal remedies, and wellness treatments by appointment only. The wellness center also offers a regular Vinyasa Flow class; call for prices and location. ⊠ *40 Ala Malama St., Suite 206, Kaunakakai* ☎ *808/553–3930* ⊕ *www.molokai-wellness.com.*

Molokai Lomi Massage

SPAS | Allana Noury of Molokai Lomi Massage has studied natural medicine for nearly 40 years and is a licensed massage therapist, master herbalist, and master iridologist. She will come to your hotel or condo by appointment. ⊠ *Kaunakakai* ☎ *808/553–8034* ⊕ *molokaimassage.com.*

Whale-Watching

Although Maui gets all the credit for the local wintering humpback whale population, the big cetaceans also visit Molokai December–April. Mokuhooniki Island at the east end serves as a whale nursery and courting ground, and the whales pass back and forth along the south shore. This being Molokai, whale-watching here will never involve floating amid a group of boats all ogling the same whale.

BOATS AND CHARTERS

Alyce C.

WILDLIFE-WATCHING | Although this six-passenger sportfishing boat is usually busy hooking *mahimahi* (dolphinfish) and marlin, the captain will gladly take you on an excursion to admire the humpback whales or other points of interest around the Island. ■TIP→ **The price is based on the length of the trip: 1/2 day, 3/4 day, full day, or round-island trips.** ⊠ *Kaunakakai Wharf, Kaunakakai Pl., Kaunakakai* ☎ *808/558–8377* ⊕ *alycecsportfishing.com.*

Ama Lua and Coral Queen

WILDLIFE-WATCHING | Molokai Fish & Dive offers two boats for whale-watching. The *Ama Lua* is a 31-foot dive boat that holds up to 12 passengers, while the *Coral Queen* is a 38-footer that holds up to 25 passengers. On both boats, the crew is respectful of the whales and the laws that protect them. A two-hour whale-watching trip departs from Kaunakakai Wharf at 7 am daily (as long as minimum passenger requirements are met), from December to April. ⊠ *Molokai Fish & Dive, 53 Ala Malama St., Kaunakakai* ☎ *808/553–5926* ⊕ *molokaifishanddive.com* 🍴 *From $99 per adult.*

Fun Hogs Sportfishing

WILDLIFE-WATCHING | The *Ahi*, a flybridge sportfishing boat, takes you on two-hour whale-watching trips in the morning, December to April. ■TIP→ **No food or drink is provided.** ⊠ *Kaunakakai Wharf, Kaunakakai Pl., Kaunakakai* ☎ *808/336–0047* ⊕ *molokaifishing.com* 🍴 *From $75 per person.*

Chapter 12

LANAI

Updated by
Laurie Lyons-Makaimoku

⊙ Sights	🍴 Restaurants	🛏 Hotels	🛍 Shopping	🍸 Nightlife
★★★★★	★★★☆☆	★★★☆☆	★★★☆☆	★☆☆☆☆

WELCOME TO LANAI

TOP REASONS TO GO

★ **Seclusion and serenity:** Lanai is small; local motion is slow motion. Get into the spirit, and go home rested.

★ **Keahiakawelo (Garden of the Gods):** Walk amid the eerie red-rock spires at this Hawaiian sacred spot. The ocean views are magnificent, too; sunset is a good time to visit.

★ **Diving at Cathedrals:** Explore underwater pinnacle formations and mysterious caverns illuminated by shimmering rays of light.

★ **Dole Park:** Hang out in the shade of the Cook pines in Lanai City, and talk story with the locals for a taste of old-time Hawaii.

★ **Hulopoe Beach:** This beach may have it all—good swimming, a shady park for perfect picnicking, great reefs for snorkeling, and—if you're lucky—schools of spinner dolphins.

1 Lanai City. Quaint and quiet, this historic plantation town is home to most of the Island's residents, restaurants, shops, and businesses. Dole Park, with its stately Cook pines and picnic benches, sits in the middle of the action.

2 Manele Bay. Rest and relaxation characterize this coastal area, home to Manele Harbor, Four Seasons Resort Lanai, iconic Puu Pehe, and the golden sands of Hulopoe Beach.

3 Windward Lanai. This area is the long white-sand beach at the base of Lanaihale. Now uninhabited, it was once occupied by thriving Hawaiian fishing villages and a sugarcane plantation.

Polihua Beach

Keahiakawelo (Garden of the Gods)

Kaumalapau Harbor

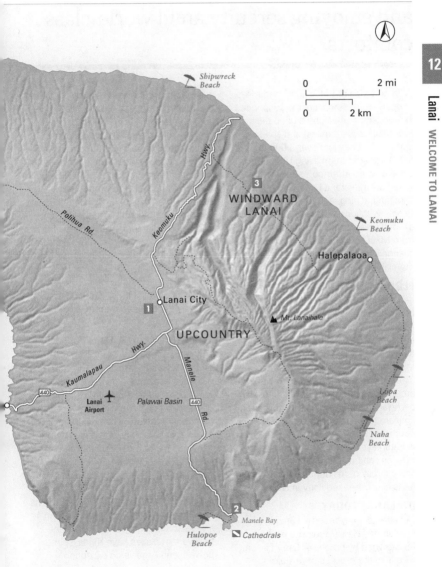

0   2 mi

0   2 km

Shipwreck Beach

Polihua Rd.

Keomuku Hwy.

3

WINDWARD LANAI

Keomuku Beach

Halepalaoa

1 Lanai City

▲ Mt. Lanaihale

UPCOUNTRY

Kaumalapau Hwy.

Manele Rd.

440

Lanai Airport

Palawai Basin

440

Lōpa Beach

Naha Beach

2 Manele Bay

Hulopoe Beach

Cathedrals

Mostly privately owned, Lanai is the smallest inhabited island in Hawaii and is a true getaway for slowing down and enjoying serenity amid world-class comforts.

With no traffic or traffic lights and miles of open space, Lanai seems suspended in time, and that can be a good thing. Small (141 square miles) and sparsely populated, it has just over 3,000 residents, most of them living Upcountry in Lanai City. An afternoon strolling around Dole Park in historic Lanai City offers shopping, dining, and the opportunity to mingle with locals. Though it may seem a world away, Lanai is only separated from Maui and Molokai by two narrow channels and is easily accessed by commercial ferry from Maui.

FLORA AND FAUNA

Lanai bucks the "tropical" trend of the other Hawaiian Islands with African *kiawe* (mesquite) trees, Cook pines, and eucalyptus in place of palm trees, and deep blue sea where you might expect shallow turquoise bays. Abandoned pineapple fields are overgrown with drought-resistant grasses, Christmas berry, and lantana; native plants *aalii* and *i lima* are found in uncultivated areas. Axis deer from India dominate the ridges, and wild turkeys lumber around the resorts. Whales can be seen November–May, and a family of resident spinner dolphins rests and fishes regularly in Hulopoe Bay.

ON LANAI TODAY

Despite its fancy resorts, Lanai still has that languid Hawaii feel. The island is 98% owned by billionaire Larry Ellison, who is in the process of revitalizing Lanai. Old-time residents are a mix of just about everything: Hawaiian, Chinese, German, Portuguese, Filipino, Japanese, French, Puerto Rican, English, Norwegian—you name it. When Dole owned the island in the early 20th century and grew pineapples, the plantation was divided into ethnic camps, which helped retain cultural cuisines. Potluck dinners feature sashimi, Portuguese bean soup, *laulau* (morsels of pork, chicken, butterfish, or other ingredients steamed in ti leaves), potato salad, teriyaki steak, chicken *hekka* (a gingery Japanese chicken stir-fry), and Jell-O. The local language is Pidgin English, a mix of words as complicated and rich as the food. Newly arrived residents have added to the cultural mix.

THE GHOSTS OF LANAI

Lanai has a reputation for being haunted (at one time by "cannibal spirits") and evidence abounds: a mysterious purple *lehua* (a native tree that normally produces red flowers) at Keahialoa; the crying of a ghost chicken at Kamoa; Pohaku O, a rock that calls at twilight; and remote spots where cars mysteriously stall, and lights are seen at night. Tradition has it that Puu Pehe (an offshore sea stack) was a child who spoke from the womb, demanding *awa* root. A later story claims it is the grave of a woman drowned in a cave at the nearby cliffs. Hawaiians believe that places have *mana* (spiritual power), and Lanai is no exception.

MAJOR REGIONS
Lanai City, Windward Lanai, and Manele Bay.
Cool and serene, Upcountry is graced by Lanai City, towering Cook pine trees, and misty mountain vistas. The historic plantation village of Lanai City is inching into the modern world. Locals hold conversations in front of Dole Park shops and from their pickups on the road, and kids ride bikes in colorful impromptu parades. Six miles north of Lanai City, Keahiakawelo (nicknamed "Garden of the Gods") is a stunning rocky plateau. The more developed beach side of the island, Manele Bay is where it's happening: swimming, picnicking, off-island excursions, and boating are all concentrated in this accessible area. Windward Lanai is the long white-sand beach at the base of Lanaihale. Now uninhabited, it was once occupied by thriving Hawaiian fishing villages and a sugarcane plantation

Planning

When to Go

Lanai has an ideal climate year-round, hot and sunny at the sea and a few delicious degrees cooler Upcountry. In Lanai City and Upcountry, the nights and mornings can be almost chilly when fog or harsh trade winds settle in. Winter months are known for *slightly* rougher weather—periodic rain showers, occasional storms, and higher surf.

Because higher mountains on Maui capture the trade-wind clouds, Lanai receives little rainfall and has a near-desert ecology. Consider the wind direction when planning your day. If it's blowing a gale on the windward beaches, head for the beach at Hulopoe or check out Keahiakawelo (Garden of the Gods). Overcast days, when the wind stops or comes lightly from the southwest, are common in whale season. At that time,

try a whale-watching trip or the windward beaches.

Whales are seen off Lanai's shores November–May (peak season January–March). A Pineapple Festival on the July 4 Saturday in Dole Park features traditional entertainment, a pineapple-eating contest, and fireworks. Buddhists hold their annual outdoor Obon Festival, honoring departed ancestors with joyous dancing, local food, and drumming, in early July. During hunting-season weekends, mid-February–mid-May and mid-July–mid-October, watch out for hunters on dirt roads even though there are designated safety zones. On Sundays, many shops and restaurants have limited hours or are closed altogether.

Getting Here and Around

AIR
Mokulele Airlines is the only commercial airline routinely serving Lanai City. Direct flights are available from Oahu; if you're flying to Lanai from any other Hawaiian Island, you'll make a stop in Kahului. Guests of the Four Seasons Resort Lanai can arrange private charters on Lanai Air.

If you're staying at the Four Seasons Resort Lanai you'll be met at the airport or ferry dock by a bus that shuttles between the resort and Lanai City.

AIRLINE CONTACTS Mokulele Airlines.
✉ *Lanai Ave., Lanai City* ☎ *866/260–7070 toll free, 808/495-4188* ⊕ *mokuleleairlines.com.*

AIRPORT CONTACTS Lanai Airport (LNY).
✉ *Lanai Ave., Lanai City* ☎ *808/565–7942* ⊕ *airports.hawaii.gov/lny.*

CAR
It's always good to carry a cell phone. Lanai has only 30 miles of paved roads; its main road, Highway 440, refers to both Kaumalapau Highway and Manele Road. Keomuku Highway starts just past Sensei Lanai and runs northeast to the

dirt road that goes to Kaiolohia (aka Shipwreck Beach) and Lopa Beach. Manele Road (Highway 440) runs south down to Manele Bay, the Four Seasons Resort Lanai, and Hulopoe Beach. Kaumalapau Highway (also Highway 440) heads west to Kaumalapau Harbor. The rest of your driving takes place on bumpy dusty roads that are unpaved and unmarked. Driving in thick mud is not recommended, and the rental agency will charge a stiff cleaning fee. Watch out for blind curves on narrow roads. Take a map, be sure you have a full tank, and bring a snack and plenty of water (including water to rinse off at the beaches, as many of the remote beaches have no showers or other facilities).

Renting a four-wheel-drive vehicle is expensive but almost essential if you'd like to explore beyond the resorts and Lanai City. Make reservations far in advance of your trip, because Lanai's fleet of vehicles is limited. Ask the rental agency or your hotel's concierge about road conditions before you set out.

Stop from time to time to find landmarks and gauge your progress. Never drive or walk to the edge of lava cliffs, as rock can give way under you. Directions on the island are often given as *mauka* (toward the mountains) and *makai* (toward the ocean).

If you're visiting for the day, Rabaca's Limousine Service or Lanai Taxi will take you wherever you want to go. Advance reservations are required.

CONTACT Rabaca's Limousine Service. ✉ *552 Alapa St., Lanai City* ☎ *808/559–0230.* **Lanai Taxi.** ✉ *Lanai City* ☎ *808/649–8330* ⊕ *facebook.com/lanaitaxi.*

FERRY
Ferries operated by Expeditions cross the channel four times daily between Lahaina on Maui to Manele Small Boat Harbor on Lanai. The crossing takes 45 minutes and costs $30 (discounts for children). Be warned: passage can be rough, especially in winter.

CONTACT Expeditions. ✉ *658 Front St., Lahaina* ☎ *808/661–3756, 800/695–2624* ⊕ *go-lanai.com.*

SHUTTLE
The high-end resorts provide free ground transportation for their guests to/from the harbor or the airport in a luxury shuttle.

Beaches

Lanai offers miles of secluded white-sand beaches on its windward side, plus the moderately developed Hulopoe Beach, which is adjacent to the Four Seasons Resort Lanai. Hulopoe is accessible by car or hotel shuttle bus; to reach the windward beaches you need a four-wheel-drive vehicle. Reef, rocks, and coral make swimming on the windward side problematic, but it's fun to splash around in the shallow water. Expect debris on the windward beaches due to the Pacific convergence of ocean currents. Driving on the beach itself is illegal and can be dangerous.

Biking

Many of the same red-dirt roads that invite hikers are excellent for biking, offering easy, flat terrain and long clear views.

A favorite biking route is along the fairly flat red-dirt road northward from Lanai City through the old pineapple fields to Keahiakawelo (Garden of the Gods). Start your trip on Keomuku Highway in town. Take a left just before Sensei Lanai's tennis courts, and then a right where the road ends at the fenced pasture, and continue on to the north end and the start of Polihua and Awalua dirt roads. If you're really hardy, you could bike down to Polihua Beach and back, but it would be a serious all-day trip. In wet weather these roads turn to mud and are not advisable. Go in the early morning or late afternoon, because the sun gets hot in the middle of the day. Take plenty of water, spare parts, and snacks.

For the exceptionally fit, it's possible to bike from town down the Keomuku Highway to the windward beaches and back. Experienced bikers also travel up and down the Manele Highway from Manele Bay to town.

Hotels

The good news is that you're sure to escape the crowds on this quaint island. The bad news is that Lanai has limited accommodation options, including the pricey Four Seasons Resort Lanai, or the (relatively speaking) affordable Hotel Lanai.

Hotel and dining reviews have been shortened. For full information, visit Fodors.com.

HOTEL AND RESTAURANT PRICES

Restaurant prices are the average cost of a main course at dinner or, if dinner is not served, at lunch. Hotel prices are the lowest cost of a standard double room in high season. Condo price categories reflect studio and one-bedroom rates.

WHAT IT COSTS in U.S. Dollars			
$	$$	$$$	$$$$
RESTAURANTS			
under $18	$18–$26	$27–$35	over $35
HOTELS			
under $181	$181–$260	$261–$340	over $340

Restaurants

Lanai has a wide range of choices for dining, from simple plate-lunch local eateries to gourmet resort restaurants.

Lanai's own version of Hawaii regional cuisine draws on the fresh bounty provided by local farmers and fishermen, combined with the skills of well-regarded chefs. The upscale menus at the Four Seasons Resort Lanai encompass European- and Asian-inspired cuisine as well as innovative preparations of international favorites and vegetarian delights. All Four Seasons Resort restaurants offer children's menus. Lanai City's eclectic ethnic fare runs from construction-worker-size local plate lunches to *poke* (raw fish), pizza, and pasta.

■ TIP➔ **Lanai "City" is really a small town; restaurants sometimes close their kitchens early, and only a few are open on Sunday.**

Lanai City

Lanai City is 3 miles northeast of the airport.

A tidy plantation town, built in 1924 by Jim Dole to accommodate workers for his pineapple business, Lanai City is home to old-time residents, resort workers, and second-home owners. With its charming plantation-era shops and restaurants kept up-to-date with new paint jobs and landscaping, Lanai City is worthy of whiling away a lazy afternoon.

You can easily explore Lanai City on foot. In its center, Dole Park is surrounded by small shops and restaurants and is a great spot for sitting, strolling, and talking story. Try a picnic lunch in the park and visit the Lanai Culture & Heritage Center in the Old Dole Administration Building to glimpse this island's rich past, purchase historical publications and maps, and get directions to anywhere on the island.

GETTING HERE AND AROUND

Lanai City serves as the island's hub, with roads leading to Manele Bay, Kaumalapau Harbor, and windward Lanai. Keahiakawelo (Garden of the Gods) is usually possible to visit by car, but beyond that you will need four-wheel drive.

Ocean views provide a backdrop to the eroded rocks at Keahiakawelo (aka Garden of the Gods).

Sights

Kanepuu Preserve

NATURE PRESERVE | Hawaiian sandalwood, olive, and ebony trees characterize Hawaii's largest example of a rare native dryland forest. Thanks to the efforts of volunteers at the Nature Conservancy and a native Hawaiian land trust, the 590-acre remnant forest is protected from the axis deer and mouflon sheep that graze on the land beyond its fence. More than 45 native plant species can be seen here. A short, self-guided loop trail, with eight signs illustrated by local artist Wendell Kahoohalahala, reveals this ecosystem's beauty and the challenges it faces. The reserve is adjacent to the sacred hill, Kane Puu, dedicated to the Hawaiian god of water and vegetation. ✉ *Polihua Tr., Lanai City* ✛ *4.8 miles north of Lanai City.*

★ Keahiakawelo (Garden of the Gods)

NATURE SIGHT | This preternatural plateau is scattered with boulders of different sizes, shapes, and colors, the products of a million years of wind erosion. Time your visit for sunset, when the rocks begin to glow—from rich red to purple—and the fiery globe sinks to the horizon. Magnificent views of the Pacific Ocean, Molokai, and, on clear days, Oahu, provide the perfect backdrop for photographs.

The ancient Hawaiians shunned Lanai for hundreds of years, believing the island was the inviolable home of spirits. Standing beside the oxide-red rock spires of this strange raw landscape, you might be tempted to believe the same. This lunar savanna still has a decidedly eerie edge, but the shadows disappearing on the horizon are those of mouflon sheep and axis deer, not the fearsome spirits of lore. According to tradition, Kawelo, a Hawaiian priest, kept a perpetual fire burning on an altar here, in sight of the Island of Molokai. As long as the fire burned, prosperity was assured for the people of Lanai. Kawelo was killed by a rival priest on Molokai, and the fire went out. The Hawaiian name for this area is Keahiakawelo, meaning the "fire of

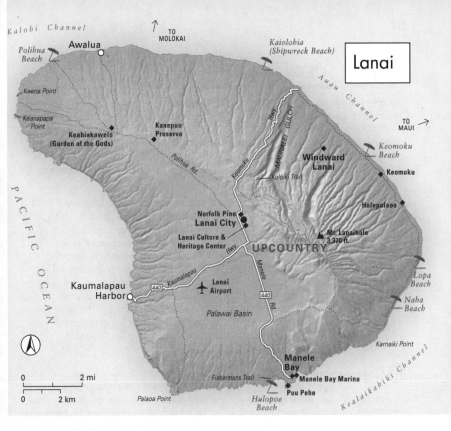

Kawelo." ⊠ Off Polihua Rd., Lanai City
✛ 6 miles north of Lanai City.

★ Lanai Culture & Heritage Center
HISTORY MUSEUM | Small and carefully arranged, this historical museum features artifacts and photographs from Lanai's varied and rich history. Plantation-era clothing and tools, ranch memorabilia, old maps, precious feather lei, poi pounders, and family portraits combine to give you a good idea of the history of the island and its people. Postcards, maps, books, and pamphlets are for sale. The friendly staff can orient you to the island's historical sites and provide directions, making this the best place to start your explorations. ■TIP→ **The Heritage Center's Lanai Guide app is a trove of information—both practical and historical—on the island's sites.** ⊠ 730 Lanai Ave., Lanai City

☎ 808/565–7177 ⊕ lanaichc.org ☒ Free
☽ Closed weekends.

Norfolk Pine
NATURE SIGHT | Considered the "mother" of all the pines on the island, this 160-foot-tall tree was planted here, at the former site of the ranch manager's house, in 1875. Almost 30 years later, George Munro, the manager, observed how, in foggy weather, water collected on its foliage, dripping off rain. This led Munro to supervise the planting of Cook pines along the ridge of Lanaihale and throughout the town in order to add to the island's water supply. This majestic tree is just in front of Sensei Lanai. ⊠ Sensei Lanai, 1 Keomuku Hwy., Lanai City.

The Story of Lanai

Rumored to be haunted by hungry ghosts, Lanai was sparsely inhabited for many centuries. Most of the earliest settlers lived along the shore and made their living from fishing the nearby waters. Others lived in the Upcountry near seasonal water sources and traded their produce for seafood. The high chiefs sold off the land bit by bit to foreign settlers, and by 1910 the island was owned by the Gay family.

When the Hawaiian Pineapple Company purchased Lanai for $1.1 million in 1922, it built the town of Lanai City, opened the commercial harbor, and laid out the pineapple fields. Field workers came from overseas to toil in what quickly became the world's largest pineapple plantation. Exotic animals and birds were imported for hunting. Cook pines were planted to catch the rain, and eucalyptus windbreaks anchored the blowing soil.

Everything was stable for 70 years, until the plantation closed in 1992. When the resorts opened their doors, newcomers arrived, homes were built, and other ways of life set in. Today, most of the island is owned by billionaire Larry Ellison, and vast areas remain untouched and great views abound. Although the ghosts may be long gone, Lanai still retains its ancient mysterious presence.

🍴 Restaurants

In Lanai City you can enjoy everything from local-style plate lunches to upscale gourmet meals. For a small area, there are a number of good places to eat and drink, but remember that Lanai City mostly closes down on Sunday.

Blue Ginger Café

$ | **ECLECTIC** | This cheery Lanai City institution offers simply prepared, consistent, tasty food. Local paintings and photos line the walls inside, while townspeople parade by the outdoor tables. **Known for:** comfort food; fresh-baked bread and pastries; authentic local cuisine. ⑤ *Average main: $12* ⊠ *409 7th St., Lanai City* ☎ *808/565–6363* ⊕ *bluegingercafelanai. com* ⊟ *No credit cards.*

Coffee Works

$ | **AMERICAN** | A block from Dole Park, this Northern California–style café offers an umbrella-covered deck where you can sip cappuccinos and get in tune with the slow pace of life. Bagels with lox, deli sandwiches, and pastries are served, while blended espresso shakes and gourmet ice cream complete the coffeehouse vibe. **Known for:** hearty breakfast burritos; varied drink selection; great place to vibe with locals. ⑤ *Average main: $12* ⊠ *604 Ilima St., Lanai City* ☎ *808/565–6962* ⊕ *coffeeworkshawaii.com* ⊗ *Closed Sat. and Sun.*

No Ka Oi Grindz Lanai

$ | **HAWAIIAN** | **FAMILY** | A local favorite, this lunchroom-style café has picnic tables in the landscaped front yard where diners can watch the town drive by, plus a few more tables in the no-frills interior. The menu includes local favorites like kimchi fried rice and massive plate lunches, plus daily specials. **Known for:** large portions; reasonable prices; local comfort food. ⑤ *Average main: $10* ⊠ *335 9th St., Lanai City* ☎ *808/565–9413.*

Pele's Other Garden

$$ | **ITALIAN** | Small and colorful, Pele's is a deli and bistro all in one. For lunch, sandwiches or daily hot specials satisfy hearty appetites; at night, it's transformed into a busy bistro, with an intimate back-room

bar where entertainers often drop in for impromptu jam sessions. **Known for:** quaint atmosphere; good beer and wine selection; tasty thin-crust pizzas. ⑤ *Average main: $22* ⊠ *811 Houston St., Lanai City* ☎ *808/565–9628* ⊕ *pelesothergarden.com* ⊘ *Closed Sat. and Sun.*

Hotels

Hotel Lanai

$$$$ | HOTEL | Built in 1923 to house visiting pineapple executives, this historic inn is like new following a massive renovation. **Pros:** porches attached to several rooms; walking distance to town; bathrooms include Toto bidet toilets. **Cons:** can be very noisy; small rooms; far from beach. ⑤ *Rooms from: $389* ⊠ *828 Lanai Ave., Lanai City* ☎ *800/795–7211 toll free, 808/565–7211* ⊕ *hotellanai.com* ⌧ *10 rooms, 1 cottage* ⎮◎⎮ *Free Breakfast.*

★ Sensei Lanai, a Four Seasons Resort

$$$$ | RESORT | This exclusive wellness retreat is the pinnacle of Hawaii luxury. Guests create customized itineraries and experiences to meet their goals including spa services, wellness activities, and various Island excursions for anywhere from two days to an entire month. Beautifully manicured grounds include a mix of native and imported plants, one of the largest private art collections in the state, and an incredible sense of serenity not found in many other places. Guests can dine at Sensei by Nobu or the Koele Garden Bar or use signing privileges at nearby Four Seasons Lanai. **Pros:** onsen outdoor baths; walking distance to Lanai City; unique private spa hales. **Cons:** activity registration can sometimes be problematic; guests must be aged 16+; not in the price range of the average traveler. ⑤ *Rooms from: $880* ⊠ *1 Keomoku Hwy., Lanai City* ☎ *800/819–5053 toll free, 808/565–2000* ⊕ *fourseasons.com/sensei* ⌧ *96 rooms* ⎮◎⎮ *No Meals.*

⬤ Shopping

A cluster of Cook pines in the center of Lanai City surrounded by small shops and restaurants, Dole Park is the closest thing to a mall on Lanai. Except for high-end resort boutiques and pro shops, it's the island's only shopping option. A morning or afternoon stroll around the park offers an eclectic selection of gifts and clothing, plus a chance to chat with friendly shopkeepers. Well-stocked general stores are reminiscent of the 1920s, and galleries and a boutique have original art and fashions for everyone.

CLOTHING

★ The Local Gentry

MIXED CLOTHING | Spacious and classy, this store has clothing for every need, from casual men's and women's beachwear to evening resort wear, shoes, jewelry, home decor, accessories, and hats. There are fancy fashions for tots and a selection of original Lanai-themed clothing and accessories as well. Proprietor Jenna Gentry Majkus will mail your purchases. ⊠ *363 7th St., Lanai City* ☎ *808/565–9130* ⊕ *facebook.com/thelocalgentrylanai.*

FOOD

Pine Isle Market

GENERAL STORE | One of Lanai City's two all-purpose markets, Pine Isle stocks everything from beach toys and electronics to meats and vegetables. The staff is friendly, and it's the best place around to buy fresh fish. ⊠ *356 8th St., Lanai City* ☎ *808/565–6488.*

Richard's Market

FOOD | Richard's is the best spot to find quality meats, fine wines, and imported gourmet items. There's also a deli, poke bar, bakery, and fresh fish selections, as well as produce from Lanai's Sensei Farms. ⊠ *434 8th St., Lanai City* ☎ *808/565–3780* ⊕ *facebook.com/LanaiRichardsMarket.*

GALLERIES
Lanai Art Center

ART GALLERIES | Local artists display their work at this dynamic center staffed by volunteers (hours are a bit flexible because of this). Workshops in pottery, photography, woodworking, and painting welcome visitors. The gift shop sells Lanai handicrafts and special offerings, the sale of which underwrites children's art classes. The gathering spot also hosts occasional special events for the community. ⊠ *339 7th St., Lanai City* ☎ *808/565–7503* ⊕ *lanaiart.org* ⊗ *Closed Sun.*

★ Mike Carroll Gallery

ART GALLERIES | The dreamy, soft-focus oil paintings of award-winning painter Mike Carroll are inspired by island scenes. His work is showcased along with those of other local artists and visiting plein air painters. You can also find handcrafted jewelry, functional art, and other accessories. ⊠ *443 7th St., Lanai City* ☎ *808/565–7122* ⊕ *mikecarrollgallery. com.*

GENERAL STORES
Lanai City Service

FOOD | Lanai's only gas station is a convenient stop to fill your belly, too. The on-site Plantation Deli is famous for its massive sandwiches packed with quality ingredients, as well as other delicious items. Snacks, beer, and souvenirs and friendly faces round out the selection. ⊠ *1036 Lanai Ave., Lanai City* ☎ *808/565–7227.*

⊛ Activities

HIKING

Only 30 miles of Lanai's roads are paved, but red-dirt roads and trails, ideal for hiking, will take you to sweeping overlooks, isolated beaches, and shady forests. Take a self-guided walk through Kane Puu Preserve, Hawaii's largest native dryland forest. You can also explore the Munro Trail over Lanaihale with views of plunging canyons (currently closed for repairs), or hike along an old coastal fisherman trail, or head out across Koloiki Ridge. Wear hiking shoes, a hat, and sunscreen, and carry a windbreaker, cell phone, and plenty of water.

Koloiki Ridge

HIKING & WALKING | This marked trail starts behind Sensei Lanai and takes you along the cool and shady Munro Trail to overlook the windward side, with impressive views of Maui, Molokai, Maunalei Valley, and Naio Gulch. The average time for the 4.2-mile round trip is two hours. Bring snacks, water, and a windbreaker; wear good shoes; and take your time. *Moderate.* ⊠ *Lanai City.*

ZIP-LINING
★ Lanai Adventure Park

ZIP-LINING | FAMILY | For an afternoon of adventure this park features on-site and off-site activities for the whole family. Options include zip-lining over Kaiholena Valley, a kid-friendly two-story aerial adventure, guided e-bike tours (location determined by skill of everyone in your party), and a guided hike of Koloiki Ridge Trail. Excursions offer plenty of cultural and historical information, giving guests the opportunity to learn more about Lanai. ⊠ *1 Keomoku Hwy., Lanai City* ☎ *808/563–0096* ⊕ *lanaiadventurepark. com* ⊠ *$50–$120 depending on activity.*

Manele Bay

Manele Bay is 9 miles southeast of Lanai City and 10 miles south of the airport.

Manele Bay is an ocean lover's dream: Hulopoe Beach offers top-notch snorkeling, swimming, picnicking, tide pools, and sometimes spinner dolphins. Off-island ocean excursions depart from nearby Manele Small Boat Harbor. Take the short but rugged hike to the Puu Pehe (Sweetheart Rock) overlook, and you'll enjoy a bird's-eye view of this iconic Lanai landmark.

One of the pools at Four Seasons Resort Lanai

GETTING HERE AND AROUND

You don't really need a car to get around Manele Bay as the resorts provide shuttle service from the airport and to other areas, but having a car would be useful for exploring other areas of the island.

◉ Sights

Manele Bay Marina

MARINA/PIER | Ferries from Maui dock four times a day, and visiting yachts pull in here, as it's the island's only small boat harbor. Public restrooms, grassy lawns, and picnic tables make it a busy pit stop—you can watch the boating activity as you rest. ⊠ *12 Manele Rd., Lanai City.*

Puu Pehe

NATURE SIGHT | Often called Sweetheart Rock, this isolated 80-foot-high islet is steeped in romantic Hawaiian lore. The rock is said to be named after Pehe, a woman so beautiful that her husband kept her hidden in a sea cave. One day, the surf surged into the cave, and she drowned. Her grief-stricken husband

buried her on this rock and jumped to his death. It is also believed that the enclosure on the summit is a shrine to birds, built by bird-catchers. Protected shearwaters nest in the nearby sea cliffs July–November. ⊠ *Hwy. 440, Manele, Lanai City.*

⬆ Beaches

★ Hulopoe Beach

BEACH | **FAMILY** | A short stroll from the Four Seasons Resort Lanai, Hulopoe is one of the best beaches in Hawaii. The sparkling crescent of this Marine Life Conservation District beckons with calm waters safe for swimming almost year-round, great snorkeling reefs, tide pools, and sometimes spinner dolphins. A shady, grassy beach park is perfect for picnics. If the shore break is pounding, or if you see surfers riding big waves, stay out of the water. In the afternoon, watch Lanai High School students heave outrigger canoes down the steep shore break and race one another just offshore. To get here, take Highway 440 south to the bottom of the hill and turn right. The road dead-ends at the beach's parking lot. **Amenities:** parking (no fee); showers; toilets. **Best for:** snorkeling; surfing; swimming. ⊠ *Off Hwy. 440, Lanai City.*

🛏 Hotels

★ **Four Seasons Resort Lanai**

$$$$ | **RESORT** | **FAMILY** | With stunning views of Hulopoe Bay and the astonishing rocky coastline, this sublime retreat offers beachside urban chic decor with meticulously curated artwork from across Polynesia, Micronesia, and Hawaii and manicured grounds that feature an array of native Hawaiian plants and species. **Pros:** nearby beach; outstanding restaurants and high-tech amenities; rental vehicles available on property. **Cons:** need a car to explore the area; not all guest rooms have coast views; 20 minutes from town. ⑤ *Rooms from: $2005* ⊠ *1 Manele Bay Rd., Manele, Lanai City* ☎ *808/565–2000, 800/819–5053* ⊕ *fourseasons.com/lanai* ⤻ *213 rooms* ⫶◯⫶ *No Meals.*

🍽 Restaurants

Dining at Manele Bay is reliant on the range of options provided by the Four Seasons Resort Lanai, from informal poolside meals to relaxed eclectic dining.

★ **Nobu Lanai**

$$$$ | **JAPANESE** | Chef Nobuyuki "Nobu" Matsuhisa offers his signature new-style Japanese cuisine in this open-air, relaxed luxury venue that features a lounge, outdoor tables, and a sushi bar overlooking Hulopoe Bay. This is fine dining without the stress, as black-clad waiters present dish after dish of beautifully seasoned, raw and lightly cooked seafood from local waters, or flown in directly from Alaska and Japan. **Known for:** Nobu's famous miso cod; exceptional levels of service; 15-course Teppanyaki experience. ⑤ *Average main: $40* ⊠ *Four Seasons Resort Lanai, 1 Manele Bay Rd., Lanai City*

☎ *808/565–2832* ⊕ *noburestaurants.com/lanai* ◯ *No breakfast, lunch.*

ONE FORTY

$$$$ | **AMERICAN** | Named after the island's 140 square miles, this ocean-view restaurant serves prime cuts of beef and the freshest local fish in airy comfort on a terrace that overlooks the wide sweep of Hulopoe Bay. Retractable awnings provide shade on sunny days, and comfy rattan chairs, potted palms, and tropical decor create an inviting setting. **Known for:** decadent and delicious seafood tower; poke prepared tableside; tasty upscale breakfasts. ⑤ *Average main: $55* ⊠ *Four Seasons Resort Lanai, 1 Manele Bay Rd., Lanai City* ☎ *808/565–2000* ⊕ *fourseasons.com/lanai* ◯ *No lunch.*

VIEWS at Manele Golf

$$ | **AMERICAN** | A stunning view of the legendary Puu Pehe rock only enhances the imaginative fare of this open-air restaurant, which also has great views of frolicking dolphins from its terrace. Tuck into a Hulopoe Bay prawn BLT, the crispy battered fish-and-chips with Meyer lemon tartar sauce, or any one of the tempting salad options. **Known for:** superb service; house-made ice cream sandwiches; fabulous cocktails. ⑤ *Average main: $26* ⊠ *Four Seasons Resort Lanai, 1 Manele Bay Rd., Manele, Lanai City* ☎ *808/565–2230* ⊕ *fourseasons.com/lanai* ◯ *No dinner; closed Mon.*

🏃 Activities

GOLF
Manele Golf

GOLF | You'll need to be a Four Seasons Resort Lanai guest to play at this renowned course. Designed by Jack Nicklaus in 1993, the course sits right over the water of Hulopoe Bay. Built on lava outcroppings, the five-tee course is on every good golfer's bucket list due to its challenging nature and beauty. Three holes are positioned on cliffs, utilizing the Pacific Ocean as a natural water hazard,

Some holes at Manele Golf use the Pacific Ocean as a water hazard.

while other shots must navigate challenging gorges and ravines to get to the hole. Unspoiled natural terrain provides a stunning backdrop, and every hole offers ocean views. Early-morning tee times are recommended to avoid the midday heat. ☒ *Four Seasons Resort Lanai, Challenge Dr., Manele, Lanai City* ☏ *808/565–4000* ⊕ *fourseasons.com/lanai* ☒ *$385 for resort guests* ⚹ *18 holes, 7039 yards, par 72.*

HIKING

Fisherman's Trail

HIKING & WALKING | Local anglers still use this trail to get to their favorite fishing spots. The trail takes about 1½ hours (4.4 miles round trip) and follows the rocky shoreline below the Four Seasons Resort Lanai. The marked trail entrance begins at the west end of Hulopoe Beach. Keep your eyes open for spinner dolphins cavorting offshore and the silvery flash of fish feeding in the pools below. The condition of the trail varies with weather and frequency of maintenance; it can be slippery and rocky. Take your time, wear a hat and enclosed shoes, and carry water. *Moderate.* ☒ *Manele, Lanai City.*

Puu Pehe Trail

HIKING & WALKING | Beginning to the left of Hulopoe Beach, this trail travels a short distance around the coastline and then climbs up a sharp rocky rise. At the top, you're level with the offshore stack of Puu Pehe and can overlook miles of coastline in both directions. The trail is not difficult, but it's hot and steep. Be aware of nesting seabirds and don't approach their nests.

⚠ **Stay away from the edge, as the cliff can easily give way.**

The hiking is best in the early morning or late afternoon, and it's a perfect place to look for whales in season (November–May, peak season January–March) and to catch a stunning sunset. Wear a hat and enclosed shoes, and take water so you can spend some time at the top admiring the view. *Moderate.* ☒ *Manele, Lanai City.*

SCUBA DIVING

When you have a dive site such as Cathedrals—with eerie pinnacle formations and luminous caverns—it's no wonder that scuba-diving buffs consider exploring the waters off Lanai akin to a religious experience.

Cathedrals

SCUBA DIVING | Just outside Hulopoe Bay, Cathedrals is the best cavern dive site in Lanai. Shimmering light makes the many openings resemble stained-glass windows. A current generally keeps the water crystal clear, even if it's turbid outside. In these unearthly chambers, large *ulua* (giant trevally) and small reef sharks add to the adventure. Tiger sharks may appear in certain seasons. ⊠ *Manele, Lanai City.*

SNORKELING

Snorkeling is the easiest ocean sport available on the island, requiring nothing but a snorkel, mask, fins, and good sense. Borrow equipment from your hotel or purchase some in Lanai City if you didn't bring your own. Wait to enter the water until you are sure no big sets of waves are coming, and observe the activity of locals on the beach. If little kids are playing in the shore break, it's usually safe to enter.

■ TIP➜ To get into the water safely, always swim in past the breakers, and in the comparative calm put on your fins, then mask and snorkel.

The best snorkeling on Lanai is at **Hulopoe Beach** and **Manele Small Boat Harbor.** Hulopoe, which is an exceptional snorkeling destination, has schools of manini that feed on the coral and coat the rocks with flashing silver. You can also easily view *kala* (unicorn fish), *uhu* (parrot fish), and *papio* (small trevally) in all their rainbow colors. Beware of rocks and surging waves. At Manele Harbor, there's a wade-in snorkel spot beyond the break wall. Enter over the rocks, just past the boat ramp.

⚠ Do not enter if the waves are breaking.

SPAS

Hawanawana Spa

SPAS | No two experiences are alike at Hawanawana Spa, where every treatment is tailored to your individual desires. Spa and salon services—like the Ocean Potions Ritual or Lanai Tai Signature Scrub—feature locally inspired ingredients and techniques. Massages are also available in couples' suites and poolside. The spa also offers a wide range of yoga (including aerial yoga), fitness, and meditation classes. ⊠ *Four Seasons Resort Lanai, 1 Manele Bay Rd., Manele, Lanai City* ☏ *808/565–2088* ⊕ *fourseasons.com/lanai* ⊠ *$240 for 60 minute massage, Ocean Ritual $460 per person for two hours.*

SURFING

Surfing on Lanai can be truly enjoyable. Quality, not quantity, characterizes this isle's few breaks. Be considerate of the locals, and they will be considerate of you—surfing takes the place of megaplex theaters and pool halls here, serving as one of the island's few recreational luxuries.

★ Lanai Surf School & Safari

SURFING | Nick Palumbo offers the only surf instruction on the island. The Lanai native is a former Hawaii State Surfing Champion, so you're in good hands—he and his staff are highly experienced and are great with beginners. Stand-up paddleboard lessons and rentals are also available. Experienced riders can rent surfboards overnight, and kids can enjoy the surf with boogie boards, also available to rent. ⊠ *Hulopoe Beach Park, Lanai City* ☏ *808/649–0739* ⊕ *lanaisurfsafari.com* ⊠ *Lessons from $200.*

Windward Lanai

Windward Lanai is 9 miles northeast of Lanai City; 17 miles northeast of the airport.

The eastern shore of Lanai is mostly deserted. A few inaccessible *heiau*, or temples, rock walls and boulders marking old shrines, and a restored church at Keomuku reveal traces of human habitation. Four-wheel-drive vehicles are a must to explore this side of the isle. Pack a picnic lunch, a hat and sunscreen, and plenty of drinking water. A mobile phone is also a good idea.

GETTING HERE AND AROUND

Once you leave paved Keomuku Highway and turn left toward Kaiolohia (Shipwreck Beach) or right to Naha Beach, the roads are dirt and sand; conditions vary with the seasons. Mileage doesn't matter much here, but figure on 20 minutes from the end of the paved road to Shipwreck Beach, and about 45 minutes to Lopa Beach. A four-wheel-drive vehicle is necessary to visit these remote areas.

Sights

Halepalaoa

BEACH | Named for the whales that once washed ashore here, Halepalaoa, or the "House of Whale Ivory," was the site of the wharf used by the short-lived Maunalei Sugar Company in 1899. Some say the endeavor failed because the sacred stones of nearby Kahea Heiau were used for the construction of the cane railroad. The brackish well water turned too salty, forcing the sugar company to close in 1901, after just two years. The remains of the *heiau*, once an important place of worship for the people of Lanai, are now difficult to find through the *kiawe* (mesquite) overgrowth. This is a nice place for sunbathing and whale-watching, but it's not easy to get to—a 4WD vehicle is definitely required. Take Highway 440

(Keomuku Highway) to its eastern terminus, then turn right on the dirt road and continue south for 5½ miles. ⊠ *On dirt road off Hwy. 440, Lanai City.*

Keomuku

RUINS | There's a peaceful beauty about the former fishing village of Keomuku. During the late 19th century, this small Lanai community served as the headquarters of the Maunalei Sugar Company. After the company failed, the land was abandoned. Although there are no other signs of previous habitation, its church, Ka Lanakila O Ka Malamalama, built in 1903, has been restored by volunteers. Visitors often leave some small token, a shell or lei, as an offering. Take Highway 440 to its eastern terminus, then turn right onto a dirt road and continue south for 5 miles. The church is on your right in the coconut trees. ⊠ *On dirt road off Hwy. 440.*

⊕ Beaches

Kaiolohia (Shipwreck Beach)

BEACH | The rusting World War II tanker abandoned off this 8-mile stretch of sand adds just the right touch to an already photogenic beach. Strong trade winds have propelled vessels onto the reef since at least 1824, when the first shipwreck was recorded. Beachcombers come to this fairly accessible beach for shells and washed-up treasures, and photographers take great shots of Molokai, just across the Kalohi Channel. A deserted plantation-era fishing settlement adds to the charm. It's still possible to find glass-ball fishing floats as you wander along. Kaiolohia, its Hawaiian name, is a favorite local diving spot. Beyond the beach, about 200 yards up a trail past the Shipwreck Beach sign, are the Kukui Point petroglyphs, marked by reddish-brown boulders.

■ **TIP→ An offshore reef and rocks in the water mean that it's not for swimmers, though you can play in the shallow water on the shoreline.**

To get here, take Highway 440 to its eastern terminus, then turn left onto a dirt road and continue to the end. **Amenities:** none. **Best for:** solitude; windsurfing. ⊠ *Off Hwy. 440, Lanai City.*

Lopa Beach

BEACH | A difficult surfing spot that tests the mettle of experienced locals, Lopa is also an ancient fishpond. With majestic views of West Maui and Kahoolawe, this remote white-sand beach is a great place for a picnic.

⚠ **Don't let the sight of surfers fool you: the channel's currents are too strong for swimming.**

Take Highway 440 to its eastern terminus, turn right onto a dirt road, and continue south for 7 miles. **Amenities:** none. **Best for:** solitude; sunrise; walking. ⊠ *On dirt road off Hwy. 440.*

Naha Beach

BEACH | An ancient rock-walled fishpond—visible at low tide—lies where the sandy shore ends and the cliffs begin their rise along the island's shores. Accessible by four-wheel-drive vehicle, the beach is a frequent dive spot for local fishermen.

⚠ **Treacherous currents make this a dangerous place for swimming.**

Take Highway 440 to its eastern terminus, then turn right onto a sandy dirt road and continue south for 11 miles. The shoreline dirt road ends here. **Amenities:** none. **Best for:** fishing; walking. ⊠ *On dirt road off Hwy. 440, Lanai City.*

Polihua Beach

BEACH | This often-deserted beach features long wide stretches of white sand and unobstructed views of Molokai. The northern end of the beach ends at a rocky lava cliff with some interesting tide pools and sea turtles that lay their eggs in the sand. (Do not drive on the beach and endanger their nests.) However, the dirt road leading here has deep sandy places that are difficult in dry weather

The Coastal Road ◉

Road conditions can change overnight and become impassable due to rain in the Upcountry. Your car-rental agency will give you an update before you hit the road. Some of the spur roads leading to the windward beaches from the coastal dirt road cross private property and are closed off by chains. Look for open spur roads with recent tire marks (a fairly good sign that they are safe to drive on). It's best to park on firm ground and walk in to avoid getting your car mired in the sand.

and impassable when it rains. In addition, strong currents and a sudden drop in the ocean floor make swimming dangerous, and strong trade winds can make walking uncomfortable. Thirsty wild bees sometimes gather around your car. To get rid of them, put out water some distance away and wait. The beach is in windward Lanai, 11 miles north of Lanai City. To get here, turn right onto the marked dirt road past Keahiakawelo (Garden of the Gods). **Amenities:** none. **Best for:** solitude; sunrise; walking. ⊠ *East end of Polihua Rd., Lanai City.*

🏃 Activities

SCUBA
Sergeant Major Reef

SCUBA DIVING | Off Kamaiki Point, Sergeant Major Reef is named for big schools of yellow- and black-striped *manini* (sergeant major fish) that turn the rocks silvery as they feed. There are three parallel lava ridges separated by rippled sand valleys, a cave, and an archway. Depths range 15–50 feet. Depending on conditions, the water may be clear or cloudy. ⊠ *Lanai City.*

Index

Photo Credits

Front Cover: Design Pics Inc / Alamy Stock Photo [Description: Outrigger canoes on the north end of Kihei; Kihei, Maui, Hawaii, United States of America]. **Back cover, from left to right:** Kriss Russell/PhotoGen-X\LifeJourneys/iStockphoto. Tane-Mahuta/ iStockphoto. MNStudio/ iStockphoto. **Spine:** RonTech2000/iStockphoto. **Interior, from left to right:** Paulacobleigh/Dreamstime (1). MNStuio/ iStockphoto (2-3). Shane Myers Photography/ Shutterstock (5). **Chapter 1: Experience Maui:** Tor Johnson/Hawaii Tourism Authority (HTA) (6-7). Svecchiotti/Dreamstime (8-9). Idreamphotos/Dreamstime (9). Dance Show/O'ahu Visitor's Bureau (9). MNStudio/Dreamstime (10). Mama's Fish House (10). AllExits/Stockphoto (10). Hinatea Sportfishing (10). Dave Sansom 2015 (11). Chandanaroy/Dreamstime.com (11). Michael Gordon/Shutterstock (11). Grand Wailea Maui (11). Max Earey/Shutterstock (12). Kelly Headrick/Shutterstock (12). Johnbronk/ Dreamstime (12). Derek van Vliet/Flickr (12). Reinhard Dirscherl / Alamy Stock Photo (13). Thediver123/Dreamstime (14). James Wright/ Dreamstime (14). EQRoy/Shutterstock (14). Blue Hawaiian Helicopters (14). David Lloyd(Annedave)/ Dreamstime (15). Alex Schmitt/Shutterstock (15). Digital94086/iStockphoto (20). Steven Gaertner/iStockphoto (21). MNStudio/iStockphoto (22). P_L_photography/iStockphoto (22). Tor Johnson/Hawaii Tourism Authority (22). Vacclav/iStockphoto (22). Jeremy Christensen/ iStockphoto (22). 7Michael/iStockphoto (23). Joflorece/iStockphoto (23). ShaneMyersPhoto/ iStockphoto (23). Joe West/Shutterstock (23). Tor Johnson/Hawaii Tourism Authority (HTA) (23). Marilyn Gould/Dreamstime (24). Douglas Peebles Photography / Alamy Stock Photo (24). Ancha Chiangmai/Shutterstock (24). Pr2is/ Dreamstime (24). Vfbjohn/ Dreamstime (24). Eddygaleotti/Dreamstime (25). Caner CIFTCI/Dreamstime (25). Elmar Langle/iStockphoto (25). Big Island Visitors Bureau (BIVB) / Kirk Lee Aeder (25). Koondon/Shutterstock (25). Brent Hofacker/Shutterstock (26). Hawaii Tourism (26). Dana Edmunds (26). Magdanatka/ Shutterstock (27). Big Island Visitors Bureau (BIVB) / Kirk Lee Aeder (27). Lost Mountain Studio/Shutterstock (28). Alla Machutt/iStockphoto (28). Hawaii Tourism Authority (HTA) / Brooke Dombroski (28). Temanu/Shutterstock (28). Mongkolchon Akesin/ Shutterstock (28). Hawaii Tourism Authority (HTA) / Heather Goodman (29). Olgakr/iStockphoto (29). Hawaii Tourism Authority (HTA) / Dana Edmunds (29). Hawaii Tourism Authority (29). Hawaii Tourism Authority (HTA) / Heather Goodman (29). Cathy Locklear/Dreamstime (31). HVCB_photo01a (32). Thinkstock LLC (33). Linda Ching/HVCB (35). Sri Maiava Rusden/HVCB (35). Leis Of Hawaii/leisofhawaii.com (36). Kelly Alexander Photography (36). Leis Of Hawaii /leisofhawaii.com (36). Leis Of Hawaii/leisofhawaii.com (36). Leis Of Hawaii/ leisofhawaii.com (36). Kelly Alexander Photography (36). Tim Wilson [CC BY 2.0]/ Flickr (37). Douglas Peebles Photography / Alamy Stock Photo (38). Douglas Peebles Photography / Alamy Stock Photo (38). Dana Edmunds/ Polynesian Cultural Center's Alii Luau (38). Douglas Peebles Photography / Alamy Stock Photo (38). Purcell Team / Alamy Stock Photo (38). Hawaii Visitors and Convention Bureau (39). Hawaii Visitors and Convention Bureau (39). Hawaii Visitors and Convention Bureau (39). Oahu Visitors Bureau (39). **Chapter 3: West Maui:** Mike7777777/ Dreamstime (57). Joe West/Shutterstock (69). CJ Anderson/Flickr, [CC BY-ND 2.0] (82). **Chapter 4: South Shore:** Mike Brake/Shutterstock (89). Igokapil/ Dreamstime (106). Mike7777777/Dreamstime (109). EQRoy/Shutterstock (111). Chapter 5: Central Maui: NIntellectual/iStockphoto (117). Derek Robertson/Shutterstock (123). Maridav/Shutterstock (129). **Chapter 6: Upcountry:** EpicStockMedia/iStockphoto (133). Artazum/ Shutterstock (143). Vlue/Dreamstime (145). 7Michael/iStockphoto (148). Laroach/Dreamstime (149). EstivillmI/Dreamstime (150). **Chapter 7: North Shore:** Arkanto/Shutterstock (153). Tracy Immordino/Shutterstock (163). Diane39/iStockphoto (165). **Chapter 8: Road to Hana:** Ehabaref/iStockphoto (167). Arkanto/Shutterstock (177). ShaneMyersPhoto/iStockphoto (178). Dejetley/Shutterstock (180). **Chapter 9: East Maui:** Chilkoot/iStockphoto (183). **Chapter 10: Maui Activities:** Jesole/Dreamstime (191). Peter Rimkus/Dreamstime (215). Ron Dahlquist/HVCB (217). Shane Myers Photography/Shutterstock (218). Orxy/Shutterstock (220). Gert Vrey/Dreamstime (220). Shane Myers Photography/Shutterstock (221). Manuel Bálesteri/Shutterstock (228). Featurecars/Dreamstime (231). **Chapter 11: Molokai:** Kridsada Kamsombat/iStockphoto (233). Michael Brake/iShutterstock (242). Ralf Broskvar/Shutterstock (246). Ralf Broskvar/Dreamstime (248). Reimar/ Shutterstock (253). Norinori303/Shutterstock (255). Greg Vaughn / Alamy (259). **Chapter 12: Lanai:** Islandleigh/Dreamstime (261). Aleksei Potov/Shutterstock (268). Courtesy of Four Seasons/Resort Lanai (273). Golf Club/Hawaii Tourism Japan (HTJ) (275). **About Our Writers:** All photos are courtesy of the writers.

*Every effort has been made to trace the copyright holders, and we apologize in advance for any accidental errors. We would be happy to apply the corrections in the following edition of this publication.

Notes

Notes

Fodor's MAUI

Publisher: Stephen Horowitz, *General Manager*

Editorial: Douglas Stallings, *Editorial Director;* Jill Fergus, Amanda Sadlowski, *Senior Editors;* Kayla Becker, Brian Eschrich, Alexis Kelly, *Editors;* Angelique Kennedy-Chavannes, *Assistant Editor*

Design: Tina Malaney, *Director of Design and Production;* Jessica Gonzalez, *Graphic Designer;* Erin Caceres, *Graphic Design Associate*

Production: Jennifer DePrima, *Editorial Production Manager;* Elyse Rozelle, *Senior Production Editor;* Monica White, *Production Editor*

Maps: Rebecca Baer, *Senior Map Editor;* Mark Stroud (Moon Street Cartography); David Lindroth, *Cartographers*

Photography: Viviane Teles, *Senior Photo Editor;* Namrata Aggarwal, Neha Gupta, Payal Gupta, Ashok Kumar, *Photo Editors;* Eddie Aldrete, *Photo Production Intern;* Kadeem McPherson, *Photo Production Associate Intern*

Business and Operations: Chuck Hoover, *Chief Marketing Officer;* Robert Ames, *Group General Manager;* Devin Duckworth, *Director of Print Publishing*

Public Relations and Marketing: Joe Ewaskiw, *Senior Director of Communications and Public Relations*

Fodors.com: Jeremy Tarr, *Editorial Director;* Rachael Levitt, *Managing Editor*

Technology: Jon Atkinson, *Director of Technology;* Rudresh Teotia, *Lead Developer*

Writers: Laurie Lyons-Makaimoku, Syndi Texeira

Editors: Lola Augustine Brown, Angelique Kennedy-Chavannes

Production Editor: Monica White

Copyright © 2023 by Fodor's Travel, a division of MH Sub I, LLC, dba Internet Brands.

Fodor's is a registered trademark of Internet Brands, Inc. All rights reserved. Published in the United States by Fodor's Travel, a division of Internet Brands, Inc. No maps, illustrations, or other portions of this book may be reproduced in any form without written permission from the publisher.

20th Edition

ISBN 978-1-64097-513-2

ISSN 1559-0798

All details in this book are based on information supplied to us at press time. Always confirm information when it matters, especially if you're making a detour to visit a specific place. Fodor's expressly disclaims any liability, loss, or risk, personal or otherwise, that is incurred as a consequence of the use of any of the contents of this book.

SPECIAL SALES

This book is available at special discounts for bulk purchases for sales promotions or premiums. For more information, e-mail SpecialMarkets@fodors.com.

PRINTED IN CANADA

10 9 8 7 6 5 4 3 2 1

About Our Writers

 Laurie Lyons-Makaimoku began travel writing in 2014, soon after receiving her master's degree in New Media Journalism. She started by sharing the secrets of some of Austin's best food, festivals, celebrities, entertainment, events, and locales, eventually as the editor of Austin.com. Eventually, after moving to Hawaii Island in 2016, she had the opportunity to start writing about the special place that she now called home in publications like Fodor's, The Matador Network, and Local Getaways. After marrying into a Hawaiian family Laurie developed a deep passion for ethical, sustainable travel, especially how it affects the quality of life and land in the Islands. Family travel, as well as food and beverage, are also some of her favorite things to write about. When she's not island-hopping to take in all she can throughout Hawaii's diverse landscapes, Laurie spends most of her weekends exploring tidepools and the dynamic shoreline of East Hawaii, chasing sunshine on the west side of the Island, and constantly growing her knowledge of and palate for the eclectic cuisines that make up Hawaii's ever-evolving food scene. She shares her home with her husband, two children, and a menagerie of rescue animals.

 Syndi Halualani Texeira is a native Hawaiian, small-town girl who was born and raised on Hawaii Island. Though she has traveled the world, including living in California, Washington, D.C., New York, Paris, and Monaco, her heart always belongs to Hawaii. After working with two of the most prominent media firms in the nation, Syndi has made her way back home to Hawaii, focusing her professional efforts on helping visitors embrace culturally sensitive and regenerative travel to Hawaii. Syndi enjoys time with her ohana, and her pets, traveling, reading, and advocating for indigenous rights. She also serves as Executive Director of a Hawaii Island nonprofit animal rescue organization.